Corpus Stylistics

CW01496871

To Eszter and Jacqui, who have always wanted a book about corpus stylistics.

CORPUS STYLISTICS
THEORY AND PRACTICE

Dan McIntyre and Brian Walker

EDINBURGH
University Press

Edinburgh University Press is one of the leading university presses in the UK. We publish academic books and journals in our selected subject areas across the humanities and social sciences, combining cutting-edge scholarship with high editorial and production values to produce academic works of lasting importance. For more information visit our website: edinburghuniversitypress.com

© Dan McIntyre and Brian Walker, 2019

Edinburgh University Press Ltd

The Tun – Holyrood Road, 12(2f) Jackson's Entry,
Edinburgh EH8 8PJ

Typeset in Sabon by
Servis Filmsetting Ltd, Stockport, Cheshire, and
printed and bound in Great Britain.

A CIP record for this book is available from the British Library

ISBN 978 1 4744 1320 6 (hardback)
ISBN 978 1 4744 1322 0 (webready PDF)
ISBN 978 1 4744 1321 3 (paperback)
ISBN 978 1 4744 1323 7 (epub)

The right of Dan McIntyre and Brian Walker to be identified as the authors of this work has been asserted in accordance with the Copyright, Designs and Patents Act 1988, and the Copyright and Related Rights Regulations 2003 (SI No. 2498).

Contents

Figures

Tables

Boxes

Acknowledgements

Some of the material in this book was originally developed for short courses in corpus stylistics that we have taught over the years. These include Summer Schools for the Poetics and Linguistics Association, held at University College Roosevelt (UCR), Netherlands (2012) and the University of Maribor, Slovenia (2014), as well as two separate short courses at UCR (2015 and 2016) and a short course at the Universidad Pedagógica Experimental Libertador, Venezuela. We are grateful to Michael Burke (UCR), Tomaz Onic (Maribor), Simon Zupan (Maribor) and Rosa Lopez de D'Amico (Venezuela) for inviting us to teach these courses, and to all the students who attended them.

We have benefited from the critical insights of a significant number of colleagues as we were writing this book. Jane Demmen, Erica Gold, Lesley Jeffries, Michaela Mahlberg, Rocío Montoro, Louise Nuttall, Hazel Price and Rebecca Woods read and commented on early drafts of the manuscript. We are grateful to them all for their help and advice.

Francine de Jager, Elliott Land and Hazel Price helped construct the HUM corpus which we refer to in various chapters. Without this all too inadequate acknowledgement, theirs would truly have been a thankless task. Muhammad Alsuweed generously gave us access to his Dickens Complete Corpus (DCC), for which we thank him too. We are also grateful to Ian Johnston of the University of Salford's Archives and Special Collections for arranging access to Salford's Arthur Hopcraft Papers, which facilitated the preparation of the *Tinker Tailor Soldier Spy* corpora used in Chapter 6, and for permission to reproduce a page from Hopcraft's draft script.

For technical advice and permission to reproduce screenshots of AntConc, WordSmith Tools, Wmatrix, BYU Corpora and Multilingual Corpus Toolkit, we thank (respectively) Laurence Anthony, Mike Scott, Paul Rayson, Mark Davies and Scott Piao. We would also like to record our sincere thanks to Mark Bratt, Chris Butler, Erica Gold and Aleksei Nazarov for their sound advice on mathematics and statistics, and for patiently taking the time to answer (often again and again) our statistics-related questions. It goes without saying that we are responsible for any errors we may have made in this regard.

At Edinburgh University Press we would like to thank Laura Williamson, Richard Strachan, Rebecca Mackenzie and Joannah Duncan. We are also very grateful to Eliza Wright, our copyeditor, for her meticulous and conscientious work on the text.

Parts of this book draw on the following previously published work: Chapter 1: McIntyre, D. (2015) 'Towards an integrated corpus stylistics', *Topics in Linguistics* 16(1): 59–68; Chapter 2: McIntyre, D. (2018) 'Irony and semantic prosody revisited', in Jobert, M. and Sorlin, S. (eds) *The Pragmatics of Irony and Banter*, pp. 81–99. Amsterdam: John Benjamins. Chapter 8: McIntyre, D. and Walker, B. (2011) 'Discourse presentation in Early Modern English writing: a preliminary corpus-based investigation', *International Journal of Corpus Linguistics* 16(1): 101–30; McIntyre, D. and Walker, B. (2012) 'Annotating a corpus of Early Modern English writing for categories of discourse presentation', in Manzano, F. (ed.) *Unité et Diversité de la linguistique*, pp. 87–107. Les Cahiers du Centre d'Etudes Linguistiques. Lyon: Atelier intégré de publication de l'Université Jean Moulin – Lyon 3. We are grateful to Manuel Jobert, Sandrine Sorlin and Štefan Beňuš for permission to reuse this material. We would also like to thank Matt Smith of Rebellion for arranging permission for us to reproduce a panel from *2000AD* in Chapter 3. Similarly, we are grateful to Nicholas Owen of Rogers, Coleridge and White Literary Agency for permission to reproduce Adrian Henri's poem 'Tonight at Noon' in Chapter 7.

On a personal level, we thank Eszter and Jacqui for putting up with us as we were writing this book. (In fact, we thank them for putting up with us full stop.)

Finally, Bernard Hulke tried to help but ultimately we relied on email.

D. M. and B. W.
July 2018

1

Combining corpus linguistics and stylistics

1.1 Introduction

Until fairly recently, *corpus stylistics* was an unusual collocation.[1] Its first attested use in print is most likely as the title of Semino and Short's (2004) corpus-based study of speech, writing and thought presentation in twentieth-century English writing, though Louw (1989) lays claim to having initiated the practice. Before this, it seems, the combination of corpus linguistic techniques with stylistic analysis was a fringe activity at best and certainly not a practice deserving of its own specialist label. Nonetheless, despite for a long time enjoying only peripheral status within linguistics and literary studies, the practice of corpus stylistics has grown in recent years, to the extent that it is fast becoming a recognisable field within stylistics generally. Evidence of this can be seen in the increasing number of encyclopedia articles discussing its practice (see, for example, Mahlberg 2013a; McIntyre 2013a) and in the small but growing number of monographs demonstrating the approach (e.g. Fischer-Starcke 2010; Toolan 2009; Ho 2011; Mahlberg 2013b; Hoover et al. 2014; Demjén 2015). In addition, there are a number of books describing approaches to text analysis that would be recognised by most stylisticians as clearly fitting the general remit of this emerging area (see, for instance, Adolphs 2006). Corpus stylistics, then, is on the rise.

As with any developing area, the possibilities that lie ahead are part of what makes the field exciting and intriguing. But coupled with this is the concurrent issue that faces any new area, namely its lack of a clear definition and its as yet not fully developed analytical methods.

The aim of this book is to address these problems directly by outlining a systematic approach to the techniques of using corpora in stylistic analysis and explaining the theoretical and methodological issues that underlie this practice. The book primarily addresses researchers in stylistics. Our aim in this initial chapter is to persuade those more sceptical stylisticians that corpora can offer valuable insights for stylistic analysis; for readers already convinced of this, the chapter offers an overview of the field as it currently stands, a brief history of its development and a consideration of how corpus stylistics differs from corpus linguistics more generally. Towards the end of the chapter we provide a working definition of corpus stylistics that we then exemplify throughout the rest of the book.

We begin this chapter by discussing some basic concepts from corpus linguistics and how they apply to corpus stylistics. Included in this discussion is a central question: 'what is a corpus?' This is an important question because it is often the case that the data studied in corpus stylistics does not constitute a corpus by the usual terms of corpus linguistics. We argue that the remit of corpus stylistics necessitates a less prototypical definition of a corpus than linguists such as Sinclair (2005) would allow, and that this is unproblematic so long as the researcher is aware of the analytical ramifications of this (we discuss in detail what these are and how to take account of them in Chapter 4). This leads us on to a discussion of the set of practices that defines corpus stylistics itself. Here we outline the historical development of corpus stylistics and consider the important issue of its disciplinary status. Whether corpus stylistics is indeed a sub-discipline of stylistics, or whether it is best described more modestly as a methodology for carrying out stylistic analysis, is an argument that mainstream corpus linguists will themselves recognise as one that has that has raged for many years with regard to corpus linguistics (see Hardie and McEnery 2010). The general summary of corpus linguistics that we provide serves as a background to our argument for the value of the corpus approach in stylistic analysis. Ultimately, our aim in this book is to demonstrate how integrating corpus methods into stylistics can improve the systematicity and rigour of stylistic analysis. What we also argue is that qualitative analysis is an integral component of good corpus stylistics. With this in mind, sections 1.5 and 1.6 of this chapter consider the integration of corpus techniques with qualitative stylistic approaches. In particular we consider the relationship between corpus stylistics and cognitive stylistics and argue that corpus techniques can support cognitive stylistic work and vice versa. We also argue against some of the criticisms that have been made of cognitive stylistics from corpus stylisticians.

We end this chapter by outlining the aims and structure of the book, in order to make clear the incremental development of our argument concerning the nature of corpus stylistics.

1.2 What is a corpus?

The words *corpus* and its plural *corpora* are Latin in origin, in which language they mean 'body'. This original meaning is metaphorised when we use the term in linguistics, with *corpus* referring to 'a body of language data'. In short, a corpus is a collection of texts but one which has been put together according to strict criteria. McEnery and Wilson, in their introduction to corpus linguistics, define a corpus as:

> a finite body of text, sampled to be maximally representative of a particular variety of a language, and which can be stored and manipulated using a computer. (McEnery and Wilson 2001: 73)

It is representativeness that is arguably the defining criterion of a corpus, since the aim of corpus linguistics is to be able to determine evidence that allows for generalisations to be made about the particular type of language under investigation. So, for instance, corpus linguists researching twenty-first-century spoken British English will need to ensure that the corpus they are studying is indeed a good representation of that particular language type if their findings are to be applicable to twenty-first-century spoken British English generally. Likewise, for a corpus analysis of the differences between teenage and adult speech patterns to be reliable, the corpus itself would need to be a reliable representation of teenage and adult dialogue; and this necessitates a balanced representation of the two variables in the population from which the sample is drawn (e.g. in terms of other variables such as social context and geographical region). This need for representativeness is emphasised in Sinclair's definition of a corpus:

> A corpus is a collection of pieces of language text in electronic form, selected according to external criteria to represent, as far as possible, a language or language variety as a source of data for linguistic research. (Sinclair 2005: 16)

The need for following strict criteria when constructing linguistic corpora is so crucial to the practice of corpus linguistics that Sinclair devotes a considerable amount of space to discussing what *doesn't* count as a corpus. It is worth summarising this here, since this has particular relevance to the practice of corpus stylistics.

According to Sinclair (2005), there are at least five types of language database that are often misconstrued as akin to linguistic corpora: (1) the worldwide web; (2) archives; (3) collections of citations; (4) collections of quotations; and (5) individual texts.

Sinclair explains that the reason the worldwide web does not constitute a corpus is because we cannot know for certain what its dimensions are. Because it has not been designed with the purpose of linguistic analysis in mind, we do not know how big it is or of what population it is a sample. Added to this is the fact that it is constantly changing as webpages are frequently updated, added, removed or in some cases censored (see Renouf et al. 2004 for further discussion of such issues). This is not to say that the worldwide web is not a useful resource for researchers studying language, and notable attempts have been made to exploit it as a resource for corpus linguistic inquiry (see Kehoe et al.'s 2006 description of the WebCorp tool for searching language on the web). However, it is important to be clear about its limitations with regard to the issues of representativeness and balance.

It is for similar reasons of representativeness and balance that an archive does not constitute a corpus. Archives are put together with the primary aim of preserving primary source documents held to be of long-term cultural, historical or political significance. While such documents may indeed be valuable in linguistic terms, the terms by which they are selected for inclusion in an archive are likely to differ significantly from those that a corpus linguist would employ when compiling a corpus for linguistic research.

Items 3 and 4 on Sinclair's list, collections of citations and quotations, are not corpora because they are partial. That is, they are short selections from texts, whose importance is centred on their propositional content rather than their relation to and position within a larger text.

Finally, Sinclair points out that an individual text cannot be considered a corpus, since corpora are designed to be representative of particular language varieties. And a single text cannot fulfil this function alone. If we return to McEnery and Wilson's definition of a corpus, we can see the same point being made:

> a corpus in modern linguistics, in contrast to being simply any body of text, might more accurately be described as a finite-sized body of machine-readable text, sampled in order to be maximally representative of the language variety under consideration. (McEnery and Wilson 2001: 32)

In corpus stylistics, particularly in authorship studies, such large-scale corpora are often used. For example, Mahlberg's (2013b) study of the fiction of Charles Dickens uses a large corpus designed to be representative of Dickens's fictional prose generally. Indeed, in some cases, corpora built for corpus stylistic research are able to achieve the kind of completeness that is not possible when studying naturally occurring language. That is, a corpus of fictional texts might constitute an entire population rather than being simply a small sample. Fischer-Starcke's (2010) study of Jane Austen's work, for instance, uses a corpus consisting of the entirety of Austen's six full-length novels rather than representative samples from them. But it is also the case that much work that goes under the term corpus stylistics is focused on individual texts. Mahlberg and McIntyre (2011), for instance, is a corpus-based study of Ian Fleming's novel *Casino Royale* while Stubbs (2005) is a corpus analysis of Joseph Conrad's *Heart of Darkness*. Like Sinclair, Louw (2008) objects to the description of such work as corpus analysis, preferring instead the term *digital stylistics*. It may be argued that *digital stylistics* better encompasses the range and varied uses of digital resources within stylistics to investigate literary and other texts. However, in our view there are numerous problems with the term. One issue is that the term *digital* is almost unrestrictedly vague, opening up the possibility that any kind of stylistic research that involves any type of non-analogue technology counts as digital stylistics. Given that very few stylisticians work only with quill pen and parchment any more, this seems disobligingly unspecific. This is a problem that has also been identified with the increasingly popular field of *digital humanities*, of which Ramsay says:

> the term can mean anything from media studies to electronic art, from data mining to edutech, from scholarly editing to anarchic blogging, while inviting code junkies, digital artists, standards wonks, transhumanists, game theorists, free culture advocates, archivists, librarians, and edupunks under its capacious canvas. (Ramsay 2013: 239)

It is because of the problematic all-encompassing nature of the term *digital* that we prefer to avoid it in relation to stylistics. Instead, we opt for *corpus stylistics* on the grounds that the word *corpus* serves as a specific reminder of the various methodological and theoretical borrowings from corpus linguistics that is key to its practice (see Mahlberg 2007b). And unlike Sinclair and Louw, we see no problem in describing studies of single texts as corpus stylistics. We explain our reasoning in full in Chapter 4.

1.3 A brief history of corpus linguistics

Since corpus stylistics is inextricably linked with the development of corpus linguistics, it will be useful to provide a brief overview of how the latter field developed.

Although the term *corpus linguistics* was not commonly used until the late 1960s, some linguists had been engaged in what might be seen as early forms of this work since the beginning of the twentieth century. The German scholar Franz Boas, for instance, was an early pioneer of what we might term field linguistics and was one of the first linguists to recognise the value of corpora for advancing our understanding of language and how it works. His far-sightedness is revealed in this quotation from his book, *Race, Language and Culture*:

> While until about 1880 investigators confined themselves to the collection of vocabularies and brief grammatical notes, it has become more and more evident that large masses of texts are needed in order to elucidate the structure of languages. (Boas 1917: 1)

Boas's lead was followed by other eminent scholars such as Leonard Bloomfield, whose description of Austronesian Tagalog, a language of the Philippines, was corpus-based; Charles Hockett, who worked on Potawatomi, a Central Algonquian language spoken around Wisconsin, and later went on to formulate his well-known series of 'design features' of language; and Zellig Harris, who strongly emphasised the importance of results being derived from data and was an early pioneer in what we now know as Discourse Analysis. Harris's involvement in this nascent corpus linguistics is particularly interesting given the direction that his most famous student, Noam Chomsky, would later take. Indeed, it was the publication of Chomsky's (1957) *Syntactic Structures* that sounded the death-knell for corpus linguistics in the USA, before it had even properly begun. The Chomskyan approach to language, with its focus on non-empirical methods, quickly became the dominant paradigm within linguistics, particularly in the USA. A consequence of this was that the study of naturally occurring language (which is, of course, what corpus linguists are interested in) was to a large extent sidelined.

However, despite Chomsky's massive influence on linguistics, some linguists continued to pursue the idea of studying language by describing naturally occurring data. William Labov's work in sociolinguistics, for example, demonstrated the fundamental importance of linguistic performance for understanding the symbiotic relationship between language, society, and societal structures and hierarchies. Such developments were partly in response to the fact that Chomsky's ideas about linguistic structure, which were illustrated by invented examples, often turned out not to adequately describe instances of real language in use.

The first significant project in what we might term modern corpus linguistics was the Survey of English Usage, instigated by Randolph Quirk at University College London in 1959. The Survey led to the creation of a corpus of one million words of written and spoken British English, made up of 200 text samples of 5,000 words each. The corpus data was all on paper and indexed on file cards. Each text sample was manually annotated for prosodic and paralinguistic features, and file cards for each sample recorded grammatical structures. Searching the corpus thus meant a trip to the Survey to physically search through the many filing cabinets in which the corpus data was stored.

Shortly after the Survey of English Usage had been initiated, Nelson Francis and Henry Kučera of Brown University in the USA began work on what would eventually become known as the Brown Corpus. This was a one million word collection of written American English, compiled from texts published in 1961. Unlike the Survey Corpus, the Brown Corpus was electronic. Kučera and Nelson published an analysis of the corpus in 1967, titled *Computational Analysis of Present-Day American English*. The project gave rise to numerous findings about the nature of language that would have been impossible without recourse to corpus data. As an example, one of these findings was that the frequency of any given word in the corpus was inversely proportional to its rank position. For instance, the most frequent word in the Brown Corpus is *the*, which accounts for approximately 6 per cent of all the words in the corpus. The next most frequent word is *of*, which accounts for approximately 3 per cent of all the words in the corpus – that is, half of the percentage frequency of *the*. Kučera and Nelson's findings confirmed Zipf's Law (Zipf 1935), which states that the most frequent word in a given text sample will occur approximately twice as often as the second most frequent, which will occur approximately twice as often as the third most frequent, and so on.

The success of the Brown Corpus led to the creation of other similarly structured corpora. In 1970, Geoffrey Leech, together with a group of colleagues at Lancaster University in the UK, embarked on the creation of a corpus of written British English to match the structure of the Brown Corpus. By 1976, the corpus was still incomplete, due in no small part to the difficulties of obtaining copyright permission to use the corpus's constituent texts. Ultimately, it took two further years and the combined efforts of three universities – Lancaster, Oslo and Bergen – to finish the corpus. It was completed in 1978 and became known as the LOB Corpus, after the initial letters of the universities involved in its creation. Because LOB paralleled the structure of the Brown Corpus, it was ideal for comparing British and American English. Later on, the Brown family of corpora was extended by the addition of FROWN (Freiberg-Brown; written American English from 1991), the charmingly named FLOB (Freiberg-Lancaster-Oslo-Bergen; written British English from 1991) and, most recently, BE06 (written British English from the early years of the twenty-first century) and BLOB ('Before LOB'; one million words of written British English from the 1930s).

While corpus linguists such as Quirk, Jan Svartvik (who had also worked on the Survey), Kučera and Nelson, Leech and Stig Johansson (another member of the LOB team) were interested primarily in grammar, John Sinclair, the first Professor of Modern English Language at the University of Birmingham, was primarily interested in what corpora could reveal about meaning. His earliest investigations in this area had taken place prior to his appointment at Birmingham, in a project known as *English Lexical Studies* undertaken at the University of Edinburgh in 1963 with his colleagues Susan Jones and Robert Daley. Sinclair analysed a small corpus of spoken and written English with the aim of investigating the relationship between words and meaning. This was the beginning of Sinclair's conviction that words are not the core unit of meaning in language. If this sounds counter-intuitive, it is because most people's understanding of how language works has largely been shaped by traditional accounts of grammar. In *English Lexical Studies* (recently republished in a new edition edited by Krishnamurthy 2004) Sinclair began to explore the idea that meaning is best seen as a property of words in combination. For example, the negative meanings associated with the word *commit* are not inherent in the word itself but arise from the fact that the word *commit* is often found in descriptions of negative events (e.g. 'commit crime'). In this work, Sinclair was building on J. R. Firth's concept of collocation (the notion that some words have a tendency to co-occur with other words more often than would be expected by chance alone). Sinclair's work on collocation and what corpora can reveal about meaning were instrumental in the COBUILD (Collins Birmingham University International Language Database) project which he initiated at Birmingham in 1980. COBUILD resulted in the creation of the Bank of English corpus of around 650 million words which was the data source that underpinned a series of dictionaries and grammars edited by Sinclair and his team, including the *Collins COBUILD English Language Dictionary* (1987), the *Collins COBUILD English Grammar* (1990) and the *Collins COBUILD English Dictionary* (1995).

In 1991, a consortium including research teams from Oxford University, Lancaster University and the British Library began work on the British National Corpus (BNC). This corpus consists of 100,000,000 words of written and spoken British English from the later part of the twentieth century (constituent texts were produced between the 1960s and the 1990s). The corpus was completed in 1994. Part of the process of creating the BNC involved annotating the data for part-of-speech. This process, commonly known as tagging, involves assigning a code (or 'tag') to every word in the corpus to indicate what part-of-speech it is (e.g. possessive pronoun, coordinating conjunction, wh-determiner, etc.). Part-of-speech tagging is done automatically using specialist software and has been a staple of methodologist corpus linguistics (for a definition of which, see Chapter 3) since the days of the Brown Corpus, when early tagging software achieved a success rate of around 70 per cent on the Brown data. Tagging of the BNC was done using a part-of-speech tagging system called CLAWS (Constituent Likelihood Automatic Word-tagging System), the latest version of which (CLAWS4) has a success rate of around 97 per cent.[2] Notwithstanding the fact that its constituent texts are no longer contemporary and it suffers from a lack of balance in the amounts of spoken and written data it contains, the BNC remains one of the best representative samples of naturally occurring language currently available. Indeed, it has been used as a model for many other national corpora, including the American National Corpus, Hungarian National Corpus, Russian National Corpus and others. Part of the success of the BNC is likely to lie in the fact that it can be accessed through various platforms. Originally, it was released with search engine software known as SARA (SGML Aware Retrieval Application), later updated to XAIRA (XML Aware Indexing and Retrieval Architecture). Since then, further projects have made it accessible via web front-ends such as CQPWeb (Corpus Query Processor, hosted at Lancaster University) and Mark Davies's BYU-BNC website (hosted at Brigham Young University), which we discuss further later in this book. Davies's website also provides access to a range of other large corpora, including COCA (Corpus of Contemporary American English) and COHA (Corpus of Historical American English).

The tagging of the BNC (and other corpora) for part-of-speech information is a way of adding value to a corpus. Tagging, however, is not restricted to part-of-speech information. Indeed, any aspect of language can be tagged in a corpus, though whether this can be done automatically depends on whether the focus of the annotation is a formal feature of language. For example, it is relatively straightforward to tag for part-of-speech, since the grammatical rules of a language can be used to determine the likelihood of a word belonging to a particular part-of-speech category. Tagging for stylistic categories – say, speech presentation – on the other hand, is much more difficult to do automatically, since categories such as direct speech (*He said, 'I love corpus linguistics!'*) and free indirect speech (*He loved corpus linguistics!*) are for the most part functional rather than formal categories; consequently, annotation of this type needs to be done manually. The value of annotation, however, is that it allows us to quantify other features of language (e.g. prosody, clause type, etc.) which can give us insights into how language works as a system.

Recent advances in tagging have involved the development of a system for annotating corpus data for semantic information. Paul Rayson's *Wmatrix* software package (see Rayson 2003, 2008, 2009) automatically assigns a semantic tag (as well as a part-of-speech tag) to every word in whatever corpus is uploaded. This allows the user to search the corpus not just for words but also for particular semantic fields. Current work in this area is aimed at improving the tagger so that it is able to disambiguate between possible meanings of homonyms, as well as cope with older varieties of English.

Advances in computing power are having a significant effect on the development of tools and technologies for corpus linguistics. At the same time, corpus techniques are finding their way into other disciplines and the broader field of digital humanities is developing fast. Recent advances include the development of multimodal corpora such as that built as part of the University of Nottingham's *HeadTalk* project (Knight et al. 2008, 2009). This focused on the construction of a corpus of video streams of an academic supervision session, marked-up to indicate aspects of body language. This allowed researchers to investigate the relationship between language and gesture. Since then, developments in multimodal corpus creation and analysis have increased considerably and look set to be part of the future of corpus linguistics (for examples of such work, see Knight 2011; Adolphs and Carter 2013; Lin 2017).

Other recent work in digital humanities has seen projects aimed at integrating corpus linguistics and geographical information systems (GIS). For example, Gregory et al. (2015) have carried out work extracting place-names from a corpus, searching for the semantic collocates of these names (we will explain the term *collocate* in Chapter 2), and creating maps that allow users to visualise how concepts such as war and money are distributed geographically. This interdisciplinary research builds on similarly focused work combining methods from the disciplines of history and geography, such as that of Southall et al. (2009).

What is striking about recent research in this area is the extent to which computational and corpus linguistics have become the driving force behind such work. While interdisciplinarity is ever more prevalent and key to all of these recent developments, language and linguistics remains at the heart of corpus-based research. And corpus construction continues in order to facilitate new insights into language structure and use. Love et al. (2017), for instance, describe the construction of the 2014 spoken BNC, an 11.5 million word corpus of orthographically transcribed British English conversations, recorded between 2012 and 2016. And work is currently under way on the construction of a new BNC of contemporary written British English.[3]

1.4 The emergence of corpus stylistics and problems with its definition

Corpus linguistics, then, has a long history compared with corpus stylistics. Although the use of computers in literary studies is not new (notwithstanding the fact that stylistics encompasses the study of non-literary language too), it is only recently that the approach has started to impinge on the mainstream.

One of the earliest significant computational studies in stylistics is Burrows's (1987) investigation of character idiolect in the work of Jane Austen. In this early example of a corpus study of literary texts, Burrows analyses only what he terms 'inert' or grammatical words (1987: 2), such as personal pronouns, auxiliary verbs, prepositions, conjunctions, adverbs and articles, in Austen's novels. These words, Burrows argues, have 'light [...] to shed on the meaning of one novel or another; on subtle relationships between narrative and dialogue [...] and character' (1987: 2). Burrows notes that 'statistics does have a distinct bearing on questions of importance in the territory of literary interpretation and judgement' and goes on to show that 'statistical evidence is a useful point of departure [for understanding how] words play a role in shaping literary character' (1987: 2, 37). As an exemplar, Burrows (1987: 3) suggests that Henry Tilney and Isabella Thorpe (characters from *Northanger Abbey*) have dissimilar counts of inert words: Henry uses *the* and *of* more than Isabella, while Isabella uses *I* and *not* more than Henry. Burrows explains that 'the effects must colour every speech they make and leave *some* impression in the minds of her [Austen's] readers' (1987: 4). Burrows also suggests that pronoun usage can be indicative of ideas of society, status and intimacy. For example, Fanny Price's use of *we* 'marks the wanted solitariness of her life at Mansfield Park' (Burrows 1987: 18).

Burrows and his associates have, over the years, extended their methodologies for the computational analysis of literary texts. Craig (1999), for instance, looks at character in the plays of Ben Jonson, while McKenna and Antonia (1996) compare the internal monologues of three characters (Molly, Stephen and Leopold) in James Joyce's *Ulysses*. By testing the statistical significance of the most frequent words in the word-lists, McKenna and Antonia show how common word usage can form distinctive patterns for different characters. They go on to demonstrate that through the analysis of the three characters' words it is possible to establish the 'distinct idioms that characterise the interior monologues of each of them' (McKenna and Antonia 1996: 65), and that the common words in the monologues help in the understanding of the characters.

Around the same time as Burrows was working on his statistical analyses of Austen, Louw (1989) was approaching the corpus analysis of literature from what might be called a Firthian perspective. Drawing on the work of the British linguist J. R. Firth, developed by Sinclair in his COBUILD work, Louw was concerned with accounting for the creation of meaning in literary texts, specifically through the investigation of collocation. His approach is exemplified in Louw (1993), where he provides persuasive evidence of the potential for meaning to be transferred from surrounding words to a node word in a phenomenon he terms semantic prosody. One of his examples concerns the phrase *bent on* in David Lodge's novel *Small World*, which Louw shows to have an ironic effect in context as a result of its being used in reference to the practice of self-improvement. This is in contrast to the more common usage of the phrase in reference to semantically negative activities (e.g. *bent on self-destruction*). Louw's work on semantic prosody has had significant influence within corpus linguistics generally (see, for example, Hunston 2007) and we outline it in full in Chapter 2.

Unsurprisingly, given his adherence to Sinclair's definition of a corpus, Louw's work in corpus stylistics has primarily utilised large representative corpora as comparators for determining meaning in individual texts (see, for example, Louw 1993). This is what O'Halloran (2007) terms corpus-assisted stylistics, which we discuss further in Chapter 2. Many stylisticians, however, have made valuable steps forward through the corpus analysis of individual texts alone (i.e. without reference to a comparator – or reference – corpus of standard language such as the BNC or Bank of English). Culpeper (2002), for instance, investigates keywords (statistically over-represented words when compared against a norm) in Shakespeare's *Romeo and Juliet*, demonstrating through text-internal comparisons of character dialogue how these help to establish lexical and grammatical patterns for a number of the main characters in the play. This is on the grounds that keywords can be strong indicators of character traits because they can act as what Enkvist (1973) terms style markers (Culpeper 2001: 199). Culpeper (2009) extends this work by using the Wmatrix (Rayson 2009) software package to tag not only parts-of-speech in the play but semantic categories too. Culpeper finds that key semantic categories reveal patterns of metaphor in Romeo's speech which contribute substantially to his characterisation.

This approach of using tagged data to facilitate stylistic analysis is one that has had significant take-up within stylistics. Walker (2011), for example, is a study of characterisation in Julian Barnes's novel *Talking It Over* while McIntyre (2010) applies similar methods in the analysis of Quentin Tarantino's screenplay *Reservoir Dogs*. And Ho (2011) looks beyond characterisation to compare the original and revised editions of John Fowles's novel *The Magus*, making use of tagged data to identify differences in stylistic effects between the two texts. These projects report the findings of corpus analyses of data that has been tagged automatically for parts-of-speech and semantic categories. Semino and Short (2004), on the other hand, is a major investigation of a corpus manually tagged for function-based categories of speech, writing and thought presentation. Semino and Short (2004) analyse a 260,000 word corpus of English prose writing (small by the standards of modern corpus linguistics but significant in corpus stylistics given the laborious nature of hand annotation; we discuss these techniques further in Chapter 8). This resource enables them to test the model of speech and thought presentation originally presented in Leech and Short (1981) and, by so doing, to identify not just semantic norms for the various categories but quantitative norms too.

The work of corpus stylisticians such as Louw (1993), Semino and Short (2004) and Mahlberg (2013b) highlights one of the key benefits of using corpus methods in stylistics. This is the capacity that corpora have to shed light on what constitutes the background against which linguistic items can be foregrounded. For a long time in stylistics, identifying background norms was semi-subjective at best, with some stylisticians (e.g. Freeman 1970) even going so far as to say that it would never be possible to calculate these. Corpus linguistic software and analytical methods have allowed stylisticians to tackle this problem head on.

Since the late 1980s, then, a body of work has emerged in stylistics which is marked by its use of corpus linguistic methods and technology. As a result, the term *corpus stylistics* has found its way into popular usage to describe the kind of work that uses corpus tools in the service of stylistic analysis. However, while the term itself is becoming more prevalent in stylistic circles, as yet there appears to be no common consensus on what corpus stylistics is, how one goes about it, or how it differs from corpus linguistics. For the term to have relevance and proper currency, it is important that these questions be addressed. This is our aim in this book.

There are a number of problems with many current definitions of corpus stylistics, not least of which is the tendency to define it rather narrowly as the analysis of literary texts using corpus linguistic techniques. This is the definition used by both Fischer-Starcke (2010) and Ho (2011), for example. However, if this is all that corpus stylistics is then it is difficult to see a justification for the use of a distinct term to describe it. Corpus linguistic work that focuses on phonetic analysis (e.g. Honga et al. 2014) is not commonly known as corpus phonetics, nor is corpus-based syntactic analysis (e.g. Ai and Lu 2013) generally referred to as corpus syntax. Corpus linguistics as understood from the methodologist position (see Hardie and McEnery 2010) is nothing more than a methodology for linguistic analysis and, as such, can be applied to any area of language study. That is, the same methods and analytical tools are used regardless of the sub-discipline of linguistics they are being applied to. For corpus stylistics to be deserving of the label, there must be something more to it than the simple application of corpus linguistic tools in the analysis of literary texts.

A second problem with many current definitions of corpus stylistics is an implicit assumption that traditional (i.e. non-corpus-based) stylistics lacks rigour. Fischer-Starcke (2010), for example, discussing the application of corpus methods in the analysis of Jane Austen's prose, notes that '[n]ew insights into the data can be gained since (1) the data is studied in a systematic and detailed way and (2) a larger number of units of meaning in language is analysed than in literary studies' (Fischer-Starcke 2010: 11). While Fischer-Starcke's second point is true (corpus tools do indeed afford the opportunity to identify units of meaning in language that would be difficult to unearth through manual qualitative analysis), her first point is an implicit misrepresentation of traditional stylistic methods. The aim of stylistics has always been to produce analyses of texts that are falsifiable, systematic and rigorous. The analytical checklists presented in Short (1996a) and Stockwell (2010) are aimed squarely at ensuring systematicity, while Leech and Short's (1981) now classic *Style in Fiction* is a watchword for rigour and detail. The point is that corpus linguistic techniques are not necessary to make stylistic analysis systematic and detailed; good stylistics should already be so. What corpus techniques offer are new ways of examining texts that can supplement insights gained via traditional methods (what Carter 2010 affectionately calls 'steam stylistics'). Corpus stylistics is not in and of itself any more or less systematic than traditional stylistics, so systematicity cannot be seen as a distinguishing feature of the practice. To put it another way, systematicity is a necessary condition of corpus stylistics, but not sufficient to distinguish it from any other kind of stylistics.

A third issue with many current definitions of corpus stylistics is one that extends to stylistics generally, and this is the definition of the discipline as the study of the language of literature. Stylistics emerged out of the work of the Russian Formalists at the turn of the twentieth century (Busse and McIntyre 2010), and one of the earliest concerns of this movement was to isolate the linguistic properties of literary language. It was quickly discovered, however, that *literary language* is something of a misnomer, since there is nothing in the language of literary texts that is not found in myriad other text-types. There is, then, no reason why stylistics should not also be practised on non-literary texts; and indeed it is (see, for example, the early work of Crystal and Davy 1969, the critical stylistic work of Jeffries 2007 and 2010a, and the sociolinguistically inclined work of Coupland 2007). Stylistics is best understood as the linguistic study of style (Leech and Short 2007: 11) and how this can be affected by such non-linguistic variables as, for example, genre, author, historical period, and so on (Jeffries and McIntyre 2010: 1). While literature remains the primary object of study for most stylisticians, there is no intrinsic reason why this should be the case and so the definition of corpus stylistics as the corpus linguistic study of literary language is unacceptably reductive (see McIntyre and Price 2018a for a fuller discussion of this issue). A suitable definition of corpus stylistics needs to take this into account while acknowledging that literature remains the object of study for most stylisticians.

All of this is to say that if corpus stylistics is to be useful as a descriptor, and if we are to make the case for it having the kind of status that distinguishes it from mainstream corpus linguistics, we must be clear about what it is that sets it apart from other corpus-related work. Over the course of this book, we will argue that corpus stylistics is indeed different from corpus linguistics, and that an understanding of the techniques of corpus stylistics may well have beneficial effects for corpus-derived analysis of all types. To this end, we define corpus stylistics as the application of theories, models and frameworks from stylistics in corpus analysis. Subsequent chapters will aim to demonstrate the practice of corpus stylistics to exemplify this definition, as well as consider related work which may not fit it exactly but which has a value to the stylistics enterprise.

1.5 Style and stylistics

In the previous section we defined stylistics as the linguistic study of style in language and how this is influenced by particular non-linguistic variables. While we assume most readers will be familiar with at least the basic tenets of stylistics, for the purposes of clarity we will set out some of the fundamental concepts here, since we view these as integral to the practice of corpus stylistics.

To further explain the object of study for stylistics, Short (1996a) makes a useful distinction between authorial style and text style. The former is what non-stylisticians often assume to be the preserve of stylistics: that is, the study of the linguistic idiosyncrasies of individual writers. Stylometry, or authorship attribution as it is also known, is indeed practised within stylistics (see, for example, Hoover 2017; Evans 2018) though it is by no means the most prominent area of research. This is not to dispel its significance. Authorship attribution is, for instance, of major importance to forensic linguistics (see, for example, Wright 2003). Nonetheless, most stylisticians are interested first and foremost in text style. This is the study of how the linguistic choices evident in a text contribute to the overall meanings and effects of that text. Of course, it will always be the case that text style and authorial style are interconnected, since whatever linguistic choices are present in a text are there because of decisions made consciously or unconsciously by a writer. The issue, then, is one of focus, with most contemporary stylisticians concentrating on the analysis of text style. And at the core of such analyses is the concept of foregrounding.

Although stylistics traces its roots to the Russian Formalist literary critical movement prevalent at the turn of the twentieth century, it was not until the 1960s that it began to cultivate the theoretical and methodological approaches that would later see it develop into a sub-discipline of linguistics. Important early work in this respect includes Nowottny's (1962) ground-breaking introduction to linguistic criticism, *The Language Poets Use*, and Fowler's (1966) *Essays on Style and Language*. Both drew on the Russian Formalist notion of *ostranenie*, translated by Shklovsky ([1917] 1965) as *defamiliarisation*, meaning the act of making strange. The purpose of defamiliarisation is to enhance our perception of the ordinary by making the familiar seem unusual. For example, defamiliarising effects can be seen in art movements such as impressionism and cubism, both of which aim to make us see elements of the world that we would not otherwise be aware of. And just as defamiliarising effects can be observed in visual art, so too can they be seen in texts. Drawing on the concept of defamiliarisation,

Mukařovský ([1932] 1964) developed the notion of foregrounding to explain the means by which defamiliarising effects can be achieved in language. In essence, foregrounding is achieved when the perceived norms of language are broken. This can happen either as a consequence of deviation (i.e. unexpected irregularity in language) or parallelism (unexpected regularity; see Jakobson 1960), and foregrounding may be achieved formally (by breaking descriptive linguistic rules at the levels of grammar, phonetics and semantics) or functionally (by deviating from expectations with regard to pragmatics).

Throughout this book, we draw on these basic principles of foregrounding, deviation and parallelism, using them to underpin the corpus stylistic analyses that we present in each chapter. Indeed, we contend that these principles are necessary components of corpus stylistics as an enterprise, and our analyses aim to illustrate this argument. And while we do discuss certain aspects of authorial style, text style is our primary object of study.

1.6 Corpus stylistics versus cognitive stylistics

Corpus stylistics is by no means the only recent major development in the field of stylistics. Cognitive stylistics has been (and continues to be) one of the most significant movements in stylistics over the last two decades, though its roots go back even further (West 2010). Its popularity stems in part from the democratising principles on which it is founded and which arise from its concern with how real readers respond to texts, including both literary and popular fiction. While cognitive stylistics aims to develop theories and models of the reading process that can be extrapolated to all readers, it is careful that such theories and models are able to explain individual readers' responses to texts. In this respect cognitive stylistics is concerned with the individual. Corpus stylistics, on the other hand, is concerned with discerning patterns in language use through the study of large quantities of language data, and while this may sometimes provide evidence for individual interpretations of specific texts (see, for example, Jeffries and McIntyre's 2010 corpus-informed stylistic analysis of the Roger McGough poem, 'italic'), it is not primarily concerned with accounting for the practices of individual readers. Rather, it is aimed at generalising about linguistic behaviour beyond the sample studied. Consequently, corpus stylistics and cognitive stylistics are concerned with different (though often related) issues. This is perhaps one reason why corpus stylistics has to date made few inroads into cognitive linguistics and stylistics; for reasons of focus, cognitive stylisticians have often assumed that corpus methods have little to offer to the cognitive enterprise. Peter Stockwell, for example, a cognitive stylistician of considerable renown, has explained that only recently has he seen the potential of corpus stylistics for augmenting his own cognitively oriented work (personal communication; see also Mahlberg et al. 2014), and that this is largely as a consequence of improvements to both software and analytical methods (since then, the interdisciplinary work of Mahlberg and Stockwell has been instrumental in raising the profile of corpus stylistics; see, for example, Mahlberg et al. 2016). Added to this is the fact that doing corpus stylistics involves familiarising oneself with corpus linguistic software (assuming, that is, that the analyst is not sufficiently skilled in programming to develop their own; see Gries 2010 for a criticism of the over-reliance on commercially available software), principles of statistics, techniques of data collection and storage, and data manipulation. It is, then, easy to see why many cognitive stylisticians have taken the view that corpus stylistics is not for them.

However, it should also be noted that corpus stylistics has, from some quarters at least, been reluctant to take on board insights from cognitive work. In some cases this reluctance has extended to outright hostility. This is a problem because it is often the case that without insights from other areas of stylistics, corpus stylistics can become simply an exercise in counting linguistic patterns, with no means of accounting for the interpretative significance of these. Indeed, one of the factors that has arguably made corpus stylistics unattractive to some stylisticians is the fact that some corpus stylistic 'analyses' fail to engage sufficiently at a functional level for meaningful interpretations of the data to be made. It is interesting to note that this is the kind of criticism that was made of some stylistics in its early days. Sinclair's (1966) stylistic analysis of Larkin's poem, 'First Sight', for example, was heavily criticised for being mechanistic rather than interpretatively revealing (see Vendler 1966; Melia 1974), a criticism that is now sometimes levelled at contemporary stylistic work that makes use of corpus methods. Nonetheless, some corpus stylisticians have been similarly critical of cognitive stylistics for a number of reasons. One of the most vocal critics has been Louw, who has been vehement in his criticism of the cognitivists. Here he is being interviewed on the issue:

> cognitivists (Stockwell 2002; Gavins and Steen 2003) will tell you that you have a schema for *pubs* and that as a result you know that you can purchase food and drink in them. We accept this form of claptrap far too readily and the system behind it works because most of us will never see the *proof* of what only

a corpus can show: that the most frequent collocates of *pub* are the terms *groups*, *chains* and *organisations*. Pubs organise our drinking habits and their own profitability, far more than anything else they do, and only a corpus will show you that. (Louw 2011: 179)

There are a number of problems with Louw's argument, however. First of all, evidence from the corpus that *pub* collocates with *groups*, *chains* and *organisations* does not, in and of itself, falsify the concept of a schema. A schema is a structured collection of world knowledge stored in our long-term memory (Eysenck and Keane 2010: 403–6) and while some specific concepts from schema theory (such as the notions of scripts and frames; see Jeffries and McIntyre 2010 for a summary) may be difficult to confirm empirically, experiments in psycholinguistics and neuroscience have found evidence for the existence of some kind of schematic structuring of linguistic knowledge. Evidence for the existence of a schema of some kind can also be found in the fact that when talking to someone from the same culture as us, there are a number of elements of world knowledge that we can take for granted, a pub being one of these. Put simply, we do not need to explain what pubs are when we use the word; we can instead simply assume that our addressee will possess the requisite background knowledge to be able to understand what we are talking about. Collocation, then, does not refute schema theory. Indeed, one of its effects may even be to tune (Rumelhart and Norman 1976) an analyst's schema.

Louw's criticism of cognitive work extends beyond that concerned specifically with stylistics. Louw is seemingly dismissive of any endeavour which does not embrace empiricism, asking, 'What price are we to set upon "theories" that specialise in telling you what you already know in the hope of keeping you away from the empiricism in which truth manifestly resides and is easily revealed?' (2011: 179). Louw is right in counselling against the unquestioning acceptance of claims that lack evidence. However, while empiricism can validate or invalidate such claims, in some cases so too can logic; that is, empiricism is not the be all and end all when it comes to demolishing mentalistic theories and models. Furthermore, the assumption that cognitive stylistics eschews empiricism is simply not true. While many cognitive theories are indeed difficult to test, significant work has been done on precisely this topic (see, for example, the work of Sandford and Emmott 2012 on testing the psychological reality of the processing of narratives). The sweeping aside of all non-empirically derived theories also seems short-sighted when we consider their value in other disciplines. Physics, for instance, has made substantial steps forward as a result of the postulation of non-empirically derived theories such as String Theory (see Polchinski 1998).

There is, then, a danger in setting corpus stylistics in opposition to cognitive stylistics. The two endeavours are not mutually exclusive and if we follow this path, we are likely to overlook significant insights that might be gained in one area and have relevance for the other. To this end, we also argue that neither corpus stylistics nor cognitive stylistics should be aiming for disciplinary isolation. Rather, they should be practised with the aim of establishing a new mainstream in stylistics, so that it becomes inconceivable that a corpus stylistic analysis that would benefit from a cognitive dimension ignores this, and vice versa.

1.7 Aims of the book

The aim of this book is to advance the discipline of stylistics by (1) demonstrating the potential of utilising corpus linguistic methods in stylistic analysis, and (2) making the case for corpus stylistics as a well-defined practice distinct from corpus linguistics more generally. We argue that corpus analytical techniques have much to offer to stylistics, and have the potential to improve the insights, generalisability and potential for falsification of stylistic analyses. The book is addressed primarily to stylisticians, particularly those who may be new to the use of corpora in stylistics. In this respect, we hope that the book may be valuable to undergraduate students, postgraduates and established researchers alike. It is not, however, an introduction to stylistics in general, and we have assumed a certain level of familiarity with the basic concepts of stylistics described in section 1.5. (For readers unfamiliar with these, there are many useful introductions to stylistics, including, among many others, Short 1996a; Jeffries and McIntyre 2010; Simpson 2014.)

We aim to show how off-the-shelf corpus linguistic software might be employed in the service of stylistic analysis (there is, of course, a strong case to be made for developing the programming skills that would make a reliance on existing software unnecessary, though we concentrate here on the use of existing programs, since this is an obvious starting point for those new to corpus studies). Moreover, we make a case for corpus stylistics as a distinctive and theoretically sound approach to text analysis. While there are a number of books that explain how to use corpus software for text analysis (see, for example, Adolphs 2006 Baker 2006), there has to date been no book that combines this with a theoretical account of the nature of corpus stylistics as an approach

And while the book is aimed primarily at stylisticians, we hope that corpus linguists will also see a value in the application of stylistic theories, models and analytical frameworks in the analysis of corpus data. At the heart of stylistics is the notion of choice; only where there is a choice from a range of linguistic options can style emerge. And since this concept of choice applies equally to the kind of data that corpus linguists tend to be interested in, it should be clear why stylistic insights are also likely to be of value to corpus linguistics.

1.8 Structure of the book

Although theory and practice are interwoven throughout this book, there is a broad distinction between the first half and the second half. The first five chapters cover key theoretical and methodological issues in corpus stylistics, from corpus building to analytical methods. Chapters 6 to 9 then demonstrate the application of these concepts in particular sub-fields of stylistics (cognitive, pedagogical and historical stylistics, and the application of stylistics in the solution of real-world problems). This is done with the aim of making a clear case for corpus stylistics as a distinctive analytical practice. Chapter 10 then draws together the arguments made throughout the book in order to offer a definition of corpus stylistics that is founded on the theoretical and methodological arguments introduced and illustrated in each chapter. And since we are particularly concerned to encourage more stylisticians to adopt corpus methods, each chapter except the first and the last features at least one case study (often alongside a range of other analytical examples). Moreover, Chapters 2 to 9 also include numerous step-by-step guides to carrying out particular elements of corpus analysis. These are presented in a series of numbered boxes. Some of these are replication tasks, aimed at allowing you to obtain for yourself the results we discuss. Others provide instructions on how to carry out a particular analytical technique on your own data. The aim behind these boxes is to be open about our own methodological processes and to encourage the development of the practical analytical skills needed to do corpus stylistic analysis independently. Throughout the book we make use of three corpus linguistic software packages in particular. These are AntConc (Anthony 2018), WordSmith Tools (Scott 2016) and Wmatrix (Rayson 2009). In addition, we also make use of a variety of other tools, including Multilingual Corpus Toolkit (Piao et al. 2002) and BYU-BNC (Davies 2004–). These are discussed at various points, with many of the numbered boxes explaining how to carry out particular analytical techniques using these packages.

The book is structured as follows. Having outlined the origins of corpus stylistics and its relation to corpus linguistics, in Chapter 2 we demonstrate the possibilities of using large, publicly available corpora and off-the-shelf software to support the qualitative analysis of short texts. This is a useful first step for anyone wishing to explore the potential of corpus stylistics, since it does not involve the labour-intensive creation of corpora from scratch and impressive results can be obtained quickly. In demonstrating this approach, we discuss in more detail the work of Louw (1993) and O'Halloran (2007). We explain the value of examining concordance lines from large corpora in order to shed light on localised meanings in texts, and we describe and critique Louw's concept of semantic prosody. We demonstrate the potential of this kind of analysis in a corpus-informed discussion of a short extract from a sketch by Alan Bennett, Peter Cook, Jonathan Miller and Dudley Moore, a sketch that formed part of their famous satirical revue show of 1960, *Beyond the Fringe*.

In Chapter 3 we move beyond the use of existing large corpora and focus on how to construct corpora of texts for stylistic analysis. We discuss corpus design and describe the process of collecting and storing data before going on to discuss techniques of annotation and mark-up (known generally as *tagging*). Here, we concentrate particularly on the manual annotation of data for stylistic categories. Our data in the case study in this chapter is a corpus of 'Judge Dredd' comic strips from the comic *2000AD*, which we use to demonstrate how manual annotation for components of a comic can be used to explore diachronic developments in this area in comics. This choice of data is intended to demonstrate that corpus stylistics can be practised equally well on multimodal texts.

Chapter 4 steps back from the practical business of corpus-building to consider what must precede this. In this chapter we discuss how to go about developing research questions for a project in corpus stylistics, how such questions relate to project aims and objectives, and how to develop and test hypotheses. While we do not suggest that a top-down approach such as that described in this chapter is the only way of going about corpus stylistics, we argue that it offers a way of carrying out the kind of tightly controlled project that can generate significant insights into stylistic techniques and effects. We demonstrate this through an analysis of the authorial style of Ernest Hemingway, comparing corpus-derived insights against the intuitive reactions of literary critics to his work. We argue that the objective insights provided by a corpus stylistic analysis supersede the subjective and unfalsifiable observations that are to be found in much literary criticism of Hemingway's work. In addition, we suggest that such insights have much to offer to non-linguistically inclined literary critics by stimulating new research questions.

Having demonstrated some of the key techniques of corpus analysis, in Chapter 5 we move on to consider more complex procedures utilising insights from statistics. We begin by explaining the need for statistical analysis in stylistics before going on to outline some of the main statistical tests used in corpus stylistic research. We concentrate particularly on procedures for calculating keyness (a measure of the extent to which a linguistic item is over- or under-represented in comparison with its distribution in a comparator corpus) and collocational strength. We explain the principles that underlie such statistical techniques and show how insights gained from such tests can be valuable in stylistic analysis, particularly with regard to identifying background norms in language. The case study in this chapter also shows the value of keyness analysis for selecting small samples from a corpus for qualitative stylistic analysis. We use the techniques introduced in the chapter to select a text sample from David Peace's novel *1974* (Peace 1999) which we then analyse both qualitatively and quantitatively.

Having outlined the tools and techniques of corpus stylistics, Chapters 6 to 9 exemplify these further by providing additional examples of what corpus stylistic analysis is and how it differs from mainstream corpus linguistic analysis. Chapter 6 examines the issue of characterisation in the 1979 BBC TV drama *Tinker Tailor Soldier Spy*. In particular, we compare the dialogue with the associated deaf and hard-of-hearing subtitles, paying attention to the potential effects on characterisation of differences that exist between the two. We use a cognitive stylistic model of characterisation to direct our analysis, and by so doing we show the potential of corpus methods to be used in conjunction with cognitive stylistics. This chapter further highlights the importance of qualitative analysis in corpus stylistics; quantitative findings have limited value on their own, and to be used to their greatest potential they need to be combined with the insights that only qualitative analysis can provide.

Chapter 7 focuses on the use of corpora for pedagogical stylistics. We explore the possibilities of using corpora both for teaching stylistics and for developing practical classroom activities. We argue that this approach has particular relevance to the foreign-language classroom, and we demonstrate how the corpus stylistic analysis of Adrian Henri's poem 'Tonight at Noon' might be used with second-language learners of English to teach linguistic norms in Standard English. In this respect, Chapter 7 constitutes an example of pedagogical corpus stylistics.

In Chapter 8 we discuss the extent to which corpus techniques can shed light on aspects of historical style. We consider some of the practicalities of collecting and analysing appropriate data and discuss how linguistic observations might be linked to external socio-political and socio-cultural events. To exemplify the techniques of historical corpus stylistics, we offer analyses of discourse presentation in Early Modern English fiction and news writing, and modality in Early Modern journalism.

Chapter 9 concentrates exclusively on the analysis of non-literary texts, with the specific aim of demonstrating the real-world impact that can be gained from corpus stylistic analysis. We discuss an external project that we have carried out for the UK Green Party, where insights from corpus stylistic analysis were used to provide this organisation with practical suggestions for addressing problems concerning their external representation in the press.

In Chapter 10 we offer a summary of what we see as the main techniques and analytical methods of corpus stylistics, and offer our own view of its definition and status. We finish by speculating on what the future may hold for this new and fascinating form of stylistics.

Finally, Appendix 1 provides a list of useful corpora for corpus stylistic analysis, along with a list of the specialised corpora constructed for this book, while Appendix 2 details the variety of corpus tools available to support corpus stylistic research. These appendices are necessarily selective but will provide an entry point to exploring the wide range of resources currently available to corpus stylisticians.

Notes

1. Collocation is defined by McEnery et al. as 'the characteristic co-occurrence of patterns of words' (2006: 345). We discuss collocation fully in Chapter 2.
2. See <http://ucrel.lancs.ac.uk/claws/> (last accessed 20 August 2018).
3. See <http://cass.lancs.ac.uk/bnc2014> (last accessed 20 August 2018).

2

Using corpora to support qualitative stylistic analysis

2.1 Introduction

One measure of the extent to which corpus linguistics has become mainstream is the degree to which it has been accepted as a methodology by numerous sub-disciplines of linguistics. In addition to the use of corpora in lexicology, syntax and semantics (around which disciplines corpus linguistics was arguably developed), it is now common to find corpus techniques employed in almost all other areas of language study. For instance, much contemporary research in child language acquisition is now informed by corpus data: at the time of writing, over 11,000 articles listed on Google Scholar utilise the CHILDES (Child Language Data Exchange System) database. Similarly, corpora and corpus analytical techniques have been embraced in, for example, sociolinguistics (Baker 2010), translation studies (Mikhailov and Cooper 2016), English language teaching (Timmis 2015) and even phonetics, where the construction of large spoken corpora has revolutionised research in forensic speech science (see, for example, Gold et al. 2017). Another measure of the importance of corpus linguistics is the extent to which it has influenced the development of sub-disciplines of language study. Historical linguistics, for instance, has been transformed by corpus linguistic techniques, which have made it possible to observe patterns of linguistic change in the recent history of languages that would have been impossible to discern prior to the advent of corpus tools (see, for instance, Nevalainen 2012; Nevalainen et al. 2016). And by the same token, corpus analytical techniques have the potential to transform stylistics by initiating a step-change in how we carry out stylistic analysis.

In this chapter, we show how even fairly basic corpus analytical techniques have much to offer to the stylistician.

It is only comparatively recently that corpora have begun to be used in stylistics. In 1970 Freeman felt able to write confidently that Bloch's (1953) definition of style as deviation from frequency norms was 'a chimera' (1970: 5). Freeman's confidence in this regard arose from his certainty that '[t]he "frequency distributions and transitional probabilities" [Bloch 1953: 40] of natural language are not known and never will be' (1970: 5–6). But even prior to Freeman's statement, nascent work in corpus linguistics had begun to show that this was simply not true (see, for example, Kučera and Francis's 1967 ground-breaking *Computational Analysis of Present-Day American English*, based on the Brown Corpus). And since Freeman's statement, corpus linguistic and stylometric analysis has clearly demonstrated the capacity for determining frequency norms based on large-scale representative samples of language data (see, for example, Biber 1988, 2006; Conrad and Biber 2001; Hoover 2017). But in addition to his statement that such quantitative data could never be obtained, Freeman also claimed that even if it could, this would 'constitute no particularly revealing insight into either natural language or style' (1970: 6). This chapter sets out to show how, in relation to stylistics, the opposite is true.

We focus in this chapter on the concept of what O'Halloran (2007) terms 'corpus-assisted' analysis, something that we prefer to call 'corpus-informed' stylistics. This essentially means using pre-existing large-scale corpora to support the stylistic analysis of single texts or textual extracts. For people new to corpus stylistics, one of the most straightforward ways of beginning to integrate corpus methods and stylistic analysis is to use such existing large corpora to support or challenge an intuitive response to a text. This is what we do in this chapter, where we introduce the BYU interface (developed by Mark Davies at *Brigham Young University*) to the British National Corpus (BNC) and use it as an external norm against which to compare a single text. In explicating corpus-informed stylistics, we pay particular attention to the concept of semantic prosody, outlined briefly in Chapter 1. This concept is inextricably linked with the concepts of collocation and concordancing, which we explain in full later on in this chapter.

We begin with a brief illustration of the value of collocational analysis for stylistics before going on to a fuller discussion of the concept of semantic prosody, taking into account the various criticisms that have been levelled at it. And in order to show how corpus-informed stylistics can support the analysis of very small textual extracts, we end the chapter with a stylistic analysis of a short excerpt from a sketch by

Alan Bennett, Peter Cook, Jonathan Miller and Dudley Moore, entitled 'Aftermyth of war' (Bennett et al. 1987). Our overall argument is that corpus-informed stylistics offers a means of testing intuitive claims about style, thereby invalidating the position held by Freeman (1970).

2.2 Strolling with intent: an exercise in corpus-informed stylistics

In John Le Carré's novel *A Legacy of Spies* (2017), the narrator is recalling the story his mother told him of how she and his father first met, at a wedding where she was a bridesmaid:

> After the ceremony, so her story goes, she and a fellow bridesmaid, the better for a glass or two of champagne, played truant from the reception and, still in their finery, took an evening stroll along the crowded promenade, where my father was also *strolling with intent*. (Le Carré 2017: 2; our emphasis)

An interesting stylistic element of the above passage is the complement in the final subordinate clause. What is the significance of the narrator describing his father as 'strolling *with intent*'? Why not say 'strolling along' or simply 'strolling'? In short, why does Le Carré choose this particular formulation over the range of other possibilities? And what effect does this choice have? One method of determining this it to look at occurrences of the phrase in a corpus and observe any patterns in its usage. This in essence is corpus-informed stylistics: using the insights to be gained from a large-scale corpus to inform our claims about the likely reasons for and effect of a particular stylistic choice.

There are 283 occurrences of the phrase *with intent* in the BNC (to replicate our search, follow the steps outlined in Box 2.1). In 270 of these instances, *with intent* is used in the context of law-breaking and/or causing injury or another form of distress to a third party (see Figure 2.1). Examples include 'with intent to injure the plaintiffs', 'with intent to defraud', 'with intent to endanger life' and 'with intent to injure, aggrieve or annoy the victim'. Given the prevalence of this pattern, it is not beyond the realms of possibility to suppose that when we read the phrase 'strolling with intent' in Le Carré's novel, we draw unconsciously on our schematic knowledge of how the phrase *with intent* is used in everyday life and that this information shapes how we interpret the passage. That is, when the narrator describes his father as 'strolling with intent', we are likely to interpret this as meaning that he was strolling with an ulterior motive in mind, one which was likely to have a negative impact on someone else.

No. Concordance line

No.		with intent	
1	' conspired amongst themselves and others to defraud the plaintiffs, and	with intent	to injure the plaintiffs, by a scheme for extracting moneys from the plaintiffs by
2	A person commits the latter offence if he' by any false pretence...	with intent	to defraud, obtains from any other person any chattel, money, or valuable
3	suggested as a definition of theft:' To steal is unlawfully, and	with intent	to defraud, by taking, by embezzlement, by obtaining by false pretences,
4	likely to endanger life (section 2), and the possession of explosives	with intent	to endanger life (section 3). The latter offence is an inchoate offence
5	. The latter offence is an inchoate offence of a familiar kind: possession	with intent	, in circumstances where an innocent reason for possessing explosives is fairly
6	is little difficulty in holding that a person caught in possession of explosives	with intent	to endanger life has sufficiently crossed the threshold of criminality to justify
7	the Firearms Act 1968. Section 16 contains an offence of possessing a firearm	with intent	to endanger life, which corresponds to the offence under section 3 of the Explosives
8	of a slightly different type. Section 18 penalizes the possession of a firearm	with intent	to commit a crime or to resist arrest: this is a more specific variation
9	imprisonment. # (b) Wounding or Grievous Bodily Harm (GBH)	with intent	# Section 18 of the Offences against the Person Act 1861 creates a serious offence
10	the fault requirements, the one most commonly relied on in prosecutions is'	with intent	to cause grievous bodily harm'. The meaning of 'intention' here is
11	as recklessness is proved. But there is an alternative fault element:'	with intent	to prevent the lawful apprehension or detainer of any person'. Whilst the policy
12	penalties, and three of them may be mentioned here. One is assault	with intent	to rob, which, like robbery, carries a maximum of life imprisonment:
13	in effect, an offence of attempted robbery. Another aggravated offence is assault	with intent	to resist arrest or to prevent a lawful arrest, contrary to section 38 of
14	substances. Section 22 penalizes the use of any overpowering drug or substance'	with intent	to enable the commission of an arrestable offence' (maximum sentence of life impr
15	. Section 24 penalizes the administration of any poison or noxious thing,'	with intent	to injure, aggrieve or annoy the victim' (maximum sentence of five years
16	the field between attempted murder and common assault: causing serious injury	with intent	to cause serious injury; causing serious injury recklessly; and causing injury either
17	to cause serious injury; causing serious injury recklessly; and causing injury either	with intent	or recklessly. Separate offences for cases involving police-officers and children
18	. Third, why are there two separate offences of causing serious injury --	with intent	, or recklessly -- when the two mental states are combined in a single offence
19	is' a definite moral and psychological difference' between causing serious injury	with intent	and causing serious injury recklessly, and that this difference should be reflected
20	have done is something' more than merely preparatory' to sexual intercourse,	with intent	to have unlawful sexual intercourse without the woman's consent. Whether the
21	submission, made by a defendant charged with the possession of a hacksaw blade	with intent	to do criminal damage to the perimeter fence of the US naval base at Brawdy
22	proved that the damage resulted from an act or omission of the carrier done	with intent	to cause damage or recklessly and with knowledge that damage would probably
23	The 1948 Genocide Convention prohibits a wide variety of acts committed	with intent	to destroy a national, ethnic or religious group. This only confirms already-existing
24	person any writing, sign... which is threatening, abusive or insulting...	with intent	to cause another to believe that immediate violence will be used... or to provoke
25	winding up it appears that any business of the company has been carried on	with intent	to defraud creditors of the company or other persons, or for any fraudulent pu
26	law, the Court of Appeal was satisfied that the articles had been published	with intent	to interfere with the administration of justice. This case also indicates that one of
27	could leave the building, and later charged them with possession of cannabis,	with intent	to supply. The defence alleged abuse of process. Held, granting the applications
28	haps the more specific question to be asked is whether the charges of possession	with intent	were brought solely for the purpose of retaining the applicants in custody. Would
29	Auld and Judge JJ.: July 16,1991. The appellant was convicted of wounding	with intent	. His defence was that of self-defence; he alleged that the victim had attacked
30	. Facts: pleaded guilty to placing an imitation bomb in a department store	with intent	to induce a belief that it was likely to explode or ignite. The appellant
31	to two offences of robbery, one of attempted robbery and two of assault	with intent	to rob. The appellant was concerned with another youth aged 17 in a number
32	the car which is the subject of the order. Causing grievous bodily harm	with intent	-- premeditated attack involving blows to the leg with a hammer, causing fractur
33	24 (m.). Facts: convicted of causing grievous bodily harm	with intent	. The offender had a dispute with the victim as a result of the sale
34	, Hodgson and Buckley JJ.: November 6,1991. F was charged with wounding	with intent	and affray. The prosecution case was that the victim, R, came with

Figure 2.1 Concordance of negative *with intent* from the British National Corpus

35	. November 4,1991. Facts: pleaded guilty to robbery, having a firearm	with intent	and driving while disqualified. The offender went by motorcycle to a small branch
36	JJ. January 27,1991. Facts: convicted of robbery and possessing a firearm	with intent	to commit an indictable offence. The offender and his accomplice went to a sub-
37	and Jowitt JJ. January 17,1992. Facts: pleaded guilty to possessing heroin	with intent	to supply. The appellant was found in possession of 1.03 grammes of heroin.
38	44 (m.) Facts: pleaded guilty to causing grievous bodily harm	with intent	. The appellant's 18 year old daughter was indecently assaulted by the father of
39	by Serious Fraud Office -- Applicant charged with carrying on business of company	with intent	to defraud creditors -- Whether power of Director to compel answers to questio
40	knowingly been a party to the carrying on of the business of the company	with intent	to defraud its creditors, contrary to section 458 of the Companies Act 1985.
41	on of the business of a company called Wallace Smith Trust Co. Ltd.	with intent	to defraud creditors of the said company contrary to section 458 Companies Act
42	a computer, in contravention of section 1(1) of the Act of 1990,	with intent	to commit a further offence of false accounting. On a submission of no case
43	the Act of 1990 the words' causes a computer to perform any function	with intent	to secure access to any program or data held in any computer,' in
44	plain and ordinary meaning, were not confined to the use of one computer	with intent	to secure access into another computer; so that section 1(1) was contravened w
45	1(1) was contravened where a person caused a computer to perform a function	with intent	to secure unauthorised access to any program or data held in the same computer
46	lows:' Count 1. Statement of Offence:Securing unauthorised access to a computer	with intent	to commit a further offence, contrary to section 2(1) of the Computer Misuse Act
47	to a computer in contravention of section 1(1) of the Computer Misuse Act 1990	with intent	to commit a further offence, namely, false accounting contrary to section 17(1) (
48	1990 dishonestly and with a view to gain for himself or another, or	with intent	to cause loss to another, falsified a document required for an accounting purpose,
49	ction 2(1) it was necessary to establish that the offender had used one computer	with intent	to secure unauthorised access into another computer. The judge upheld the sub
50	actual wording of the subsection:' Causing a computer to perform any function	with intent	to secure access to any program or data held in any computer."
51	there does not have to be the use by the offender of one computer	with intent	to secure unauthorised access into another computer; (iii) there is no ambiguity
52	offence if -- (a) he causes a computer to perform any function	with intent	to secure access to any program or data held in any computer; (b
53	an offence under section 1 above (' the unauthorised access offence')	with intent	-- (a) to commit an offence to which this section applies; or
54	2(1), it was necessary to establish that the offender had used one computer	with intent	to secure unauthorised access into another computer. The judge upheld that s
55	actual wording of the subsection;' causing a computer to perform any function	with intent	to secure access to any program or data held in any computer.' A
56	, there does not have to be use by the offender of one computer	with intent	to secure unauthorised access into another computer. The words used are not a
57	words. They are,' he causes a computer to perform any function	with intent	to secure access to any program or data held in any computer.' Mr.
58	ainant was injured, the appellant was charged with causing grievous bodily harm	with intent	, contrary to section 18 of the Offences against the Person Act 1861. At
60	another person, not being a servant or agent of the owner,	with intent	to do damage or # (iii) # was due wholly to the negligence
61	any rights over the goods. If I snatch your hat from your head	with intent	to steal it, that is conversion as well as trespass, but if I
62	, sign or other visible representation which is threatening, abusive or insulting,	with intent	to cause that person to believe that immediate unlawful violence will be used ag
63	as it appears to be on first reading, by the opening words'	with intent	'If a person acts with the intention of frightening or provoking, there
64	Part. Section 4(1) provides that the offence is committed if the defendants act	with intent	to cause a person to believe that immediate unlawful violence is about to be used
65	person to believe that immediate unlawful violence is about to be used, or	with intent	to provoke such unlawful violence. This probably repeats the existing law. In add
66	changes the existing law, making the offence more difficult to prove. #	with intent	# The current meaning of the word' intent' has been discussed in connection
67	from another is not an assault for the purposes of the offence of assault	with intent	to resist an arrest. # The mental element for assault on a constable #
68	charge gives the defendant the choice of jury trial. The offence of assault	with intent	to resist arrest -- whether by a policeman or a civilian -- remains indictable,
69	under the age of 18 out of the possession of her parent or guardian	with intent	that she shall have sexual intercourse, are restricted in the same fashion. It
70	of taking an unmarried girl of 18 out of the possession of her parent	with intent	to have sexual intercourse, and concluded that little would be achieved by doing s

Figure 2.1 Continued

Concordance line

No.			
71	the offence of taking an unmarried girl out of the possession of her parents	with intent	to have sexual intercourse should include both boys and girls provided that they a
72	boy or girl under 16 or a severely mentally handicapped person of either sex	with intent	to have unlawful sexual intercourse or take part in an act of gross indecency.
73	section 3(1) as well as for the offence of administering drugs to a woman	with intent	to stupefy her and enable a man to have sexual intercourse with her. Parliament
74	indecent assault upon his spouse, or an attempt to commit, or assault	with intent	to commit rape or indecent assault upon his spouse (except as an accessory)
75	on bigamy. In the remaining three, which did involve rape or assault	with intent	to commit rape, the jury was directed that' Both the charges require an
76	plead guilty to lesser offences such as assault, assault and battery and assault	with intent	to commit rape which carry low penalties. Surprisingly similar findings were made
77	ffences. 23 were convicted of a related non-sexual offence ranging from burglary (	with intent	to rape) to assault occasioning actual bodily harm. Furthermore, of those convic
78	provides as follows:' Sexual Assault Category 1 – inflicting grievous bodily harm	with intent	to have sexual intercourse with another who maliciously inflicts grievous
79	(1) Any person who maliciously inflicts grievous bodily harm upon another person	with intent	to have sexual intercourse with the other person shall be liable to penal servitude
81	. Sexual Assault Category 2 – inflicting actual bodily harm, etc.,	with intent	to have sexual intercourse. S.61C. (1) Any person who --;
82	odily harm upon another person by means of an offensive weapon or instrument,	with intent	to have sexual intercourse with the other person shall be liable to penal servitude
83	or (b) threatens to inflict actual bodily harm upon another person,	with intent	to have sexual intercourse with a third person who is present or nearby shall be
84	of 20 years, is confined to the malicious infliction of grievous bodily harm	with intent	to have sexual intercourse either with the victim or with a third party who is
85	its maximum penalty of 12 years, covers the infliction of actual bodily harm	with intent	to have sexual intercourse with the victim or a third party who is present or
86	nearby. It also covers a threat to inflict such harm upon a person	with intent	to have sexual intercourse with that person provided that the threat is made with
87	. Where, however, the defendant threatens one person with actual bodily harm	with intent	to have sexual intercourse with another, no offensive weapon or instrument is n
88	akes it an offence maliciously to inflict grievous bodily harm upon another person	with intent	to have sexual intercourse. However, it is precisely where the infliction of grievo
89	committed where the defendant inflicts actual bodily harm upon the complainant	with intent	to have sexual intercourse. Actual bodily harm need not be serious harm and it
90	. For example, the defendant may argue that the injury was not inflicted	with intent	to have intercourse but occurred after consensual intercourse or was inflicted dur
91	ory 2 with threatening the complainant with an offensive weapon or instrument	with intent	to have sexual intercourse, he may state that he brandished a knife to persuade
92	assertion of consent would generally amount to a denial that injury was inflicted	with intent	to have sexual intercourse. It may be concluded, therefore, that the advantages
93	order to promote the trade interests of the Association and its members and not	with intent	to injure, and so long as the money, fine or penalty demanded was
94	ere subjected to force. This subsection creates two offences: robbery and assault	with intent	to rob. Robbery is essentially an aggravated form of theft. All the elements
95	' (p.270). One minor change is that the crime of assault	with intent	to rob, at present found in s.8, is transferred out of the part
96	payment, whether his own liability or another's: or (b)	with intent	to make permanent default in whole or in part on any existing liability to make
97	whole or in part on any existing liability to make a payment, or	with intent	to let another do so, dishonestly induces the creditor or any person claiming pa
98	from him, dishonestly makes off without having paid as required or expected and	with intent	to avoid payment of the amount due shall be guilty of an offence. (
99	to pay but leaves without doing do. (e) The phrase '	with intent	to avoid payment ' is read as meaning ' with intent never to pay'
100	The phrase ' with intent to avoid payment ' is read as meaning '	with intent	never to pay '; Allen 1985AC 1029 (HL). On the facts
101	(pause) sent to prison for five years plus six months for possessing a firearm	with intent	to endanger life. July nineteen eighty eight escape from prison at (-----) with one
102	received a prison sentence er for in fact being in possession of a firearm	with intent	to endanger life. (pause) He reminded me of the circumstances of the incident res
103	. Bourne, of Maidenhead Road, Bristol, denies causing grievous bodily harm	with intent	. The hearing was adjourned until today. # Man saw hit-run driver kill wife
104	explosion in Bridle Lane, Soho, on April 6 and possessing a revolver	with intent	to resist arrest. Mr Don Dovaston, assistant chief constable of Derbyshire, named
105	, Soho, central London, on April 6, and possessing a revolver	with intent	to resist arrest. Canning and Lamb were flanked by police in the oak-panelled cour

Figure 2.1 Continued

	Left context		with intent	Right context
106	said. The lower-tier offence should cover simple hacking and the other, hacking		with intent	to steal or damage. The gravity of the second would be reflected in heavier
107	orised entry into a computer system, an aggravated offence of unauthorised entry		with intent	to commit or assist in serious crime, and a further serious offence of altering
108	of pounds on security to deter simple unauthorised access. The offence of hacking		with intent	to commit serious crime -- including all serious forms of dishonesty, serious offenc
109	forces in west Belfast, and of possessing an AK 47 rifle and ammunition		with intent	to endanger life. Daniel Joseph McBrearty, 36, from Londonderry, is to
110	, Dunbar, East Lothian, admitted attempting to murder her and assaulting her		with intent	to rape. An earlier court hearing was told that the woman awoke one morning
111	jury also found Danny Palmer, aged 17, guilty of grievous bodily harm		with intent	and cruelty to the seven-month-old baby who died in Whittington Hospital, north
112	of Belfast, was charged with having two rifles, a pistol and ammunition		with intent	to endanger life; possessing information likely to be useful to terrorists and raising
113	south London, was jailed for eight years for possessing 501 grams of cocaine		with intent	to supply. The judge ordered seizure of his assets totalling 36,200 or Fraser would
114	gsworth was jailed for three years after he admitted causing grievous bodily harm		with intent	, wounding, assault causing actual bodily harm and two offences of burglary. Mr
115	, culpable homicide, rape, child abuse, possession of a deadly weapon		with intent	to use it, assault which results in permanent serious injury to body or mind
116	. They also denied trying to murder three police officers and possessing a rifle		with intent	to endanger life. Both were remanded in custody. # 40 held in dole
117	found 4,000 in a bedside cabinet. Eubank was found guilty of possessing drugs		with intent	to supply. He was remanded in custody and will be sentenced in four weeks
118	on. He admits burglary. Both men deny alternative charges of unlawful wounding		with intent	and unlawful wounding of the two PCs. The trial continues. # Sooty sweeps
119	Cleve, and Winter, 19, of Cheltenham, deny manslaughter and arson		with intent	. The trial continues. # Aunt's pity saves death drive girl # A
120	one was killed.' Harre, of Walworth, London, denied arson		with intent	to endanger life but admitted reckless arson. Jailing him for three and a half
121	, but the jury failed to reach a verdict on alternative charges of wounding		with intent	and causing actual bodily harm. The charges arose from an incident in Cypress
122	, 18, of Marine Parade, Dovercourt, faces a charge of wounding		with intent	to inflict grievous bodily harm on Brian Kelsey. Mr Kelsey, who is thought
123	no fixed address, denies kidnapping, attempted murder and administering poison		with intent	on March 20 last year. The judge, Mr Justice Humphrey Potts, told
124	jury he will direct them to acquit the man of rape and administering poison		with intent	to endanger life following submissions by the defence. The jury was told yesterd
125	sending an article'. The original charge was of sending a fake bomb		with intent	, but the charge was amended because of the man's mental state. Pryse-Jones
126	ton-Rogers, of Calkewood Lane, Rickinghall, guilty of causing grievous bodily harm		with intent	. He had denied the offence. Assistant recorder Paul Downes remanded him in cus
127	the car. He was acquitted of rape, attempted murder, administering poison		with intent	and kidnapping. He admitted unlawful imprisonment and sex with an under-age g
128	guilty of wounding Mr Lay, 19, of Anderson Walk, Bury,		with intent	to cause him grievous bodily harm. During the two-day trial the court heard how
129	of the most serious offences known to criminal law – you wounded your friend		with intent	to do him really serious injury.' He said the youth had drunk a
130	g grievous bodily harm and one had also been charged with possessing a firearm		with intent	to endanger life. The two accused men are due to appear before Chelmsford ma
131	urders, three attempted murders and six charges of causing grievous bodily harm		with intent	. Many of the youngsters who survived were left mentally and physically handica
132	Becky's twin sister Katie, and 11 alternative counts of grievous bodily harm		with intent	to injure. # Call to young musicmakers # MUSICIANS across Essex are being invited
133	of Hopkins Mead, Chelmsford, are charged with attempted grievous bodily harm		with intent	to injure two men at the pub that night. Rank is additionally charged with
134	three counts of attempted murder, planting a bomb and possession of explosives		with intent	on February 24,1991. The Crown lawyer said the court would hear that the pro
135	store in Chesterfield on May 7. The boy was also charged with arson		with intent	to endanger life in connection with an incident at Chesterfield library on Monday.
136	ns, Carrickfergus, was also accused of unlawfully wounding Kathleen Williamson		with intent	to cause her grievous bodily harm on the same date. # Electricity powers ahead
137	y have also pleaded not guilty to causing the explosion and possessing explosives		with intent	to endanger life. The court heard that the IRA victim was in the habit
138	Wilson pleaded guilty to three charges of possession of drugs, one of possession		with intent	to supply and two charges of unlawfully supplying drugs. # Lifestyle A defence l
139	accused also deny charges of conspiring to cause an explosion, having the bomb		with intent	and possessing it in suspicious circumstances. The three all refused to give evid
140	offences from 1988-1990. # Planned Beck also denies conspiracy to possess rifles		with intent	to endanger life between February and June 1991. Crown counsel said the defenc

Figure 2.1 Continued

Concordance line		
141	can not be named, denied unlawfully administering a poison alleged to be LSD	with intent	to injure, aggrieve or annoy on May 13. She was found guilty,
142	four police charges – two for possession of the drugs and two for possession	with intent	to supply. A defence solicitor said McHugh bought the drugs with compensation h
143	cstasy, three months for possessing amphetamines, six months for having Ecstasy	with intent	to supply and three months for having amphetamines with intent to supply. All t
144	having Ecstasy with intent to supply and three months for having amphetamines	with intent	to supply. All the jail terms are to run concurrent. Said a Drug
145	had pleaded guilty at Liverpool Crown Court to wounding Brian Daly, 24,	with intent	. David Owen, prosecuting, said the men were fighting outside the Volunteer pub
146	ffences involving blackmail, attempting to pervert the course of justice, wounding	with intent	and assault. Prosecuting counsel Mark Brown claimed at Liverpool Crown Court:'
147	ot Drive, pleaded guilty at Liverpool Crown Court yesterday to possessing the drug	with intent	to supply. David Owen, prosecuting, told how police officers called at Potter
148	Ainsworth, 24, of Acrefield Road, Woolton, denies possessing the drug	with intent	to supply. Christopher Cornwall, prosecuting, told Liverpool Crown Court that pol
149	fences involving blackmail, attempting to pervert the course of justice, wounding	with intent	and assault. # Police hunt for street attacker # POLICE are appealing for witnesses
150	ffences involving blackmail, attempting to pervert the course of justice, wounding	with intent	and assault. Mark Brown, prosecuting, claimed Grugel' by the use of
151	e 22 year-old occupier, has been charged with supplying cannabis and possession	with intent	to supply and has been bailed to Wrexham Magistrate's Court on July 14.
152	. Dunsheath, of Elmridge, Tanhouse, Skelmersdale, pleaded guilty to wounding	with intent	to resist arrest, destroying the Volvo which was written off, and attempted theft
153	received a cut finger. Redmond denied attempted murder but admitted wounding	with intent	. Defence counsel Brian Hicks QC said that Redmond's wife had forgiven him.
154	es in Birkenhead today charged with attempting to administer noxious substances	with intent	to endanger life. The male nurse, who is not being named, is
155	. Dunsheath, of Elmridge, Tanhouse, Skelmersdale, pleaded guilty to wounding	with intent	to resist arrest, destroying the Volvo which was written off, and attempted theft
156	day charged with attempting to administer noxious substances to a young patient	with intent	to endanger life. Dominic Rymer, 25, a nurse at Arrowe Park Hospital
157	id he had been illegally sub-letting the flat. Ainsworth denied possessing the drug	with intent	to supply. He said he had been living with his parents in Fazakerley,
158	Caernarfon, was found not guilty, at Caernarfon Crown Court, of wounding	with intent	and unlawful wounding. The jury had heard during the four-day trial that Daly and
159	ppeared before Teesside Crown Court and admitted causing grievous bodily harm	with intent	, wounding, two offences of assault causing actual bodily harm and two offences
160	, having a shotgun when he is prohibited for life, possessing a firearm	with intent	to endanger life, making threats to kill and criminal damage. # Shop raided
161	rtly afterwards and a policeman smelled petrol on him. Simpson had denied arson	with intent	to endanger life and arson being reckless as to whether life was endangered. A
162	is cleared after drug find # A DRIVER was yesterday acquitted of possessing LSD	with intent	to supply after 1,800 worth of the drug was found in his car boot.
163	, was also charged with aggravated burglary, entering a house as a trespasser	with intent	to rape and having a knife as an offensive weapon. He was remanded in
164	day by Chester-le-Street magistrates yesterday charged with grievous bodily harm	with intent	, reckless driving and other motoring offences following an incident in which a pol
165	Judge William Hannah, at Teesside Crown Court, after he admitted possessing LSD	with intent	to supply. # Car theft: # Terence Dowse, 25, of Hamilton
166	, causing grievous bodily harm with the intent to resist arrest and criminal damage	with intent	to endanger life. Another youth was being questioned by police last night. Three
167	d assault causing actual bodily harm, two offences of damaging property, assault	with intent	, affray and having an offensive weapon. Judge Angus Stroyan QC placed Harker o
168	believing it stolen, making a false instrument, namely a cover note,	with intent	to induce someone to accept it as genuine, using a motor without insurance,
169	tor without insurance, forging or altering an insurance certificate, using insurance	with intent	to deceive, fined 350 plus 30 costs, licence endorsed, disqualified for one
170	efield, appeared before Sedgefield magistrates yesterday charged with possession	with intent	to supply 400 Ecstasy tablets worth 800 at Coxhoe in March. They were remanded
171	Avenue, Whinney Banks, Middlesbrough, was charged with grievous bodily harm	with intent	. He was granted conditional bail by Teesside Magistrates. Now the CPS has to
172	red before Teesside magistrates on Monday on a charge of grievous bodily harm	with intent	and was bailed. Just hours later, Mr Dearlove died of his injuries in
173	Darlington magistrates yesterday charged with possessing 36,000 worth of heroin	with intent	to supply. # Nick video: # Former EastEnders star Nick Berry is preparing
174	wounding. Dempsey, of Grange Road, Middlesbrough, was cleared of assault	with intent	to rob. MacPherson, of Elmstone Gardens, Hemlington, was convicted of assault

Figure 2.1 Continued

Line	Left context	Node	Right context
175	rob. MacPherson, ot Elmstone Gardens, Hemlington, was convicted of assault	with intent	to rob. Bull men were cleared on the direction of Judge Angus Stroyan,
176	of blackmail if, with a view to gain for himself or another or	with intent	to cause loss to another, he makes any unwarranted demand with menaces; and
177	-(a) he enters any building or part of a building as a trespasser and	with intent	to commit any such offence as is mentioned in sub-section (2) below;
178	because the former includes the latter when the accused is charged with entering	with intent	to steal or inflict grievous bodily harm: see Whiting (1987) 85 Cr
179	the Cunningham form as to the infliction of some harm. The term '	with intent	' in s.9(1) (a) would seem to require purpose, a narrower meaning
180	no battery. (The offence would be one of administering a noxious thing	with intent	to injure or annoy contrary to s.24 of the OAPA.) Consent is a
181	any means whatsoever wound or cause any grievous bodily harm to any person...	with intent	... to do some grievous bodily harm to any person or with intent to resist
182	... with intent... to do some grievous bodily harm to any person or	with intent	to resist or prevent the lawful apprehension or detainer of any person shall be gui
183	, and differs from s.20 in the need for the ulterior intent ('	with intent	to ') and in the different verbs for committing the grievous bodily harm (
184	wounding: the offence is not satisfied by wounding (or causing GBH)	with intent	to wound. Such facts fall within s.20 (if the GBH was inflicted)
185	wording of s.18 should be noted. It is an offence to cause GBH	with intent	to prevent lawful apprehension. If the accused hits a constable while resisting arr
186	his head on a kerbstone causing serious injury, he is guilty of GBH	with intent	. He need not intend GBH. The term ' unlawfully ' in both sections
187	' Section 18 requires proof of a further state of mind: '	with intent	to do some GBH '. Coleridge CJ said in Martin that ' maliciously '
188	were caused. The accused was charged with one form of s.18, wounding	with intent	to resist arrest. The court corrected the trial judge by holding that Cunningham ap
189	a possible charge. In s.18 the prosecution must prove that the accused acted	with intent	to do some GBH or resist arrest or prevent apprehension or detainer. In Belfon
190	of the ulterior intent do not sit happily together in s.18: causing GBH	with intent	to do GBH may be more serious than causing GBH with intent to resist arrest
191	causing GBH with intent to do GBH may be more serious than causing GBH	with intent	to resist arrest yet the crime and punishment are the same. Because s.18 is
192	are the same. Because s.18 is expressed in terms of ' cause GBH	with intent	to do GBH ', the Court of Appeal in Mowatt opined that the term
193	or possible outcome. If, however, the indictment is based on GBH	with intent	to resist arrest, ' maliciously ' is not superfluous. If the accused seriously
194	Wilson, approved by the House of Lords in Savage. # POSSESSING ANYTHING	WITH INTENT	TO COMMIT AN OFFENCE UNDER THE OAPA # Section 64 of the OAPA penalises
195	penalises any person who has ' in his possession... any... thing,	with intent	thereof ' to commit an offence under the Act. The Law Commission's draft
196	to resist arrest (cl. 77) are redrafted. The crime of assault	with intent	to rob, found in s.8 of the Theft Act 1968, is taken out
197	had ceased to reside in the premises. (3) If any person	with intent	to cause the residential occupier of any premises -- (a) to give up
198	astily rearrested, George for countless frauds, and Joseph for wounding the porter	with intent	to kill. Both were convicted and sentenced to hang, ironically for a mass
200	denied limitation if the casualty was due to' An act or omission done	with intent	to cause loss or reckless to such loss occurring ' -- Merchant Shipping Act 1979
201	I don't think they'd move me on. (SP:PS0CJ) Are you loitering	with intent	? (unclear) (pause) (SP:PS0CG) I wouldn't look (pause) I like those, I would
202	to be formally charged on four counts of kidnapping and four counts of assault	with intent	to commit grievous bodily harm. The case arises out of the death of fourteen
203	inch kitchen knife. Lewis who's twenty, admitted a charge of wounding	with intent	to cause grievous bodily harm. When sentencing him at Oxford Crown Court tod
205	murder and is observed with some nicety on the matter of recklessness or assault	with intent	to cause bodily harm. The element of' mens rea' -- that is
206	f Customs &; Excise. He knew the wording by heart:Attempt to export equipment	with intent	to evade prohibition then in farce by the Provision of the Export Control and Good
208	get out of my house, do you hear?' He lurched forward	with intent	to swipe at her but lost his balance and was thankful to fall heavily back
213	the corridor was a kitchen and across it I could see young Dennison loitering	with intent	outside the window.' Looo-ees,' Lloyd cooed.' It's your
214	to anybody. You're the kind of dealer who gets caught. Possession	with intent	to supply. First offence. Six months inside. There is another problem.
217	ehaviour beyong belief.' Today Mills pleaded guilty to causing grvous bodily harm	with intent	, two cases of aggravated vehicle taking, driving while disqualified and without ins
218	picious circumstances. # A fourteen year old boy has been charged with wounding	with intent	after a boy of the same age was stabbed in the back. The victim

Figure 2.1 Continued

No.	Concordance line		
219	's from Pittville Circus in Cheltenham, is also accused of having a firearm	with intent	to commit an indictable offence and an earlier assault on the seventeen year old g
220	istol appeared before South Gloucestershire Magistrates, charged with possession	with intent	to supply and being concerned in the supply of illegal drugs. He's been
222	Georgia Griffiths pleaded guilty to supplying LSD and possessing amphetamines	with intent	to supply. But it was claimed in court she was not a drug dealer
223	raids in North Oxfordshire. Six people have been charged with possession of drugs	with intent	to supply others. The big fear from police at the moment is availability of cheap a
224	the burden of proof implicity. Laws used to specify offences such as loitering	with intent	or malicious wounding, so that it was up to the prosecutor to prove the
225	cheekbone for the rest of his life. Riley admitted causing grievous bodily harm	with intent	and assault causing actual bodily harm. Duncan Smith, prosecuting, said Mr Mur
226	Darlington magistrates yesterday charged with possessing 36,000 worth of heroin	with intent	to supply. The case was adjourned until June 26 and Rahim was remanded in
227	found Jones, of Tyne Crescent, guilty of possessing LSD, possessing LSD	with intent	to supply it and possessing cannabis resin. Sentence was adjourned for a social in
228	peared before Teesside Crown Court charged with possessing LSD, possessing LSD	with intent	to supply and possession of cannabis resin. Jones, of Tyne Crescent, Darlington
229	and burglary while Howard is charged with burglary, possession of class B drugs	with intent	to supply and dishonestly obtaining and receiving goods. They were both released
231	to six years, with a further year for possessing five petrol bombs	with intent	, taking a car without consent and making off without payment, offences uncon
232	of attempted murder and 11 alternative charges of causing grievous bodily harm	with intent	. All but four relate to children and babies who were patients on Ward 4
233	rdering four children and attempting to murder and causing grievous bodily harm	with intent	to ten children and a 73-year-old woman. The charges include the murder of Be
234	weeks. She is accused of attempting to murder and causing grievous bodily harm	with intent	to Katie Phillips, Becky's twin, Kayley Desmond, 14 months, Paul
235	of four children, attempting to murder 11 other people and causing grievous bodily harm	with intent	. Mr Goldring told the jury on the second day of the trial, which
236	three other children, and attempting to murder and causing grievous bodily harm	with intent	to ten children and a 73-year-old woman. Mr Taylor, of Grantham, said
237	ld woman. She also denies 11 alternative charges of causing grievous bodily harm	with intent	. Allitt was with Liam constantly the night he died and the prosecution at Nottin
238	n Sunderland, Tyne and Wear, this morning charged with causing criminal damage	with intent	to endanger life. PC John Robinson, 37, suffered multiple skull fractures and
239	ght men were before the court charged with conspiracy to cause criminal damage	with intent	to endanger life arising from the injury to PC Robinson on the A183 near Sunderl
240	y. The youngsters have been charged with conspiracy to commit criminal damage	with intent	to endanger life. Eight others have been remanded in custody until 3 March on
241	Larkin and Mark Whitehouse on 7 June. They also deny possessing a rifle	with intent	to endanger life. Mr Nutting said Magee and O'Brien were stopped by PC Goodm
242	homicide of Mr Buckley on 10 April last year. The charge stated that	with intent	to defraud the Sun Alliance Insurance Group, and while acting with the dead man
243	Trustee Savings Bank, Jedburgh, in December last year together with others,	with intent	to steal. Witnesses told the court how they had discovered the cylinders and two
244	, 31, was found guilty of three charges of possessing explosives and arms	with intent	to endanger life. Connolly denied the charges but the court heard that swabs tak
245	at Westrock Drive in west Belfast. He was also convicted of having possession	with intent	to endanger life of a cache of explosives and arms found at another house five
246	18 months after admitting illegal possession of the drug, valued about 1,000,	with intent	to supply. Simpson also admitted driving while disqualified and without insurance
247	denies breaking into the Jedburgh TSB on 6 December last year with others,	with intent	to steal. The court had heard how the raid had had been abandoned after a
248	Buckley, 44, on 10 April last year. It is claimed that	with intent	to defraud the Sun Alliance Insurance Group and while acting with the dead man,
249	denies supplying heroin, offering to supply the class A drug and possessing 800	with intent	to supply. He has lodged a special defence naming another person in connection
250	, was jailed for three years. He admitted possessing cannabis worth about 800	with intent	to supply it. # Outdoor centre staff given eight days' warning on jobs
251	breaking into the bank on 6 December last year were involved. # Lung-cancer	with intent	to steal. Police believe at least four other men were involved. # Lung-cancer
252	Street, Leith. The court heard that on 10 April last year,	with intent	to defraud the Sun Alliance Insurance Group, the two men started a blaze which
253	do you prove when a player went in for a tackle he did it	with intent	to harm his opponent?' It will just end up with long, protracted
255	Punch (deleted:address) Nelmes pleaded guilty to inflicting grievous bodily harm	with intent	when he appeared at Gloucester Crown Court in September last year. The court

Figure 2.1 Continued

#			
256	itional haunt of busloads of Day-Glo-rucksacked European schoolchildren loitering	with intent	to spend their last tenner on a Sex Pistols T-shirt. The area has not
257	or a number of other offences, including manslaughter, armed robbery, wounding	with intent	, arson, rape, Kidnapping, and causing an explosion. In 1957 there
259	representation, namely... which is threatening abusive or insulting, # 5. #	with intent	to cause that person to believe that immediate unlawful violence would be used a
260	the level of his intelligence have been aware?' # 5. #	with intent	to cause that person to believe that immediate unlawful violence would be used a
262	, lewdly and obscenely # 3. # expose your person # 4. #	with intent	to insult a certain female named... # (B) MEANING OF TERMS #
263	part of the body will suffice for this offence. # 4 #	with intent	to insult a certain female named.' This point means that the accused must
264	by a witness. Hunt v DPP 1990Crim LR 812. # 4. #	with intent	to insult a certain female named... The intent can best be proved by an
265	illegal drug can be charged by the police with the offence of ' possession	with intent	to supply '. This charge automatically takes the case to a higher court,
266	casual postscript. If the defendant is clearly guilty of a crime like wounding	with intent	, and only doubtfully guilty of murder, it is sensible to start with the
267	g former MP George Anyona, had been charged with holding a seditious meeting	with intent	to overthrow the government. Anyona immediately announced his intention of s
268	pain is substantial and the human agent has acted wantonly or maliciously, and	with intent	. A man who, for the sheer fun of it, intentionally torments and
269	er a policeman arresting someone under the' being a suspected person/loitering	with intent	' power -- who sued him. You'd see fellows in the middle of
270	take them inside, lock them up -- be a' suspected person loitering	with intent	to carry out a felony'. Until some clever solicitor come along and he
271	using a weapon which causes actual injury; # Grievous bodily harm: (	with intent	); Manslaughter; # Murder; and # Theft: dishonestly appropriating property belo
272	reinstated that year. Then she was fired and taken to court, charged	with intent	to damage property and the possession of arms. The entire thing was entirely tr
273	later he was back in court charged with being in possession of a gun	with intent	to commit a robbery. And a few years after that his sticky career came
274	tholomew -- were acquitted at the Old Bailey of charges of blackmail and assault	with intent	to rob. According to the Clarkes' evidence in the Old Bailey court,
275	The following month' John Ward' was given a life sentence for shooting	with intent	to murder. At that stage Susan Grey revealed his true identity for the 100
278	e night the neighbours report us to the NSPCC for malicious blinding of offspring	with intent	are over. Yes, we had purchased the yellow polystyrene shampoo guard from Mot
279	unauthorised access to a computer in contravention of s 1(1) of the 1990 Act	with intent	to commit a further offence of false accounting. S 1(1) provides that' a
280	. The relevant words are' he causes a computer to perform any function	with intent	to secure access to any program or data held in any computer'. To
281	in the present case, a person caused a computer to perform a function	with intent	to secure unauthorised access to any program or data held in the same computer.
282	in question was proven to have resulted from its act or omission' done	with intent	to cause such loss, damage or delay, or recklessly and with knowledge that
283	. As the hon. Member for Leyton knows, the maximum penalty for wounding	with intent	to cause grievous bodily harm is life imprisonment. A life sentence is mandatory if

Figure 2.1 Continued

give opposite view!!

But what of the instances of *with intent* from the BNC that don't appear to have this meaning? These can be seen in Figure 2.2. What we can observe here is that there are some grammatical differences between these examples and those that appear to be negatively charged. Figure 2.1 shows that in those examples in which *with intent* seems to have a negative meaning, it tends either to be a followed by an infinitive (e.g. 'with intent to have unlawful sexual intercourse') or to be followed by nothing at all ('The appellant was convicted of wounding with intent'). In both cases, *intent* functions as the head of a noun phrase. In Figure 2.2, seven of the 13 examples follow these grammatical patterns (examples 199, 207, 209, 254, 258, 276 and 277), and we will return to these momentarily. The other six, however, are different. In examples 204, 210, 212 and 216, *intent* functions as an evaluative adjective qualifying a subsequent noun phrase; in these instances, there does not appear to be any negative meaning implied. And in examples 211 and 215, *intent* functions as a noun but is not followed by an infinitive; again, the same element of negativity does not appear to be present in these two examples (we are aware that this is a fairly subjective assertion; we will return to this issue in section 2.3). For these reasons, we can reject these examples on the grounds that they are not exemplars of the phenomenon that is being drawn upon to interpret the phrase 'strolling with intent'.

Let us return now to the seven examples from Figure 2.2 that do follow the same grammatical patterns as observed in Figure 2.1. We will first deal with those examples which are not followed by an infinitive. These are examples 207, 209 and 277. In each, the specific intent is not specified and so, as when we interpret the Le Carré example, we draw on our schematic knowledge of prototypical usage to fill in the meaning gap. Example 277 in particular is similar to the Le Carré one, in that the context specifies that the intent is applied to a situation that is markedly less serious ('holding a teapot') than those observable in the examples from Figure 2.1 (compare 'Causing grievous bodily harm with intent' and 'strolling with intent'). Louw (1993) suggests that such usages can be indicative of irony. We explore this further in the next section.

This leaves us with four examples of *with intent* followed by an infinitive that do not seem to carry the negative implications to be found in the examples in Figure 2.1. These are 199, 254, 258 and 276. Example 276 can be rejected because *with intent* occurs as a subordinate clause at the beginning of a sentence; that is, it does not follow the grammatical patterns observed in Figure 2.1 and for this reason does not convey a negative implication. In 199, we can observe the same possibility of irony as in 207, 209 and 277. Here the intent is 'to titillate'.

interesting! how does it make that assumption?

No.	Concordance line		
199	an that exclamation mark. So there. Quentin Oates # UNAUTHORISED RETURNS #	with intent	to titillate # 'You can always rely on the Modern Review to ask the really
204	water under the blue eyes of Sergeant Collier, who was looking at them	with intent	curiosity like a man staring at a two-headed dog in a freak show.'
207	growth. Each severed section seems alive independently. A few loose slices quiver	with intent	. As for the atomized material -- well, I don't know. That
209	to gaze. Recognition halted their breath for an instant. He was there	with intent	. With news or with questions. Lesley came towards him, veering from the
210	not enough for him.' And?' He watched her flushed face	with intent	eyes and she didn't even try to look away.' I realised that
211	daylight. They looked at the prince, and passing by him, fastened	with intent	upon Hotspur's watching face, as yet impassive.' 'Your Grace, my
212	feet. But his head, Julian thought, staring up into his face	with intent	and passionate attention, was a death's-head, drawn and pale about hollow eyes.
215	, until just a few inches separated them, staring down into her eyes	with intent	written all over his face.' No!' She backed away, one
216	streaming loose and silken down her slender back, and Damian would watch her	with intent	eyes as she moved around the house, his eyes eating her up as she
254	, in Roman and later times, deposits were often made in temple precincts	with intent	to recover them later, in the belief that hallowed ground would provide special pr
258	the foregoing paragraph the pronoun' he' was used, but of course	with intent	to include, mutatis mutandis, the female. For convenience throughout this paper,
276	obtain; and in doing this, have spared neither Cost nor Pains.	with intent	to make the Love of Gardening more general, and the understanding of it more
277	from the teapot, held slightly aloft and repeatedly ritualistically, and no doubt	with intent	, half-way through the conversation. On this occasion, we got straight down to

Figure 2.2 Concordance of non-negative *with intent* from the British National Corpus

So what of 254 and 258? These match the grammatical pattern for negativity observed in Figure 2.1 and the object of the intent in each case does not appear to be non-serious (thereby discounting the possibility of an ironic interpretation). And in neither example is *with intent* used in the context of causing injury or distress to someone. We would argue, then, that in these cases, because of the shared grammatical pattern with the example in Figure 2.1, and because of the absence of a possible ironic reading, in interpreting 254 and 258 the transfer of meaning from the prototypical negative usage of *with intent* is likely. The difference here is that this interpretation is likely to be erroneous, stemming as it does from an uncontrolled piece of writing.

To return to the Le Carré example, examining concordance lines has given us an insight into how the phrase 'strolling with intent' is likely to be interpreted by readers. Its characterising function also becomes more obviously apparent in terms of what it reveals about the character of both the narrator's father and the narrator himself (i.e. the fact that he is comfortable with presenting his father in a slightly unfavourable light and the possibility of irony also being present in his narration). Just as importantly, looking at the examples from the corpus that do not appear to convey negative meaning has allowed us to develop a more precise understanding of the particular pattern in which the negatively charged meaning of *with intent* is triggered. This, then, is a brief example of one aspect of corpus-informed stylistics. But our examination of concordance lines has been a fairly subjective process. In the next section, then, we consider how such an analytical process can be improved by drawing on the theoretical concepts of collocation and semantic prosody.

2.3 Collocation and semantic prosody

The concept of semantic prosody was first introduced in a ground-breaking paper by Louw (1993). The term, he explains, is analogous with the phonological phenomenon identified by Firth (1955), whereby certain phonological characteristics can transcend segmental boundaries (Louw 1993: 158). Louw gives the example of the word *Amen*, arguing that the vowels in this word take on a nasal quality because of their proximity to the nasal consonants /m/ and /n/. Following Firth (1957), Louw (1993) explains that a similar phenomenon can occur with regard to the transfer of meaning between words in close proximity to one another. In explaining this phenomenon, he draws on the concept of collocation (that is, the tendency of words to co-occur). As Firth puts it:

Box 2.1 Searching BYU-BNC for the phrase *with intent*

BYU (Brigham Young University) Corpora at <https://corpus.byu.edu/> is a website run by Mark Davies that provides a web front-end search tool for exploring a range of large corpora. The analysis in section 2.1, above, uses the British National Corpus (BNC), a 100 million word corpus of British English from the early 1990s. To generate the search results discussed in 2.1, take the following steps.

1. Go to https://corpus.byu.edu/bnc/.
2. Click on the **ACCOUNT** tab and register to use the BYU corpora.
3. Once you have done this, click on the **SEARCH** tab at the top of the screen and type *with intent* into the search box, as shown in this screenshot:

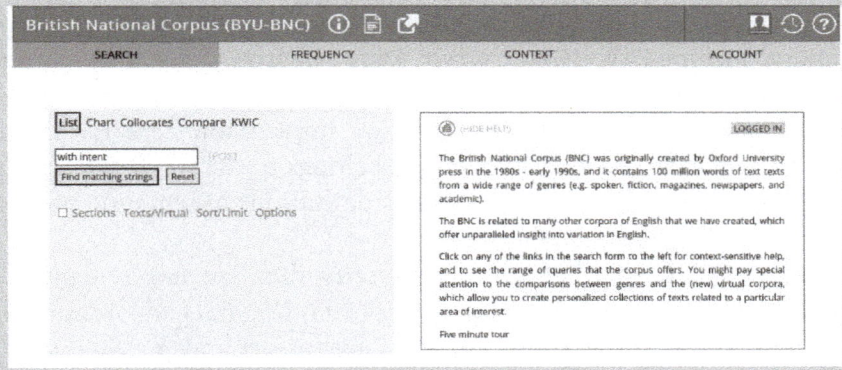

4. Now click **Find matching strings**. You will see the following:

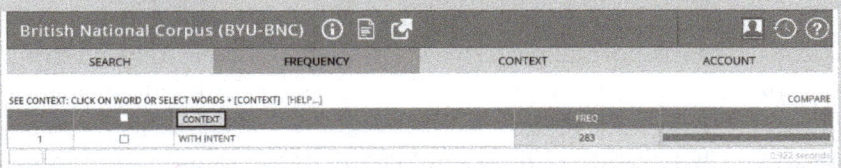

5. Click on WITH INTENT to view the 283 concordance lines for this phrase.

> Meaning by collocation is an abstraction at the syntagmatic level and is not directly concerned with the conceptual or idea approach to the meaning of words. One of the meanings of *night* is its collocability with *dark*, and of *dark*, of course, collocation with *night*.
>
> (Firth 1957: 196)

The above summary is an extended version of Firth's rather more succinct and well-known statement that 'you shall know a word by the company it keeps' (1957: 179). To illustrate what Firth means, Louw (1993) refers to the final line of Philip Larkin's poem 'First Sight', which is concerned with the experiences of newborn lambs in winter. The poem concludes with the claim that these lambs have no capacity to grasp what lies in store for them as the year progresses, and that what is to come will be 'Utterly unlike the snow'. Louw claims that this final line, and the word *utterly* in particular, is suggestive of 'the myriad cruelties of the world the lambs have just entered' (1993: 161). This is on the grounds that the habitual collocates of the word *utterly* are overwhelmingly negative. Louw cites evidence from the original 18 million word COBUILD corpus, where the collocates to the right of *utterly* include *demolished, destroyed, meaningless, stupid, terrified* and so on. There are very few semantically positive collocates. On the basis of having observed this pattern, Louw argues that *utterly* takes on the semantic meaning of its overwhelmingly negative collocates, causing us to interpret the final line of Larkin's poem as meaning that nothing good is in store for the lambs. (Louw's implication here is that the negative semantic prosody in question belongs to the word *utterly*; this is a point of contention in other conceptualisations of semantic prosody which we will explore further below.)

What, then, of the collocates of *utterly* that are not semantically negative? There are just four in Louw's (1993) original concordance and Louw explains that these four instances are foregrounded (Mukařovský [1932] 1964) because they break the established pattern. Moreover, the functional effect of this foregrounding is irony; when something semantically positive follows *utterly*, we cannot take it at face value because we are so used to the normal pattern of negativity. One of Louw's examples is that of a Nazi Stormtrooper described as being 'confident, well-trained and utterly dedicated' (1993: 164). Louw's definition of irony matches Simpson's (2011: 39), in which he claims that irony arises when we perceive a difference between 'what is asserted and what is meant'.

Louw's (1993) discussion of semantic prosody has been influential in both corpus linguistics and stylistics, and its potential value for the purposes of identifying verbal irony should be clear. However, the concept is not uncontroversial, as the following section explains.

2.3.1 Semantic prosody as one aspect of extended units of meaning

Semantic prosody is a consequence of collocation, the tendency of words to co-occur. Of course, words co-occur all the time in language but of particular interest to linguists are high-frequency collocates. Collocates are those words that appear within a particular span (or 'window') of the node or target word. Four words to the left and right of the node word is a typically used span, though Mason (1999) points out that not all words influence their environment in the same way. Mason argues for the use of variable spans as a result. While collocational behaviour can be assessed purely by reference to the frequency of collocates (as in Louw 1993), it is more reliable to calculate the statistical significance of collocates. This is because simple frequency is not necessarily indicative of collocational strength. A collocate which co-occurs with the node word much more frequently than it does with other words will be a stronger collocate than one which frequently co-occurs with lots of other words in addition to the node. Collocational strength can be tested by calculating a Mutual Information (MI) score. Scores of three and above are indicative of strong collocation (we explain this in more detail in Chapter 5). Claims for semantic prosody, then, need at least to be based on the statistical significance of collocates. Moreover, as Stubbs (2007) explains, semantic prosody (which he prefers to call *discourse prosody*, the reasons for which will be discussed below) is a pragmatic feature and needs to be seen as just one element of the structure of an extended unit of meaning. Stubbs's (2007: 179) model of such a structure is based on Sinclair's (1998), which is made up of four elements – collocation, colligation, semantic preference and semantic prosody – and explained by Sinclair as follows:

> Collocation (at present) is the co-occurrence of words with no more than four intervening words.
> [...]
> Colligation is the co-occurrence of grammatical phenomena. (Sinclair 1998: 15)
> [...]
> Semantic preference is the restriction of regular co-occurrence to items which share a semantic feature, for example that they are all about, say, sport or suffering.
> [...]
> The semantic prosody of an item is the reason why it is chosen, over and above the semantic preferences that also characterise it. (Sinclair 1998: 20)

As an example, consider the most frequent collocates of the phrasal verb *get away with* in Table 2.1 (see Box 2.2 for the process for replicating these results). *Get away with* collocates with nouns such as *anything*,

Table 2.1 Collocates of *get away with* in the BNC (9 word window; minimum frequency = 3)

	Collocate	Frequency	All	%	MI
1	can	137	229,823	0.06	3.46
2	could	79	158,325	0.05	3.20
3	let	68	33,038	0.21	5.25
4	anything	25	27,172	0.09	4.08
5	murder	22	5,434	0.40	6.22
6	allowed	21	12,207	0.17	4.99
7	wo[a]	16	15,312	0.10	4.27
8	able	16	29,454	0.05	3.32
9	lucky	11	3,872	0.28	5.71
10	letting	8	2,158	0.37	6.09
11	managed	5	7,238	0.07	3.67
12	em[b]	4	1,949	0.21	5.24
13	killers	3	370	0.81	7.22
14	behaving	3	589	0.51	6.55
15	lets	3	847	0.35	6.03
16	treating	3	1,305	0.23	5.40
17	crimes	3	1,688	0.18	5.03
18	hopefully	3	1,824	0.16	4.92
19	literally	3	1,911	0.16	4.85
20	whenever	3	2,993	0.10	4.21

[a] Won't.
[b] Them.

murder and *crimes*. Its colligational preference is for modal structures (e.g. *can*, *could*) and it has a semantic preference for being preceded by words from the semantic field of ability (e.g. *allowed, able, letting, managed, lets*). But what of its semantic prosody? It is not obviously positive or negative, and might best be described as one of censure or disapproval; but this would seem to be dependent on the viewpoint of the speaker or writer (we discuss this issue further, below).

This is a problematic issue that Hunston (2007) identifies with Louw's (1993) conception of semantic prosody. So too do Morley and Partington when they state that 'semantic prosody can give the reader or listener an insight into the opinions and beliefs of the text producer' (2007: 140; see also Partington 2004). In addition, Hunston (2007) identifies a number of other issues with the concept of semantic prosody.

First, she argues, in line with Sinclair (2004: 37), that semantic prosodies are distinguishing characteristics of extended units of meaning rather than properties of individual words (the word, rather, is the core of a longer sequence of co-occurring items). To illustrate this point,

Box 2.2 Searching BYU-BNC for the most frequent collocates of *get away with*

1. Click on the **Collocates** option.
2. Enter *get away with* in the **Word/phrase** box.
3. Enter an asterisk in the **Collocates** box. (N.B. An asterisk acts as a wildcard, and stands for any character; i.e. this search tells the software to extract any collocate of *get away with*, regardless of whether it is a noun, verb, adjective, etc.)
4. Click on 4 to the left and 4 to the right in the box below.
5. Ensure that the **SORTING** box is set to **FREQUENCY**.
6. Set the **MINIMUM** box to **MUT INFO** (i.e. mutual information), check the box to the right of that and insert **3** into the box to the right of that one.

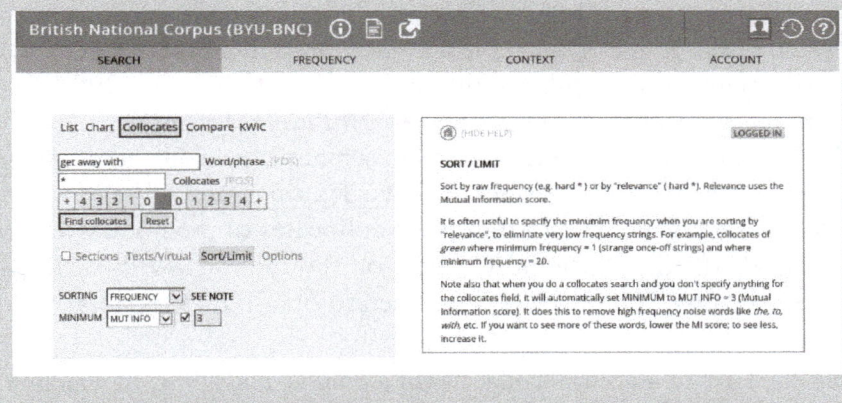

7. Now click **Find collocates**.

Hunston (2007) refers to the word *persistent*, arguing that its semantic prosody varies according to the particular unit of meaning of which it is a part. By way of example, she points out that when *persistent* is followed by a noun phrase (e.g. '*persistent* drug users', '*persistent* errors'), the semantic prosody is negative. However, when *persistent* is used predicatively (as in the examples 'Con men and charlatans are so thick and so *persistent*', 'But she is so *persistent* that Beth – that they end up – they have a real break, a very good conversation') it has the capacity to generate both negative (as in the first example) and positive (as in the second) semantic prosodies.

Hunston makes two further, and related, points about semantic prosody: (1) that a binary approach, wherein semantic prosodies are either positive or negative, would seem to be an over-simplification of how attitudinal meaning works (Hunston 2007: 256); and (2) that semantic prosodies are likely to vary according to the point of view of the reader. To explore these issues further, we need to consider the distinction between semantic prosody and semantic preference.

2.3.2 Semantic prosody versus semantic preference

Hunston (2007: 266) points out that the term *semantic prosody* is often used to refer to two different phenomena: the first is the discourse function of a unit of meaning and the second is the attitudinal meaning of words or phrases. Using the term to refer to what are in actual fact two distinct concepts is likely to give rise to confusion and so Hunston (2007: 266) favours two different terms. She explains that her preference is to retain the term *semantic prosody* to refer to the discourse function of a unit of meaning. This is in line with Sinclair's own use of the term. To refer to the propensity of a lexical item to frequently co-occur with items that express particular evaluative meanings, Hunston (2007: 266) prefers the term *semantic preference* or *attitudinal preference.*

To explore the difference between semantic prosody and semantic preference, we can consider the two lexical items *job* and *career*. Table 2.2 shows the first 15 adjectival collocates of the node word *job* in the BNC (British National Corpus) of 100 million words of British English (see Box 2.3 for the process used to obtain these results).

Table 2.2 First 15 adjectival collocates of *job* in the BNC (9 word window) in order of collocational strength

	Collocate	Frequency	All	%	MI
11	off-farm	15	80	18.75	6.69
12	well-paid	13	77	16.88	6.54
15	unenviable	8	85	9.41	5.69
1	full-time	108	2,158	5.00	4.78
2	part-time	77	2,046	3.76	4.37
6	thorough	28	1,081	2.59	3.83
10	vacant	16	785	2.04	3.49
4	marvellous	32	1,746	1.83	3.33
5	decent	30	1,724	1.74	3.26
8	worthwhile	24	1,435	1.67	3.20
3	temporary	61	3,740	1.63	3.16
7	boring	25	1,632	1.53	3.07
9	fantastic	17	1,113	1.53	3.07
13	hardest	9	587	1.53	3.07
14	terrific	9	618	1.46	3.00

Box 2.3 Searching BYU-BNC for adjectival collocates of *job* in order of collocational strength

1. Click on the **Collocates** option.
2. Enter *job* in the **Word/phrase** box.
3. Click on **POS** (part-of-speech) to the right of the **Collocates** box and selected **adj.all** from the drop-down menu (note that this inserts the part-of-speech tag for general adjectives in to the Collocates box; this tells the software only to extract collocates of *job* that are adjectives).
4. Click on 4 to the left and 4 to the right in the box below.
5. Ensure that the **SORTING** box is set to **FREQUENCY**.
6. Set the **MINIMUM** box to **MUT INFO** (i.e. mutual information), check the box to the right of that and insert **3** into the box to the right of that one.
7. Now click **Find collocates**.

These can be compared with the first 15 collocates for *career* in the same corpus, shown in Table 2.3 (to generate these results, use the same settings as described in Box 2.3 but change the search term to *career*).

Stubbs (2007: 178) explains that by examining collocates, we can identify the *semantic preference* of the node word; that is, the lexical

Table 2.3 First 15 adjectival collocates of *career* in the BNC (9 word window) in order of collocational strength

	Collocate	Frequency	All	%	MI
3	distinguished	79	2,452	3.22	5.70
12	glittering	17	610	2.79	5.49
7	promising	28	1,492	1.88	4.92
4	academic	69	4,762	1.45	4.54
15	managerial	15	1,329	1.13	4.18
6	racing	32	3,173	1.01	4.02
1	successful	105	10,564	0.99	4.00
5	entire	43	4,633	0.93	3.90
10	varied	22	2,829	0.78	3.65
2	professional	83	10,842	0.77	3.62
14	full-time	16	2,158	0.74	3.58
9	brilliant	24	3,332	0.72	3.53
8	acting	27	4,638	0.58	3.23
13	musical	17	2,934	0.58	3.22
11	subsequent	22	4,334	0.51	3.03

field(s) from which its collocates are drawn. For example, Tables 2.2 and 2.3 indicate that jobs and careers are both discussed in terms of workload (*full-time*, *part-time*), desirability (*unenviable*, *varied*) and industry (*musical*, *managerial*, *off-farm*). However, the semantic prosody arising from the units of meaning in which the two words are used is arguably different, in that the strongest collocates (i.e. MI 5+) of *career* are more positively evaluative than those of *job*, which are either negatively evaluative or purely descriptive. And while *job* does attract semantically positive collocates, those of *career* arguably have higher-status association (e.g. *distinguished*, *glittering*). According to Sinclair (1998), semantic preference describes the lexical relationship between the node word and its collocates (from which it is possible to derive the lexical field that Stubbs 2007: 178 describes), while semantic prosody describes the discourse function of the unit of meaning. Sinclair explains that semantic prosody conveys 'a subtle element of attitudinal, often pragmatic meaning' and that '[t]he semantic prosody of an item is the reason why it is chosen, over and above the semantic preferences that also characterise it' (1998: 20). To return to the example of jobs and careers, a career might be seen as something to aspire to more than a job because of the more strongly positive semantic prosody associated with the units of meaning in which *career* turns up. These reasons might well determine which word is chosen by a writer; for instance, it is possible to imagine that graduate recruitment agencies might well favour the term *career* over *job* for the reasons described above.

Semantic prosody is defined by Louw as 'a form of meaning which is established through the proximity of a consistent series of collocates' (2000: 57). This is consistent with Sinclair's, Stubbs's and Hunston's definitions but it is easy to see how it might lead to confusion and the running together of semantic prosody and semantic preference, since it makes no clear reference to the fact that semantic prosodies belong to units of meaning and not to individual words.

Sinclair (1998) and Stubbs (2007), who prefers the term discourse prosody to semantic prosody, both use the concept of semantic prosody in their accounts of the structure of units of meaning. What Louw (1993) does is to take the concept and apply it to account for the projection of irony in texts. One of Louw's (1993) now well-known examples of how, in his view, semantic prosody can give rise to irony comes from David Lodge's (1984) satire on academic conferences, the novel *Small World*. The extract that Louw quotes is as follows:

> The modern conference resembles the pilgrimage of medie-
> val Christendom in that it allows the participants to indulge

themselves in all the pleasures and diversions of travel while appearing to be austerely bent on self-improvement. (Lodge 1984: 1; qtd in Louw 1993: 164)

Louw (1993) argues that *bent on* generates an ironic effect as a result of its semantic prosody. He cites the evidence in the concordance in Figure 2.3 to support his argument, stating that '[a]lthough the corpus rises only to a modest total of ten citations for *bent on*, the seven cited [in Figure 2.3] are sufficiently negative to suggest the consistency of background that Lodge needed in order to create the desired effect' (Louw 1993: 165).

There are a number of issues worth pointing out with Louw's claims. The first is that he appears to run together the notions of semantic prosody and semantic preference, to the extent that it is difficult to know whether he views semantic prosody as a property of words or as a feature of units of meaning (in the case of his *utterly* example, it would appear to be the former, since he states that '*utterly* has an overwhelmingly "bad" prosody' [Louw 1993: 160]). The second is that it is debatable whether Louw's interpretation of the semantic value of the collocates of *bent on* would be shared by all readers. This relates to Hunston's (2007) point about semantic prosodies being likely to vary according to a reader's perspective. We can see this if we consider the concordance in Figure 2.3. With regard to line 1, for example, it is not clear why 'bent on defending themselves' should be evaluated negatively. At the very least, more context is needed to determine the subject of the verb phrase and what they are defending themselves against. Being *bent on* defending one's legal rights, for instance, would be more likely to be interpreted as a positive move than being *bent on* defending oneself after, say, having said something clearly racist or sexist.

Given the problems of just ten examples from the original 18 million word COBUILD corpus, Louw then turns to a 37 million word corpus (later incorporated into the 455 million word Bank of English, a subset of the 4.5 billion word COBUILD corpus). Here he finds 103 examples

```
1   them were so   bent   on   defending themselves and on distinguishin
2   meant is hell  bent   on   destroying Bristish Leyland, aided and abe
3   side, seemed   bent   on   getting down my collar and up the trouser
4   of the crowd   bent   on   harrying the speakers, often for a laugh
5   nt. They are   bent   on   'improving' and perfecting existing weapons
6   n or persons   bent   on   mayhem had not so for chosen to resort to
7   ated figure,   bent   on   the same routine. Thereafter every Mamous
```

Figure 2.3 Collocates of *bent on* in the 18 million word COBUILD corpus identified by Louw (1993: 165) as semantically negative

of *bent on* and argues that these reveal a clearer profile of the negative semantic prosody of the phrase. Louw cites every third instance and asserts that '[t]his concordance shows that the pursuits that people are *bent on* are almost always negative or unpleasant in some way' (1993: 166). There are two issues here. The first is that we do not have access to the full concordance, only every third line, so it is impossible to know whether the unseen lines might falsify Louw's claim (this is not to suggest any dishonesty on Louw's part, only that his results are not open to falsification). The second is that Louw says that the semantic prosody of *bent on* is 'almost always' negative. This, of course, is not a precise account of the frequency of a negative profile; more importantly, without precise numbers, Louw's assertion is, once more, not open to falsification.

These criticisms aside, Louw's claim is that in those instances where *bent on* is used with semantically positive collocates (usually, he says, invoked by the collocate immediately to the right of *bent on*), the 'normal' semantic prosody is transferred. This results in the projection of irony since there is a clash between the semantically positive nature of the collocate and the transferred semantic prosody which is negative; in effect, there is, in Simpson's (2011) terms, a clash between what is asserted and what is meant.

Louw's discussion of the concept of semantic prosody has undoubtedly been influential in both corpus linguistics and stylistics, and the above criticisms should not be seen to detract from the value of his initial work in this area. Certainly, his research provides a working hypothesis for how irony is generated in texts. But it would seem to be the case that the concept of semantic prosody is improved (that is, made more specific and reliable) by separating it out from the concept of semantic preference. Consequently, this distinction needs to be considered in any analysis of irony that draws on Louw's approach. Furthermore, the reliability of a semantic profile is increased by the use of statistical tests of collocational strength. And the notion that semantic prosodies are either positive or negative would seem to be something of an over-simplification. Louw himself, in his discussion of the *bent on* example, refers to the concordance lines as being 'sufficiently negative' (1993: 164), suggesting that negativity is not an all or nothing quality. With these issues in mind, in the next section we demonstrate the stylistic application of the concepts of collocation and semantic prosody. We use these concepts to explore the possible projection of irony in a short extract from a sketch called 'Aftermyth of war'. Following Sinclair (1998), Stubbs (2007) and Hunston (2007), we take *semantic prosody* to refer to the discourse function of a unit of meaning and *semantic preference* to refer to collocational patterns.

2.4 Case study: irony in 'Aftermyth of war'

In 1961, the comedian Peter Cook opened a nightclub in London which became famous for comedy that satirised the British establishment. With no small amount of irony, Cook called it *The Establishment*. The comedian's reputation as a leading satirist had been cemented the previous year with the premiere of *Beyond the Fringe*, the stage revue that Cook, along with his fellow comedians Alan Bennett, Jonathan Miller and Dudley Moore, had written and starred in. *Beyond the Fringe* quickly became famous for its no-holds-barred approach to the objects of Cook and his fellow performers' satire. No one up to that point had so obviously lampooned authority figures such as the Royal Family and the Prime Minister of the day in so public a domain. 'Aftermyth of war' is a sketch from the show that satirises British attitudes to the Second World War. In it, a narrator explains to the audience Britain's role in the war and summarises various key events, such as the Battle of Britain. The other performers act out short scenes which illustrate the narrator's main points. As with all the other sketches in *Beyond the Fringe*, 'Aftermyth of war' was performed with minimal scenery, with the performers dressed in nondescript clothing (white shirt, grey trousers and grey sweater), augmented only occasionally with more obvious elements of costume (e.g. hats). Towards the end of the sketch, Alan (Bennett) enters and summarises very quickly how the war ended:

> **Alan** But the tide was turning, the wicket was drying out. It was deuce – advantage Great Britain. Then America and Russia asked if they could join in, and the whole thing turned into a free-for-all. And so, unavoidably, came peace, putting an end to organised war as we knew it. (Bennett et al. 1987: 78)

The sketch as a whole centres on a significant irony: that the people charged with ending the war do not, in fact, want it to end because they are rather enjoying it. We will argue that the extract above contains a verbal irony that supports this general interpretation. The question is: how is this irony projected textually and how are readers likely to recognise this?

Simpson defines verbal irony as 'the perception of a conceptual paradox, planned or unplanned, between two dimensions of the same discursive event' (2011: 39). Simpson further notes that this core definition incorporates two sub-definitions, which he explains as follows:

Sub-definition 1: Irony is a perceived conceptual space between what is asserted and what is meant

Sub-definition 2: Irony is a perceived mismatch between aspects of encyclopaedic knowledge and situational knowledge (with respect to a particular discursive event) (Simpson 2011: 39)

We can first note that Alan implicates that the end of the war was a bad thing. This is conveyed in his statement, 'so, unavoidably, came peace'. *Unavoidably* has a semantic preference for negative collocates, as can be seen in the concordance in Figure 2.4.

What the concordance suggests is that processes described using the adverb *unavoidably* are usually negative in the sense of being unwelcome or undesirable to the speaker or writer (e.g. *unavoidably delayed, unavoidably detained, unavoidably distorted, unavoidably contaminated*). *Peace*, then, is an unusual collocate of *unavoidably*. Furthermore, the statement that 'so, unavoidably, came peace' generates a conversational implicature (Grice 1975) as a result of flouting the maxim of manner. This is because *unavoidably* clashes collocationally with descriptions of peace coming, since the norm is only to use this adverb to describe attitudinally negative processes. Consequently, Alan's description of the coming of peace is a decidedly odd (and consequently unclear) way of expressing the situation. The resultant implicature is that Alan believes that had it been possible to avoid peace, this would have been the better course of action. This is discoursally deviant. War is generally acknowledged to be an undesirable state, therefore putting an end to it should, in normal circumstances, be seen as something desirable. We can also note that the maxim of quality is broken here. Despite the fact that *peace* is the agent of the clause, the statement that peace came unavoidably cannot possibly be true (the state of affairs must have come about as a result of human intervention to some degree). Alan may, of course, be deluded, in which case he is infringing (see Thomas 1995) the maxim rather than flouting or violating it. At the discourse level of author addressing reader, however, the statement is clearly a flout and the implicature likely to be a satirical comment on leaders not taking responsibility for their actions.

In addition to the Gricean implicatures, what is also unusual is the statement that peace put an end to 'organised war'. This too generates a conversational implicature – that war is acceptable so long as it is organised. 'Organised war' seems intuitively to be another collocational clash and this again is something that can be investigated with recourse to corpus data. In the BNC, for instance, *war* appears as a collocate of

Figure 2.4 Concordance of *unavoidably* in the BNC

Left context	Node	Right context
look at things that we would like to do, and set our priorities.	Unavoidably,	we have to delay some decisions, we put off other decisions, we
their previous occupant, may have had something to do with it as well.	Unavoidably	detained in a traffic snarl-up in Park End Street, Dennis couldn't be with
as soon as she got back to the hotel. The Rome-bound train had been	unavoidably	delayed in Montreux after a small avalanche had blocked the track five miles further up
mmered out his compliments and made the speech he had prepared about Dom Joo being	unavoidably,	detained in Lisbon by pressing affairs of state. Sara turned to her father.
there, directly in her way, unavoidable, smiling passively, uncomfortably, yet	unavoidably,	was Lady Henrietta, dutifully offering herself for an exchange with her hostess.
ies in his life, and certain involvements, but those business obligations which do	unavoidably	devolve upon him he has always observed punctiliously. There are money matters
Voice over Saving premature babies has its costs. Weeks on a life support machine	unavoidably	damaged Jade's lungs. She's wholly dependant for breath on the oxygen bottle
still matters. For the rest of Europe this assertion of German nationhood has its	unavoidably	bitter dimension. Britain has spent the last 100 years fighting against the facts of
ency Medical Rescue Units that the city maintains to deal with such accidents were	unavoidably,	delayed in getting to the scene. Four out of five of their rescue vehicles
are considering the scope and shape of a common foreign policy -- and therefore,	unavoidably,	common defence and security policies as well. Not all Americans enjoy what they
d the propane/butane fuel mix makes it suitable for colder seasons. At present the	unavoidably	large cartridge makes life complicated for backpackers trying to limit their fuel load to what
study tool for the committed student or collector of Caro, but its presentation is	unavoidably	prosaic: one misses the nuance and audacity of Caro if his works are reproduced
on our children; that they are becoming even more radical than we were and	unavoidably	so. One of the teachers was saying that you give children pieces of paper
thought too cheeky a dig at Marshall and Celestion. Though many assembly jobs are	unavoidably	labour intensive, computers and automation are a vital part of the Peavey philosophy.
cials box and those standing behind the Speaker's Chair should not be shown except	unavoidably	as part of wide-angle shots; # (b) # shots which show the
However, it can not be proved or disproved in any final way and is	unavoidably	a political statement. None the less, it is necessary to make explicit what
between the CPS, the police and the courts. In the formative stages,	unavoidably	perhaps, relationships were tense and difficult, with a great deal at stake in
the fact that in this case the point of law has not been served but	unavoidably	deserved. If we pretend there can be law when it is not clear what
the treatment sessions. The therapist will otherwise receive a one-sided and often	unavoidably	distorted view of the relationship, and it is less likely that worthwhile change will
difficult to define the absolute composition of fasting gastric juice since it is	unavoidably	contaminated by saliva, and often bile and pancreatic uice, and because mucus may
. The cap that happened to get overlooked returns the reader's gaze blankly yet	unavoidably,	like the bill from a restaurant abroad which the conspirators find when they turn
e overwhelming majority of recruits to the best jobs at the airport are recruited,	unavoidably	it seems, outside Shetland (as yet the Shetland workforce does not have the
ve of it in piecemeal fashion, recognising particular boundaries as and when it is	unavoidably	necessary to do so. It is not therefore assumed that people have a'
co-existing initiatives, boundary definitions and the fact that any assessment is	unavoidably	interim. Despite these complications this assessment of the MDC experience will focus
treated without doubling the historical part of this book.) The treatment will be	unavoidably	brief. It should serve the purpose, however, of providing a sense or
free trade unions'', autonomous publishing houses'and so forth. All of this	unavoidably	suggested that the' central question in the debates now under way in the country
similarities between them and other critical practices. Psychological knowledge is	unavoidably	ambiguous, and this is especially clear when it involves relatively ill-defi
ined ultimately in terms of our impairment, which qualifies us for admission to an	unavoidably	disadvantaged category of people. # Material abnormality # For all its deficiencies, the
lives, even if it were possible, unless perhaps they were crises which might	unavoidably	lead to the person becoming trapped into a highly stressful lifestyle. Perhaps, for
treasured by those present at the death-bed and recorded for the benefit of those	unavoidably	absent. For the dying man to lapse into a state of stupor or incoherence
wever in order to cling with grim determination to the ancient beliefs which quite	unavoidably	preceded intelligent religious thought, religious leaders have refused to accept the fact.
oercion to achieve, can be most effective. Nevertheless, the training is sometimes	unavoidably	accompanied by the infliction of punishment in some form or other, but as is
have already been mentioned. There might have been more of these. ITV was	unavoidably	vulnerable to the impact of economic recessions upon advertising revenue (for instance, revenue
shipped on board of a man-of-war he becomes as insignificant as a midshipman must	unavoidably	be from his humble situation. I see the error -- yet I can not
te activities through an underground body called the Communist Group. Progress was	unavoidably	slow but they set up and directed most of the subversive organisations. The

crown -- to consult his parliament, the meeting of which on this occasion was
thought too cheeky a dig at Marshall and Celestion. Though many assembly jobs are
between four people, which is much more difficult for the speechreader. If,
over the Community even more and if the club was reduced to eight she would
ious thematic culmination of everything he had done before, but also represented,
indicate one choice from the candidates listed. # 12. # Where any Member is
e Party outside Parliament would be outraged; the Sovereign would be seen, however
would speak on behalf of the parents. This was not easy, and they
Do come home at the agreed time; if you're going to be
a small number of portable machines, to be booked out to staff who must
ALONE ON A DATE # How do you share a date when your paramour is
answer is that it never can -- at least, not completely. Multimedia is
the spread of affluence, and the sheer rapidity of change, have combined,
are releasing the aromatic oils into the atmosphere, tranquillity and contentment
From the outside, however, like many post-industrial conversions, the prospect is
when it is not staring back. If we lock eyes with it we are
n and with tight radii and mountable shoulders; speed control islands to interrupt
ugh heather and naked peat hags, keeping to the clifftops where possible but often
lculate returns on investment in education are laden with many assumptions and are
mouth every day or so he, beyond a certain threshold of exhaustion, falls
asked of all other employees, at all levels, around the world.'
across the vital role that' guinea pigs' perform and although the date clashes
umbers were smaller on this occasion, several of those who have come regularly had

unavoidably
unavoidably
unavoidably,
unavoidably
unavoidably,
unavoidably
unavoidably,
unavoidably,
unavoidably
unavoidably
unavoidably
unavoidably
unavoidably
unavoidably
unavoidably
unavoidably
unavoidably
unavoidably
unavoidably
unavoidably
Unavoidably,
unavoidably
unavoidably

delayed. Thereafter the tribute was only paid to grease the wheels of Anglo-papal diplomacy
labour intensive, computers and automation are a vital part of the Peavey philosophy.
three people are involved in conversation, it will help if the seating arrangements
become dominant. Accepting that a group of countries should proceed to a political or
a kind of conclusion. This was confirmed by Tunnel of Love, a
absent from the House on that day, through sickness or by being abroad,
to be taking sides. And there would be no solution in appointing a
sounded like lawyers arguing a case. Gordon Sloan, the Interim Reporter, took
late, ring your babysitter and let her know. # Do make sure your
work away from base for periods. Schedule: Inventory end 1992/93 Replacements 8 p.a.
detained on business in another town halfway across the country? Microsoft Corp chairman Bill
a complex, technical environment and many design and application matters necessarily involve an
to undermine the complex of institutions and myths that invested all pre-industrial civilisations
seep into one's outlook. # Site and soil # However, it does
prosaic. Porters South is a former three-storey beer-bottling plant, built in brick and
intimidating it, when this is the last thing we wish to do. By
long and straight stretches of road where speeds would otherwise be excessive;
descending into and scrambling out of the coves and gullies that break the ramparts,
narrow in approach; in particular, the financial return is calculated on the basis
asleep, bolt upright, with his eyes wide open. One of them admittedly
there will be further job losses -- around 250 -- in the UK and
with the A.G.M. we hope that some class-members will be willing to channel their efforts
to miss this one, and we numbered only 17 in all. The May

Figure 2.4 Continued

organised only once, and in this one instance it appears *before* the word *organised*, in the following example:

> When this war broke out organised Labour in this country lost the initiative[.]

Organised war, then, is clearly an unusual collocation and is, in stylistic terms, foregrounded as a result. By contrast, the most frequent post-modifying lexical collocate of *organised* is *crime*, which appears as a collocate of *organised* 61 times. If we could say by virtue of this association that *organised* has a negative semantic prosody, then this would explain why *organised war* is foregrounded; in effect, the negative semantic prosody of *organised crime* is being transferred to *organised war*. But this is too simplistic and reveals the problems with seeing semantic prosody as the property of a word rather than of a unit of meaning. Just below *crime*, for instance, with a frequency of 44 is *Labour*. And what of the grammatical collocates of *organised* that are ranked higher than *crime*? Table 2.4 shows the first 20 collocates of *organised* in the BNC (see Box 2.4 for the process for generating these results).

Table 2.4 Top 20 collocates of *organised* in the BNC by frequency (4 word span to the right)

Rank	Collocate	Frequency
1	the	1,209
2	by	1,187
3	and	558
4	a	437
5	in	369
6	of	358
7	to	232
8	for	202
9	on	116
10	with	115
11	as	108
12	at	87
13	into	86
14	's	76
15	that	71
16	which	65
17	this	64
18	it	62
19	an	61
20	crime	61

Box 2.4 Searching BYU-BNC for collocates of *organised* by frequency

1. Click on the **Collocates** option.
2. Enter *organised* in the **Word/phrase** box.
3. Enter an asterisk in the **Collocates** box.
4. Click on 4 to the right in the box below.
5. Click on **SORT/LIMIT** and ensure that the **SORTING** box is set to **FREQUENCY**.
6. Set the **MINIMUM** box to **FREQUENCY**.
7. Click **Find collocates**.

The *Frequency* column in Table 2.4 indicates how frequently the collocate occurs in the corpus. What we can note from observing the concordances for the collocates in Table 2.4 is that *the*, *by* and *a* are always collocates of *organised* as a verb. The rest appear as collocates of both the verb and adjective *organised*. *Organised*, then, colligates with determiners, prepositions, nouns and adjectives. So far, this has not revealed much about the locus of the intuited negative semantic prosody associated with *organised*. But Table 2.4 only shows collocates by frequency. It is also important to consider collocational strength. To this end, Table 2.5 shows the most frequent collocates that have an MI score of at least three (see Box 2.5 for search parameters). N.B. It is, of course, possible to extract collocates of *organised* by Mutual Information score alone. However, the strongest collocates in such a search occur only once and it is impossible to determine patterns of usage in single occurrences. Hence, we searched first by frequency and then examined the associated MI scores for those results.

The *Frequency* column in Table 2.5 indicates how frequently the collocate occurs in the corpus. The *All* column shows the total number of occurrences of the word in the corpus. The % column expresses this as a percentage. The *MI* column shows the MI score for the collocate, a measure of its collocational strength (recall that scores of 3+ are statistically significant). Given that in the 'Aftermyth of war' sketch, *organised* qualifies the noun *war*, it makes sense to pay particular attention to the nouns in Table 2.5. What we can observe here is that *organised* appears to have a semantic preference for nouns that specify collectives or co-operatives of some kind (e.g. *gangs*, *religion*, *groups*, *conference*, etc.). To investigate this further, we will turn next to the statistically significant noun collocates of *organised* as an adjective. These are shown in Table 2.6 (see Box 2.6 for search parameters).

Table 2.5 Top 20 collocates of *organised* in the BNC by frequency, arranged by collocational strength (4 word span to the right)

	Collocate	Frequency	All	%	MI
14	WACC	17	597	2.85	7.47
20	gangs	11	524	2.10	7.03
5	jointly	22	1,098	2.00	6.96
9	conjunction	19	1,459	1.30	6.34
2	crime	61	6,815	0.90	5.80
10	religion	19	4,305	0.44	4.78
8	institute	20	5,271	0.38	4.56
1	by	1187	505,413	0.23	3.87
16	district	15	7,806	0.19	3.58
4	groups	36	18,961	0.19	3.56
11	event	19	10,227	0.19	3.53
7	activities	21	11,360	0.18	3.52
13	lines	18	9,879	0.18	3.50
3	labour	44	26,519	0.17	3.37
15	events	16	10,214	0.16	3.28
6	basis	22	14,230	0.15	3.27
18	conference	14	9,630	0.15	3.18
17	northern	15	10,685	0.14	3.13
12	series	19	13,996	0.14	3.08
19	campaign	12	9,170	0.13	3.03

Box 2.5 Searching BYU-BNC for frequent collocates of *organised* by collocational strength (i.e. MI score of 3+)

1. Click on the **Collocates** option.
2. Enter *organised* in the **Word/phrase** box.
3. Enter an asterisk in the **Collocates** box.
4. Click on 4 to the right in the box below.
5. Click on **SORT/LIMIT** and ensure that the **SORTING** box is set to **FREQUENCY**.
6. Set the **MINIMUM** box to **MUTUAL INFORMATION**, check the box to the right of that and insert **3** into the box to the right of that one.
7. Click **Find collocates**.

Table 2.6 Statistically significant noun collocates of *organised* as an adjective in the BNC (4 word span to the right)

Rank	Collocate	Frequency	All	%	MI
1	gangs	7	524	1.34	8.68
2	religions	8	735	1.09	8.39
3	crime	60	6,815	0.88	8.08
4	religion	18	4,305	0.42	7.01
5	displays	6	1,700	0.35	6.76
6	chaos	5	1,559	0.32	6.62
7	abuse	10	3,534	0.28	6.44
8	resistance	9	3,588	0.25	6.27
9	enterprise	7	4,108	0.17	5.71
10	visits	5	2,993	0.17	5.68
11	labour	37	26,519	0.14	5.42
12	activities	14	11,360	0.12	5.24
13	games	6	5,925	0.10	4.96
14	groups	17	18,961	0.09	4.78
15	events	9	10,214	0.09	4.76
16	effort	5	7,486	0.07	4.36
17	opposition	5	8,617	0.06	4.16
18	parties	7	12,241	0.06	4.14
19	movement	6	13,052	0.05	3.82
20	workers	6	14,359	0.04	3.68
21	class	7	17,755	0.04	3.60
22	force	5	15,271	0.03	3.33
23	approach	5	15,859	0.03	3.28
24	industry	6	19,461	0.03	3.24

Box 2.6 Searching BYU-BNC for noun collocates of *organised* as an adjective

1. Click on the **Collocates** option.
2. Enter *organised* in the **Word/phrase** box and choose **adj.ALL** from the drop-down menu to the right.
3. Choose **noun.ALL** from the drop-down menu in the **Collocates** box.
4. Click on 4 to the right in the box below.
5. Click on **SORT/LIMIT** and ensure that the **SORTING** box is set to **RELEVANCE**.
6. Set the **MINIMUM** box to **FREQUENCY**, check the box to the right of that and insert **5** into the box to the right of that one.
7. Click **Find collocates**.

Based on an analysis of concordance lines for each of the collocates in Table 2.6, the closest to a discernible unit of meaning in which *organised* features, that has a negative semantic prosody, is as follows (square brackets indicate necessary components and round brackets indicate optional ones):

should display info like this too

[Ø determiner] *organised* [as an adjective] (+ adjective) + [uncountable noun]

Examples from the BNC that fit this structure include *organised crime, organised chaos, organised abuse, organised backlash, organised conspiracy, organised congregation, organised hooliganism, organised pressure, organised protest, organised terrorism, organised violence, organised disruption* and *organised cruelty*. This would explain why, for instance, such phrases as *organised religion*, say, give rise to semantically negative collocates while phrases such as *these organised highways, many organised elements* and *all organised groups* do not. However, a closer look at the results of a BNC search for this perceived unit of meaning reveals many semantically positive nouns attached to *organised*, for instance *organised football, organised antislavery, organised benevolence, organised cricket, organised theatre, organised education* and *organised charity*. Furthermore, some examples are neither obviously positive or negative, such as *organised labour, organised religion, organised resistance, organised system, organised campaign* and *organised operation* (though, as Hunston 2007: 255 notes, in some cases, semantic prosodies may vary according to the point of view of the reader; for instance, *organised resistance* may be viewed as having a positive prosody if the resistance is against something the reader perceives to be bad, such as occupation). What this shows is that the proposed unit of meaning does not fully account for why the phrase *organised war* appears to have a negative semantic prosody. It seems that this is explained by the preceding idiom *putting an end to* and by the qualifier *as we knew it*. It would appear that these heighten the semantically negative connotations that the phrase *organised war* projects.

we've already had this info but see how it's used.

There are 290 occurrences of *put* an end to* in the BNC. Figure 2.5 shows the concordance for the 17 instances of *putting an end to*. What this overwhelmingly indicates is that we put an end to undesirable activities (e.g. *drought, domineering activities, usurped authority, squabbling*, etc.). This semantic preference means that *organised war* (as distinct from the unmarked form, *war*) is also likely to be interpreted as something undesirable. The foregrounding that comes about because of

up his bag and walk out, that it was he who was	putting an end to	things. He did not, however, show any signs of picking up
Well, enough was enough. There had to be some way of	putting an end to	his domineering activities. So he thought she was explosive, did he?
years, moving water from the wet north to the dry south and	putting an end to	drought. # Otters could soon be making a comeback along the banks
really look forward to.' But so much football on TV is	putting an end to	the Saturday afternoon tradition. The final insult has been moving Coronation Street forward
all the existing buildings comprising the demised property without	putting an end to	the tenancy (Price v Esso Petroleum Co Ltd (1980) 255 EG
campaign going and decide when the critical moment should come for	putting an end to	the Coalition'. On 8 September, Churchill, hitherto a free trader
the means under God of extirpating all error and prejudice, and of	putting an end to	all undue and usurped authority in the business of religion as well as of
st humanities scholars to develop IT applications generally and by	putting an end to	territorial squabbling over who owns what encoding, interpretative or processing
rom Talbot Square to Layton Cemetery was opened on June 19th 1902,	putting an end to	the horse buses which had served the inland routes since being banned from the
s saying that the party was willing to co-operate with the army in	putting an end to	a " reign of terror " by its political rival, the Sind-based Mohajir
sumu Ishii, the late leader of the Inagawa-kai crime syndicate, in	putting an end to	a harassment campaign against Takeshita by an obscure right-wing group, Nihon Kominto.
continue, but the News International case gives legal grounds for	putting an end to	the banning of newspapers and magazines of whatever political persuasion. The irony of
o criticise the government for the little interest it has shown in	putting an end to	the import of unauthorised pirate telephones, 3m of which are now in Spain
e observer suggested had been selected' for the express purpose of	putting an end to	Chief Joseph and his band'. Malaria was rife and by the following
w passing through the town conveyed the body to London for burial,	putting an end to	a thirty-seven-year Oxbridge career during which time he had a virtual monopoly on Hebrew
sturbed -- mulching is not intended as a boon to lazy gardening by	putting an end to	the need for hoeing. The cover has to be disturbed and scratched open
to local factories and the authorities, enlisting their support in	putting an end to	the stream's pollution. The group received a grant of 300 from the

Figure 2.5 Concordance of *putting an end to* in the BNC

the unusual collocation means that *organised war* constitutes a marked form. Use of the marked form generates an implicature, via a flout of the maxim of quantity, that the unmarked form (*war*) is both undesirable *and* disorganised.

We can now turn to the qualifier, *as we kn*w it*. This appears 148 times in the BNC, with six instances of *as we knew it* (see Figure 2.6). The second and final concordance lines record slightly different usages, with *as we knew it* preceding an ellipted non-finite verb phrase and a relative clause (*as we knew it short lived* and *as we knew it would be*, respectively) so can be discounted. The others all use *as we knew it* as part of a unit of meaning in which *as we knew it* qualifies a noun phrase. The collocates of this unit of meaning (i.e. NP + *as we knew it*) are in many cases semantically negative (e.g. *death knell*, *an end*, *no more*), but what is perhaps more significant is that all uses of *as we knew it* occur in contexts in which regret is expressed. This particular unit of meaning, then, generates a negative semantic prosody, specifically one of regret. This provides further evidence for an interpretation of *putting an end to organised war* as something regrettable. Indeed, this might also be seen as support for Hunston's (2007) claim that semantic prosodies go beyond being simply positive or negative. It may be the case, for instance, that it is possible to specify positive and negative prosodies to a greater level of detail than is usually done; in this case, the negative semantic prosody can be explained in more detail as a prosody of regret.

Having examined the semantic preferences and prosodies of the constituent parts of the utterance, 'So, unavoidably, came peace, putting an end to organised war as we knew it', we can now consider the likely triggers for irony.

- The semantic preferences of *unavoidably* signal that the speaker sees the coming of peace as regrettable (i.e. a negative state of affairs); this clashes with our values and assumptions about the world and we judge the speaker to be either non-serious, ridiculous or loathsome as a result.
- The semantic preferences of *putting an end to* lead us to expect that whatever has been ended (in this case, *organised war*) is something usually considered to be negative (which, of course, war is).
- However, the semantic preferences of *as we knew it* give rise to a semantic prosody of regret, implicating that the end of 'organised war' is something to be regretted. This suggests that *organised war* is actually considered by the speaker to be a good thing.

| | as we knew it. | And part of that barn policy even were it not worthy of extra |
of the death knell of erm, (SP:HYKPSUNK) Yes. (SP:HYKPSUNK) barn policy — as we knew it. — And part of that barn policy even were it not worthy of extra
foaming waves. This was truly paradise; it had to be savoured — as we knew it — short lived. The wind began to pick up strongly; dense grey clouds
red loudspeaker. Probably # The Walkman: an end to domestic intercourse — as we knew it, — or a handy educational tool for budding DIY types? Who cares...
e Foreign Secretary has made the point several times – that Yugoslavia — as we knew it — is no more. Whether that is to be lamented or not, it
What we are seeing them is an acknowledgement that the gallery system — as we knew it — early in the eighties, has really changed. Up until now it's
the sections for which you had a responsibility was very well done, — as we knew it — would be. And your readiness to assume additional tasks like the service in

Figure 2.6 Concordance of *as we knew it* in the BNC

- The fact that *organised war* is considered by Alan to be a good thing led us to infer, via a flout of the maxim of quantity (Grice 1975), that it is only the unmarked form (i.e. *war*) that is assumed to be *disorganised* and undesirable as a result.

[handwritten margin note: look it up]

Ultimately, then, *organised war* is considered by Alan to be a good thing (compared with the 'free-for-all' that transpires once America and Russia join in). However, the irony of this position seems to arise not from the semantic prosody of the unit of meaning in which the noun phrase appears. Instead it arises because of a clash between the conversational implicature arising from the phrase *organised war* and the semantic prosody of *as we knew it*. What this suggests about the detection of irony is that it is not simply a matter of comparing a semantic prosody against a norm. In this case, it is a matter of comparing the semantic prosody of a particular unit of meaning against an implicature arising from a specific phrase and discovering that the propositional assertions of the two positions are incongruous. This is broadly in line with Simpson's assertion that verbal irony is 'a perceived conceptual space between what is asserted and what is meant' (2011: 39).

[handwritten margin note: copy this for a way of analysis]

2.5 Conclusion

[handwritten note: → this only using big corpora and not a specific on for a text.]

This chapter has introduced the concept of corpus-informed stylistics; that is, the practice of using pre-existing large corpora to support the qualitative analysis of short texts. Taking such an approach offers the stylistician a means of checking intuitions and validating (or invalidating) what might otherwise be fairly subjective claims about a text.

[handwritten margin note: these are for important when introducing methodology.]

Central to corpus-informed stylistics are concordancing and collocation. Even a simple concordance can offer considerable insight into a text, as we showed in our analysis of the John Le Carré example in section 2.2. Concordances can be revealing of potential semantic prosodies. But semantic prosodies belong to units of meaning rather than to words themselves. Statistical testing is a useful means of reducing collocation lists to a manageable size for qualitative analysis, as well as a mechanism for determining not just frequency but strength of collocation.

With regard to the case study in section 2.4, what we aim to have shown is how collocation analysis can offer significant insights into even very small amounts of text. What our case study also reveals is that while semantic prosody can be used in the identification of irony in texts, (1) the concept needs to be separated out from the simple concept of semantic preference and (2) semantic prosodies in and of themselves are not necessarily enough to explain the creation of irony. As suggested above, the irony generated by the line from 'Aftermyth of war' arises from a complex interplay of stylistic effects. These include the semantic prosodies of *putting an end to* and *as we knew it*, and, particularly, the clash between the semantic prosody of *as we knew it* and the pragmatic implicature arising from the phrase *organised war*. In addition, the Gricean implicatures generated by the flouts of the maxims of manner and quality in relation to the use of the adverb *unavoidably*, work to convey the deviant mind style (Fowler 1977) of the character, which constitutes a further clash, this time between what the character Alan considers to be normal and what the reader is likely to believe. Our analysis of semantic preferences and prosodies in the line in question can also be used to express more clearly the irony conveyed by the sketch as a whole. It is not that the characters are enjoying the war so much as the fact that they are enjoying the organisation of it. Indeed, the sporting metaphors in the extract analysed (e.g. 'the wicket was drying out', 'It was deuce – advantage Great Britain') suggest an underlying conceptual metaphor of WAR IS A GAME, with rules to be followed and fair play expected (see Lakoff and Johnson 1980) for a discussion of cognitive metaphor theory). One possible extrapolation from our analysis is that the satire as a whole is a comment on what is perceived by the writers as a British propensity for being more concerned with following correct processes than actually reaching the goals that those processes are intended to realise. The sketch may be seen as debunking some of the mythologising of the Second World War by those who were lucky enough to survive it and who then carried some backward-looking and triumphalist attitudes over into the 1950s and 60s.

What our analysis suggests is that semantic prosody, while a useful tool in the identification of verbal irony, cannot be the sole locus of irony. Irony is dependent on a clash of expectations, and this clash can happen at various linguistic levels in addition to syntax and semantics. Our analysis, for instance, indicates the importance of conversational implicature. Furthermore, we can note that verbal irony is discoursal in the sense that it is created over a longer stretch of text, so irony is unlikely to be identifiable in a single unit of meaning. Our analysis and discussion of semantic prosody provides further evidence that a simple binary distinction between positive and negative prosodies seems unlikely. Indeed, it is possible to imagine the semantic prosody of a particular unit of meaning as having a more experiential semantic value; for example, censure, approbation or disgust. This might in turn suggest that whether we identify a unit of meaning as having semantic preferences or a semantic prosody could well depend on the stance or viewpoint of the reader. This points to the need for experimental testing of readers' responses to postulated semantic prosodies. Indeed, we would suggest that such an investigation, at the intersection of corpus linguistics and stylistics, would be a fruitful area for future research.

Ultimately, then, what we hope to have demonstrated in this chapter is that corpus-informed stylistics is about more than the simple application of corpus analytical techniques to stylistically interesting data. In addition to this, we need to consider the stylistic concept of foregrounding, as well as be mindful of a range of other (pragmatic) stylistic tools of analysis to fully interpret the results of a corpus search. Corpus software offers no analytical panacea for stylistics but what it does provide is a means of seeing patterns in data that would not be observable through purely qualitative analysis. It is also possible to go beyond the type of analysis we have provided in this chapter. Chapter 3 begins to explain how.

3

Constructing and annotating corpora

3.1 Introduction

In the last chapter we introduced corpus-informed stylistic analysis which involved using readymade corpora to help support intuitions about short sections of texts. Corpus-informed analysis is characterised by the indirect use of corpus linguistics for the analysis of texts, where the target text is typically being analysed manually. The manual analysis is supported, where necessary, by the findings and insights from large reference corpora that are chosen for their suitability to test and potentially explain particular language intuitions, or answer particular questions about the target text. Over the following chapters, we explore a corpus-based approach (Tognini-Bonelli 2001) to stylistic analysis, where texts under investigation are analysed directly using corpus linguistic methods and tools. We discuss corpus-based stylistics more fully in Chapter 4, but we introduce it here since this approach typically necessitates preparing electronic versions of the texts for direct analysis via corpus tools and/or creating corpora in order to answer specific research questions. A corpus-based approach might also mean adding electronic codes to a text or corpus (i.e. mark-up) that record, for example, the results of analysis, which can then be interrogated using computer tools in order to discern patterns.

This chapter focuses on how to prepare texts for electronic analysis and the principles behind the construction of corpora. In explaining this, we discuss sourcing and storing textual data, and adding electronic mark-up to the data automatically, semi-automatically and manually. We also consider copyright and ethical issues when compiling collections of texts into corpora. At the end of the chapter, in our second case study, we illustrate the advantages to be gained from electronic corpus mark-up. We do so via an analysis of the comic strip 'Judge Dredd', which features in the comic *2000AD*. In particular, we show how corpus techniques can enable quantitative insights that supplement qualitative commentaries on this particular comic strip.

3.2 Designing a corpus: representativeness, sampling and balance

Over this and the following section we discuss the methodological considerations associated with designing and building corpora. We will discuss representativeness and sampling, drawing on Biber (1993), as well as the notion of balance. We will begin, though, by returning to the definitions of a corpus that we drew upon in Chapter 1:

> A corpus is a collection of pieces of language text in electronic form, selected according to external criteria to represent, as far as possible, a language or language variety as a source of data for linguistic research. (Sinclair 2005: 16)

> [A] finite-sized body of machine-readable text, sampled in order to be maximally representative of the language variety under consideration. (McEnery and Wilson 2001: 32)

Both these definitions remind us that a corpus is a collection of language examples drawn from a particular language variety that aims to represent the entirety of that language variety. By differentiating between *language* and *language variety* Sinclair's definition hints at the fact that corpora can be both general (and represent a 'whole' language by including texts from many different genres and registers) as well as more constrained. As we saw in Chapter 1, some corpora can be extremely constrained and, for example, contain only the works of a single author such as Dickens or Austen. Some corpora are therefore more specialised than others (see McEnery et al. 2006: 60), and this suggests that the term *language variety* needs be understood in very broad terms. This matches the view from sociolinguistics where according to Holmes (2013: 6) *language variety* is used to mean 'language in context'. Holmes goes on to say that although this definition is 'broad', the term is nevertheless 'very useful [...] because it [...] covers all the different realisations of the abstract concept "language" in different social contexts' (2013: 6). Language variety, then, when used in a definition for a corpus can be seen as any grouping of language examples that are delimited by any number of non-linguistic parameters ('external criteria' in Sinclair's terms). These parameters could be, for instance, geographical boundaries (national and international), mode/medium of communication (spoken or written, or some form of computer-mediated communication), domain (social context or setting), genre, author and so on (see McEnery et al. 2006: 80 for an alternative view). However, it is worth noting that whether or not the language examples which fall within these sorts of specified non-linguistic boundaries amount to a distinct variety needs to be established through analysis. As we will see in the following sections, another way to think of *language variety* within the definition of a corpus is as a *language population*, and a corpus as a sample from a language population. This is because within social science more generally, the entirety of whatever phenomenon is being studied is usually referred to as the population. A population can be defined and delimited in any number of ways as we will see in the next section where we consider what is meant by *representing* a language population (and therefore a language variety).

3.2.1 Representativeness

We noted in Chapter 1 that representativeness is essential for producing a reliable corpus. This is because, even though corpora can be extremely large, usually they will never hold every single example of a particular language or language variety. There are some exceptions to this, of course, because, as we have already noted above, corpora do not necessarily have to aim to represent very broadly defined language varieties (such as British English, which might be described as a whole language). They can also aim to represent more narrowly defined language varieties which are delimited, for example, by domain (social context or setting), genre and/or date of publication/production. Where a particular language variety is very narrowly defined (e.g. the published output of a single author), this would embody a finite amount of data which, in theory, could be collected in its entirety (assuming it is accessible and retrievable). However, when we consider other less narrowly defined language varieties, such as prose fiction, print news journalism, text messages, doctor–patient interactions or written British English, it would be practically (and theoretically) impossible to collect every single example of these that exists. Instead, we need to collect a selection of examples that aim to represent such varieties.

   The term *represent* is usually understood to mean that, proportionally, there should be the same quantity of any item we care to examine in the sample as there is in the population. So a corpus should contain the same proportional quantity of any particular linguistic item (e.g. a particular word or grammatical part-of-speech) as the language population it is sampled from. Of course, the only way to be absolutely sure whether a particular linguistic item occurs proportionally the same number of times in a corpus as it does in the entire language population it aims to represent is to count the number of occurrences in each. However, we have already established that unless the language variety and therefore the population is finite and retrievable, this is almost impossible and definitely impractical. So, with few exceptions, we can never know for sure whether any corpus we build is accurately representative or not. Both McEnery and Wilson (2001) and Sinclair (2005) recognise this when they state, respectively, that a corpus should be 'maximally representative', and representative 'as far as possible'. Therefore, we can only strive to be as representative as is practically possible. Knowledge of the language variety under investigation coupled with careful corpus design can help us to build corpora that, while not necessarily being complete pictures of the language they contain, are nevertheless sufficiently representative to be able to reveal general linguistic tendencies within that language variety.

3.2.2 Sampling and balance

We established in the last section that since it is usually practically impossible to investigate very broadly defined language varieties, corpus building inevitably involves gathering together enough examples of the language variety in question to adequately represent it. In this section we look more closely at the process of selecting and collecting examples, which is usually referred to as sampling.

An important initial step in any sampling is to constrain and define the population that will be the target for the research and from which examples will be drawn. For a corpus, defining a population means defining and constraining in clear terms the language variety that is being investigated. A language variety can be seen, then, as a language population from which a sample will be drawn, and can be constrained using various parameters; for example, mode (spoken/written), geographical location, and/or of date(s) of production. Further definition, according to Hunston (2002: 28), typically involves breaking down the language variety under investigation into its constituent parts, which requires detailed knowledge of the variety being studied and careful consideration of what amounts to a 'constituent part'. This is important because decisions about which constituents comprise a language variety will impact on the choice of sampled texts, and dictate what the corpus actually represents rather than what it was meant to represent. Biber (1993: 243) suggests that when establishing the constituents of a language variety, non-linguistic parameters should be used so that no assumptions are being made about the linguistic nature of the variety prior to analysis of the corpus of sample texts. Biber (1993), for example, suggests that a language variety could be defined by the genres it contains since genres are not defined by their linguistic make-up. For example, the Brown Corpus (Francis and Kučera [1964] 1979) and LOB Corpus (Johansson et al. 1978) aim to represent written American English (AmE) and written British English (BrE) respectively. These two language varieties (populations) were constrained in terms of mode (written), location of production (USA and UK) and date of publication (1961). The designers of the two corpora then used four broad categories to define written American and British English: *press*, *general prose*, *learned writing* and *fiction*. These categories were further subdivided in 15 genres. For example, the *press* category is subdivided into *reportage*, *editorial* and *review*.

Having defined a language variety (and therefore a language population) that will be sampled from in terms of a series of constraints and constituents, the next stage is to establish a sampling frame from which to draw samples. The sampling frame is a list of identifiable members of a population from which it is possible to sample. The items in a sampling frame are sometimes referred to as sampling units (Lavrakas 2008), and in the case of building a corpus that represents a language variety these units are texts (this has consequences for certain assumptions that are made in the statistical analysis of corpus data, as we discuss in Chapter 5; see in particular note 7 in that chapter). A sampling frame is needed for each of the constituents that define a language variety. So, the LOB and Brown corpora use 15 genres to define the language varieties they aim to represent, and each of these 15 genres requires a sampling frame. This method, known as stratified sampling, ensures that each of the constituents that represent the language variety is represented in the desired proportions (we will say more about this later in this section).

The sampling frame is likely to be (considerably) smaller than the actual population of texts that make up a language variety. This is because not all texts are retrievable or known about. For example, the population definition of the language varieties represented by the Brown and LOB corpora incorporates unpublished writing, which includes, for instance, company reports and university documents. We can see that compiling a list of unpublished texts created in industry, government, education and so on would be practically impossible, and that any such list would only contain the unpublished texts that are known about and that can be accessed. So, the sampling frame represents what is the practical reality for collecting examples. That is, while it would be desirable to sample from the entire language variety, in reality that will rarely be possible (we will see in Chapter 8 that this is also a particular problem when dealing with older varieties of languages).

The problem of knowing about the existence of texts can be less troublesome with published written materials, such as books, because bibliographies can be obtained and used to formulate lists of items to sample from. Indeed, to create a sampling frame for parts of the LOB Corpus, the creators used the information contained in *The British National Bibliography Cumulated Subject Index, 1960–1964* for books and *Willing's Press Guide, 1961* for periodicals. Whatever means are used to build a sampling frame, it should reflect as closely as possible what has been defined as the language variety.

A further possible issue with creating a sampling frame is that in some situations it is not always straightforward deciding on what counts as a text. For example, when dealing with interactions on internet bulletin boards or Twitter feeds it might not be obvious where one text begins and ends. This matter would depend on the type of corpus being built and would need to be resolved at the start of the project. Whatever is decided, it is important to be consistent throughout the collection process.

Assuming that we can create a sampling frame (i.e. a list of texts) for each of the constituents that represent the language variety, the next task is to create the sample by selecting a subset of texts from each of the sampling frames. One way to accomplish this is through random sampling, which is a type of probabilistic sampling (Guthrie 2010), whereby every sample item in the frame has equal probability of being chosen for inclusion in the corpus. If we do this for each of the constituents that make up the language variety, this is known as stratified random sampling. An alternative approach is simple random sampling, whereby a single sampling frame is created containing one long list of texts from all the constituents that define the language variety, and a random sample is generated from this one list. However, as Biber (1993: 244) explains, a problem with this approach is that because items are chosen at random from anywhere on the list, and any text has an equal chance of being selected, it is possible that not all constituents will be represented in equal (or in the desired) proportions. As a consequence, some of the constituents in the sample (and therefore in the eventual corpus) might be under-represented while others are over-represented, which could mean that the corpus is not balanced. We will say more about balance in the next section.

Microsoft Excel can be used to create a random sample and the steps required to do this are described in Box 3.1.[1] For stratified random sampling, the steps need to be repeated for each of the constituents that define the language variety. For example, for the Brown and LOB corpora there was a sampling frame for each of the 15 genres that formed part of the language variety (and therefore language population) definition. This guaranteed that each genre was represented in the proportions described by the population definition.

Building corpora, then, necessitates thinking carefully about the language population that the corpus aims to represent. As Biber notes, a careful definition of the population is crucial because 'it is not possible to identify an adequate sampling frame or to evaluate the extent to which a particular sample represents a population until the population itself has been carefully defined' (1993: 244). Creating a constituent hierarchy of the language variety helps to define the variety, and therefore the population, that will be sampled from and the eventual textual content of the corpus. Being clear about this at the start of a project ensures that a corpus is as representative as possible of the language variety in question.

Box 3.1 Using Excel to create a random sample

1. Enter the sample frame (i.e. the list texts) into the first column in an Excel worksheet.
2. In the first cell in the next empty column type in the following function:
   =rand( )

3. Press return and the *rand* function will generate a random number between 0 and 1.
4. Now double click on the small box in the bottom right-hand corner of the cell. This will generate random numbers for the whole column.

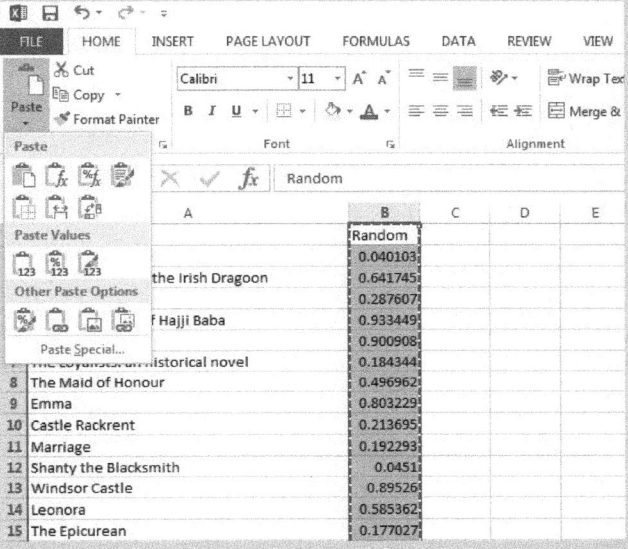

5. Select the whole column of random numbers by clicking the column label at the top of the column ('B' in the screenshot), and then copy the contents of the column.
6. With the column still selected, open the **Paste** drop-down menu, and choose the first option in **Paste Values**, which is to paste number values only. This means that instead of each cell in the column containing a function to generate a random number, it will contain a random number.

NOTE: If step 6 is missed, every time the random number column is refreshed, a new set of random numbers will be generated, and this would cause step 7 (below) not to work.

7. Select the two columns containing the list of sampling items and the random numbers.
8. Click on **sort and filter**, and choose **custom sort** from the drop-down menu.
9. Make sure the sort is using the random number column, and click **OK**.

Sorting by the random numbers means that the sampling items (the texts) are arranged in a random order. The number of items required for the sample can now be drawn from the list starting from the top down.

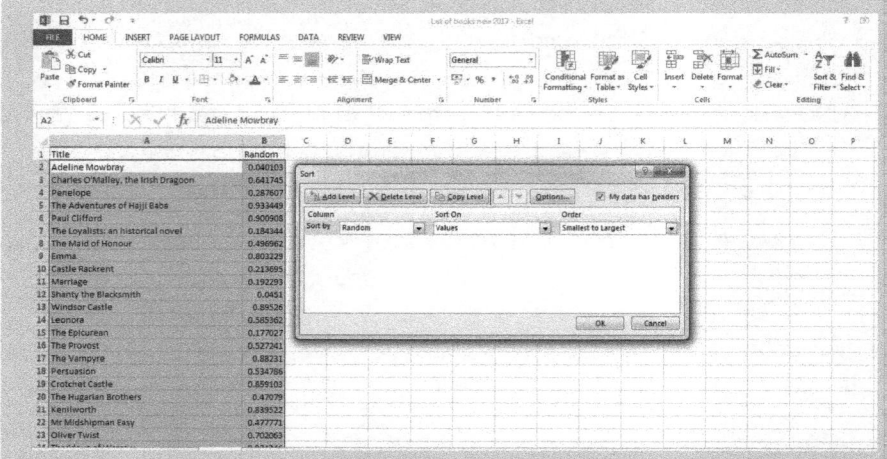

That is, if the sample required 20 items, simply take the first 20 items from the list because their random ordering means that they have come from anywhere in the original full list.

3.2.3 Sample size and more about balance

Having defined what constitutes the language variety under investigation and, if necessary, constructed a stratified sampling frame, the next consideration is sample size. This means deciding on the number of sample units (i.e. texts) and/or the number of words that are needed to represent each sampling stratum (and therefore each constituent that defines the language variety). This, then, is the 'how much?' question, to which there is, unfortunately, no simple answer. The language variety under investigation will have a bearing on this question. For example, in a corpus that attempts to represent the language of text messages, it is likely that the key to representativeness is collecting samples of texts from a large number of different respondents. Consequently, the constituents that define the language variety (and therefore the sampling strata) would probably need to include gender, age and different social contexts (so, not just 17-year-old college students, for instance). The number of texts collected from each person might be quite small, if one assumes that a person is consistent in their texting style (which might not be the case, of course), but the number of respondents would ideally be quite large. The latter is likely to be governed by the investigator's ability to persuade many different people from different walks of life to contribute examples of text messages (and there are also ethical considerations associated with this, which we discuss later in this chapter). A further matter relating to the 'how much?' question is whether to use whole texts or extracts of texts. If extracts of texts are used, the size of each extract in words will also be an important consideration. These decisions might be influenced by practical issues such as the amount of time available for text collection.

Clearly, the more texts (or extracts of texts) that are in a corpus, the more representative the corpus is likely to be, provided the texts are distributed across the constituents specified in the hierarchy that defines the language variety. The distribution of texts (in terms of number and size) raises the issue of balance. Sinclair describes balance as a vague notion and goes on to say that '[r]oughly, for a corpus to be pronounced balanced, the proportions of different kinds of text it contains should correspond with informed and intuitive judgements' (2005: 8). Balance, then, is open to interpretation, but nevertheless requires careful thought. While it seems reasonable to accept that texts should be distributed across the full range of constituents, an important consideration is whether the distribution should be equal, or proportioned according to some other principle. In order to create balance, the distribution of texts across the components of a corpus does not necessarily have to be equal. This is an important point and one that is often misunderstood. To be clear, a balanced corpus is not necessarily a corpus in which each component is represented by an equal number of texts. Rather, a balanced corpus can be one in which the number of texts assigned to each constituent reflects the frequency of these constituents in the actual language population as a whole. For example, the relative popularity of some texts or genres might influence the number of texts collected for each constituent. Therefore, a corpus of text messages might contain more texts written by, say, 15–20-year-olds if there is evidence to suggest that this age group sends more texts than any other age group. This, then, would be an informed judgement about balance. Similarly, in a corpus that contains twenty-first-century British written fiction, we might want to argue for the inclusion of British soap opera scripts, since these fictional texts are not only very popular (if viewing figures are anything to go by) but also produced in large quantities (many soap operas are screened on a daily basis). Given the production volumes and reception numbers of these texts, one might also argue that there should be a greater proportion of these texts in the corpus than other fictional texts that are considered to have more literary value but which are less popular. Of course, there are problems with defining popularity (taking into account viewing figures, sales figures and website hits, for example) and literary value (possible criteria being literary critical consensus, reader response and/ or awards), and these would have to be resolved at the start of the project.

However, Biber points out that proportional sampling (i.e. sampling that reflects actual frequencies of text production and reception in the population) 'provide[s] no representation of relative importance that is not numerical' (1993: 247–8), meaning that some genres, such as news broadcasts, might be more influential (in some way) than other more frequently populated genres. Biber also notes that such corpora would be unsuitable for linguistic analysis because comparison between constituents within the corpus would be a problem if the corpus contains varying amounts of text representing different genres.

Therefore, when answering the 'how much?' question, it is important to consider whether the amounts of texts in each component of a corpus should be equal, or whether they should attempt to reflect actual proportions in the total population of the language variety as a whole. These sorts of decisions should be made at the corpus design stage and explained in any documentation accompanying the corpus (see Leech 2011).

Another consideration relating to the 'how much?' question is whether to include whole texts or extracts from texts. Sinclair (2005) suggests that whole texts should be used in a corpus, because a part of a text cannot represent the whole since position within a text affects language choices. That is, language choices available at, say, the start of a text (e.g. *Dear Madam*; *In this chapter we will ...*; *Fire fighters battle mile-wide moorland inferno*; *Can I speak to the homeowner?*) are different from the choices available at the end (e.g. *Yours sincerely*; *In summary, this chapter ...*; *The cause of the fire has still not been established*; *Goodbye and thank you for your time ...*). Therefore, a corpus that contains just the beginnings of texts will not adequately represent that constituent; at best it will only represent the start of texts within that constituent. Biber (1993: 248–52), however, suggests that representing a genre is better achieved using many small extracts of texts of approximately 1,000 words each. He explains that this is because '[o]ccurrences of new types decrease throughout the course of a text. The frequency of new types is consistently higher in cross-text samples than in single-text samples' (Biber 1993: 252). Lexical variety therefore increases if the corpus contains more texts, even if those texts are extracts/samples of larger texts. The size of the extracts used will depend on the focus of the investigation, because common linguistic features can be 'reliably represented by relatively short text segments', while '[r]are linguistic features [...] require longer text samples for reliable representation' (Biber 1993: 252). According to Biber, then, a genre can be represented efficiently by choosing to collect samples from many different texts. However, because of the issues noted by

Sinclair (2005), and discussed above, using extracts of texts needs to be managed carefully, with samples being selected from different portions of a text. This might mean randomly selecting multiple extracts from across the whole text (we suggest how to achieve this sort of sampling later in this chapter).

One potential problem with Sinclair's suggestion of collecting whole texts is that if variation in text size within the corpus is large relative to the size of the corpus, then it is likely that larger texts, or even one very large text, will skew any results obtained from the corpus. That is to say, one unusually large text might impose a disproportional influence on any results obtained from the corpus. This again raises the issue of balance whereby we need to consider not only the number of texts that represent a constituent of the language variety, but also the total number of words. For example, ten text messages are likely to amount to fewer words than ten emails. One possible solution to this issue is to make the corpus bigger so that the effects of very large texts are watered down. However, this might not be possible due to external limits such as time. Biber's suggestion of using text extracts is an alternative solution, but this needs careful management due to the phenomena described above concerning language choices being affected by text position.

If we decide that a particular number of whole texts will represent each constituent of the language variety, then the number of constituents and the number and size of texts within each constituent will dictate the eventual size of the resulting corpus (which is usually measured in words). With this approach, the number of texts is determined at the design stage, but the size of the corpus is not known until it is built. Alternatively, the final corpus size can be decided upon first, and then enough texts gathered until that size is reached. If we use the examples of Brown and LOB again, these corpora were designed to contain one million words each, spread over 15 genre categories. The size of each genre category was fixed at 2,000 words. This approach meant that genres that tend to contain texts larger than 2,000 words (e.g. General Fiction) were mainly represented by extracts of texts, while other genres, where the texts tend to be less than 2,000 words (e.g. Press: Reportage), were largely represented by a number of complete texts (if we assume that, for example, a single news report from a newspaper counts as a complete text) that together totalled the required number of words. Therefore, the approach adopted for designing and building a corpus can be influenced by the nature of the genres and texts that define and aim to represent the language variety under investigation.

When building a corpus, the aim is to collect enough samples of a language variety to represent the *entirety* of that variety (in whatever way it is constrained and defined). Having an appreciation of what the entire language variety consists of helps to answer the 'how much?' question. So too does an appreciation of the purpose of the corpus and whether it is going to be used, for example, to study linguistic items that are likely to occur frequently or infrequently (e.g. definite/indefinite articles versus five-syllable words in English language). Giving careful thought to the constituent structure (as described above) and to the aims of the research is consequently a valuable use of time.

3.3 Building a corpus: collecting and handling data

It should be clear by now that a corpus contains electronic texts. Building a corpus therefore means collecting or making electronic versions of texts. This can be straightforward if the texts are already available in electronic format, but a very time-consuming endeavour if they are not, since this will necessitate either scanning paper versions of texts and converting them to electronic format via optical character recognition (OCR) or keying in the text manually. Whether or not electronic versions of the required texts are available will depend very much on what the corpus is representing. For example, a corpus of spoken data will very likely require manual transcription of recorded speech. There are numerous online repositories of texts, such as the Oxford Text Archive or Project Gutenberg, where electronic versions of texts can be located, and these can be useful resources for corpus building, especially if out-of-copyright materials are required. Notice, though, that using a repository can, to some extent, dictate what a corpus contains – and therefore what a corpus represents. The web is also a useful repository of data, and corpus utilities such as Multilingual Corpus Toolkit (MLCT) (Piao et al. 2002) and WordSmith Tools 4: Webgetter can help to build corpora from data contained in webpages. However, it might be that there is no alternative but to manually type in the corpus data.

It is not possible to cover all the different scenarios for corpus building in this short section. Instead, based on questions frequently asked by our students, we focus on some of the practicalities of handling corpus data and suggest some useful tools that can help. We also discuss the important topics of copyright and ethics.

3.3.1 Converting and cleaning data files

Assuming that it is possible to locate electronic versions of required texts, these might not be in the correct format for use with corpus software. Corpus data needs to be in the form of plain text files, which means that the file contains no formatting features embedded into the file; it just contains text. This is mainly because most corpus tools can only process files that are in this plain text format. So, while electronic versions of texts might be available, they might need converting to plain text. Common file formats are those associated with word-processing software such as Microsoft Word, where files can be .doc, .docx or .rtf. Converting these files to plain text is fairly straightforward since the 'Save as' function in Word provides this option. Another commonly used file format is portable document format (PDF). These files can be converted to plain text using Adobe Acrobat Reader DC using the 'Save as other' function. An alternative option is AntFileConverter (Anthony 2017a), which is freeware for converting .doc, .docx and PDF files to text. If files contain non-Latin characters (such as Chinese, Japanese, Greek or Arabic), then it will be necessary to save the plain text files using UTF-8 encoding, which is an international standard that will cater for all character sets. However, it is also worth checking what sort of encoding is required by the corpus tool that will be used to analyse the data.

It is also important to be aware that file conversion only works where the text is machine-readable or prepared from a machine-readable source. PDF files can contain scanned facsimiles of a text that, while digital, are not machine-readable and cannot be converted to a text file. In such situations, OCR software is required to convert the text to machine-readable format. However, not all texts are suitable for OCR software. If the copy is poor quality, printed in an embellished font, or contains characters that the software does not recognise, then OCR will be of limited or no use. We return to this problem in Chapter 6, where we analyse a script from a TV drama, and again in Chapter 8, where we discuss historical corpus stylistics.

Once files have been downloaded and where necessary converted, the data might need to be cleaned and any non-data text removed. Sometimes the resulting converted files can contain numerous corruptions, spurious characters and line breaks. For example, where a PDF presents the text in multiple columns, these might not be successfully converted into running text in a plain text file; instead the sequencing of the text might become muddled. In such situations the file will require manual editing. Another issue to be aware of is that downloaded files often contain extra information, such as page headers and footers, page numbers and details about the data source which are not required in the corpus. This non-data therefore needs to be removed from the files, which, if there is a lot of data, can require considerable manual effort. A useful tool for editing plain text data files is Notepad ++, which is freeware with a number of powerful utilities that can make editing tasks less time-consuming. We introduce Notepad ++ again in the next section, along with another corpus tool.

3.3.2 Splitting and merging corpus files

Occasionally, corpus files need to be split or merged. For example, if (as Biber 1993 suggests) a corpus is to contain extracts of texts rather than whole texts, then this will require random sampling of extracts from across a text. One way to achieve this is to select a page number at random, find the start of the first full sentence on that page and then transcribe the desired number of words from that point. In order to ensure that samples came from across the text, the text would first need dividing into at least three sections (beginning, middle and end) and then extracts randomly selected from each section. Alternatively, using AntFileSplitter (Anthony 2017b), a data file could be divided into extracts containing the desired number of words from which the required number of extracts could then be randomly selected. The procedure for doing this can be found in Box 3.2 (WordSmith Tools also incorporates a file splitter in its numerous file utilities). Once files have been split using AntFileSplitter, a random sample can be selected and added to the corpus. A stratified sample that ensures a spread of extracts from across the text can be achieved by first splitting the text into the required number of larger extracts, and then splitting each of these down into further smaller extracts of the required sample size, and then sampling from each set of extracts.

Box 3.2 Using AntFileSplitter

1. Select an input file by clicking on the **Choose** button in the top left-hand corner of the screen. An **open target file(s)** dialogue box will open. Use this to locate and open the required file.
2. The name of the input file(s) will appear in the left-hand window on the screen.
3. Select a directory for the output files using the **Choose** button in the top right-hand corner of the screen. A **choose output directory** dialogue box will open. Use this to locate and select the folder where the output files will be created.
4. Select the desired number of words for each split using the **split size (in tokens)** drop-down menu (the default is 1,000).

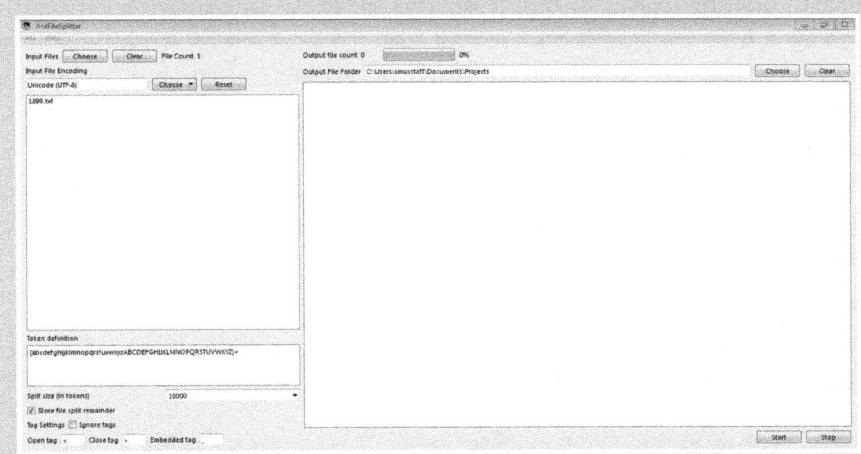

5. Tick **Store file split remainder** if a file is required that contains the remaining words from the end of the text after all the splits have been completed.
6. If the text is tagged, tick **Ignore tags** if they need to be excluded from the word count.
7. Now click **Start**.

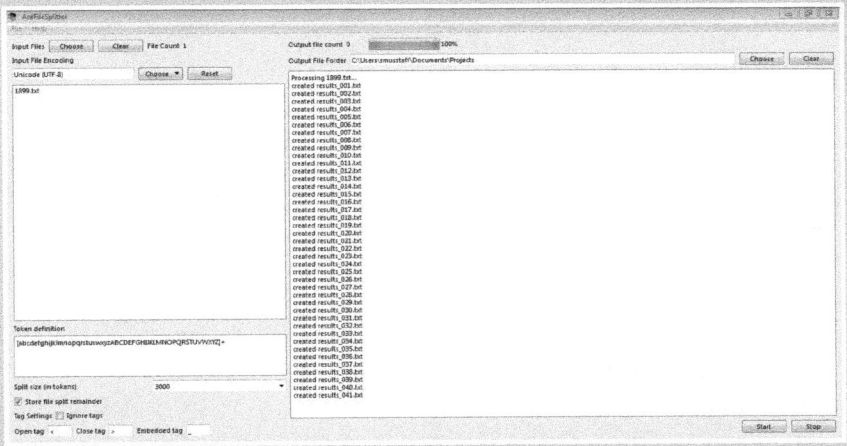

The list of files resulting from the splitting appears in the large right-hand window. This list can be used to create a random selection by selecting the list using **Ctrl A**, copying the list (**Ctrl C**), and then pasting the list (**Ctrl V**) into an Excel spreadsheet. Then follow the steps in Box 3.1.

It can also be useful to *merge* corpus files into one big file, especially in cases where corpus tools are not able to process multiple files (e.g. Wmatrix [Rayson 2009]). One possible procedure for achieving this using Notepad++ is set out in Boxes 3.3 and 3.4. This method uses what is known as a plugin, which is an extra utility that must be installed into Notepad++. The procedure for doing this, which is straightforward, is explained in the boxes. WordSmith Tools 7 (Scott 2016) also includes a file merger in its file utilities.

Box 3.3 Downloading Notebook++ plugin

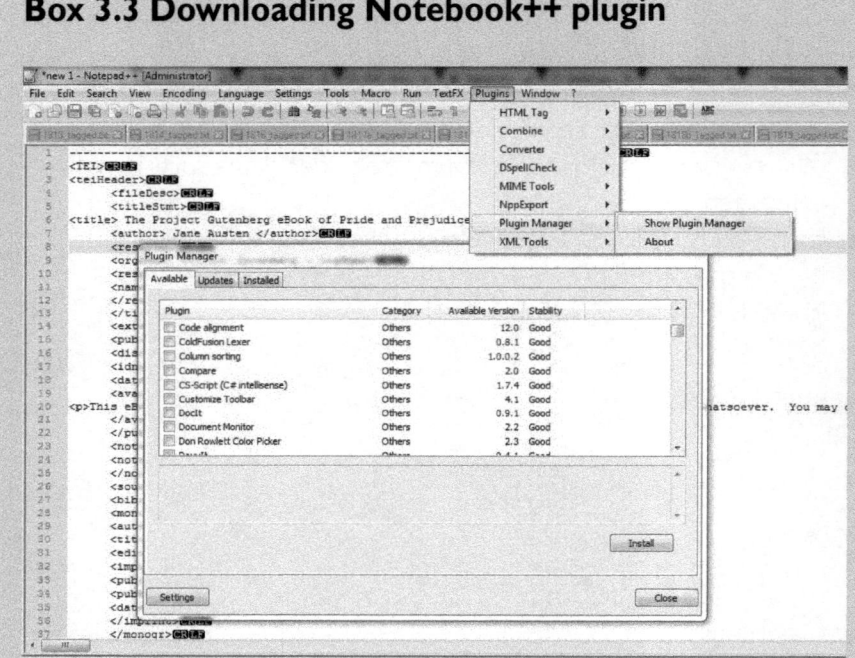

1. Click on the **Plugin** tab at the top of the screen.
2. If **Combine** is not included in the list of plugins in the drop-down menu, select **Plugin** 3) **Manager** and then select **Show Plugin Manager**.
3. A dialogue box will appear showing a list of available plugins.
4. Find **Combine** in the list of plugins and tick the box next to it.
5. Click on **Install**.
6. **Notepad++** will install **Combine** and then restart itself. Once the installation is complete, click on the **Plugins** tab and **Combine** should be on the list of available plugins.

Box 3.4 Merging files using 'combine' in Notebook++ I

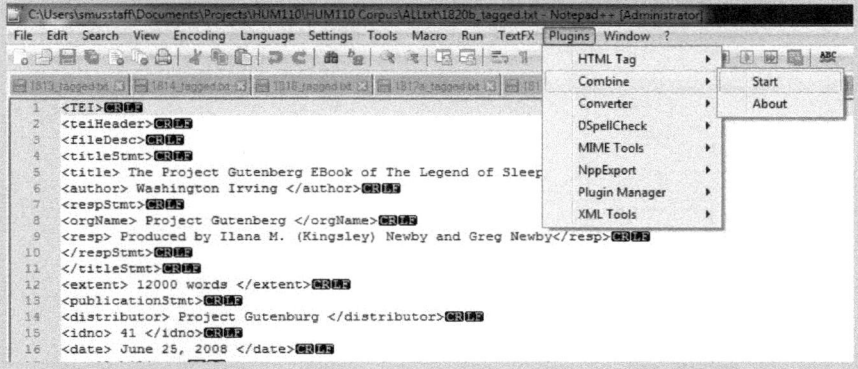

1. Open all the files that require merging.
2. Click on **Plugins** and choose **Combine** from the drop-down menu, and then select **Start** from the side menu.

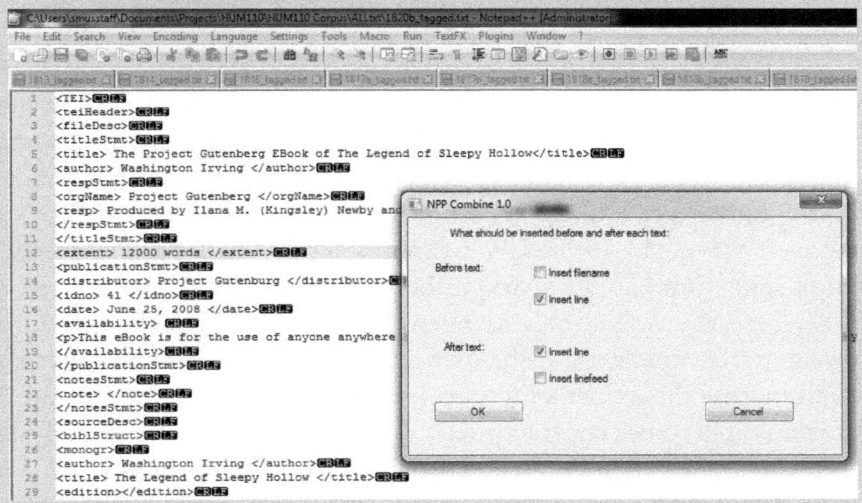

3. In the pop-up menu, tick any of the options as required, such as inserting a line between each file when it is merged.
4. Then click **OK**, and the open files will be merged into one new file.

5. The new file containing the merged content of all the other files appears at the end of the open files, and has the name New1.

3.3.3 Copyright

Copyright permission is required for any texts that are in copyright that are to be used in a corpus.[2] This includes prose fiction, poetry, drama, newspaper articles and song lyrics. Even if texts are published online, the copyright rules still apply. Copyright law is different in different regions of the world. In the US, it extends across the copyright owner's lifetime plus another 50 years, although for works published before 1978 where the copyright was renewed after 28 years, the period of copyright after the death of the owner is 75 years. In the EU, copyright extends across the owner's lifetime, plus another 70 years.

It is possible to use short extracts of texts for research (provided that the research is for non-commercial purposes) under what is known as fair dealing. Fair dealing permits the use of extracts without submitting a copyright permission request. As a rough guide, fair dealing allows the use of up to 400 words from a journal article or book chapter, but no more than a total of 800 words from an edition of a journal or a whole book (even then, different publishers may have different views on what constitutes fair dealing). For other genres, including newspapers and magazines, poems and song lyrics, fair dealing possibilities are even more vague and it is a good idea to seek permission for such texts. As long as you are not intending to make a profit from your corpus, there is a good chance that permissions will be granted, but without permission you cannot legally disseminate a corpus. Therefore, building a corpus that contains copyright material is likely to be a considerable undertaking and is something to be borne in mind at the design stage of a project.

3.3.4 Ethics

There are extensive guidelines for ethics which can be found on numerous websites, including those of the British Association for Applied Linguistics (BAAL), the Economic and Social Research Council (ESRC), and the Association of Internet Researchers (AoIR). We also recommend consulting the 'Professional and ethical codes for socio-economic research in the information society' document, available on the website of the Respect Project, which is a project funded by the European Commission's Information Society Technologies (IST) Programme.[3]

Ethical research is summarised by the ESRC through six core principles:[4]

1 'research should aim to maximise benefit for individuals and society and minimise risk and harm';
2 'the rights and dignity of individuals and groups should be respected';
3 'wherever possible, participation should be voluntary and appropriately informed';
4 'research should be conducted with integrity and transparency';
5 'lines of responsibility and accountability should be clearly defined';
6 'independence of research should be maintained and where conflicts of interest cannot be avoided they should be made explicit'.

We can see from these principles that ethics relates to all aspects of research, from design stage and data collection to the analysis and reporting of results, as well as how we as researchers conduct ourselves in the research process and in the wider community. Our focus in this section, however, is on ethical considerations required for data collection, since these are the ethical issues that relate most obviously to corpus building.

Although stylistics is traditionally associated with the analysis of fictional texts, the applied nature of stylistics as a sub-discipline of linguistics means that it is also (increasingly) interested in non-fiction, and any type of language data, both written and spoken, is open to stylistic scrutiny. Such non-fiction data might include, for example, naturally occurring conversations, interviews, focus group discussions, questionnaires, readers' responses to fiction, and social media interactions. Once data is elicited or collected from informants, then the notion of ethics, particularly relating to ESRC principles 2, 3 and 4, outlined above, becomes important. Research that involves collecting data from people is bound by a series of ethical considerations, which can be summarised by the following statement from the guidelines issued by BAAL:

> Applied linguists should respect the rights, interests, sensitivities, privacy and autonomy of their informants in all research contexts, including those in which users' rights are not so clear-cut, such as easily accessible internet sites. (BAAL 2016: 4)

Therefore, any data collection that involves informant participation should bear in mind the ethos set out above. The latter part of the quotation hints at the increasing amount of data that is gathered from the internet, and the ethical questions that collecting and using such data can raise, some of which we will mention below.

BAAL note that the 'the cornerstone of ethical research' is informed consent. This is the practice of obtaining consent from informants to use their language output as data *prior* to the data being collected and *after* being informed about the research as fully as is practically possible or appropriate. Informants can therefore make an informed decision about whether they wish to participate in the research or not. Such consent is reasonably straightforward with some forms of data such as, for example, questionnaires, reader response surveys and spoken interactions in focus groups, since informants must be solicited and can be presented with all relevant information concerning the research, which they can acknowledge with a signature. However, informed consent becomes less straightforward in some situations. For example, when collecting spoken data in a public place, it is likely to be impossible to locate all the people that might appear on the recording whose language might potentially end up in the dataset. McEnery and Hardie (2012: 60–9) also note the situation where consenting participants who are collecting naturally occurring spoken data using a portable (lapel) microphone might not inform their interlocutors fully or at all about the research, making any such data ethically problematic.

Informed consent can also be a problem when data is downloaded from online forums, chatrooms and other platforms for computer-mediated communication (CMC), such as Twitter and Facebook. Firstly, whether consent is needed in such situations is debateable since much of what can be found on the internet is arguably in the public domain. The general guidance here is that if potential data is password-protected, then it is not public domain and cannot be used without consent. However, this is not a rule and so should not be applied by default. Even if it is decided that consent is not needed, behaviours such as signing up to and 'lurking' in a chatroom in order to be able to collect data could be viewed as covert research and therefore unacceptable. In effect, this is a form of deception, since the researcher is posing as a 'normal' chatroom user. Secondly, in certain online/CMC situations it might not be clear who the participants are or how to contact them, so asking for consent is likely to be difficult. Additionally, if there are thousands of participants (as on certain Twitter feeds), then the task of asking for consent might become extremely difficult and practically impossible. While there appear to be no specific guidelines on how to deal with these sorts of problems, generally researchers should do what they reasonably can to inform participants about their research and how the data will be used, and provide an opportunity for participants to withdraw. For example, Demmen et al. (2015), following Seale et al. (2010) take the view that data from publicly accessible, non-password protected websites does not require informed consent from contributors. Nevertheless, they informed users of a forum from which they gathered data about their research and gave them the opportunity to signal their withdrawal from the project. In a similar way, King (2009) uses the notion of implied consent when compiling a corpus of online chatroom data. Here, chatroom participants were offered the opportunity to say if they did not want their contributions to be used as data, and if no reply was received, then consent was inferred.

An important potential problem with informed consent is the Observer's Paradox, whereby respondents/informants are aware that they are being studied and change their language performance accordingly. This can alter the phenomenon being studied and, at worse, make the data unusable. Gathering examples of language data from informants without their knowledge – known as covert research – is now acknowledged as unacceptable, although ESRC guidance in the Framework for Research Ethics states:

> Covert research may be undertaken when it may provide unique forms of evidence that are crucial to the research objectives and methodology or where overt observation might alter the phenomenon being studied. The broad principle should be that covert research should not be undertaken lightly or routinely. It is only justified if important issues are being addressed and if matters of social significance which cannot be uncovered in other ways are likely to be discovered. (ESRC 2015: 31)

So, in certain special, socially significant (but unspecified) circumstances, covert research is allowable, but should be handled carefully in order to address the key ethical consideration set out by BAAL, quoted above.

Another option proposed by BAAL for helping alleviate the Observer's Paradox is justified deception. Deliberate deception is generally unacceptable but in specific circumstances it can be justified to the extent that some details about the specific purpose of the research are withheld until after the data is collected. This might involve a situation when a particular linguistic phenomenon is being studied but informants are not told what that phenomenon is in case they are primed in some way to use (or avoid) the phenomenon during the research. So, participants would know that their language is being studied, but they would not know what particular aspect until the end of the process. Again, deception should be handled carefully, sensitively, and only used where there is no risk of harm to participants.

Also important in data collection from informants is the right to anonymity, so even where informed consent is obtained (or implied), the data must be anonymised. This can also raise a number of practical problems, not least if there is a considerable amount of data to be processed. The extent of the anonymisation must also be considered (e.g. whether any personal names, place or institutional names mentioned should be omitted) so that there is no way in which participants can be identified by their contributions.

As we noted at the start of this section, there are numerous guidelines for ethical research, which can be consulted if there is any doubt about whether research practices are ethical or not, particularly in the area of data collection from informants (for more discussion of ethical issues relating to corpora, see also McEnery and Hardie 2012: 60–9).

3.4 Adding metadata to a corpus: mark-up and annotation

Having prepared an electronic version of a text, or constructed a corpus of texts, a useful and sometimes necessary next step is to add metadata. Metadata is extra information that tells us something more about the corpus data; in essence, it is data about data. In this section we discuss the different kinds of metadata that can be added and the forms they can take. Our focus here is on corpora but what we describe applies equally to single texts.

First of all, it is generally a good idea to add some metadata about the texts that make up the corpus – what Burnard (2004) refers to as 'descriptive metadata'. This information might include the medium of the text, publication date, data collection date, author, speaker, and so on. Additionally, 'administrative metadata' (Burnard 2004) can also be added to provide details about the production of the file; for example, date of production, notes about the data source and, if relevant, the person who transcribed the data. These kinds of metadata are typically inserted manually at the start of every file that makes up a corpus to form what is known as a header. We describe in more detail the form that headers can take later on in this section. The exact content of the metadata is down to the corpus builder, but the aim should be to provide users of the corpus with the information that will enable them to interpret the results of any analyses of the corpus. For example, knowing in detail about the contents of a corpus will enable someone using it to know to what extent the results from their investigations are generalisable or not.

Secondly, depending on the research objectives and the reasons for building the corpus, metadata can be added which results from some sort of (linguistic) analysis. Leech (1993) refers to this kind of metadata as 'corpus annotation' (see also McEnery and Hardie 2012: 13), which he defines as 'the practice of adding *interpretative* (especially linguistic) information to an existing corpus' (1993: 275; original emphasis). The example often used to illustrate this is part-of-speech (POS) or grammatical annotation, where a label is added to every word in a corpus to indicate the grammatical category it belongs to. POS annotation can be carried out automatically using computer software, with reasonably low error rates, and we discuss this in more detail later in this section. Annotation is not restricted to POS information, though. Indeed, any aspect of language can be tagged in a corpus, though whether this can be done automatically depends on whether the focus of the annotation is a formal feature of language or not. POS annotation, for example, can be relatively straightforward because the particular POS category that a word is likely to belong to can be determined by descriptive grammatical rules. However, if we were interested, say, in how individual occurrences of modal auxiliary verbs function in a text (e.g. whether a modal form conveys deontic or epistemic modality), we would not be able to tag for this automatically because modal categories are functional rather than formal and rely for their interpretation on the surrounding co-text. Consequently, annotation of this type would have to be done manually.

Other kinds of metadata can also be added to a corpus to provide information about structural elements of the data, such as paragraph breaks, the beginnings and ends of chapters, or (in transcriptions of spoken discourse or play texts) the identity of the speaker and where each turn in a conversation starts and stops. This sort of information can be useful for projects that require comparisons between different elements of the data (such as first and last chapters) or different textual entities (such as characters in a play). Additionally, graphological information can be added, such as indications of font size, or whether underlining, or bold or italic font is used. While this sort of information might be present in the original text, it will not be represented orthographically in the plain text corpus files, since these do not encode any formatting features. If required for the research objectives, then metadata is needed to make these graphological/typographical phenomena explicit.

The types of metadata that can be added to corpora are referred to by a variety of different terminology. As we have already seen, Leech (1993) distinguishes between annotation (interpretative information) and other information, but notes that with transcribed spoken data this distinction is less easy to make. McEnery and Hardie (2012: 29–30) use 'linguistic annotation' to mean metadata that results from linguistic analysis, and 'textual mark-up' for metadata that provides structural and graphological information.[5] Our view is that *metadata* is a generic term that refers to any added data that describes corpus data, while *mark-up* is a hypernymic term that encompasses any type of meta-data added to a corpus, including descriptive information contained in headers. Mark-up can relate to a variety of different aspects of the data but can be narrowed down terminologically; for example, McEnery and Hardie's (2012) term *textual mark-up* refers to formatting and structural metadata, while Burnard's (2004) *editorial mark-up* informs the corpus user of, for example, transcribing decisions or gaps in the data. Annotation, as Leech (1993) and McEnery and Hardie (2012) suggest, can be seen as a particular type of mark-up, relating to specialised linguistic information that results from linguistic analysis using various language models external to the text.

Figure 3.1 summarises the different types of mark-up discussed in this section, and our view that mark-up is a general term covering all types of additional information that can be added to a corpus. The diagram does not present an exhaustive list of potential mark-up but just some of the possibilities.

The process of adding metadata to a corpus can be referred to as marking-up, encoding, annotating or tagging (we will explain why this last term is used in due course). Sometimes these terms are used interchangeably even though for some corpus linguists they describe slightly different phenomena. Whatever the terminology, it is worth reflecting that adding metadata to a text or corpus involves, to some degree, an interpretative process. As Burnard notes, adding metadata is 'best regarded as the process of making explicit a set of more or less interpretive judgments about the material of which it is composed' (2004: 35). Sperberg-McQueen et al. make a similar point, saying that

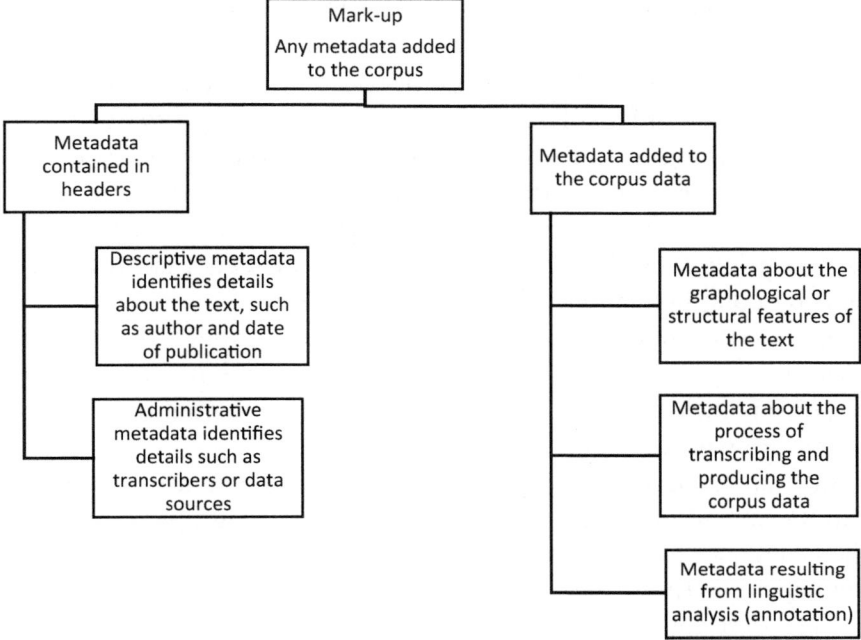

Figure 3.1 Types of metadata that can be added to a corpus

metadata 'reflects the understanding of the text held by the transcriber' (2000: 215) and encodes the transcriber's interpretation of elements of the text. This should be borne in mind when using a marked-up/ annotated corpus. We will see, though, that the value of mark-up is that it allows us to quantify particular features of language which can give us insights into a text (or corpus of texts) that we might not otherwise have been able to obtain.

3.4.1 The format of mark-up and annotation

The basic idea of marking-up a corpus is to label stretches of textual data with special codes that provide extra information about that stretch of data. The mark-up we add might result from some sort of linguistic/stylistic analysis of the corpus (e.g. labelling occurrences of the word-form *could* as a modal auxiliary verb, or marking sections of discourse presentation). The mark-up records the results of the analysis directly into the data. This is rather like using coloured highlighter pens to mark different sections of a paper text, in order to record particular issues. To use another analogy, mark-up can be likened to sticking post-it notes into a book to mark what you consider to be important chapters or sections, to enable you to return to them quickly. The advantage of electronic mark-up is that it increases the ease with which it is possible to reuse and share the products of your analytical effort. With electronic mark-up the text is coded with labels that are machine-readable and usable by computer software, as well as being meaningful to the human eye. So, whatever is marked-up in a corpus can very straightforwardly be quantified and extracted for further analysis or comparison with other data using corpus tools. Also, by using a standard coding format that is widely used and understood by computer applications, it is possible for computer software to separate the codes from the data, so that even though the codes are added directly to the data, they do not interfere with it. This is important, given Sinclair's (2005) concerns about the potential for metadata to interfere with the analytical process.

Mark-up is added to corpus data using what are usually referred to as tags. For this reason, the process of marking-up is sometimes called tagging. Typically, tags are in the style of eXtensible Mark-up Language (XML), which is a widely used computer language designed for data description with numerous applications across many fields. XML allows you to define your own tags and label them in whatever way suits you, so that any mark-up you add to your corpus can consist of self-descriptive labels that potentially make them understandable to anyone who wants to use your data, and not just computer software.

XML mark-up consists of start and end tags. These tags are used to enclose sections of data within what are known as elements: the tags mark the start and the end of an element and the data they enclose is the content of the element. Sometimes, the terms *tag* and *element* are used interchangeably.

Figure 3.2 demonstrates that start tags consist of a left angle bracket (<), followed by the element name, which can contain letters and numbers but no spaces, and finish with a right angle bracket (>). End

```
<ExampleElement1>some content consisting of alpha-numeric characters,
i.e. text</ExampleElement1>
<ExampleElement2 Attribute1="extra information">some content consist-
ing of alpha-numeric characters, i.e. text</ExampleElement2>
<ExampleElement3 attribute1="information"/>
<ExampleElement4>
    <EmbeddedElement>more content here</EmbeddedElement>
    <EmbeddedElement>more content here</EmbeddedElement>
</ExampleElement4>
...
```

Figure 3.2 Examples of XML tags

tags take the same format as start tags except that the left angle bracket is immediately followed by a forward slash (/). Other than the extra forward slash, start and end tags must be exactly the same in their format (e.g. the same spelling and capitalisation). If they are not, then the tags are not well formed and this will cause problems later when used by computer applications. In-between the start and end tags is usually the content of the element, which typically would be sections of the text being tagged or, in the case of headers, additional descriptive information (see below).

Figure 3.2 also shows that elements can optionally contain attributes. When used, these form part of the opening tag of an element and consist of the attribute name, which is made up of alpha-numeric characters but no spaces, followed by an equals sign and then the attribute content (or attribute value), which is made up of alpha-numeric characters, including spaces, and enclosed in either single or double quotation marks (but not a mixture of the two). Attributes can provide additional information about the element and therefore about the data the element is marking-up. For example, if we were interested in the modal auxiliary verbs (of which there is generally agreed to be a small finite number in English), we could tag every instance in a corpus using the following start and end tags:

<modal> ... </modal>

With this example, various different forms within a text or corpus are tagged as sharing the same function. If we were interested in providing more functional information about the modal auxiliary verbs in a text (e.g. whether they are deontic or epistemic), we could use attributes to do this:

<modal type="epistemic"> ... </modal>
<modal type="deontic"> ... </modal>

Here, the tagging labels various forms in the text or corpus as (1) being a modal auxiliary and (2) conveying a particular type of modality. While the tagging of (1) can be automated, tagging for (2) cannot, and would require manual analysis of the surrounding co-text, informed by a framework for the analysis of modality. Notice that we have chosen to call the attribute 'type', but we could have chosen any label (e.g. 'function' or 'force'). Notice also that we have chosen to populate the attribute with full word-forms (i.e. 'epistemic' or 'deontic'), but we could have easily used codes, such as 'D' and 'E' to indicate deontic and epistemic modality respectively.

The penultimate example in Figure 3.2 (ExampleElement3) demonstrates a situation where an element is empty (i.e. no textual data is enclosed by tags) and that in such situations it is possible to omit an end tag. Instead, the mark-up consists of just one tag that is a combination of both an opening and closing tag. The tag consists of left angle bracket, followed by a name, an attribute, which contains some information, and closes with a forward slash and a right angle bracket. We will see how these special tags can be used in the following section.

Finally, Figure 3.2 also demonstrates that it is possible to embed elements within elements. This can help to show structural features within a text and we will see how that can work in future examples.

3.4.2 Descriptive metadata: headers

As we noted earlier, it is often a good idea to add metadata about the texts in a corpus (e.g. author, date of publication, page numbers sampled) to assist others who might want to use the corpus, as well as for future reference. This sort of information forms a header, which is separated from the corpus data using XML mark-up. Figure 3.3 shows one option for a header where the information about the text is sandwiched between a start and end tag. Here the header is made up of several elements, and the metadata makes up the content of these elements. Figure 3.4 demonstrates a slightly different format for the same information, where the metadata is incorporated into a series of four elements using an attribute. Here, the elements have no content, and so can be opened and closed using a special single tag that ends with a slash and an angle bracket.

Typically, computer tools used to analyse corpora (e.g. AntConc, Wmatrix, Wordsmith Tools) are designed to ignore anything enclosed in angle brackets. The problem with the header shown in Figure 3.3 is that the content of the tags (i.e. the information about the text) is not enclosed in angle brackets. For some computer tools this will mean

```
<header>
<publication title> Jane Eyre </publication title>
<author> Charlotte Brontë</author>
<publication date> 16/10/1847 </publication date>
<pages sampled> 38–53 </pages sampled>
</header>
...
```

Figure 3.3 An example of a simple header

```
<header>
<publication title = "Jane Eyre"/>
<author = "Charlotte Brontë"/>
<publication date = "16/10/1847"/>
<pages sampled = "38–53"/>
</header>
...
```

Figure 3.4 An example of a simple header using attributes
and empty elements

that while the tags will be ignored, the tag content will not be, and will instead be treated as part of the data. This will mean, for instance, that, using the example in Figure 3.3, a wordlist generated by some software will contain the words 'Charlotte' and 'Brontë'. However, with the header option in Figure 3.4, information about the text is part of the start tags and therefore enclosed by angle brackets and so will be ignored by the corpus tool being used.

A further option is shown in Figure 3.5, where the metadata is held in multiple attributes in just one element. Again, the element has no content, so can be opened and closed within the same tag.

This type of header would again mean that the metadata is ignored by most corpus tools. However, such an approach might not be appropriate for all applications. The choice of header (and other tagging) will depend on which applications will be interacting with the corpus data and metadata. Software that is intended to provide a front end to a corpus might need the structural information that elements describe in the data, and might have more difficultly manipulating attributes compared with elements.

```
<header>
<TextDesc publication title = "Jane Eyre" author = "Charlotte Brontë"
publication date = "16/10/1847" pages sampled = "38–53"/>
</header>
...
```

Figure 3.5 An example of a simple header using one element
and multiple attributes

3.4.3 Automatic annotation

As we noted above (and in Chapter 1), some annotation, such as that for part-of-speech/grammatical category, can be done automatically using specialist software. An example of a POS annotation program (or tagger) is the Constituent Likelihood Automatic Word-tagging System (CLAWS), developed over many years at Lancaster University.[6] Automatic POS taggers use a variety of methods to tag words for grammatical category. Firstly, word-forms are looked up in a computerised dictionary or lexicon. In cases where the word-form in question could belong to more than one category (e.g. 'dogs' could be a plural noun or third-person singular verb), the part-of-speech is worked out based on the surrounding word-forms using one of two methods:

- Rule-based: the computer is given rules about what tags can and cannot possibly follow one another and uses these to work out the correct tag.
- Probabilistic (or stochastic): the computer uses information about how frequently tags follow one another to work out what the correct tag is likely to be.

Although automatic taggers use a combination of methods to identify grammatical categories, they are not 100 per cent accurate (CLAWS is 96–7 per cent accurate), so it can be necessary to manually check any automatically annotated texts (to indicate the importance of this, if a tagger with 97 per cent accuracy is used to tag a one million word corpus, around 30,000 words will be mistagged).

Taggers assign codes to the data from what is known as a tagset, which is a predesigned list of category-identifying codes. In the case of CLAWS, the codes identify categories of word class. The number of categories will depend on the nature of the phenomenon being described (e.g. parts-of-speech) and the degree of specificity required. For example, a POS tagset could include very broad categories of, say, noun, verb, adjective, adverb, and so on. However, a text annotated in this way would probably be of limited use. For example, differentiating between different types of verb (modal auxiliary, other auxiliary, lexical) is likely to provide greater analytical possibilities. The CLAWS tagger uses a tagset with over 160 possible tags and therefore 160 different grammatical categorisations. For example, the tagset differentiates between different types of verb (lexical, auxiliary, etc.) and also breaks these categories down further to mark base, participle and infinitive forms. The codes that mark these categories are made up of alpha-numeric characters, with upper-case letters. For example, the tags to mark verbs all start with a 'V', lexical verbs all begin with 'VV', past tense lexical verbs have the code 'VVD', -ing participles have the code 'VVG', and so on.[7] Other categories of verbs (e.g. *do*) have tags that follow a similar pattern: 'VDD' marks the past tense of *do*; 'VDG' marks the -ing participle form (i.e. *doing*).

CLAWS (in common with some other automatic taggers) does not use XML to add codes to a corpus. Instead, tagset codes are added to words with a connecting underscore character, as illustrated by this short extract from the beginning of *Jane Eyre*:

> There_EX was_VBDZ no_AT possibility_NN1 of_IO taking_ VVG a_AT1 walk_NN1 that_DD1 day_NNT1 ._. We_PPIS2 had_VHD been_VBN wandering_VVG ,_, indeed_RR ,_, in_II the_AT leafless_JJ shrubbery_NN1 an_AT1 hour_NNT1 in_II the_AT morning_NNT1 ;_; but_CCB since_CS dinner_NN1 (_(Mrs._NNB Reed_NP1 ,_, when_CS there_EX was_VBDZ no_AT company_NN1 ,_, dined_VVD early_RR)_) the_AT cold_JJ winter_NNT1 wind_NN1 had_VHD brought_VVN with_IW it_PPH1 clouds_VVZ so_RG sombre_JJ ,_, and_CC a_AT1 rain_NN1 so_RG penetrating_JJ ,_, that_DD1 further_ RRR out-door_JJ exercise_NN1 was_VBDZ now_RT out_II21 of_II22 the_AT question_NN1 ._.

This sort of mark-up is also widely understood by computer software, so can be used (and ignored if necessary) in similar ways to XML tags.

It is also possible to automatically tag texts semantically. For example, the UCREL (University Centre for Computer Corpus Research[8]) Semantic Analysis System (USAS), also developed at Lancaster University, assigns semantic tags to each word in the text or corpus (see Wilson and Thomas 1997). The semantic framework used by USAS is based on McArthur's (1981) *Longman Lexicon of Contemporary English* but has undergone many revisions during its development. The tagset used by USAS is based on a semantic hierarchy of 21 major semantic fields, which expand to 232 finer semantic categories. In Chapter 9, we describe USAS in more detail, and demonstrate how semantically tagged data can be used to enhance the analysis of a corpus of political texts.

3.4.4 Manual annotation

Not all annotation can be added automatically and, as stylisticians, it is often appropriate and necessary to add annotation manually, since there are numerous types of analysis that we might want to carry out on corpus data that cannot be automated. This is especially true when an analysis assesses the function of textual elements within the corpus data. As we have already mentioned, annotating the function of modal auxiliary verbs is one example where manual annotation would be necessary since computer software cannot currently assess the difference between, for example, deontic and epistemic modality. These language functions can be recorded in the data using the sorts of XML tags we described above. We provide an example of analysing modal function in a corpus more fully in the second case study in Chapter 8.

One particular corpus stylistic project that demonstrates the usefulness of manual annotation for stylistics is that carried out over a number of years by Semino and Short (2004) on speech, writing and thought presentation. The project team built a corpus of about 260,000 words of written British English, which consists of 120 text samples of around 2,000 words, distributed equally across three genres: prose fiction, newspaper new reports and auto/biography (Semino and Short 2004: 19).[9] The corpus was annotated in the first instance using the model of speech and thought presentation posited by Leech and Short (1981). This was a manual endeavour since not all discourse presentation is marked formally, and where it is (such as quotation marks indicating direct forms of speech presentation) the forms used are not consistent across texts. The process of analysis and annotation tested the existing model on both fiction and non-fiction and eventually led to the model (and therefore the annotation scheme) being developed and refined. A major development was the addition of a separate discourse presentation scale for writing presentation, as well as new categories for speech and thought presentation (Semino and Short 2004: 222–3). Using annotation made the process of analysis and re-analysis more practically manageable, with analytical decisions recorded directly in the data, thereby allowing it to be assessed more easily against other similarly tagged examples. The annotation also made the quantification and comparison of speech, writing and thought presentation categories more straightforward, once the tagging was complete, and this resulted in an indication of what the quantitative norms are for the different discourse presentation categories across three different genres of written British English. We return to this study in Chapter 8, where we use a similar annotation scheme to tag a parallel corpus of Early Modern English texts.

3.4.5 Mark-up and annotation summary

Adding mark-up can be a very useful way of recording analyses and encoding them into the text or corpus under analysis in a way that can be utilised by corpus tools and other computer software. Not all corpus linguists share this view, though. Some make the case that annotation imposes analyses on corpus data rather than allowing the data to speak for itself (for further discussion of this, see McEnery and Hardie 2012: 147–62). Such a view typically aligns with what is sometimes referred to as a neo-Firthian approach to corpus linguistics, which takes the view that rather than being simply a methodology, corpus linguistics is actually a sub-discipline of linguistics and, as such, constitutes a distinct theoretical approach to language. Our view, consistent with that of many other linguists, is that corpus linguistics is better seen as a methodology. However, we do not see that one approach to corpus linguistics necessarily excludes the other (we discuss this further in Chapter 4). As stylisticians we analyse texts using numerous frameworks and theories. Mark-up that electronically encodes the results of such analyses has the advantage of enabling us to automate pattern searches within corpora based on the encoded results. Mark-up can also assist in finding anomalies or errors in analyses, and enabling analyses to be shared and tested by others. Also, mark-up adds information to the data in a way that does not interfere with the data, and when required it can be ignored by corpus tools so that the raw data is preserved.

3.5 Summary: suggested steps to building a corpus

To summarise our discussion so far in this chapter, here are a set of suggested steps for building a corpus:

1 Decide on what language variety the corpus is aiming to represent and therefore what will be in it. Consider whether there might be any practical or ethical problems relating to the data that will eventually be in the corpus.
2 Create a hierarchical model of the constituent parts (possibly genres/sub-genres) of the language variety.
3 Consider whether each constituent part should have equal standing in the corpus, or whether some parts will contain more texts than others.
4 Decide whether whole texts will be collected, or extracts, or both.
5 Create a sampling frame (or multiple sampling frames for stratified sampling), and produce a random sample.
6 Locate and gather the data that comprises the sample. This can be a very time-consuming step, depending on the nature of the texts being created/collected. For instance, gathering spoken

texts will require a number of further steps including making audio recordings of the spoken data and then transcribing them.

7 Make and keep a security copy of the text in its original form. This copy might be electronic, paper or audio/visual, depending on the nature of the text(s) being collected.

8 Make and keep an electronic, plain text format copy of the text. This format is the simplest electronic format and, at the moment, a requirement of most corpus tools. It is also the most portable, flexible and future-proof format, so is a good bet for archive copies of the corpus. If required, the plain text copies can be converted into other formats.

9 It might be necessary to clean the text before using a corpus tool to process it. This might mean removing any spurious characters from the text left over from the conversion to plain text format. It might also mean that certain everyday characters (e.g. ampersands and currency symbols such as £ and €) might not be recognised by the software, and might need to be converted to some other format (e.g. XML-entities such as &amp and &pound). The manual for the software you are using should tell you what to do.

10 Add some information about the text at the beginning of the text file in the form of a header.

11 Add further mark-up as required by the investigation (e.g. POS annotation). Keep copies of the corpus before the mark-up is applied, and make copies afterwards.

12 Once you have a working copy of the corpus, *make a copy of it!* Ideally, you should make copies along the way as you build the corpus. This means that you can always go back if something goes wrong at some stage.

13 Keep notes of what you do and why you are doing it. Record decisions about corpus design, the data you use, where you got the data from, any annotation you apply to it, and so on. These notes will act as an *aide-memoire* during the process of writing up results, and will help others see and understand what you did.

3.6 Case study: investigating the *2000AD* comic strip 'Judge Dredd'

This case study uses two small corpora of comic strip data to demonstrate how mark-up can assist in the analysis of the data they contain. The corpora comprise just the lexical data (i.e. no pictures) from several episodes of the comic strip 'Judge Dredd' (as featured in the comic *2000AD*) from two points in time: 1977 and 2002. The part of the study we discuss here demonstrates how using XML tags can help to describe the lexical composition of the comic strip more precisely by separating the data into predefined categories, which can then be compared diachronically. As we will see, even though we are only looking at the words, our analysis necessarily takes into account visual aspects of the text in order for us to make decisions about marking-up the data.

Aside from our general interest in this popular comic strip, *Judge Dredd* was chosen for this study for four reasons:

1 'Judge Dredd' is one of the longest running comic strips in British comic history. It began in in 1977 and has continued almost without a break to the present day.[10]
2 The longevity and popularity of both the comic (*2000AD*) and the Judge Dredd character establishes 'Judge Dredd' as culturally significant.
3 The creator of 'Judge Dredd', John Wagner, has contributed episodes of the comic strip over the 25-year period, meaning that it is possible to keep the author variable in the data constant.
4 Crucially, we had access to comic data and from two points in the comic's history: 1977 and, 25 years later, 2002.

Perhaps the most important factor of this study (and other studies) is the access to data. Without data, no research project can begin. Having access to data from two points in time (1977 and 2003) enabled us to make diachronic comparisons and investigate which (if any) language features of the comic strip had changed and which remained stable.

3.6.1 Scope of the study

In this case study we analyse only the words of one comic strip; there is no analysis of the pictures. Our analysis is therefore limited but nevertheless constitutes a useful starting point that highlights important language features of the written component of the text. In order to carry out a study of comic strip language with generalisable results, we would need to build a corpus that somehow represented all comic strips. This would mean including representative samples from every comic strip type, which might be defined by intended audience age (adult, adolescent, child), gender, possibly some sort of classification reflecting content (action/adventure, humorous), and so on, while taking into consideration factors such as authorship and country of origin. This would be a considerable undertaking and would present the sorts of 'pragmatic' issues that Hunston (2002: 29) discusses, such as data availability, permission to use data, decisions concerning classification, and so on. As we have already mentioned, access to data is crucial for any study. We used comic data that was readily available to us (back issues of *2000AD*) and we selected the best-known comic strip from that data ('Judge Dredd'). Therefore, our corpus at best represents just one example of a comic strip. While this may not seem particularly useful in terms of general statements about genre style, it is a starting point from which it might be possible for further studies to proceed. For these reasons this study cannot make general claims about the language of comic strips. Nonetheless, it is consistent with a focus in stylistics on specific texts, and allows for the examination of text style in a specific example of the comic strip text-type.

3.6.2 Building the corpora

Our very first step in building our corpora was to obtain permission from the comic's current owner, *Rebellion Developments*, to use the words from 'Judge Dredd' in our research. Once permission was secured, we began to collect an appropriate amount of data to represent each time period (i.e. 1977 and 2002). What amount counts as appropriate is clearly debatable and this was the point in the project where we needed to ask the 'how much?' question. Our answer was very much driven by the data we had available and our research goal, which was to compare 'Judge Dredd' episodes from an early point in its history with episodes from a later point in time. We decided to make comparisons of the first 12 months in the comic strip's history and a 12-month period 25 years later. Within those 12-month periods, we used only the stories written by John Wagner, in order to control any variability that might be attributable to author. This resulted in our collecting 17 episodes and just over 11,000 words of data from 1977 into a corpus we named JD77. We matched that number of words as closely as we could from the 2002 data, which resulted in our collecting 19 episodes into a corpus we named JD02. We were, to some extent, restricted by the data we had available but nonetheless felt that a 25-year gap was sufficient for us to investigate diachronic changes in style. The word counts for both corpora can be found in Table 3.1. The final column of the table shows the mean number of words per comic, which indicates that the comic strip in 1977 consisted of more words than in 2002. This begins to indicate a possible change in storytelling style, whereby the comic strip producers rely more on images to convey stories in the later comics.

Table 3.1 Corpus profiles and average number of words per story

Corpus name	Years used	No. of words	No. of texts	Mean words/story
JD77	1977	11,674	17	687
JD02	2002	11,276	19	593

In order to create our corpora we needed to convert the paper comic strip data to machine-readable data. This could not be achieved by scanning so we manually typed the words from each episode we had selected into separate Word files, which we subsequently converted to plain text files. At the start of each file we added a data header that provided a record of what the file contained, for example:

> <head>
> <TextDesc   ComicTitle="2000AD"   PubDate="02102002"
> ComicEdition="Prog   1311"   ComicStrip="Judge   Dredd"
> ComicStripTitle="Zoom Time" Author="John Wagner"/>
> </head>

We wanted to encode information about the data into our transcriptions, and we found that adding XML mark-up as we typed was the most efficient way to proceed (rather than transcribing first then marking-up later). The mark-up we added aimed to indicate different textual components of the comic strip (for descriptions of comic strip components, see Eisener 1996; McCloud 1994: 153–5; Sabin 1996; Saraceni 2003: 7–11), which include: panels – the usually rectangular areas that the comic strip is divided into on the page; balloons – the usually ovoid shapes that contain words either spoken or thought by characters; and captions – the usually rectangular frames within the panel that contain words that typically belong to some sort of narrator. The purpose of our mark-up was to describe, using tags, in which of the comic components the words in the texts occurred. From the outset we decided to distinguish between speech balloons and thought balloons as these describe different discourse phenomena (see Semino and Short 2004). We began, therefore, with four possible category tags with which to mark-up our data. We soon found, however, that in order to account for all the words in the comic strip data, these categories were insufficient. Firstly, the data contained onomatopoeic or sound symbolic words that indicate that a noise is being produced (e.g. gunfire), and these could occur anywhere in the panel. And secondly, some words constituted writing presentation (Semino and Short 2004), such as letters or notes, but also signs, notices, placards, books, and so on (cf. McCloud's 1994 notion of 'montage', Unser-Schutz's 2011 concept of 'background text' and Walsh's 2012 'diegetic text'). The resulting tags for these categories are detailed below:

<c> caption text</c>
<sb> speech balloon </sb>
<tb> thought balloon </tb>
<wp> writing presentation </wp>
<sfx> sound effects </sfx>

These components have a functional bearing on the words we transcribed that relate to storytelling elements (e.g. narration and discourse presentation). We applied the mark-up on the basis of the visual presentation of the text within the components in question. In other words, if text appeared in what looked like captions, then the words were marked as caption text. It is worth noting that this mark-up is not perfect. It records an act of interpretation and analysis, which is not without problems. We can illustrate this by explaining some of the tagging decisions made for one panel, which is shown in Figure 3.6.

Within the corpus, the transcribed data for this panel was tagged as follows:

<panel>
<c>AFTER THE CEREMONY JUDGE TEX CONDUCTED DREDD AND HIS ROBO-SERVANT WALTER ON A TOUR OF LUNA-CITY ...</c>

Figure 3.6 A panel from 'Judge Dredd' 1977 (Judge Dredd® © 2018 Rebellion A/S. Judge Dredd is a registered trademark. All rights reserved. Reproduced by permission of the copyright holder)[11]

```
<sb>WE USE HOVER-BIKES UP HERE BECAUSE THE LOW
GRAVITY MAKES NORMAL ONES UNSTABLE!</sb>
<sb>LOOK, JUDGE DWEDD – THAT'S THE WEMAINS OF
THE FIRST MOON LANDING CRAFT!</sb>
<sb>A BRAVE MONUMENT – DEFACED. THE PEOPLE
HERE ARE A LAWLESS BUNCH.</sb>
<wp>ARMSTRONG AND ALDRIN APOLLO JULY 1969
<add>EAT AT MOONIES</add>
</wp>
<wp>MOONIES BEBOP</wp>
<wp>MOONIES SODAS</wp>
<wp part="F" desc="incomplete" note="probably MOONIES
BAR">ES BAR</wp>
</panel>
```

The panel in Figure 3.6 depicts a scene on Luna-City 1, one of a number of cities constructed on the moon's surface. Judge Dredd and his robot, Walter, are being given a tour by the incumbent lawman, Judge Tex. The scene in the panel includes writing presentation in the form of signage for bars and a sign commemorating the first Apollo moon landing, which has been partially obscured by graffiti but is still readable. The signs ('MOONIES BEBOP' and 'MOONIES SODAS') help to show that Moonie, a mysterious, reclusive character, owns a lot of businesses and is an important figure in the city. The graffiti helps to underline this, as well as indicate that lawlessness is a problem in the city. One of the bar signs ('ES BAR') is cut off by the edge of the panel so some of the writing is missing. Our assumption is that the full sign says 'MOONIES BAR' due to the pattern established throughout the rest of the writing presentation in the panel. The transcription and subsequent tagging of caption and speech balloon data was straightforward; the writing presentation, however, required careful consideration due to the graffiti on the commemoration plaque and only half of the sign for Moonies Bar being visible. For the former, we used our <wp> tag to show the original wording on the plaque, and then within that tag embedded an <add> tag to show the addition of extra words in the form of graffiti. For the latter we used a <wp> tag with the addition of 'part', 'dec' and 'note' attributes. The part attribute contains the value 'F' for final (other possible values are 'M' for medial and 'I' for initial). The 'desc' (description) and 'note' attributes can contain any value. We found the guidelines and suggestions proposed by Burnard (2014) helpful in developing a tagging strategy for this panel, and the extra tags and attributes we used were adopted from the Text Encoding Initiative (TEI) encoding scheme.[12]

3.6.3 Results of the preliminary analysis

In this section we show how words are distributed in comic strips from both eras based on the tagging that we added to the corpora. The mark-up divides the lexical data into five textual components: caption, speech balloon, thought balloon, sound effect and writing presentation. From this mark-up we calculated the number of words in each of these components for each corpus. We normalised these totals by converting them to percentages so that we could make comparisons between the corpora. Figure 3.7 shows the results of these calculations.

From the breakdown of the two corpora shown in Figure 3.7 we can see that most of the words in each of the corpora are in speech balloons, suggesting that lexically the majority of the narrative is conveyed through presentation of characters' spoken words. However, while the JD77 data is predominantly made up of words in speech balloons, the percentage of just over 71 per cent is lower than that in JD02, which stands at over 86 per cent. The second largest category in both corpora is captions, with words in captions making up just over 20 per cent of the data in JD77, which is double the total 10.1 per cent in JD02. The word totals for speech balloons and captions indicate an overall quantitative trend in both datasets, suggesting the predominant

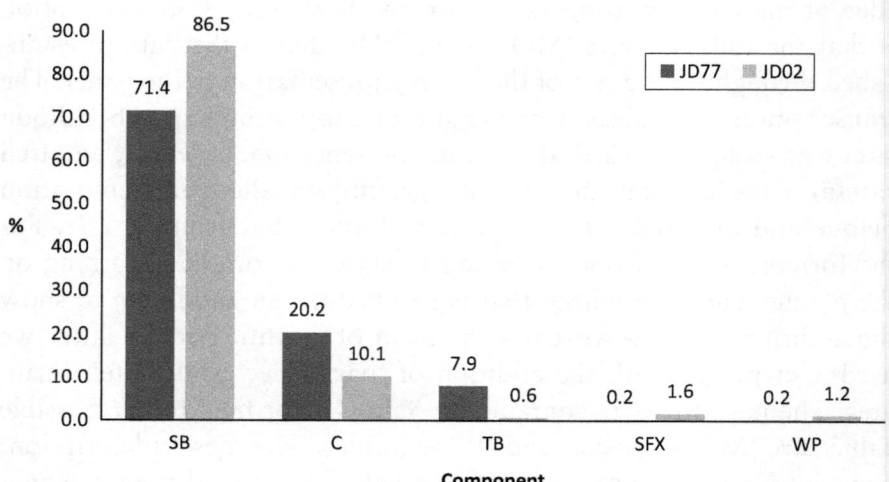

Figure 3.7 Percentage totals of words in each text category for JD77 and JD02

lexical mode of storytelling is via character speech and captions. This trend appears to be a stable feature of the data used to represent this comic strip. In order to ascertain how widespread this convention is across the genre more generally, more comic strips would need to be analysed in a similar manner. There is a noticeable difference in the datasets between the numbers of words used in thought balloons: in JD77 this is almost 8 per cent, but in JD02 the figure is only 0.6 per cent (which equates to 63 words out of the whole corpus). This indicates that within the data we used to represent 'Judge Dredd' in the two time periods, characters' thoughts are used less in the overall narrative. The figures for sound effects and writing presentation are very low in both corpora but in both cases there are more examples in JD02 than there are in JD77.

3.6.4 Further analysis

The next stage in our analysis is to look more closely at each of the textual components in order to investigate the differences. At this stage we use the quantities derived from our tagging to find a focus for qualitative analysis. There is only space here to briefly explore difference in captions.

There are fewer captions in the JD02 data compared with the JD77 data. The small size of our datasets made it possible to make manual comparisons, particularly once the data was split into its constituent components. We found that the captions in the JD77 data match the prototypical and documented assumptions (see, for instance, Saraceni 2003) about this comic component being akin to third-person narration. For example, some captions contain long noun phrases that act as descriptors for the images contained in the panel, helping to explain what the reader is looking at, such as the following:

> <c>MEGA-CITY 1. VAST METROPOLIS OF THE 22ND CENTURY.</c>

Other captions account for temporal gaps in the narrative or simply describe ongoing action within a panel using past tense verbs, whereby the people involved in the action can be seen in the image. For example:

> <c>TWO TROGGIES WERE LEFT TO GUARD THE WORK SQUAD. THE MINUTES TICKED BY ... </c>
> <c>DREDD PULLED AWAY SOME OF THE RUBBLE</c>

Additionally, a number of captions are short and contain adverbials, prepositional phrases or conjunctions that respectively position the action in the panel temporally, spatially or sequentially, such as:

> <c>SUDDENLY ...</c>
> <c>MEANWHILE, IN THE STUDIO ...</c>
> <c>LATER ...</c>
> <c>A WEEK LATER ...</c>
> <c>ON THE ROOF ...</c>
> <c>AND SO ...</c>

We manually compared the lexis in the captions from JD77 and JD02, and found that the lexical items *suddenly*, *meanwhile* and *later* appear 10, 6 and 14 times respectively in the JD77 captions but are not used at all in the JD02 captions. This finding in itself suggests that the captions in JD02 function differently. Indeed, we found that, unlike the captions in JD77, a number of captions in JD02 contain what appears to be free indirect thought. For example:

>
> <c>DREDD HAD THE BIT BETWEEN HIS TEETH. HE WOULDN'T LET UP. THEY'D LOOK INTO BUBBA O'KELLY, FIND THE CONNECTION.</c>
> <c>HE'D TRIED TO PUT THINGS RIGHT, ONLY MADE THEM WORSE. KILLED A CIVILIAN -</c>
>

The image in the panel contains just one character, Judge Michael de Klerk, who is involved in a conspiracy to kill criminals without trial, and at this point in the story he is coming to the realisation that Judge Dredd is about to find him out. However, even though Dredd is not present in the panel, the first caption in the panel provides a description of Dredd, referring to him by name in the first sentence and then by anaphoric reference via the pronoun *he* in the second sentence. The pronoun shifts to *they* in the third sentence and probably refers to the justice department, generally. The description found in the first sentence makes use of the simple past tense, a tense which is prototypically used for narration. The epistemic modal auxiliary verb *would* used in the second and third sentences expresses the conditional mood and suggests possibility and/or prediction of future actions, and therefore does not provide a description of ongoing action of the type associated with third-person narration. The caption therefore describes a state of affairs that exists spatially and temporally beyond the panel. In the second caption there is a second use of the pronoun 'he' but this time it does not refer back to 'Dredd', but refers instead to de Klerk. For readers familiar with the story, this becomes apparent in the second sentence due to reference to actions carried out by de Klerk in the recent past. Within the captions in this panel there is reference to people and situations not present in the panel, a switch in pronoun referent, and the use of the past perfect aspect. These features are consistent with the blend of narration and characters' discourse associated with free indirect discourse (in this case, free indirect thought) which is described by, for example, Leech and Short (1981), Short (1996a) and Semino and Short (2004). Below are some further illustrative examples of this phenomenon in JD02 from two different stories:

```
<p>
<c>SOMETIMES YOU GET A FEELING ... BAD THINGS
ARE IN THE WIND.</c>
</p>
<p>
<c>EVERYTHING   TO   LIVE   FOR.   NO   SECRET
ATTACHMENTS,  NO  BIG  OUTSIDE  INTERESTS.  A
PERFECT, SELF-CONTAINED LITTLE LIFE.</c>
<c>JUST  ONE  LOUSY  UNCLE  WHO  DIDN'T  CARE
ENOUGH ...</c>
<c>CUT IT OUT.</c>
</p>
```

There are no examples of this phenomenon in the JD77 corpus, suggesting a change in the style and function of captions between the two points in time described in the two datasets.

Clearly, this represents only a starting point in terms of a more detailed analysis of the corpus data, using the quantitative analysis as a focus. Importantly, though, our qualitative analysis is informed by an existing stylistic framework, which enables us to describe more precisely and make sense of the results obtained from our quantitative analysis.

3.6.5 Case study summary

The sorts of quantitative comparisons we carried out in this case study were made more possible through the tagging. The study aims to demonstrate, using small corpora, how breaking texts down into constituent elements allows for finer-grained comparisons. In other words, the tagging makes comparisons between individual components of two corpora (e.g. 1977 speech balloons vs 2002 speech balloons) practically more straightforward. The results from the study suggest a general trend between the two datasets, whereby speech balloons and captions are the most frequent lexical categories, but also indicate differences. From these findings we were able to focus on one particular component of the comics in order to explore the features in more detail.

Our initial analyses of the corpora (done to develop the system of mark-up) were based on what the various textual components looked like. That is, if a component looked like a speech balloon, then the words within it were tagged as speech balloon data, and so on. However, as we saw with the captions in the JD02 corpus, this approach ignores the function of the words that occur within the visually identified component. So, some captions contained third-person narration while some contained, for example, free indirect thought. This suggested that a further level of mark-up was required to take into account the functions of the comic components. Adding mark-up, therefore, can be a cyclical endeavour that is first informed by the text as well as models that help to inform an interpretation of elements of the text (in this case the traditional and well-documented inventory of comic components). The results from such initial mark-up can then inform further tagging or amendments to existing annotation.

3.7 Conclusion

In this chapter we have dealt with designing and building a corpus and in doing so introduced the concept of a population and the notion of sampling from that population. The idea behind sampling is that whatever results are obtained from a sample can be generalised to the population the sample came from. In effect, a sample aims to be a mini version of the population. We went on to introduce the idea of adding metadata to a corpus using annotation, and described the different sorts of metadata that can be added. We noted that metadata can add value to corpus data and make the corpus useful for different types of linguistic enquiry. In the case study we put into practice some of the data collection and annotation methods, and discussed some of the issues that different data can present. We used the case study in particular to demonstrate the sorts of useful findings annotation can generate and how these can lead to further, more focused and detailed analyses. The comparative analysis that we carried out, of course, was guided by a general research question which asked, 'What, if any, are the differences between the 1977 and the 2002 data and what are the stylistic effects of such differences?' Formulating clear research questions and hypotheses is key to producing replicable and falsifiable stylistic analyses. In the next chapter, we explore the process of developing these in more detail.

Notes

1. It is possible to create a random sample using other software, such as SPSS, and free-to-use websites such as www.random.org. The latter will create a random sample from a list of up to 10,000 sample items.
2. Information in this section is drawn from <https://www.gov.uk/using-somebody-elses-intellectual-property/copyright>, <https://www.gov.uk/guidance/exceptions-to-copyright>, <https://www.copyrightservice.co.uk/copyright/> and <https://global.oup.com/academic/authors/author-guidelines/copyright-permissions/> (all last accessed 14 September 2018).
3. See <http://www.respectproject.org/main/index.php> (last accessed 20 August 2018).
4. See <https://esrc.ukri.org/funding/guidance-for-applicants/research-ethics/our-core-principles/> (last accessed 20 August 2018).
5. McEnery and Hardie (2012) only use the term *metadata* to refer to the descriptive metadata that is contained in headers.
6. See <http://ucrel.lancs.ac.uk/claws/trial.html> (last accessed 20 August 2018).
7. The full tagset can be found at <http://ucrel.lancs.ac.uk/claws7tags.html> (last accessed 20 August 2018).
8. Formerly 'University Centre for Research on the English Language', hence UCREL.
9. The Lancaster Speech, Writing and Thought Presentation Written Corpus is available for download from the Oxford Text Archive; see Appendix 1 for details.
10. The publishers of *2000AD* in 1977 were IPC/Fleetway. Now, Rebellion Developments publish *2000AD* both in paper format and online at: <http://www.2000adonline.com> (last accessed 20 August 2018).
11. We are grateful to Rebellion for granting permission to reproduce this panel.
12. The Text Encoding Initiative is a consortium that provides

guidelines for creating and encoding machine machine-readable texts. It has developed and continually maintains a comprehensive encoding scheme. See <http://www.tei-c.org> (last accessed 20 August 2018).

4

Testing hypotheses and answering research questions

4.1 Introduction

In Chapter 2 we showed how it is possible to use pre-existing large corpora to support the qualitative stylistic analysis of text fragments. When such an endeavour is carried out in pursuit of insights into the significance of particular stylistic choices in the text, this practice constitutes corpus-informed stylistics. In this chapter we broaden the parameters of corpus stylistics by exploring the possibilities of subjecting the target text itself (i.e. the text we are particularly interested in analysing) to corpus analysis. That is, rather than comparing a small section of our target text with a pre-existing corpus (i.e. a reference corpus), we instead treat the target text (or, indeed, texts) as a corpus in its own right. This allows us to use corpus analytical techniques to discover patterns in the text(s) that would not be discernible through qualitative analysis alone. To this end, in this chapter we begin to utilise the insights from Chapter 3 concerning sampling and representativeness, as we consider how to analyse not just single extracts but also collections of texts.

We refer to this practice of treating the target text (or collections of texts) as a corpus in its own right as corpus-based stylistics. When analysing a corpus stylistically, although it is possible to approach the task with no particular agenda concerning what we want to investigate, we advocate concentrating any analysis on answering a specific research question or addressing a specific hypothesis. This chapter, then, builds on the corpus-informed approach described in Chapter 2 by discussing the philosophy behind corpus-based stylistic analysis. We explain methods for generating hypotheses and candidate research questions before moving on to consider the practice of developing a robust and replicable analytical method to test/answer these. Here we focus particularly on methodological issues shared by both corpus linguistics and stylistics, namely objectivity, rigour, replicability and falsifiability. We discuss how stylistics has dealt with these issues and the extent to which corpus linguistic methods increase the potential for addressing these. We also make clear that these issues apply equally to qualitative analysis and that here stylistics has a contribution to make to corpus linguistics. We illustrate these points with reference to our third case study, a corpus-based analysis of Ernest Hemingway's authorial style. In so doing, we introduce two more software packages for corpus analysis, WordSmith Tools (Scott 2016) and Wmatrix (Rayson 2009). WordSmith provides valuable descriptive statistics for uploaded corpora, while the particular value of Wmatrix is its capacity for automatically annotating texts for part-of-speech (POS) and semantic information. In this chapter we make particular use of Wmatrix's POS tagger; and in so doing we lay the groundwork for the more complex Wmatrix analyses that follow in subsequent chapters. We begin, though, with a brief discussion of the nature of a corpus. In corpus stylistics, some licence is often taken with how a corpus is defined, and it is worth being clear on both the pros and cons of doing this. We then clarify our use of the term *corpus-based* through consideration of the distinction between this and *corpus-driven* linguistics.

4.2 Corpora in stylistics

In Chapter 1 we discussed the definition of a corpus, noting that representativeness is a key criterion. Corpus linguists tend to be primarily concerned with making generalisable claims about language use based on the analysis of a sample of language data. For generalisability to be possible, such samples have to be representative of whatever language variety is under scrutiny. It is for this reason that Sinclair (2005) claims that an individual text cannot constitute a corpus. However, in stylistics, it is not always the case that we want to make generalisable claims of the kind made in corpus linguistics. Of course, corpus stylisticians do sometimes construct corpora that are intended to be representative of a particular stylistic variety (see, for example, Green's 2017 Corpus of the Canon of Western Literature, as well as the corpora analysed in Chapters 8 and 9). And in the related field of stylometry, representativeness is just as important a criterion as it is in corpus linguistics (see, for instance, Hoover 2017). But it is also true that what many stylisticians are interested in is what Short (1996a) calls text style; that is, the style observable in a single specific text. This may or may not be connected to authorial style. For example, Stubbs's (2005) corpus stylistic study of Joseph Conrad's *Heart of Darkness* is concerned with providing textual justification for well-established interpretations of the novella, and offering new insights into the language and meaning potential of the text. In this respect, Stubbs's focus is on explicating issues concerning this text in particular, such as how the story is told and how the characters are projected. He does not seek to make claims about Conrad's authorial style in general terms. Because of his specific interest in *Heart of Darkness*, there is no need for Stubbs to construct a corpus that is a representative sample of Conrad's output as a novelist.

Despite being focused on one text in particular, Stubbs's (2005) analysis does make use of other texts in the form of a reference corpus. In this respect, Stubbs's (2005) study is an example of what Adolphs (2006) calls *inter*-textual analysis. But some studies of text style do not even utilise separate reference corpora. Adolphs (2006) calls such cases *intra*-textual analysis, where the focus is entirely on extrapolating particular information from one text in order to generate insights relating to that text alone. An example of a corpus stylistic analysis of intra-textual variation is Culpeper's (2009) study of keywords (as well as key parts-of-speech and key semantic domains) in Shakespeare's *Romeo and Juliet*. We introduce the notion of keyness in full in Chapter 5, but in brief a keyword is one that is more frequent in one text than it is in another. Keyness studies are often inter-textual in nature, in that a target corpus is compared against a reference corpus. Culpeper's (2009) study, however, compares the dialogue of individual characters against the dialogue of all the other characters in *Romeo and Juliet*. In this respect, the play serves as both the target text and the reference corpus. Among Culpeper's (2009) findings are the fact that *if, or, would* and *yet* are all keywords for Juliet; that is, they occur more frequently in Juliet's speech than they do in the speech of the other characters. Culpeper (2009) notes that the findings from his keyness analysis are relevant to understanding characterisation in the play. For example, Juliet's keywords reflect her tendency as a character towards uncertainty and anxiety.

Both Culpeper's (2009) and Stubbs's (2005) studies illustrate the value of using corpus analytical techniques on single texts. So we might ask: what precisely is the nature of Sinclair's (2005) objection to the use of the term *corpus* to describe single texts? This is partly that its dimensional restrictions do not allow for generalisations to be made about the language variety that it represents. But in addition, it is also possible to be knowledgeable about a single text in a way that it is impossible, given its size, to be knowledgeable about the contents of a corpus. This has potential analytical implications. For example, it may well be that a corpus-based stylistic analysis of a single text is also informed (consciously or unconsciously) by the researcher's qualitative familiarity with it. To the extent that this might impact on the objectivity of the analysis, Sinclair (2005) is right to draw attention to the distinction between corpora and single texts. Nonetheless, for ease of reference we do on occasion use the term *corpus* when discussing single texts; but in such instances we make quite clear that our focus is indeed on a single text and not a corpus in the traditional sense. In such cases, the potential complicating factors associated with the corpus stylistic analysis of single texts should be borne in mind. In theoretical terms, we agree with Sinclair in cautioning against extending the term *corpus* to encompass single texts too.

4.3 The concept of corpus-based and corpus-driven linguistics

The first section of this chapter introduced the concept of *corpus-based* stylistics and defined it as the practice of analysing a target text using corpus methods (as opposed to using a pre-existing corpus to support or challenge a qualitative analysis of a text extract). Before we proceed any further with this concept, however, it is worth briefly discussing the origins of the phrase *corpus-based*, since our usage here differs somewhat from that to be found in mainstream corpus linguistics.

Tognini-Bonelli (2001) contrasts corpus-*based* with corpus-*driven* linguistics. The distinction between these two analytical procedures (as described by Tognini-Bonelli 2001; see also Francis 1993) is that the former uses corpus analysis to validate existing theories and hypotheses, while the latter uses the results of corpus analysis to formulate new, corpus-derived theories and hypotheses. For example, the 100 million word BNC contains part-of-speech information that was added to the corpus automatically using a POS tagger. But the POS information that the tagger contains is based on a non-corpus-derived grammar. The upshot of this is that what we learn about the grammar of English by studying the BNC will always be constrained by the model of grammar that the POS tagger uses. Retrieving information about prepositions, for instance, will only ever allow us to observe those lexical items that have been identified as prepositions by the tagger. We will not be able to observe any instances of potential prepositional meaning in words that have not already been tagged as having this function. This, then, is corpus-*based* linguistics, that is, using non-corpus-derived theories and analytical frameworks to inform a corpus analysis.

By contrast, corpus-*driven* linguistics is not constrained by existing theories or analytical frameworks. Rather, the aim is to identify patterns in the raw (i.e. unannotated) corpus data that might then be used to formulate new theories of whatever aspect of language we are studying. Sinclair's work on lexis and meaning (1991; see also 2004) is a prime example of corpus-driven linguistics, and it is worth briefly explaining this so as to be clear about the distinguishing characteristics of a corpus-driven approach to data analysis.

Sinclair (2004) explains that a particular problem in linguistics – one that arises as a result of the excessive attention paid to written (as opposed to spoken) language – is that we have a tendency to see words as discrete units. This, obviously, is because words on a page are separated by spaces. Words, of course, are formed from morphemes but whether we see words or morphemes as the basic unit of language, the important point is that, traditionally, linguists have focused on how these basic units combine, that is, their interest has been in grammar. Meaning, by contrast, was (and still is in some quarters) assumed to be a separate property of words, distinct from this focus on structure. This view, however, ignores the significant role that structure plays in generating meaning. As Sinclair points out, '[w]ords enter into meaningful relations with other words around them, and yet all our current descriptions marginalize this massive contribution to meaning' (2004: 25). For example, dictionaries often treat phrasal verbs (e.g. *give in*) as anomalies to be dealt with separately from single unit lexical items. Accounting for the meanings of phrasal verbs is difficult using the standard hierarchical model of language which sees morphemes combine to form words, words combine to form phrases, phrases combine to form sentences and so on. This is because phrasal verbs seem to cut across these category boundaries. And while the meanings of some phrasal verbs seem to be entirely different from the meanings of their component parts (e.g. *brush up on*), others do not (e.g. *look for*). To explain such meanings, we need to understand how words relate to each other semantically. Since we are used to examining constraints on syntactic structure, there is no reason in principle why we should not extend this consideration to constraints on lexical relations (Sinclair 2004: 28). For example, *strong tea* is an acceptable formulation whereas **powerful tea* is not.[1] The reason we can have *strong* but not *powerful* before *tea* is not down to syntactic constraints (after all, English allows adjectives to pre-modify nouns). It must, then, be due instead to lexical restrictions.

The notion of lexical constraints forms the core of collocational studies (see, for example, the case study in Chapter 2) and is at the heart of the concept of a unit of meaning. Sinclair's (2004) point is that it is only through corpus-driven analysis that we can identify such structures. As an example, Sinclair (2004: 30–5) shows how the meaning of the expression *naked eye* can only be explained by determining the unit of meaning in which it is typically found. Through observation of concordance lines for *naked eye*, Sinclair explains that the collocational and colligational patterns, in conjunction with patterns of semantic preference, suggest the following unit of meaning: 'visibility + preposition + *the* + *naked* + *eye*' (2004: 33). This unit of meaning generates such usages as 'too faint to be seen with the naked eye', 'is not really visible to the naked eye' and 'could be seen by the naked eye'. In addition, Sinclair (2004: 33) notes an associated semantic prosody of difficulty. The point is that the meaning of *naked eye* arises from the sum total of the elements of the unit of meaning; it is not inherent in the phrase itself. And the constraints on lexical relations predict that a usage such as 'delicious to the naked eye' would be unlikely and unacceptable (except in deliberately creative formulations).

On the basis of such corpus-driven analysis, Sinclair (2004) formulates what he terms the idiom principle. According to this principle, words have meanings which derive from their collocational patterns. That is, meaning is not necessarily inherent in individual words but is dependent on the particular patterns that words form. Consequently, constructing sentences is not a matter of inserting individual words into open grammatical slots (as suggested by the slot/filler model of structuralist grammar), or of generating sentences according to an underlying set of grammatical rules (as proposed by generative grammar). According to the idiom principle, speakers do not have a free choice in which words they use (e.g. speakers are constrained to say *strong tea* as opposed to *powerful tea*). Instead, they select from a set of pre-existing patterns. In essence, we form utterances by relying primarily on the idiom principle. Only when this principle fails to offer an option do we fall back on what Sinclair (2004) calls the open-choice principle.

Sinclair's corpus-driven work on lexis has been hugely influential, giving rise to, for instance, lexical priming theory (Hoey 2004) and pattern grammar (Hunston and Francis 1999; Hunston 2015), the grammar that underpins the Collins COBUILD series of dictionaries and grammar books (see Chapter 1). Hunston and Francis (1999: 22) further point to the role of the idiom principle in the interpretation of utterances. They explain that an example like *I must confess* can be interpreted either as a single item, under the idiom principle (in which case it means something like, 'I am about to tell you something embarrassing to me'), or as a string of individual items, according to the open-choice principle (in which case it means 'I am obliged to inform you of some wrongdoing on my part'). It is down to the hearer to decide which principle generates the most appropriate interpretation. To take a similar example, consider the expression *I have to say*. Under the open-choice principle, this would be interpreted as meaning 'I am required to inform you.' But under the idiom principle, the meaning is something like 'I wish to emphasise the following statement.' This can be seen in the concordance lines from the BNC, shown in Figure 4.1.

The difference between the two is that the meaning generated by the idiom principle interpretation belongs to the sequence as a whole, which means that its component words cannot be altered without affecting this meaning. For instance, changing the pronoun and tense (e.g. *he had to say*) would preclude the idiom principle interpretation.

The point behind this explanation of Sinclair's work and the work of Hunston and Francis (1999) is that the insights into grammar that they offer could only have been gained through corpus-driven analysis. A corpus-based analysis of an automatically POS-tagged corpus would very likely have failed to reveal these patterns because of the influencing effects of the non-corpus-derived grammar used by the tagger. This, then, is the distinction between corpus-based and corpus-driven linguistics. Nonetheless, while this distinction is useful in heuristic terms, it should be borne in mind that in practice there are often overlaps between the two approaches. Hardie and McEnery (2010) see the distinction as the difference between viewing corpus linguistics as a methodology (the corpus-based position) and seeing it as a distinct sub-discipline of linguistics (the corpus-driven position). Hardie and McEnery (2010) refer to the first view as the methodologist position and the second as the neo-Firthian position (based as it is on the theoretical work of J. R. Firth; see Chapter 2). They further point out that the two traditions have an equally long history and suggest that the distinction between them seems likely to diminish over time as neo-Firthian discoveries such as pattern grammar converge with cognitive linguistic theories. Construction grammar, for instance, is a cognitive linguistic theory of language structure that shares many similarities with pattern grammar, as suggested by Hank's definition of a construction as 'a linguistic element that cannot be broken down into smaller units without loss of meaning' (2008: 226; for more on construction grammar, see Fillmore et al. 1988; Croft 2001; Goldberg 1995, 2006; Hilpert 2014). The difference is that pattern grammar is based solely on observable instances of language in use, whereas construction grammar is focused

(SP:F7FPSUNK) Okay. (SP:F7FPS000) Yes, (unclear) that will. (SP:F7FPSUNK) And	**I have to say**	my experience it leaves me to doubt, I know I'm a cynic sometimes
place over the (unclear) (pause) erm (pause) we have immediately re-secured,	**I have to say**	there's been about fifty erm (pause) tickets out to re-secure those (pause) those,
(SP:PS23B) I'll gladly suggest it. But er (SP:PS23A) (unclear)2. (SP:PS23B)	**I have to say,**	I I won't take no bets as to what we (laughing) actually get
erm a, a range of options. (SP:H49PSUNK) Mhm. (SP:PS1XD)	**I have to say,**	relatively er in an erm unbiased as unbiased as they could be. Er
city football club, because they are concerned, and have been	**I have to say**	for many years, so it's not unusual. (SP:H49PSUNK) (unclear) (SP:PS1XE) (unclear) the
yesterday, to which the answer, I mean I'm afraid	**I have to say**	th-- th-- the glib answer is, why are you telling me you need a
organized is different. (SP:HM6PSUNK) It, again I have to,	**I have to say**	(SP:HM6PSUNK) (unclear) (SP:HM6PSUNK) that (unclear) talk about the company of which I'
being in this (unclear) together. (SP:HUTPSUNK) Yes. (SP:HUTPSUNK) Yes,	**I have to say**	I enjoyed it far more than I expected. (SP:HUTPSUNK) I actually enjoyed it.
see if we can erm, if that, because, because	**I have to say**	that although you know part of reading (-----)' s letter, erm, I
important and I think it's, there's er actually,	**I have to say**	er I detect (-----) in (-----)' s letter because I am quite sure that
ith the brick (unclear) and the flints. (SP:HYKPSUNK) (unclear) (SP:HYKPSUNK)	**I have to say**	there's a little bit grieving in the way (pause) (SP:PS3CJ) Oh, yeah,
are (pause) two of the most important for people. (SP:HYYPSUNK) Well	**I have to say**	that as a result of last night's session I have a much healthier view
it, I really enjoy that. (cough) Meetings (pause) once again	**I have to say**	(pause) the old, old (pause) chestnut (pause) please can we start at eight o
the meetings (pause) please. Erm (pause) and that's about all	**I have to say,**	Mr Chairman. (SP:J3NPSUNK) (unclear) (SP:PS3MG) (unclear) need a proposer (unclear)2.
training staff, your, your residential staff get trained. But	**I have to say**	for Shropshire, it means one I think, er, per year, and
there is an over-supply of residential accommodation, not evenly distributed,	**I have to say**	that, that it varies, for example in Shrewsbury there's a very sizable
military term (SP:PS3MP) To fill that gap for us immediately. And	**I have to say**	to you again that the home care service is the one that is most under

Figure 4.1 Concordance lines from the BNC illustrating the idiom principle interpretation of *I have to say*

on modelling mental representations of language. Nonetheless, the clear similarities between them would suggest a converging of corpus and cognitive theories of language (for examples of the connections between pattern grammar and construction grammar, see Hennemann 2015; Hunston and Su 2017).

As Hardie and McEnery (2010) point out, then, in practice there are overlaps between corpus-based and corpus-driven approaches in corpus linguistics generally. The same is true in corpus stylistics. For this reason, it is worth clarifying our own use of the terms. We use *corpus-based stylistics* to refer to any corpus stylistic study that treats the target text as a corpus, whether annotated or not (cf. corpus-informed stylistics, which uses existing large corpora to generate insights into single short texts). We reserve the term *corpus-driven stylistics* for those studies that are exploratory in nature (e.g. those that are carried out for purposes of selecting a sample for qualitative analysis, or to generate potential research questions).

Let us now turn to another concept that has been widely discussed in both corpus linguistics and stylistics: intuition.

4.4 The value of intuition

The notion of hypothesis testing is a mainstay of stylistic analysis, though it is often not discussed in such explicit terms. In Leech and Short's (1981) seminal *Style in Fiction*, for instance, there is no reference at all to the concept of a hypothesis. What there is, however, is considerable discussion of the notion of intuition, and of the value of using stylistic analysis to test the validity of our initial impressions of a text. In effect, this is what we did in Chapter 2 when we examined concordance lines of the phrase *with intent* in order to gain an insight into the potential effects of the phrase 'strolling with intent' in the John Le Carré passage. We began with an intuition that this was a stylistically interesting phrase and we then examined concordance lines and collocates to determine the effects likely to spring from its use. Testing our intuitions is very similar to the concept of testing a hypothesis. The difference is that hypotheses are formulated more stringently than intuitions, which tend by their nature to be more general. Here, for example, are Leech and Short's initial impressions of a passage from Joseph Conrad's *The Secret Sharer* (1910):

> Our first impression of this passage is of a meticulously detailed setting of the scene for the story. The description is clearly etched, so that we can reconstruct, in our mind's eye, the whole

topography. But more than this, we have a vivid sense of the loneliness of the human observer, set apart from his surroundings, and of 'a mind energetically stretching to subdue a dazzling experience *outside* the self, in a way that has innumerable counterparts elsewhere in Conrad' [Ohmann 1966: 152]. (Leech and Short 1981: 83–4)

The impressions described in the above quotation include specific feelings that, according to Leech and Short, the text imbues in the reader. In addition, there is reference to the claims of another critic (Ohmann 1966) about Conrad's style. Leech and Short (1981: 84–90) then go on to explain the linguistic source of these impressions, pointing out, for example, the distancing effect caused by the syntactic subordination in the passage, and how this might relate to their initial impression of loneliness. Leech and Short's (1981) linguistic analysis is detailed and replicable. What is harder to evidence is a link between the stylistic features they observe and their effects on other readers. One reason for this is that the claim for an effect of loneliness is unfalsifiable. That is, if another reader claims not to encounter this feeling as they read, then it is impossible for us to say that they are wrong. The most that we can do in such a circumstance is to claim that stylistic effects in the text give rise to an impression of loneliness *for us*, while accepting that for other readers this emotional response may be different. Research in cognitive stylistics has made considerable headway in accounting for such differences of interpretation, not least through the use of schema theory to explain the source of literary impressions (see, for example, Jeffries 2001; Semino 2001; Stockwell 2002: 82–7; Lang 2009). Moreover, Short et al. (2011) have demonstrated that what are described as different interpretations would in most cases be better described as variations of the same higher-order interpretation.

  The other issue with testing the kinds of intuitions observable in the Leech and Short (1981) quotation is that such impressions rarely provide much guidance on what might constitute their linguistic source. In this respect, looking for linguistic evidence for a particular impression of a text can be likened to searching for a needle in a haystack, or trying to locate a light switch in a darkened room. For these reasons, instead of using our general impressions of a text to underpin a stylistic analysis, it is often of greater value (not to mention more manageable analytically) to use them to formulate specific hypotheses which are then amenable to more reliable testing. We should not dismiss the value of intuition in stylistics; we should simply be mindful of its limitations.

The same is true of intuition in corpus linguistics. Again, intuition has value. As McEnery and Hardie note, 'without some ability to introspect, it is doubtful whether a linguist could ever formulate a question to ask of a corpus' (2012: 26). This is a point also made by Aston (2011: 5; see also McEnery and Wilson 2001: 7). But of course, our intuition is limited, particularly concerning certain aspects of language use. As Hunston (2002: 20–1) clearly explains, we are notoriously unreliable when it comes to making intuitive judgements about the frequency of words, phrases and other linguistic structures. We are similarly unreliable at making judgements about collocations, semantic prosody and phraseology. But testing our intuitions is one of the prime purposes of doing corpus analysis. Again, this means using our intuitions to generate hypotheses and research questions. And as Aston points out, '[b]ecause intuition is unreliable, it is a good idea also to pose questions to which you think you already know the answers' (2011: 6). This is a particularly pertinent point, given one of the criticisms that is often levelled at stylistics by non-linguistically inclined literary critics; namely: what is the value of doing detailed linguistic-stylistic analysis if the results tell us nothing that a sensitive literary critic could not have told us without going to the trouble of doing such work? The answer, as Aston (2011: 6) notes, is that while we might intuitively feel that we know the effects of a particular linguistic structure, without testing this empirically we can never know for certain. This attitude has long underpinned stylistics, and is perhaps summed up most famously by Spitzer, who notes that 'to make our way to an old truth is not only to enrich our own understanding: it produces new evidence of objective value for this truth – which is thereby renewed' (1948: 38). Introspection, then, is important to corpus stylistics. But crucially its value is as a source for generating hypotheses and research questions, not as a source of data in its own right (cf. the role of intuition in early generative syntax, such as Chomsky 1957).

4.5 Hypotheses

Hypotheses might be formulated based on our intuitions, or they might stem from the literature on whatever topic we happen to be interested in. The key point is that a hypothesis aims to explain a particular phenomenon. Moreover, a hypothesis must be testable; that is, it must be formulated in such a way as to make it possible, after appropriate analysis, to reject it as an explanation of the phenomenon under investigation. For example, we might want to claim that the reason Charles Dickens is so lauded as a novelist is because he had a larger vocabulary than those of his contemporaries. This is an explanation for a particular phenomenon (that Dickens's work is distinctive) and one that is also open to testing, at least in theory. To decide whether our hypothesis is correct or not, what we would need to do is compare the size of Dickens's vocabulary with the size of the vocabularies of other novelists of the time, and see whether it is indeed the case that Dickens used a greater variety of words. A key point, though, is that we can never prove a hypothesis to be right. While this might sound counter-intuitive, the reason is that we can never know whether an additional test might prove the hypothesis to be wrong. For this reason, the scientific method focuses on proving hypotheses to be wrong, not right (this approach to hypothesis testing is a consequence of the seminal work of Popper [1959] 2002; see Chapman 2008: 28–48 for an outline of Popperian falsification in relation to linguistics, and Hughes and Sharrock 1997: 77–81 for a summary in relation to the sociology of science more generally). For example, if on comparing Dickens's vocabulary with those of his contemporaries we find that he does indeed use a greater variety of words, we still cannot say for sure that Dickens has a larger vocabulary. This is because we cannot know for certain whether another novelist, one whose work we have not examined, uses an even wider variety of words. However, if we compare Dickens's vocabulary with the vocabularies of his contemporaries, and we find that one of those contemporaries has a larger vocabulary than Dickens, then we have proved beyond doubt that our initial hypothesis was wrong (notwithstanding some of the problems associated with null hypothesis significance testing, which we discuss further in Chapter 5). We only need one instance of a nineteenth-century novelist having a larger vocabulary than Dickens to be sure of this. Such a result would then allow us to reject our initial hypothesis as a potential explanation for why Dickens's work is distinctive.

Much corpus linguistic work relies on statistical hypothesis testing (i.e. using statistical tests to determine whether there is indeed a difference between the phenomena under investigation; see Chapter 5 for a fuller discussion of statistics in corpus studies). In such cases, it is appropriate to state both a null hypothesis and an alternative hypothesis. The null hypothesis (H_0) always posits that there is no difference between the phenomena under investigation. In the case of our Dickens example, the null hypothesis would be that there is no difference between the size of Dickens's vocabulary and those of his contemporaries. The alternative hypothesis (H_a) is that there *is* a difference between the two phenomena. We could, in fact, formulate two alternative hypotheses:

H$_1$ Dickens's vocabulary is larger than those of his contemporaries.
H$_2$ Dickens's vocabulary is smaller than those of his contemporaries.

Statistical analysis can then be employed to determine whether it is possible to reject (i.e. prove wrong) the null hypothesis in favour of one of the alternative hypotheses. For example, if after analysis we find that one of Dickens's contemporaries had a larger vocabulary than him, then we can reject the null hypothesis in favour of H$_2$ (until such time as other evidence becomes available). Alternatively, if we find that there is no significant difference between the vocabulary sizes of Dickens and his fellow novelists, then we have simply failed to reject H$_0$.

Whatever the outcome of hypothesis testing, it is important to bear in mind that observing a correlation between two phenomena does not mean that one phenomenon causes the other. For example, if after experiment we are able to reject the null hypothesis in favour of H$_1$ (i.e. Dickens's vocabulary is larger than those of his contemporaries), this does not necessarily mean that vocabulary size is what causes Dickens to be so celebrated as a novelist. There may well be other variables that impact on this, which we would need to take account of.

It should be clear from the discussion above and in section 4.4 that hypothesis testing (or, in its weak form, intuition testing) is a mainstay of stylistic analysis. In the next section we explain the concept of research questions, how these should be used to direct a stylistic analysis, and the role they play in allowing us to reject hypotheses.

4.6 Objectives and research questions

The initial hypothesis stated in section 4.5 (strictly speaking, an alternative or experimental hypothesis) was that Dickens had a larger vocabulary than his contemporaries did, and that this is what makes his work so distinctive. Underpinning this hypothesis is a broader research question (what we will call an *over-arching* or *global* research question): what makes Dickens's prose distinct from that of his contemporaries? This question, however, raises a number of other questions which we would first need to answer before we are in a position to (1) either reject or fail to reject our hypothesis, and (2) posit an answer to our over-arching research question. In order to determine what these sub-questions are, we can consider the objectives (Os) we would need to achieve in order to answer our global research question, which might be as follows:

O1 Determine what makes Dickens's prose distinct from that of his contemporaries.

O2 Collect a sample of Dickens's prose.
O3 Collect a sample of the prose of Dickens's contemporaries.
O4 Count the number of words in the two samples.
O5 Determine the number of *different* words in the two samples.

What should be noticeable about these objectives is that they each have a different status within the project as a whole. O1 might be described as the project's overall intellectual objective. Os 2 and 3, on the other hand, are methodological objectives, while Os 4 and 5 are analytical objectives. In effect, to achieve these objectives, we need to answer the following research questions (*RQs*):

RQ1 What makes Dickens's prose distinct from that of his contemporaries? [Addresses O1]
RQ2 What counts as a representative sample of Dickens's prose? [Addresses O2]
RQ3 What counts as a representative sample of the prose of Dickens's contemporaries? [Addresses O3]
RQ4 How many words are in each sample? [Addresses O4]
RQ5 How many *different* words are in each sample? [Addresses O5]

It should also be clear that the answer to RQ1, our global research question, can only be posited after the other research questions have been answered. For this reason, we might refer to the other questions as *local* research questions. What should be apparent is that answering the local research questions enables us to achieve the objectives we need to meet in order to decide whether to reject or fail to reject our initial hypothesis. And whether we reject or fail to reject our hypothesis determines the answer to our global research question.

4.7 How big was Dickens's vocabulary?

The discussion in the previous two sections, concerning the size of Dickens's vocabulary relative to the vocabularies of his contemporaries, might not be particularly interesting in stylistic terms, but it is a relatively straightforward issue to investigate. We simply have to achieve the objectives described in section 4.6 in order to be able to answer the associated research questions. Since RQs 4 and 5 concern quantitative issues, we will posit both a null hypothesis and two alternative hypotheses. Recall that these are as follows:

H_0 There is no difference in the vocabulary sizes of Dickens and his contemporaries.

H_1 Dickens's vocabulary is larger than those of his contemporaries.
H_2 Dickens's vocabulary is smaller than those of his contemporaries.

RQ2 asks what counts as a representative sample of Dickens's prose. We do not have access to everything Dickens wrote in his lifetime (this would include all his personal letters, notes, shopping lists, etc.) and so whatever we examine will be just a proportion of his total output. To achieve as complete a corpus as possible, however, we used the Dickens Complete Corpus (DCC; Alsuweed 2015). As the name suggests, this is a corpus containing the entirety of Dickens's published work. Alongside Dickens's novelistic output, it also includes personal letters, poems, plays, journalism and short stories. We used everything in the DCC except the non-prose outputs. As a reference corpus, we used the HUM (Huddersfield-Utrecht-Middelburg) Corpus which aims to be a representative sample of nineteenth-century fiction.[2] So far, then, we have answered RQs 2 and 3 and achieved Os 2 and 3. The next stage is to count the words in the two corpora. However, simply counting the total number of words is not particularly informative, since (1) the two corpora are of different sizes so we are not comparing like with like, and (2) knowing the total number of words in each corpus is of less value than knowing the total number of *different* words. In effect, what we need to know about are word types rather than word tokens. A *token* is any instance of a word in a corpus. Hence, a one million word corpus contains one million tokens. A *type*, on the other hand, is a unique word. In a one million token corpus, many of those tokens will turn up more than once. There will, then, always be fewer types than tokens. To answer RQ4 (How many words are in each sample?) what we really need to know is the number of types in each corpus. The figures for the DCC and the HUM corpora are given in Table 4.1.

Of course, because the two corpora are different sizes we cannot rely on raw figures to determine which corpus has the highest number of types. What we can do instead is calculate a type-token ratio (TTR). To do this, we simply divide the number of types by the number of tokens and multiply by 100. Table 4.2 shows the results.

As can be seen in Table 4.2, the TTR is higher for the DCC corpus than it is for HUM. What this indicates is a greater degree of lexical

Table 4.1 Types and tokens in the DCC and HUM corpora

Corpus	Types	Tokens
DCC	50,119	6,144,502
HUM	83,962	13,168,635

Table 4.2 Types, tokens and type-token ratios in the DCC and HUM corpora

Corpus	Types	Tokens	TTR	STTR
DCC	50,119	6,144,502	0.82	42.99
HUM	83,962	13,168,635	0.64	43.51

variation in DCC than in HUM. However, we have to be careful of reading too much into these results since the difference between the two TTRs is not great. This is a problem that arises when calculating TTRs for large corpora and is explained by the fact that in such corpora, grammatical words (e.g. articles, prepositions, etc.) are inevitably repeated, resulting in low TTRs. For this reason, a better measure of lexical variation is a standardised type-token ratio (STTR). This can be calculated using WordSmith Tools (Scott 2016), a concordancing package for corpus analysis (see Appendix 2). The STTR is calculated by measuring the TTR for the first 1,000 words in the corpus, then the TTR for the next 1,000 words, and so on. Finally, a mean average is calculated for the TTRs, which constitutes the standardised type-token ratio. Table 4.2 also shows the STTRs for both corpora, and what is apparent from these scores is that there is even less difference between them than there is between the TTRs.

On the basis of these results, we have failed to reject the null hypothesis. In effect, our results show that there is no difference between the vocabulary sizes of Dickens and his contemporaries. This, of course, is one measure of vocabulary size. Were we to investigate this further, we may want to look at, for example, average word length, word origins, and so on, before coming to a final conclusion about whether to reject H_0. And, of course, there are myriad other factors we could consider, such as average sentence length and sentence complexity. Nonetheless, however we choose to investigate these issues, the key point is that we need to do this in an objective way.

4.8 Objectivity in stylistics

The investigation above into the size of Dickens's vocabulary demonstrates a fundamental principle of stylistics. This is the concept of aiming to be objective in analysis. That is, rather than simply asserting that Dickens's vocabulary was larger than those of his contemporaries, we tested the claim using a replicable method. In the natural sciences, the notion of trying to be objective analytically is uncontroversial. However, in some areas of the social sciences and particularly in the humanities, the concept of objectivity has been the subject of considerable debate. Stylistics in particular has been criticised for its commitment to objectivity (see, for example, Bateson 1967, 1968; Fish 1980; Mackay 1996, 1999), and so it is worth briefly clarifying what it means to be objective.

The principle objections to the stylistic enterprise have come from literary critical quarters. In some cases (e.g. Bateson 1967, 1968; Mackay 1996, 1999) they have rested on the assumption that literature as a creative artefact is inaccessible to objective study (for an explanation of why this view is mistaken, see McIntyre and Price 2018a). In others (e.g. Fish 1980), they stem from a conviction that stylistics is not the objective discipline that its practitioners claim. However, what all of these complaints have in common is that they rest on a misunderstanding of the nature of objectivity. In essence, objectivity equates to clarity. If we want to answer a research question with any confidence, then we need to be clear about the methods we intend to use to go about answering it. We need to be open about the data we are using and we need to apply our analytical methods to the data systematically. We then need to report our findings honestly. The aim behind these processes is to produce results which are falsifiable; that is, results which are open to being proved wrong. This might sound a counter-intuitive thing to want to do, since surely we want to be right! We do, of course – but the only way to achieve that in the long term is to allow other analysts to question our results. If, after being as clear as we possibly can, other linguists fail to disprove our findings, then our results stand. If, on the other hand, other linguists do manage to falsify our results, then we are wrong – and to pretend otherwise would be delusional. The only alternative to this objective approach is to make subjective assertions and to argue through force of rhetoric. The problem with this is that subjective assertions are unfalsifiable. They are not open to being proved wrong so we can never know whether a subjective assertion is accurate or not. The alternative to the objective approach, then, is no alternative at all.

Despite the problems with making subjective assertions, these are still particularly common in non-linguistically oriented literary studies. Mackay (1996) even argues in favour of a subjective approach to stylistics, missing the fact that a subjective stylistics is, by its nature, paradoxical. His reasoning, however, is based on a misunderstanding of the nature of objectivity, which leads him to accuse stylisticians of not practising objectivity at all. For example, in response to Short's claim that '[n]o analysis is objective in the sense that it is true for all time' (1996a: 358), Mackay writes:

> I read this as meaning that an analysis can be objective but not in the particular sense 'that it is true for all time'. So in what sense are we to assume that an analysis is or can be objective? How long is its shelf-life? Five years? One year? Can such an analysis be true for a fortnight? (Mackay 1999: 61)

As Short and van Peer (1999: 272) point out, Mackay's first sentence is accurate. It is indeed the case that no analysis is objective in the sense of 'true for all time'. (Short and van Peer 1999 note that it is even possible to imagine circumstances in which analytically true statements – such as 'all triangles have three sides' – might no longer hold.) Mackay's subsequent questions, however, are seriously misguided. The reason should be clear from our discussion of hypotheses in section 4.5. Recall that we cannot prove hypotheses right; we can only reject or fail to reject them. In the case of the analysis of Dickens's vocabulary size, we failed to reject the null hypothesis. However, this does not mean that we *proved* H_0. It only means that it seems reasonable to accept it until such time as further evidence comes to light that *dis*proves it (perhaps a larger, more representative reference corpus would give us different results). In this respect, Mackay's questions in the quotation above are futile. There is no need to specify a 'shelf-life' for objective analyses; the findings from an analysis can be accepted until such time as new evidence comes to light that shows them to be false.

   The other reason that Mackay (1996) opposes the objective approach is because stylisticians freely admit that achieving objectivity is impossible. Again, however, Mackay's interpretation of this point reveals a faulty understanding of their position. Mackay (1996) points out what he claims to be inconsistencies in Carter's (1982) endorsement of the objective approach. Briefly, Carter notes that we can only ever be 'relatively objective' and that there is 'no such thing as an objective criticism'; nonetheless, he is clear that stylistics is 'at least more objective' than literary critical approaches to text analysis (1982: 6, 16, 82). Mackay takes issue with these assertions as follows:

> From interpreting texts in a 'relatively objective manner', we move to the bold statement that there can be 'no such thing as an objective criticism' and then, finally, to the assurance that the 'practical stylistic approach is at least more objective' than its rivals. In the absence of 'an objective criticism', it is difficult to see how one could judge the relative objectivity of different approaches to interpreting literary texts. (Mackay 1996: 82)

What Mackay misunderstands, however, is that when Carter says there is 'no such thing as an objective criticism' (1982: 16), what he means is that no approach to criticism can be 100 per cent objective. There will always be variables that we cannot control for that might impact on our analysis (indeed, this is the reason for triangulation as a methodological tool; see Miller and Brewer 2003: 326; Baker and Egbert 2016). Crucially, though, this does not undermine the objective approach, despite Mackay's implications to the contrary. This is because it is better to aim for objectivity and fail to fully achieve it than to reject it entirely in favour of subjective assertions which can never be proved wrong. The aim for objectivity, then, is an attempt to produce falsifiable claims via replicable analytical methods, in order to avoid making subjective assertions. In the final section of this chapter, we will explore how this works in practice in an analysis of elements of the authorial style of Ernest Hemingway.

4.9 Case study: Hemingway's authorial style

Having described the basic tenets of corpus-based stylistics and the principles upon which it is founded, in this section we illustrate its practice through an analysis of a corpus of the novels of Ernest Hemingway. We begin with a brief discussion of how our hypotheses were formulated, before going on to spell out our research questions and associated analytical process. This involves a description of Wmatrix (Rayson 2009), the software we used to carry out our analysis. Finally, we discuss the value of corpus-based stylistics to the analysis of literature particularly, following Mahlberg's (2013b: 11–12) suggestion that the corpus-based approach should be integrated into what Spitzer (1948) refers to as a 'philological circle' (see the discussion in Leech and Short 2007: 12).

Ernest Hemingway is widely acknowledged to be one of the foremost prose stylists of the twentieth century, having won the 1954 Nobel Prize in Literature 'for the influence that he has exerted on contemporary style' (Nobel Foundation 2018). Nonetheless, for all their discussion of Hemingway's style, very few critics offer any concrete claims about the linguistic forms from which it is generated. All too often, any claims about Hemingway's use of language descend into the vacuous, as in Cain's assertion that: '[t]he structure of Hemingway's sentences makes the reader keenly aware of the words that he has selected and, just as much or more, the countless other possibilities that he has not selected' (2014: 80). The problem here is that this is an unfalsifiable claim. Cain offers no way of determining whether Hemingway's sentence structure does indeed make readers 'keenly aware' of the constituent words of his sentences. Nor is it clear what bearing this might have on Hemingway's style. Cain continues in this vein when he says:

> The sentence that Hemingway writes must be this way: it is as it is. Yet the sentence need not be this way: it appears stable and sounds strong but it is fragile, precarious, and vulnerable to endless revision. Each sentence is closed yet open, perfectly complete in the midst of other possibilities. (Cain 2014: 82)

Again, this is nothing more than a series of vacuous, tautological and unfalsifiable claims. In short, these assertions are of no value to the corpus stylistician since there is nothing here that can be tested; there is no way we can attempt to prove Cain wrong on these points. And if there is no way of testing whether Cain's assertions are wrong, there is no reason for us to accept that he is right. In essence, we cannot form any testable hypotheses from the claims that Cain makes. Unfortunately, this is all too often the case in literary criticism.

There does, however, appear to be something of a consensus among literary critics in their subjective assertions about Hemingway's style. Often, for example, it is characterised as 'repetitive' (Ryan 1995: 232; Balaev 2014). Meyers, for instance, asserts that: 'Hemingway's style was characterised by clarity and force. He stressed the function of the individual word, wrote five simple sentences for every complex one, used very few similes, repeated words and phrases, emphasised dialogue rather than narration' (Meyers 1985: 140). According to Meyers (1985: 74), Hemingway's authorial style was an attempt to achieve the Imagist style associated with Ezra Pound. This, perhaps, is what Cain means when he claims that Hemingway sought 'complexity through stringent simplification' (2014: 83).

Similarly, Trodd writes that '[w]ithin his form, Hemingway embedded a further commentary upon language's depleted capacity for expression. For example, his paratactic syntax – which juxtaposes clauses and like syntactic units without subordinating conjunctions – creates static, abrupt sentences that seem to stammer or bark' (2007: 8). Trodd's comments contain the same kind of tautological assertions as found in the quotations from Cain (2014), above. What does it mean, for example, to suggest that language has a 'depleted capacity for expression'? However, Trodd does at least make reference to formal features of language, which opens up at least some of his claims to testing. If, for instance, Trodd is claiming that paratactic syntax is a distinctive feature of Hemingway's style, and that subordinating conjunctions are noticeable by their absence, then we might hypothesise that subordinating conjunctions are significantly under-represented in Hemingway's writing.

While the mainstream literary establishment often seems loath to make falsifiable claims about Hemingway's style, non-academic discussions of the author's work often go to the opposite extreme, making falsifiable assertions but offering no evidence to support them. For instance, the Wikipedia site for Ernest Hemingway claims that Hemingway's syntax 'lacks subordinating conjunctions',[3] while the website Literary Devices goes even further, stating that: 'Ernest Hemingway was famous for his short, declarative sentences. He rarely even used adjectives and almost never used adverbs.'[4]

What we can observe in the literary critical commentary on Hemingway is a tension between unfalsifiable subjective assertions and unevidenced objective claims. Despite its shortcomings, then, we might use such literary critical commentary as a point of departure for formulating some research questions and testable hypotheses. We can express these as follows:

Global research question

RQ1 Are literary critical claims about Hemingway's style accurate?

Answer is dependent on answers to local RQs.

Local research questions

RQ2 Are Hemingway's sentences shorter than those of other writers?

Answer is dependent on rejecting or failing to reject the following hypotheses:

- H_0 There is no difference in sentence length between the work of Hemingway and that of other writers.
- H_1 Hemingway uses shorter sentences than other writers.
- H_2 Hemingway uses longer sentences than other writers.

RQ3 Does Hemingway repeat words more than other writers do?

Answer is dependent on rejecting or failing to reject the following hypotheses:

- H_0 There is no difference in STTR between the work of Hemingway and that of other writers.

H_1 Hemingway has a lower STTR than other writers.
H_2 Hemingway has a higher STTR than other writers.

RQ4 Does Hemingway use adjectives less frequently than other writers?

Answer is dependent on rejecting or failing to reject the following hypotheses:

H_0 There is no difference in frequency of adjectives between the work of Hemingway and that of other writers.
H_1 Hemingway uses fewer adjectives than other writers.
H_2 Hemingway uses more adjectives than other writers.

RQ5 Does Hemingway use adverbs less frequently than other writers?

Answer is dependent on rejecting or failing to reject the following hypotheses:

H_0 There is no difference in frequency of adverbs between the work of Hemingway and that of other writers.
H_1 Hemingway uses fewer adverbs than other writers.
H_2 Hemingway uses more adverbs than other writers.

RQ6 Does Hemingway use fewer complex sentences than other writers?

Answer is dependent on rejecting or failing to reject the following hypotheses:

H_0 There is no difference in frequency of subordinating conjunctions between the work of Hemingway and that of other writers.
H_1 Hemingway uses fewer subordinating conjunctions than other writers.
H_2 Hemingway uses more subordinating conjunctions than other writers.

Having outlined our research questions, we can now consider what data we need to examine in order to answer them, and what analytical methods to use. Note that we use the term *methods* as opposed to *methodology*. In stylistics, and in other areas of the humanities and social sciences, these terms are often used interchangeably. This, however, is a mistake as there are important differences between them.

A methodology consists of the theoretical ideas, principles and values that underpin a particular set of methods. As Kaplan puts it, methodology refers to 'the study – the description, the explanation, and the justification – of methods, and not the methods themselves' (1964: 18; see Stuart 2017 for a full discussion of the difference between the two terms). For our purposes, corpus linguistics constitutes a methodology which underpins and informs the use of a number of analytical methods, including, among others, frequency profiling, collocation and keyness.

RQs 2 to 6 require, in Adolph's (2006) terms, inter-textual analysis. That is, to answer them, we need to compare a sample of Hemingway's writing with a sample of the work of other writers. The first consideration, then, is what counts as a representative sample of Hemingway's writing, and what constitutes a suitable reference corpus for comparison.

We decided that our sample of Hemingway's work would be made up of his novelistic output, including novels and novellas. The only one of Hemingway's novels not included in our corpus is *The Torrents of Spring* (1926), as we were unable to obtain an electronic copy of the text. This is a pragmatic issue in the compilation of corpora that researchers often have to face, as Hunston (2002: 27) notes. The eight books that comprise our Hemingway corpus are therefore as follows:

- *The Sun Also Rises* (1926)
- *A Farewell to Arms* (1929)
- *To Have and Have Not* (1937)
- *For Whom the Bell Tolls* (1940)
- *Across the River and into the Trees* (1950)
- *The Old Man and the Sea* (1952)
- *Islands in the Stream* (1970)
- *The Garden of Eden* (1986).

In total, the Hemingway corpus consists of 783,551 words. The reference corpus we chose was formed from two existing corpora: the LOB Corpus of 1960s written British English and the BLOB Corpus of 1930s written British English (see Appendix 1 for more details of these corpora). Together, these comprise approximately two million words. We chose to combine these two corpora on the grounds that Hemingway's novel-writing career spanned the mid-1920s to the mid-1980s. Two million words of 1930s and 1960s English therefore seems an appropriate set of data against which to compare his work. Ideally, it would have been useful to compare Hemingway's work against a corpus of fiction, though for copyright reasons these are hard to come by. Wmatrix (the software used to answer some of our research questions) is pre-loaded with the BNC Written Imaginative sampler of fiction, but this is only 222,541 words in size. We therefore decided against using this on the grounds that it is smaller than our Hemingway corpus, and generally speaking reference corpora ought to be larger than target corpora (Baker 2004). In order to answer our research questions, we needed to use two pieces of software – WordSmith Tools and Wmatrix (see Appendix 2) – and a number of different methods. We describe these as we discuss the results of our analysis, below.

RQ2 Are Hemingway's sentences shorter than those of other writers?
To answer this question we used WordSmith Tools (Scott 2016). WordSmith's WordList function provides a variety of descriptive statistics about uploaded files; we used it to compare Hemingway's sentence length against sentence length in BLOB-FLOB (see Box 4.1). The results are given in Table 4.3.

What these results indicate is that Hemingway's average sentence length is indeed lower than that of other writers. Consequently, we can reject the null hypothesis in favour of H_1. This result would appear to confirm the subjective intuitions of mainstream literary criticism concerning Hemingway's sentence lengths.

RQ3 Does Hemingway repeat words more than other writers do?
To answer this question, we again used the WordList function in WordSmith, specifically the STTR calculation it provides. The results are given in Table 4.4.

Here again the result would seem to confirm the literary critics' intuitions that Hemingway repeats words more than other writers do. This is reflected in his lower STTR. We can therefore reject the null hypothesis in favour of H_1. We should be mindful, however, of the fact that STTR is just one measure of vocabulary richness, as we noted in our discussion of vocabulary size in Dickens (indeed, there are other tests of vocabulary richness that we can carry out, as we demonstrate in Chapter 5).

Table 4.3 Mean sentence lengths in Hemingway and BLOB-LOB

	Hemingway	BLOB-LOB
Mean sentence length	10.65	18.81

Table 4.4 Standardised type-token ratios in Hemingway and BLOB-LOB

	Hemingway	BLOB-LOB
STTR	35.84	39.75

Box 4.1 Using the WordList function in WordSmith Tools (Version 7)

WordSmith Tools is a licence-only software package (see Appendix 2 for details of how to obtain a copy). We used it to generate statistics for the Hemingway corpus. For copyright reasons, we cannot make the Hemingway corpus publicly available. However, the steps below explain how to generate a wordlist, which is the first step in extracting descriptive statistics about a corpus.

1. Open WordSmith Tools and click on **WordList**.

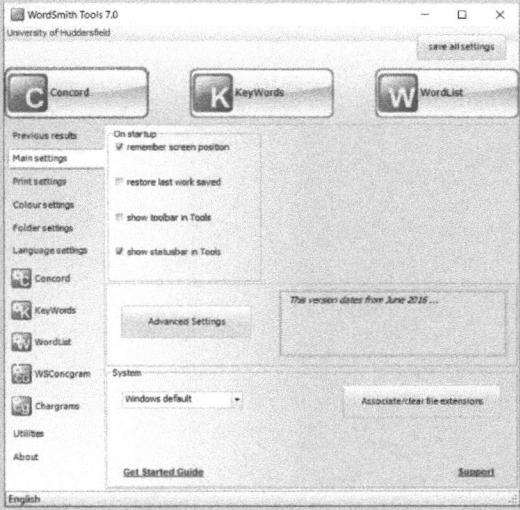

2. The WordList tool will now open up. Click on **File** and **New**. You will see the following dialogue box:

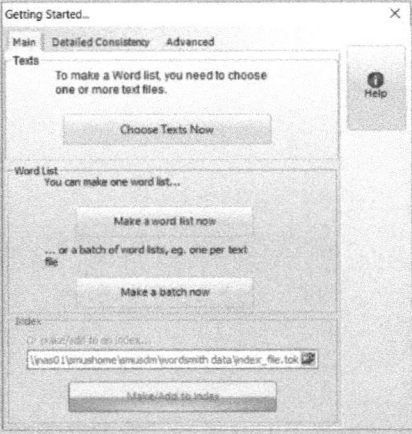

3. Click on **Choose Texts Now** and you will see the following screen:

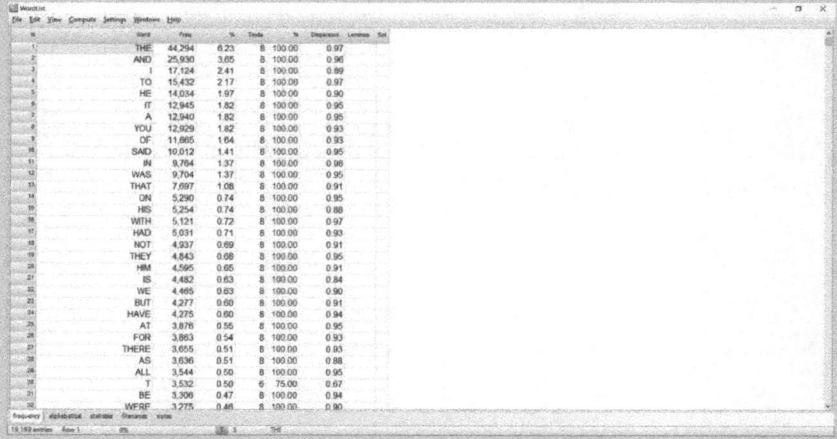

4. Use the drop-down menu in the top left of the window to locate your corpus files. Then drag and drop them from the left-hand pane to the right-hand pane and click **OK**.

5. Click **Make a wordlist** now and you will see the following screen:

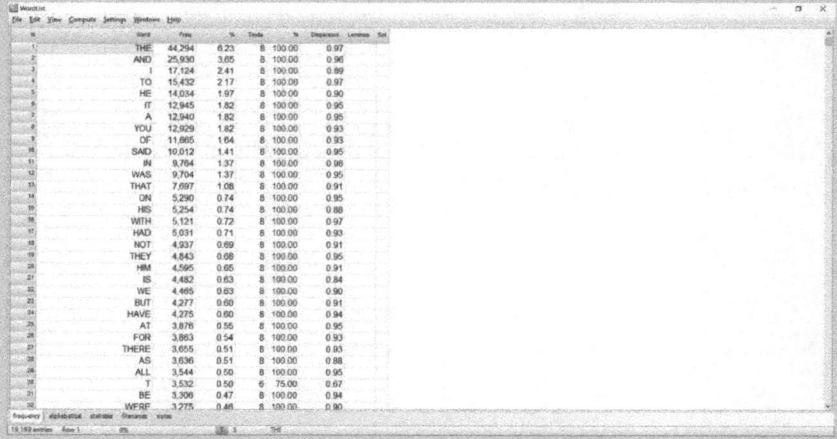

6. Click on the **Statistics** tab at the bottom of the screen to view descriptive statistics for the file(s), including word count, average sentence length and (S)TTR.

RQ4 Does Hemingway use adjectives less frequently than other writers?

Since this question asks about a particular part-of-speech, it was necessary to examine POS-tagged versions of both our target and reference corpora. To do this, we used Wmatrix (Rayson 2009). Wmatrix is a web-based corpus analysis tool that includes a built in POS tagger known as CLAWS (Constituent Likelihood Automatic Word-tagging System; see Garside 1987). Once a text or corpus has been uploaded to Wmatrix, CLAWS applies POS tags to each constituent word before a second tagger, the USAS semantic tagger (described in detail in Chapter 9), applies tags to mark what semantic category each word belongs to.

In order to answer the question of whether Hemingway uses adjectives less frequently than they are used in BLOB-FLOB, one option was to calculate a normalised frequency for this POS; that is, to determine how many adjectives there are per million words. However, a better measure is a keyness analysis. We noted in the introduction to this chapter that keywords are words that turn up in one corpus more (or, indeed, less) than they do in a reference corpus. Keyness analysis can also be applied to parts-of-speech, where it works on the same principle. Calculating keyness requires a statistical test to determine the significance of the difference between frequency in the target corpus and frequency in the reference corpus. One test that Wmatrix uses is known as log-likelihood. We discuss keyness in full in Chapter 5. For now, we can simply note that a log-likelihood score that exceeds 15.13 is significant in statistical terms (we also explain the reason for this seemingly arbitrary value in Chapter 5). What this means is that if an item has a log-likelihood score higher than this, we can be confident that it is either significantly more prevalent or significantly less prevalent in our target corpus than we would expect it to be, based on its frequency in the reference corpus. More specifically, its frequency is higher (or, in the case of negatively key items, lower) than we would expect it to be based on chance alone.

Since RQ4 asks whether Hemingway used adjectives *less* than other writers, we used Wmatrix to see whether adjectives are negatively key in the Hemingway corpus; that is, to see whether they turn up less frequently than we would expect them to do based on their frequency in BLOB-LOB. (See Box 4.2 for details of how to upload a text to Wmatrix and carry out a key POS analysis.) The results are shown in Table 4.5 and Column O1 shows the frequency of the item in the target corpus (i.e. the Hemingway corpus), while column O2 shows its frequency in the reference corpus (i.e. BLOB-LOB). Columns %1

Table 4.5 Negative key adjectives in Hemingway compared with BLOB-LOB

POS tag	O1	%1	O2	%2	LL
JJ (general adjective)	31,464	4.89	125,377	6.62	2,426.13
JJR (general comparative adjective, e.g. *older*, *better*, *stronger*)	872	0.14	3,859	0.20	127.69
JK (catenative adjective, e.g. *able* in *be able to*, *willing* in *be willing to*)	98	0.02	548	0.03	39.37
JJT (general superlative adjective, e.g. *oldest*, *best*, *strongest*)	499	0.08	1,971	0.10	36.13

and %2 shows what percentage of the target and reference corpora are made up of the item in question. The LL column gives the log-likelihood score. What we can see from the results in Table 4.5 is adjectives of all kind are under-represented in Hemingway's work, compared with their frequency in the reference corpus. We can, as a consequence of this, reject H_0 in favour of H_1.

Box 4.2 Uploading a text to Wmatrix and generating a key part-of-speech list

Wmatrix is accessible with a licence at <http://ucrel.lancs.ac.uk/wmatrix3.html>. Wmatrix can only deal with single .txt files so if your corpus consists of multiple files, these will need to be merged into one. This is a simple process that can be done using the command prompt in both Windows and Mac operating systems. A relevant Google search will generate explanations of how to do this.

1. First, upload your target corpus. To do this, click **Tag Wizard**.
2. Type your chosen filename in the **Enter new folder name** box. Use the **Browse** function to locate your file.
3. Click **Upload now**. Your file will now be tagged for POS and semantic tags. Repeat stages 1 to 3 for your reference corpus.
4. Once tagged, your file is accessible via the **My folders** option. Clicking on the relevant folder will take you to Wmatrix's analysis options. To generate a key part-of-speech list, go to **Key POS compared to:** in the **Keyness analysis** column and select your reference corpus from the drop-down menu. Now click **Go**.

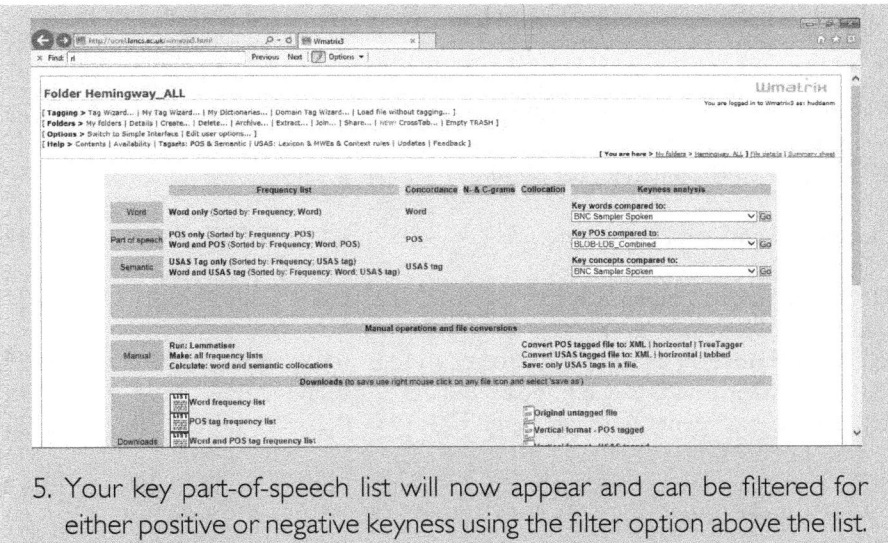

5. Your key part-of-speech list will now appear and can be filtered for either positive or negative keyness using the filter option above the list.

RQ5 Does Hemingway use adverbs less frequently than other writers?
To answer this question, we used the same key part-of-speech analysis as for RQ4, this time comparing adverb usage. The results are shown in Table 4.6.

Table 4.6 Negative key adverbs in Hemingway compared with BLOB-LOB

POS tag	O1	%1	O2	%2	LL
RGR (comparative degree adverb, e.g. *more, less*)	165	0.03	1,987	0.10	449.58
RGT (superlative degree adverb, e.g. *most, least*)	80	0.01	1,179	0.06	312.80
REX21 (two-part adverb introducing appositional constructions, e.g. *for instance*)	13	0.00	402	0.02	154.95
REX (adverb introducing appositional constructions, e.g. *namely*)	4	0.00	212	0.01	95.02
RR31 (three-part general adverb, e.g. *and so on*)	29	0.00	373	0.02	89.23
RA (adverb, after nominal head, e.g. *else, galore*)	51	0.01	464	0.02	78.53
RGQV (wh-ever general adverb, e.g. *wherever, whenever*)	2	0.00	67	0.00	26.54
RG21 (two-part general adverb, e.g. *up to, ever so*)	8	0.00	107	0.01	26.41
RR41 (four-part general adverb, e.g. *all of a sudden*)	9	0.00	99	0.01	20.60
RRT (superlative general adverb, e.g. *best, longest*)	56	0.01	293	0.02	17.56

Table 4.7 Positive key adverbs in Hemingway compared with BLOB-LOB

POS tag	O1	%1	O2	%2	LL
RT (quasi-nominal adverb of time, e.g. *now, tomorrow*)	6,715	1.04	8,255	0.44	2,668.75
RP (prep. adverb, particle, e.g *about, in*)	3,797	0.59	3,571	0.19	2,305.86
RL (locative adverb, e.g. *alongside, forward*)	4,037	0.63	5,557	0.29	1,274.34
RRQ (wh- general adverb, e.g. *where, when, why, how*)	2,922	0.45	3,962	0.21	953.32
RG (degree adverb, e.g. *very, so, too*)	4,421	0.69	8,942	0.47	400.05
RGQ (wh- degree adverb, e.g. *how*)	379	0.06	451	0.02	159.89
RR21 (two-part general adverb, e.g. *of* in *of course*)	1,595	0.25	3,857	0.20	42.92
RL22 (two-part locative adverb, e.g. *here* in *over here*)	18	0.00	7	0.00	23.87
RL21 (two-part locative adverb, e.g. *on* in *on board*)	44	0.01	50	0.00	20.11
RT31 (three-part quasi-nominal adverb of time, e.g. *from now on*)	13	0.00	4	0.00	19.49

What Table 4.6 shows is that a large number of adverb types are indeed under-used in Hemingway's work. However, in this case, this does not provide us with the requisite information to reject H_0 in favour of H_1. This is because although we find many adverbs *under*-represented in Hemingway, we also find other types to be *over*-represented. These are shown in Table 4.7.

Table 4.7 demonstrates the paucity of intuition regarding the question of adverb usage in Hemingway. Concerning this question, we cannot reject any of our hypotheses. Instead, the data necessitates us taking a more nuanced look at adverb usage in the corpus.

RQ6 Does Hemingway use fewer complex sentences than other writers?

Since the definition of a complex sentence rests on it containing a dependent clause, to answer this question we once again used Wmatrix's key POS function, this time to search for subordinating conjunctions in both our target and reference corpora. The results are shown in Table 4.8.

The results in Table 4.8 show that coordinating conjunctions are over-represented in the Hemingway corpus. Given H_1 (Hemingway uses fewer subordinating conjunctions than other writers), this result may seem understandable. If subordinating conjunctions are under-used,

Table 4.8 Keyness of coordinating and subordinating conjunctions in Hemingway and BLOB-LOB

POS tag	O1	%1	O2	%2	LL
CC (coordinating conjunction, e.g. *and*, or)	26,069	4.05	57,584	3.04	1,435.46
CCB (adversative coordinating conjunction, e.g. *but*)	3,975	0.62	8,555	0.45	257.35
CS (subordinating conjunction, e.g. *if*, *because*, *unless*, *so*, *for*)	6,485	1.01	15,621	0.82	181.16

then perhaps as a consequence coordinating conjunctions are being overused. However, what Table 4.8 also shows is that not only does Hemingway use subordinating conjunctions, they are over-represented in his work. We can therefore reject the null hypothesis in favour of H$_2$.

4.10 Conclusion

In this chapter we have explored particularly the practice of determining clear research questions. We have also discussed the importance of intuition in corpus stylistics and its value as part of the hypothesis formation process. In particular, we showed how hypothesis testing can work as a method for identifying the linguistic source of impressions about a text, thereby systematising the notion of an analysis being used to support or invalidate readers' interpretations. What the analyses in the previous section demonstrate is that by taking a methodical approach to the testing of falsifiable hypotheses, we are able to test the assertions of literary critics concerning Hemingway's authorial style. In some cases (RQs 2, 3 and 4), our evidence supports literary critical claims. In others (RQs 5 and 6), it doesn't. Ultimately, then, our answer to RQ1 (Are literary critical claims about Hemingway's style accurate?) must be 'yes and no'. And here is where Spitzer's (1948) notion of the philological circle comes to the fore. Spitzer (1948) argues that understanding literary meaning involves a constant movement between linguistic description and literary appreciation (see Leech and Short 2007: 1–4 for a summary of his position). It is not enough simply to prove literary critical positions wrong, as we have done here. We need to use such analyses as starting points for further investigation. One of our findings, for instance, was that, counter to literary critical expectations, Hemingway does use subordinating conjunctions; in fact, he overuses them compared with their frequency in our reference corpus. An interesting question at this point, then, is: why do literary critics perceive that subordination is lacking in Hemingway's work? The potential explanations for this can be used to generate further hypotheses to be tested. Is it the case, perhaps, that the overuse of coordinating conjunctions has the effect of backgrounding the subordinating conjunctions, causing them not to be perceived as salient, despite the fact that they are used just as much? Or could it be the case that subordinating conjunctions are only used in particular parts of Hemingway's novels: direct speech, perhaps, or stretches of first-person narration? In many cases, the answers to our research questions send us back to the corpus and its constituent texts to investigate particular issues further.

Given the value of corpus approaches in answering such questions, Mahlberg (2013b: 12) suggests an adaptation of Spitzer's (1948) philological circle, adding 'corpus linguistic description' between 'literary appreciation' and 'linguistic description'. Clearly, corpus methods have much to add to the stylistic analysis of literary (and non-literary) texts, though we see corpus linguistic description as simply a sub-type of linguistic description, and for preference would not view this as an additional stage in the philological circle. Nonetheless, the point is clear: corpus-based stylistics has much to offer to both the stylistician and the literary critic. In the next chapter, we discuss a key element of corpus-based stylistics: statistics.

Notes

1. This famous example comes from Halliday (1966). It may be the case that lexical constraints vary according to dialect, of course.
2. Other alternatives are available for such a study. For example, a corpus of Dickens's novels and reference corpora of nineteenth-century fiction are publicly accessible via the CLiC (Corpus Linguistics in Context) project website (Mahlberg et al. 2016). CLiC offers a web interface for studying a wide variety of corpora of nineteenth-century fiction, particularly that of Dickens.
3. See <http://bit.ly/2CG18Ae> (last accessed 20 August 2018).
4. See <http://www.literarydevices.com/syntax/> (last accessed 20 August 2018).

5

Making sense of significance

5.1 Introduction

In the previous chapter, in order to answer research questions about elements of Ernest Hemingway's authorial style, we drew on statistical information derived from our Hemingway corpus. Some of this information was fairly straightforward. For instance, we considered Hemingway's mean sentence length compared with that of the BLOB-LOB reference corpus, and we examined vocabulary size by looking at types and tokens in our target and reference corpora and comparing (standardised) type-token ratios. In effect, to answer the research questions relating to sentence length and vocabulary size, we drew on *descriptive statistics*. Descriptive statistics are so called because they describe a dataset. That is, they provide information about the basic characteristics of our sample, enabling us to begin to see patterns in our data. Determining such patterns might involve frequency profiling (establishing the most and least frequent parts-of-speech in a corpus, say) and calculating the mean, median and mode of a set of values. Mean, median and mode are all measures of what is known as central tendency (i.e. the average). The mean of a set of figures is calculated by adding all the values together and then dividing by the total number of figures; for example, we could calculate mean word length in a novel by counting the total number of characters in the book and dividing by the total number of words. However, the mean can sometimes give a skewed representation of the data. For instance, a small number of particularly long words might result in a high mean and give us a false impression of average word length. For this reason, we might also want to calculate the median word length. To do this, we would take all the words in the novel and arrange them in ascending order of length. The middle value is the median. Finally, the mode refers to the most frequent value in a dataset. In the case of the word length example, the mode would be the word length that is most frequent; for example, if most of the words in the novel are 5 letters long, then 5 constitutes the mode.

Insights from central tendency can also be supported by measuring the dispersion of values. This can be done by calculating range, standard deviation and variance. Range refers to the difference between the maximum and minimum values in a dataset. In the case of the word length example, if the longest word is composed of 20 letters and the shortest is composed of 2, then the range is 18. Standard deviation is another measure of dispersion and indicates the average distance of a particular value from the mean average. Variance is a related measure (for an explanation of how standard deviation and variance are calculated, see van Peer et al. 2012; we cover standard deviation in more detail in Chapter 8). Each of these measures gives an indication of the extent to which the values in a dataset cluster around the mean average.

Frequency profiles and measures of central tendency will only get us so far, however. To answer some of our other research questions about Hemingway's style, we needed to consider statistical information derived from more complex calculations. This involved using *inferential statistics*. For instance, we examined the keyness of particular parts-of-speech in Hemingway's writing; that is, we looked at those parts-of-speech which, as a result of a statistical test, we could be confident were either more frequent or less frequent in the Hemingway corpus than they were in the reference corpus. Calculating keyness necessitates testing for statistical significance. In essence, a significance test in a keyness analysis tells us how confident we can be that the results we observe in our data sample would also be observable in the population that our sample represents. The test does this by estimating the probability that the observed relationship between the two variables (i.e. linguistic item and corpus) is down to chance alone. This probability is expressed as a *p*-value (*p* stands for probability). For example, $p < 0.05$ indicates that there is a less than 5 per cent probability that our result is due to chance alone. Or, to put it another way, we can be 95 per cent confident that our result is indeed a significant one (though it is important to note that significance does not necessarily equate to meaningfulness; we discuss what this means in more detail later on in this chapter).

Significance tests are used to help us decide whether to reject a null hypothesis. In practice, we decide on an acceptable significance level (known as an alpha level) before we carry out the significance test. For example, we might decide we are willing to accept a 5 per cent probability of our observed result being due to chance alone. Our alpha level, therefore, would be 0.05. In such a case, any result with a p-value of less than 0.05 would be considered significant. In essence, the closer a p-value is to zero, the more confident we can be that we are seeing a significant result. And if a p-value is significant (i.e. if it is less than or equal to our predetermined alpha level), then we can reject the null hypothesis with the associated level of confidence that the p-value gives us. This, then, is inferential statistics, the purpose of which is to allow us to generalise about a population based on an analysis of a sample.

Significance testing is an important part of corpus linguistic (and, by extension, corpus stylistic) analysis. As well as underpinning keyness analysis, it is also essential for calculating collocational strength, as in the kind of analysis we described in the case study in Chapter 2. Most corpus linguistic software will perform particular statistical tests for you, so in this respect it is possible to carry out such tests without understanding the mathematics that underpins them. The danger associated with doing this is that it is easy to misinterpret the results of such tests. Moreover, the use of p-values alone has been the subject of intense debate and criticism within the social sciences generally (see, for example, Cohen 1994) and so it is always prudent to seek advice from a statistician when carrying out research that necessitates statistical analysis. We discuss p-values here because many off-the-shelf corpus software packages (e.g. Wmatrix, AntConc and WordSmith Tools) make use of them in the statistical tests they employ. Additionally, it is also important at least to understand the principles behind particular statistical tests in order to make sense of the results they generate, as well as to design projects effectively. To this end, Butler (1985) is an accessible introduction to statistics for linguistics generally, while Oakes (1998) discusses statistics in relation to corpus linguistics particularly, and van Peer et al. (2012) offer an introduction to the use of empirical research methods in the humanities more broadly.

Our aim in this chapter is to discuss some of the most common statistical tests used by corpus linguists, particularly the tests available in popular corpus linguistic software packages. We begin by returning to the issue of vocabulary size that we discussed in the previous chapter. Specifically, we explain how the vocabulary size of an author can be assessed more reliably than by the simple measurement of type-token ratios. To do this we use what is known as a t-test.

Assessing the relative size of vocabulary involves comparing one corpus against another. The comparison of corpora is also at the heart of the concept of keyness, introduced in the previous chapter. In this chapter we explore this concept in more detail and explain log-likelihood, a common statistical test for calculating keyness. Having done this, we then move on to a consideration of the statistics that underpin collocation analysis.

Our principle concern throughout this chapter is examining how we can incorporate the corpus linguistic methods that make use of such statistical tests into stylistic analysis. To this end, the case study at the end of this chapter uses the concept of keyness to address a major issue in stylistics: how to select text samples for qualitative analysis. We show how the concepts of keyness and collocation can be integrated into qualitative stylistic analysis, as well as discuss the difference between statistical and interpretative significance.

5.2 Vocabulary size

In Chapter 4 we compared Charles Dickens's prose writing against a general corpus of nineteenth-century fiction in order to determine whether or not his vocabulary was bigger than those of other nineteenth-century novelists. In so doing, we calculated a (standardised) type-token ratio ((S)TTR) for each corpus. We then compared these two ratios. However, the decision about the extent to which the STTRs differed from one another was still a subjective one. One way to improve on this decision-making method is to determine whether there is a statistically significant difference between the types present in each corpus.[1] The STTRs for Dickens (DCC; Dickens Complete Corpus) and the HUM (Huddersfield-Utrecht-Middelburg) Corpus of nineteenth-century fiction are detailed in Table 5.1.

The hypotheses that we want to test are:

H_0 There is no difference between the two corpora in terms of vocabulary size.
H_1 There is a difference between the two corpora in terms of vocabulary size.

Table 5.1 Overall types, tokens and type-token ratios in the Dickens and HUM corpora

Corpus	Types	Tokens	TTR	STTR
DCC	50,119	6,144,502	0.82	42.99
HUM	83,962	13,168,635	0.64	43

In relation to H_1, we can also add two specific research questions:

RQ1 Can we be sure that the difference between the STTRs is not by chance and therefore confidently reject the null hypothesis?

RQ2 If there is a difference, is it a big difference?

The first question concerns the reliability of our result, and we can answer it using an inferential statistic called a t-test. Specifically, we use Welch's t-test (Welch 1947), which is a variation on Student's t-test.[2] We use Welch's t-test here because it does not assume that variances in the datasets we are comparing are equal; we will explain what we mean by variance below.[3] The second question concerns what is known as effect size. This refers to the scale of our result. There are a number of possible tests that measure effect size. We demonstrate one of these in particular.

The t-test determines whether there is a significant difference between the means of two sets of figures. A significant difference is one which is not likely to be the result of chance alone (we explore the notion of statistical significance in more detail in section 5.3). The output from a t-test is a figure called the t-score, t-value or, in Microsoft Excel, t-stat. The larger the score, the larger the difference is between the datasets. In the case of our type-token calculations, the t-score determines whether there is a significant difference between the average STTR across the Dickens Corpus and the average STTR across HUM.

In order to carry out the t-test, we need more information than is set out in Table 5.1. In addition to the STTRs for each corpus as a whole, we need to know the STTRs for each novel in each corpus (DCC and HUM). Since both our corpora are made up of individual files, each consisting of one book, we can use WordSmith Tools (introduced in Chapter 4) to generate STTRs for each file. These figures are summarised in Table 5.2. There are 24 STTRs for DCC (one for each file/book) and 99 for HUM.

When assessing the differences in means between two datasets, the t-test calculation takes into account variation in scores across each dataset. Variation (statisticians use the term 'variance') relates to how much the values in a dataset fluctuate (in this case our datasets are DCC and HUM). More precisely, it relates to how spread out the values are. That is, while there might be lots of different values, these may be very close together (e.g. 43, 41, 40, 44, 45, 39, …) or, indeed, they may not (e.g. 43, 51, 19, 88, 44, 102, …). If we were to plot these two sets of made-up figures on a graph, the first set of figures would form a cluster of points, while the second set would be spread out

Table 5.2 Standardised type-token ratios for each novel in the Dickens and HUM corpora

Group 1: DCC	Group 2: HUM
45.31, 44.00, 44.14, 44.08, 44.04, 44.67, 46.72, 41.99, 43.20, 41.92, 41.17, 42.67, 40.96, 41.36, 41.62, 41.85, 41.64, 39.89, 45.44, 41.24, 43.28, 44.23, 43.51, 44.44	42.35, 49.45, 47.36, 42.39, 43.81, 42.59, 43.23, 44.59, 45.91, 45.05, 46.23, 49.05, 41.60, 45.01, 45.74, 45.75, 43.71, 45.75, 42.37, 43.79, 40.14, 41.22, 46.54, 43.09, 44.77, 48.31, 45.65, 40.93, 45.94, 46.06, 43.58, 50.68, 46.49, 39.66, 41.16, 39.25, 44.11, 40.28, 42.44, 43.32, 46.13, 44.11, 43.27, 43.34, 48.27, 43.41, 46.60, 43.15, 41.40, 44.69, 40.28, 42.71, 44.60, 42.10, 41.93, 44.75, 46.03, 41.29, 40.55, 41.68, 43.37, 45.29, 41.40, 35.84, 39.39, 44.63, 40.31, 42.71, 46.83, 39.93, 42.15, 43.48, 46.17, 44.89, 37.94, 43.89, 37.07, 44.57, 41.44, 44.73, 40.01, 42.35, 43.60, 43.51, 43.64, 43.47, 38.36, 45.54, 43.21, 43.77, 41.48, 46.42, 42.88, 45.77, 41.78, 43.97, 42.96, 39.98, 42.64

across the chart. Judging the difference in means relative to the spread of values across the dataset enables us to take a more complete view of the results.

If we look at the figures in Table 5.2, they all appear to be fairly close to each other, that is, there does not appear to be much spread. However, this assessment is somewhat subjective. A more precise way to measure variance is to obtain the mean value of the data and then see how much each value in the dataset differs from that mean. The mean of those differences is known as the standard deviation. In essence, standard deviation tells us how much variation there is in the dataset (we explain standard deviation in more detail in Chapter 8, where we use it to assess changes in the frequency of modal auxiliary verbs across the Early Modern English period). The t-stat calculation comprises a form of this statistic to make an estimation of the variance in the datasets that are being compared. This is why we need the STTRs for each of the novels in DCC and HUM. From these we can calculate the average STTR for each dataset, and work out how much variation there is between the STTRs based on that average. The t-score, then, can be summarised as follows:

$$t\text{-}score = \frac{difference\ between\ two\ means\ (mean\ 1 - mean\ 2)}{The\ variation\ in\ the\ two\ datasets\ pooled}$$

Because corpus tools tend not to include a t-test function that allows for this sort of comparison between means (although, as we will see later, it is available in some corpus tools for calculating collocates), here we will explain how to use Microsoft Excel to perform a t-test calculation, using the figures provided by WordSmith Tools (shown in Table 5.2).[4] Other statistics packages such as SPSS can also be used for t-tests, and there are a number of online calculators available.[5] To carry out a t-test using Excel, follow the steps in Box 5.1.

Box 5.1 Using Excel to carry out Welch's t-test

1. Copy the STTR output from WordSmith Tools into an Excel spreadsheet. Arrange the data into two columns in a single worksheet. The screenshot shows that we put DCC in column A and HUM in column B and included a data label in the first cell of each column (A1 and B1, respectively).

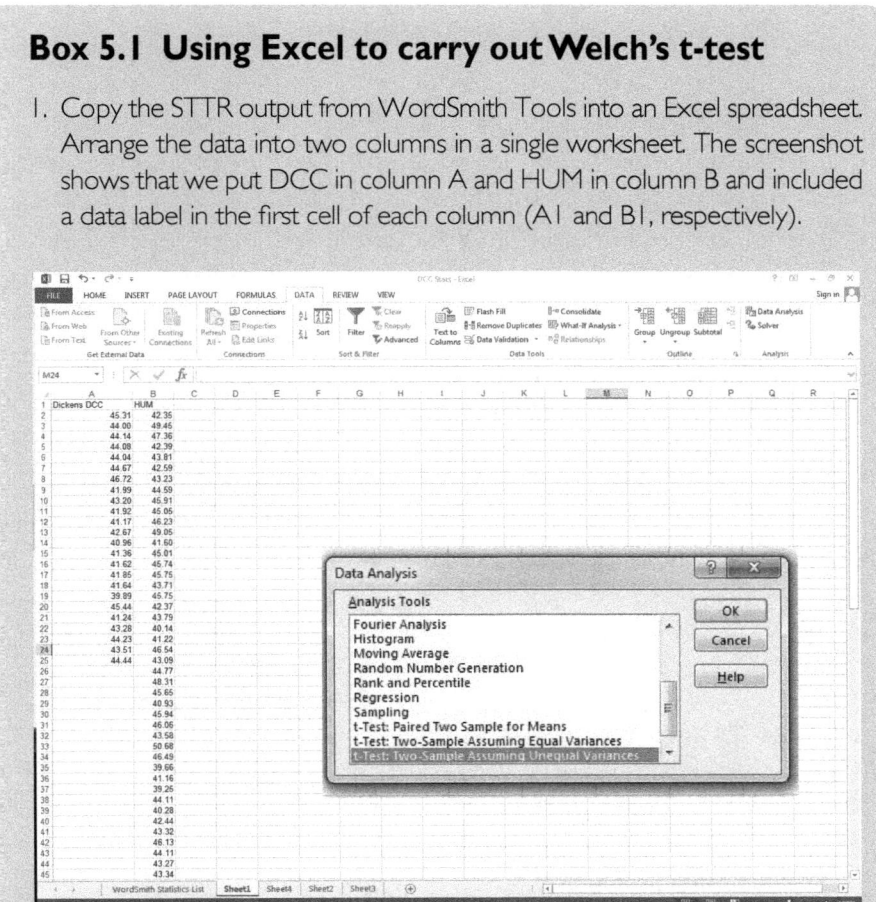

2. Click the DATA tab at the top of the sheet, and then click on **Data Analysis**. A pop-up menu will open which contains numerous tools for analysis. Select **t-Test: Two-Sample Assuming Unequal Variances**. This is an alternative name for Welch's t-test. Click **OK**, and a dialogue box will open.

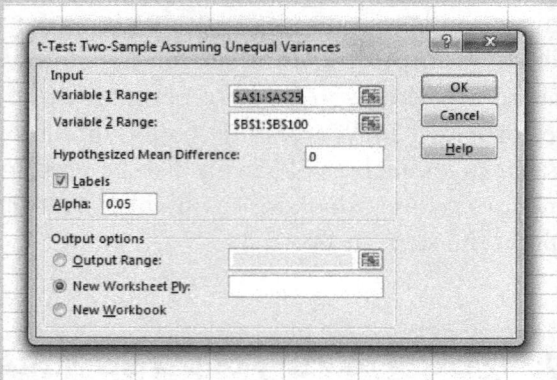

3. In the **Variable 1 Range** and **Variable 2 Range** fields, specify the range of cells that contain the data. You can do this by clicking on the first cell of a data column and then, whilst holding down the shift key, clicking on the last cell containing data in the same column. The range of cells containing the data will then appear in the dialogue box. We included the cells that contained the dataset labels *Dickens DCC* and *HUM* (i.e. cells A1 and B1), as this makes reading the output easier.

4. Specify a **Hypothesized Mean Difference** of zero. This is our null hypothesis, that is, the hypothesis that there is no difference between the two datasets.

5. Tick the **Labels** box if you included data labels in your data range (see point 3), so that Excel knows to exclude these from the calculations and only use them to label the results.

6. The **Alpha** box is used to specify what percentage of probability you are prepared to accept that the results are a chance happening (referred to by statisticians as the alpha level). The default is 0.05, which means that there is a 5 per cent probability that the results are a chance happening, and consequently a 95 per cent probability that they are not. The smaller the number in the box, the more confident we can be that the result is not a consequence of chance (e.g. 0.01 means 99 per cent confidence that the results are telling us about a real difference between the two datasets). We left the value at the 0.05 default.

7. Tick **New Worksheet Ply** so that the t-test results will appear in a new worksheet within the same workbook (you can specify a name for the worksheet in the field to the right of the toggle switch in the dialogue box).

8. Click **OK**.

	A	B	C	D
1	t-Test: Two-Sample Assuming Unequal Variances			
2				
3		Dickens DCC	HUM	
4	Mean	43.05666176	43.4444473	
5	Variance	2.89805462	6.983331671	
6	Observations	24	99	
7	Hypothesized Mean Difference	0		
8	df	53		
9	t Stat	-0.886633947		
10	P(T<=t) one-tail	0.18964081		
11	t Critical one-tail	3.251267953		
12	P(T<=t) two-tail	0.37928162		
13	t Critical two-tail	3.483777273		
14				
15				
16				

Figure 5.1 Results of the t-test of STTRs in DCC and HUM

We can see the results of the t-test calculation in Figure 5.1. This is the t-stat, which is −0.886633947. It does not matter that it is negative; that just means that the DCC average is less than the HUM average, and does not affect the interpretation of the statistic.

The t-stat is a measure of the size of the difference between the two datasets in relation to the variance within the datasets. The higher the t-stat, the greater the evidence of a difference between the two datasets. When the number is small, as with our result, it is evidence that there is no significant difference. In order to be sure, though, we need to look up our t-stat value in what is known as a table of critical values (see, for instance, the t-distribution table in Butler 1985: 172). To use these tables we need to know three pieces of information: degrees of freedom (or *df*; Figure 5.1 shows 53 for our test), alpha level (we used 0.05), and whether the test was one-tailed or two-tailed. Before considering what the results of the t-test tell us, we will briefly explain these three concepts.

Degrees of freedom is a complex concept and notoriously difficult for non-statisticians to grasp (we return to it in section 5.3.1). It refers to the number of observations (i.e. bits of information) that are free to vary when the value of a particular statistic (such as the mean) is known. For example, if the mean average of three numbers is 10 and two of those numbers are 2 and 8, then the third number must be 20. That is, only two of the three numbers are free to vary since together they predetermine what the third number must be. In the case of this example, then, there are two degrees of freedom. For a single data sample, degrees of freedom are calculated as *n* − 1 (where *n* = the number of values in the dataset). In a t-test, the number of degrees of freedom relates to sample size and consequently the inferences you can make about the population that you drew your sample from. If your sample contains only a couple of observations, then you will have less confidence about any inferences you might make about the population. However, if your data is based on a larger sample of the population and contains many more observations, then the confidence level of any inferences about the population will increase. The more degrees of freedom we have, the closer we get to a normal distribution of values within the data. A normal distribution of data is one which, if plotted on a graph, results in a bell curve (also known as a Gauss curve). We need to know the degrees of freedom in order to identify the t-value that matches best our data profile from a significance table. We stated earlier that the higher the t-stat value, the more significant the difference. However, the higher the number of degrees of freedom we have, the lower the t-stat needs to be to be significant at whatever cut-off has been chosen (i.e. the alpha value – see below).

The alpha level is more straightforward to understand. As we have already explained, it indicates the percentage probability we are willing to accept that our result is due to chance. The 0.05 level indicates a 5 per cent probability of this. Another way to think of it is that the alpha level indicates the probability of making a wrong decision and rejecting the null hypothesis when it is actually true. This is known in statistics as a Type I error.[6] To reduce the chance of a Type I error, we can lower the alpha level.

Finally, a two-tailed test assesses whether the difference between datasets is significantly bigger *and* significantly smaller, that is, it works in both directions. A one-tailed test assesses difference in only one direction, that is, whether a mean is significantly bigger *or* significantly smaller but not both. With our comparison of vocabulary, we are testing differences in both directions. Recall that our experimental hypothesis is as follows:

H$_1$ There is a difference between the two corpora in terms of vocabulary size.

That means that we are not hypothesising that Dickens's STTR is bigger than the comparator, or that Dickens's STTR is smaller than the comparator; we are being non-specific and simply hypothesising that there will be a difference. A possible one-tailed hypothesis would be:

H$_1$ Dickens's vocabulary size is bigger than that of nineteenth-century writers generally (as represented by the HUM Corpus).

Once we know our alpha level, degrees of freedom and whether the test is one-tailed or two-tailed, we can then consult a table of critical values for a t-test. We look down the significance table to find the t-score that corresponds with our *df* and alpha level. If the t-score for our data is less than the value in the significance table, then this indicates that there is no significant difference between the two datasets we have compared. Excel does all this work for us and presents two 't Critical' values for one-tailed and two-tailed results. As we can see, −0.886633947 is less than either of these values. This tells us we can be confident that the difference between the means of DCC and HUM is not significant.

Excel also provides both one-tailed and two-tailed *p*-values. Our null hypothesis was that the mean STTR of Dickens's writing is the same as our corpus of other writers. We compare these *p*-values with the alpha level that we set for the t-test, which was 0.05. If the *p*-values are less than 0.05, then we can reject the null hypothesis, which states that the datasets are the same. However, as we can see in Figure 5.1, the *p*-values are both higher than 0.05, so the null hypothesis stands.

At the start of this section we also mentioned effect size, which answers the question: 'what is the scale of the difference between the two datasets?' In this situation, the t-test has already told us that there is not a significant difference, and intuitively the datasets seem quite similar. However, we can double check with a fairly straightforward effect size statistic called Cohen's d (we introduce another effect size measure later in this chapter). Cohen's d is determined by first calculating the difference of the means of two groups (M_1 and M_2). This is done by subtracting one mean from the other, and dividing the results by the mean of the standard deviations of the two groups:

$$Cohen's\ d = \frac{(M_1 - M_2)}{SD\ average}$$

The SD average is also known as the pooled standard deviation, or SD_{pooled}, and is calculated as follows:

$$SD_{pooled} = \sqrt{\frac{\left(SD_1^2 + SD_2^2\right)}{2}}$$

The reason why the SDs are first squared before being added together and then divided by 2 is to stop negative values cancelling out positive values. For our data, Cohen's d is as follows:

$$Cohens's \ d \ = \frac{\left(43.0571 - 43.4445\right)}{\sqrt{\dfrac{\left(1.7029^2 + 2.6422^2\right)}{2}}} = \frac{-0.3874}{2.222793} = -0.17429$$

The convention for interpreting Cohen's d is as follows:

- d = 0.2 is a small effect size
- d = 0.5 is a medium effect size
- d = 0.8 is a large effect size.

We can therefore see that our result of –0.17429 (we can ignore the minus sign) is a very small effect size. Consequently, we can see that in Chapter 4 we were right *not* to reject the null hypothesis that Dickens's vocabulary was the equivalent of that of nineteenth-century novels generally. To put it simply, there is no statistical basis for saying that Dickens had a larger vocabulary than of other nineteenth-century novelists.

5.3 Keyness

Essentially, what we were doing in section 5.2 was comparing two datasets. The comparison of corpora is also at the heart of tests of keyness. We have introduced the concept of keyness already, in the case study in Chapter 4, though without explaining the statistical method that underpins it. Recall that an item which is key in a corpus is one which is significantly more or significantly less frequent than it is in a reference corpus. For example, in the case study in Chapter 4, we were able to observe that adjectives in Hemingway's writing are significantly under-represented when compared with their frequency in BLOB-LOB. One of the most common measures of keyness is the log-likelihood test and since most corpus linguistic software (e.g. AntConc and Wmatrix) uses log-likelihood as a measure of keyness, we will begin by explaining what the test does.

5.3.1 Log-likelihood

In corpus linguistics, log-likelihood is often preferred over the similar chi-square (χ^2) test because, unlike χ^2, log-likelihood does not assume a normal distribution of data (Dunning 1993: 62; see also Kilgarriff 1996 for further problems with χ^2). Recall that a normal distribution results in a bell curve when plotted on a graph. And what a bell curve indicates is that most of the data clusters around the mean average.

But consider the frequency of words in a corpus. If we presuppose a normal distribution, then what we are assuming is that the frequency of most words in the corpus will be somewhere around the mean average frequency. However, word frequency doesn't follow a normal distribution. Instead, if we look in a corpus, we are much more likely to see a few high frequency words and many more low frequency ones. For this reason, it is more reliable to calculate keyness using log-likelihood than χ^2 (for more details, see Dunning 1993; Rayson and Garside 2000).[7]

To carry out a log-likelihood test, we need to construct a contingency table. This is a table in which one variable (in our case, words) is distributed in rows, while another variable (in our case, corpora) is distributed in columns. Table 5.3 is an example.

The best way to explain how the contingency table works is to consider an example. Imagine we want to know if the word *politics* is key in our target corpus. First we would generate a frequency list for our target corpus. Then we would insert the frequency of the word *politics* into the 'Frequency of word' cell in the 'Target corpus' column. We refer to this as the *observed* frequency, since it indicates the number of times we have observed the word *politics* to appear in our corpus. The next step is to insert the total number of tokens in the target corpus into the cell marked 'Total' (still in the 'Target corpus' column). Then we subtract the frequency of *politics* from the total number of tokens and insert this figure into the 'Frequency of other words' cell (again, in the 'Target corpus' column). We then repeat the same steps for the reference corpus and insert the figures into the 'Reference corpus' column.

Having filled in the cells in the contingency table, what we then need to do is calculate the *expected* frequencies for our corpora. An expected frequency is simply the frequency we would expect to see if chance alone was responsible for the observed frequency, that is, if no other variable was responsible for the observed frequency. Consider, for example, the possibility that the observed frequency is the result of the genre of the constituent texts in the corpus. For instance, maybe it is the fact that our imagined target corpus is composed of politicians' autobiographies that causes the observed frequency to be what it is, or

Table 5.3 Contingency table for calculating the keyness of a word using log-likelihood (Rayson and Garside 2000: 3)

	Target corpus	Reference corpus	Total
Frequency of word	a	b	$a + b$
Frequency of other words	$c - a$	$d - b$	$c + d - a - b$
Total	c	d	$c + d$

perhaps it is the case that our sample is skewed. In effect, the expected frequency is derived from the frequency of our target word (or item) in the reference corpus. To calculate the expected frequency for our target corpus ($E1$), we multiply the total from the 'Frequency of word' row (i.e. $a + b$) by the total from the 'Target corpus' column (i.e. c) and divide the result by the grand total (i.e. $c + d$). This description can be represented by the following equation:

$$E1 = c \times (a + b)/(c + d)$$

(Rayson and Garside 2000: 3)

Similarly, $E2$ (the expected frequency for the reference corpus) = $d \times (a + b)/(c + d)$ (Rayson and Garside 2000: 3). The closer the expected frequency is to the observed frequency, the more likely it is that the observed frequency is a result of chance alone (or, as McEnery and Wilson 2001: 81 put it, 'simply a fluke of the sampling process'). On the other hand, the *greater* the difference between the expected frequency and the observed frequency, the more likely it is that the observed frequency is key.

If all of this is beginning to sound daunting, rest assured that if we are using corpus software to calculate keyness, we don't need to fill in the contingency table or do any of these calculations ourselves. The software does it for us and we don't see the table at all. The above description is simply an attempt to explain in as clear terms as possible what is going on behind the scenes in such calculations.

There is one more step in the calculation of keyness and this is to determine how close the expected frequency is to the observed frequency. To do this, we calculate a log-likelihood value (again, this is done automatically if calculating keyness using corpus linguistic software). We will not describe the formula by which this is done, since this involves a complex calculation that requires a considerable understanding of statistics to follow (the process is described by Rayson and Garside 2000: 3). The output from this calculation is what is important. This is called a *log-likelihood value*. The log-likelihood value tells us whether the word (or item) whose potential keyness we have been calculating is indeed key, thereby avoiding the need for us to rely on subjective judgements about such matters. To interpret the log-likelihood value, we need to consult a table of critical values, just as we did for the t-test in section 5.2. Critical values are in essence the log-likelihood values associated with particular levels of confidence. For instance, a log-likelihood value above a particular level will allow us to be, say, 95 per cent confident that what we have is a significant result and not one that is simply down to chance. One further piece of information is needed to interpret a list of critical values and this is the number of degrees of freedom associated with the data under analysis. We have already encountered degrees of freedom in our discussion of the t-test in section 5.2. If the statistical explanation there was difficult to grasp, consider an analogy. Imagine you are driving to a particular destination. If you know the speed at which you're travelling and how long your journey will take you, then you can also calculate the distance you'll cover. By the same token, if you know the distance you'll cover and the speed at which you're travelling, then you can calculate how long your journey will take you. And if you know how long your journey will take you and the distance you'll cover, then you can work out the speed at which you're travelling. There are, then, three observations here: values for speed, time and distance. If we know two of these values, we can calculate the third. And most importantly, not only can we calculate that third value, it has no freedom to vary. That is, once we know, say, values for speed and time, the value for distance is fixed. In the case of this example, then, there are 2 degrees of freedom, that is, two of these values determine the third.

If we apply this concept to the contingency table needed to calculate log-likelihood, we can see that we have four values: (1) frequency of word in the target corpus; (2) total number of words in the target corpus (minus frequency of target word); (3) frequency in the reference corpus; and (4) total number of words in the reference corpus (minus frequency of target word). And given the constraints of the row and column totals, only one of these values is free to vary. That is, if we enter a value for, say, b, then the row and column totals will predetermine what the values for the other cells must be. The number of degrees of freedom in this case, then, is 1.

As with the formula for calculating log-likelihood, there is no need for a full understanding of degrees of freedom in order to carry out a keyness analysis, though for those interested, Field (2000: 253–4) offers one of the most accessible explanations of the basic principle. Moreover, determining degrees of freedom in a keyness test is a relatively straightforward task. This is done by multiplying the number of rows in the contingency table minus one by the number of columns minus one. For the contingency table we have been working with, this is: $(2 - 1) \times (2 - 1)$, that is, $1 \times 1 = 1$. Hence, the number of degrees of freedom for our data is 1. Armed with this final piece of information, we can consult a table of critical values and determine whether our result is significant or not. For example, the critical values table (Oakes 1998: 266) indicates that for 1 degree of freedom a log-likelihood value of 3.84 is associated with a p-value of 0.05 (which indicates a 5 per cent likelihood of the result being down to chance alone). In other words, if the log-likelihood value resulting from our keyness test is 3.84 (i.e. the critical value) or higher, we can be 95 per cent confident that we are seeing a significant result.

In the social sciences, a p-value of 0.05 is generally considered the minimum necessary for confidence of a significant result. Other typically used p-values in corpus studies are: $p < 0.01$ (i.e. 1 per cent likelihood of the observed frequency being a result of chance rather than significant) and $p < 0.001$ (a 0.1 per cent likelihood of a chance result). These equate to there being, respectively, a 99 per cent and 99.9 per cent probability that the results are significant and not due to chance. Higher test values can be used if we want to increase our confidence even further and reduce the chance of a Type I error (and, as we will see, this can be a useful strategy for reducing a keyness list in order to make it manageable for qualitative analysis). The critical values associated with particular p-values are detailed in Table 5.4, which also indicates the respective levels of confidence that each conveys.

To summarise, for the result of a log-likelihood test to be considered significant it needs to be at least above the minimum log-likelihood critical value of 3.84. And the closer a p-value is to zero, the more significant the result.

Table 5.4 Log-likelihood critical values and associated p-values for 1 degree of freedom (based on Rayson et al. 2004)

Log-likelihood critical value	p-value	Percentage level of confidence in a significant result	Percentage probability that result is due to chance
3.84	0.05	95	5
6.63	0.01	99	1
10.82	0.001	99.9	0.1
15.13	0.0001	99.99	0.01

5.3.2 Log ratio

Having explained how keyness works in principle, let us now consider an example, since this will raise an issue with the use of log-likelihood statistics alone. So far, we have been discussing keyness in relation to keywords. In the case study in Chapter 4 we saw how keyness can also be calculated for parts-of-speech. In addition, Wmatrix offers a third option, which is to calculate key semantic domains (also known as key concepts). This is done using the same principles as described in Box 4.2 in Chapter 4. The only difference is that when it comes to making a comparison, we select **Key concepts** rather than **Key POS**. If we compare the Hemingway corpus against the BLOB-LOB corpus, what we find is that there are 125 semantic domains that are over-represented in Hemingway (i.e. 125 results that are over the critical value of 3.84). Here we encounter a problem. If we are not examining a keyness list with a specific aim (as we did in Chapter 4 when we identified subordinating conjunctions, for example), then we are faced with an overwhelming amount of data. It would, for instance, be a potentially huge task to examine concordance lines for each of the 125 key domains. One mechanistic solution to this problem is simply to reduce the probability of chance that we are willing to tolerate when we sift our results; that is, we can choose only to consider those results that exceed a particular log-likelihood value. For example, if we decide only to look at those results with a log-likelihood value of 15.13 or over, then this reduces the number of items in the key semantic domains list to 95. This still leaves us with a lot of data to analyse and we will consider this problem in greater detail in Chapter 6. For the moment, we will make a pragmatic decision and simply consider the top ten items in the list. These are shown in Table 5.5.

The codes in the 'Tag' column denote particular semantic domains. These are defined in the 'Domain' column. 'O1' is frequency in the target corpus and 'O2' frequency in the reference corpus. '%1' is the frequency of the key item expressed as a percentage of the target corpus (i.e. the semantic domain of pronouns makes up 15.96 per cent of the Hemingway corpus). '%2' conveys the equivalent information for the reference corpus. 'LL' is the log-likelihood value. The only one of these concepts which we have not yet discussed is 'Log ratio'.

Like Cohen's d (section 5.2), log ratio (Hardie 2014) is a measure of effect size rather than significance. To understand what a log ratio value means, we need first to be clear about what the results of a log-likelihood test convey. In essence, what a log-likelihood test tells us is how much evidence there is for a linguistic item (word, part-of-speech or semantic domain) being used more (or less) in the target corpus than it is in the reference corpus. Therefore, at the top of a keyness list is the item for which we have most evidence of there being a frequency difference between target and reference corpus. This, however, is not the same as saying that it is the item whose frequency differs *most* from the reference corpus. This is because while log-likelihood tells us how much evidence there is for there being a difference between the two corpora, it says nothing about the *size* of that difference (it may be, for

Table 5.5 Top ten key semantic domains (Hemingway compared with BLOB-LOB)

Tag	O1	%1	O2	%2	LL	Log ratio	Domain
Z8	102,604	15.96	153,044	8.08	26,789.78	0.98	PRONOUNS
Q2.1	13,279	2.07	12,740	0.67	7,849.45	1.62	SPEECH: COMMUNICATIVE
Z4	6,989	1.09	6,917	0.37	3,956.05	1.57	DISCOURSE BIN
B1	9,388	1.46	12,217	0.64	3,338.58	1.18	ANATOMY AND PHYSIOLOGY
M1	11,867	1.85	18,248	0.96	2,863.36	0.94	MOVING, COMING AND GOING
F2	2,625	0.41	1,600	0.08	2,537.23	2.27	DRINKS AND ALCOHOL
G3	4,076	0.63	3,768	0.20	2,532.39	1.67	WARFARE, DEFENCE AND THE ARMY; WEAPONS
Z6	11,090	1.72	17,494	0.92	2,496.22	0.90	NEGATIVE
X3.4	4,544	0.71	5,466	0.29	1,879.90	1.29	SENSORY: SIGHT
M2	6,590	1.02	10,096	0.53	1,605.81	0.94	PUTTING, PULLING, PUSHING, TRANSPORTING

example, that that we obtain a significant result as a consequence of having a large corpus). This is where log ratio comes in. To summarise: keyness indicates the degree of confidence with which we can reject the null hypothesis of there being no difference between the frequency of an item in the target and reference corpora. It does *not* indicate that there is necessarily a big difference in frequency between the target and reference corpora. For this we need to consider effect size. Wmatrix offers a number of effect size measures, including %DIFF (Gabrielatos and Marchi 2012), ELL (Effect Size for Log Likelihood; Johnston et al. 2006) and log ratio (Hardie 2014). We will concentrate here on log ratio.

To illustrate log ratio, let us consider how it would be calculated for a single word. As with the description of log-likelihood and Mutual Information, the process is automatic if using software that utilises log ratio statistics (this description is based on Hardie 2014):

- First, relative frequencies are calculated for our chosen word. This means working out how many times it occurs per thousand (or per million, etc.) words in both the target and reference corpora. This is done by dividing the raw frequency of the word by the total number of tokens in the corpus and multiplying by 1,000 (or whatever multiplier we choose). For example, the word *said* occurs 10,012 times in the Hemingway corpus. To determine its relative frequency, we divide 10,012 by the total number of tokens in the corpus (783,551) and multiply this by 1,000. This gives us a relative frequency of 12.78 per thousand (‰). The relative frequency of *said* in BLOB-LOB is (3,329 / 1,995,791) × 1,000 = 1.67‰.

- We then need to determine how many times bigger the relative frequency for the target corpus is than the relative frequency for the reference corpus. To do this, we divide the relative frequency for the target corpus by the relative frequency for the reference corpus. For the example of *said* in Hemingway and BLOB-LOB, this is: 12.78 / 1.67 = 7.65. This tells us that *said* occurs 7.65 times more in Hemingway than it does in BLOB-LOB. The 7.65 figure is known as the *ratio of relative frequencies*.

- The ratio of relative frequencies is then converted to a base 2 logarithm ($\log_2$). A logarithm is the power to which a number must be raised (i.e. the number of times it must be multiplied by itself) in order to get some other number. Hence, a base 2 logarithm is the number of times that the number 2 must be multiplied by itself in order to get some specific number N (in

Table 5.6 Size of frequency difference between target and reference corpora based on $\log_2$ of the ratio of relative frequencies (based on Hardie 2014)

Frequency in target (T) and reference (R) corpora	$\log_2$ of the ratio of relative frequencies
Frequency in T and R is the same	0
2 times more frequent in T than in R	1
4 times more frequent in T than in R	2
8 times more frequent in T than in R	3
12 times more frequent in T than in R	4
16 times more frequent in T than in R	5
32 times more frequent in T than in R	6
64 times more frequent in T than in R	7
128 times more frequent in T than in R	8
256 times more frequent in T than in R	9
512 times more frequent in T than in R	10
...	...

this case, N = the ratio of relative frequencies, or 7.65). The $\log_2$ of 7.65 is 2.03.[8]

- To interpret the $\log_2$ of N, consider Table 5.6. What this shows is that every time the $\log_2$ of the ratio increases by 1, this represents a doubling in size of the frequency difference between the target and reference corpus. Calculating the $\log_2$ of the ratio helps us to see the scale of the difference in size between the two corpora. Without doing this, we would have no way of comparing the ratio of relative frequencies of different words.

Effect size measures such as log ratio and Cohen's d are important because relying on p-values alone is problematic, as Cohen (1994) himself has explained. This is because null hypotheses can only be rejected on a probabilistic rather than absolute basis (see Cohen 1994 for a detailed discussion of how the misapplication of deductive syllogistic reasoning leads to problems with null hypothesis significance testing). The reporting of effect sizes is part of Cohen's proposed solution to this difficulty.

5.3.3 Log ratio as a mechanism for reducing keyness lists

Now let us return to Table 5.5 which details the top ten key semantic domains in the Hemingway corpus. Based on log-likelihood alone, the temptation is to say that the semantic domain PRONOUNS is worthy of more detailed investigation since its keyness value is so high ($p < 0.0001$). If we look at the contents of this category, there are 102,604 items. Of these, 23,322 are masculine pronouns while 5,729 are feminine. This is a substantial difference and we might want to use it as a starting point for developing research questions related to the representation and discursive construction of gender in Hemingway's writing (indeed, as Rayson 2003: ii points out, one of the particular values of Wmatrix is its capacity for generating candidate research questions). However, bearing in mind that log-likelihood only indicates the strength of evidence for a difference between two corpora (i.e. it doesn't take into account the size of that difference), we would do better to consider log ratio too. To this end, Table 5.7 shows those semantic domains whose log-likelihood value exceeds 15.13 and whose log ratio score is 2 or above (this indicates that all the key items in the table occur at least four times more in the target corpus than in the reference corpus; we could, of course, choose a higher log ratio).

The advantage of taking account of log ratio is twofold. First, it allows us to be confident that what we have is a list of those key items for which there is a substantial difference in frequency between the target and reference corpora. Second, using log ratio offers an objective means of further reducing the amount of data for qualitative analysis, while avoiding the need for arbitrary measures such as only viewing, say, the top ten items in a keyness list. The original keyness semantic domains list for the Hemingway corpus ran to 125 items. Using log ratio in conjunction with log-likelihood, we have been able to reduce this to five, a much more manageable amount of data for qualitative analysis.

What is noteworthy in Table 5.7 is that three of the key domains are related to drinking and alcohol. (N.B. In relation to category F2, ++ marks comparative forms while +++ indicates superlative forms;

Table 5.7 Key items ($p < 0.0001$) in Hemingway corpus (compared with BLOB-LOB) arranged by log ratio (> 2)

Semantic tag	O1	%1	O2	%2	LL	Log ratio	Domain
F2+++	91	0.01	3	0.00	225.07	6.48	EXCESSIVE DRINKING
F2++	171	0.03	48	0.00	267.28	3.39	EXCESSIVE DRINKING
Q2.1-	96	0.01	39	0.00	124.09	2.86	SPEECH: NOT COMMUNICATING
F2	2,625	0.41	1600	0.08	2,537.23	2.27	DRINKS AND ALCOHOL
X3.5	247	0.04	171	0.01	212.60	2.09	SENSORY: SMELL

see Piao et al. 2005 for more information on the sub-categorisation of domains.) Consequently, we may wish to claim 'drinking' as an interpretatively significant theme in Hemingway's work. Of course, non-linguistically inclined literary critics may well say that this tells us nothing we did not already know about Hemingway's novels. There are two responses to this. The first is to repeat Spitzer's point that 'to make our way to an old truth is not only to enrich our own understanding: it produces new evidence of objective value for this truth – which is thereby renewed' (1948: 38). The second and related response is to note that if the statistical test confirms what we already know to be the case, then this demonstrates the reliability of the method. This enables us to have confidence in the test's ability to reveal textual functions that may not be discoverable simply by reading the work in question.

That said, it is important to note that while statistical significance and effect size are indicators of what Baker (2006) terms *saliency*, they are not necessarily indicators of foregrounding (Mukařovský [1932] 1964; Shklovsky [1917] 1965; van Peer 1986; see also McIntyre and Price 2018a for a summary). That is, statistical significance does not necessarily equate to interpretative significance, which may be judged instead on the basis of the extent to which an item deviates from a perceived linguistic norm. Salience is important as a marker of likely candidates for qualitative analysis, and (in the case of semantic domains particularly) as a potential marker of thematic issues. But identifying keyness is not a shortcut to the identification of foregrounding. We explore this issue in more detail in the case study in section 5.5. Before we do this, however, we turn from keyness to collocation, and focus on the role of statistical tests in the interpretation of collocational information.

5.4 Collocation

As we saw in the discussion of semantic prosody in Chapter 2, collocation can be assessed relatively subjectively, simply by reading concordance lines. This approach can yield valuable insights, as in, for example, Hoey's (2007) collocational study of Philip Larkin's poem 'First Sight', Mahlberg's (2007b) analysis of the local textual functions of the phrase *sustainable development*, and Sinclair's (2004: 24–48) detailed exploration of units of meaning. Nonetheless, taking a purely manual approach to the analysis of collocation can also be problematic. The problem centres on the issue of frequency. If we look in our target corpus and observe, for example, that the word *police* has a tendency to co-occur with the word *car*, then we may intuitively feel that we have discovered a collocational relationship between the two words. However, to be sure of the importance of this collocation, we would need to know how often *police* collocates with other words too. If it is the case that *police* co-occurs with lots of other words in our corpus, then its relationship with *car* becomes potentially less noteworthy as a result. It is also the case, of course, that a word will collocate with high frequency words much more often than it will with low frequency ones.

Manual analysis of collocation does not allow us to determine the seriousness of these problems, and for this reason many corpus linguists advocate using statistical tests in collocation analysis. Statistical analyses of collocation allow us to be more confident about the nature of the relationship between particular words, in much the same way that tests of keyness offer more reliable insights into the salience of particular words than simple frequency profiling. Using statistical tests to analyse collocates is not a panacea, however, and statistical tests come with their own problems, as we will discuss. First, though, we will explain how a statistical test of collocation works. We focus here on one particular approach, the Mutual Information test, in order to explain the principle behind collocation. A wide range of other tests are available, some of which we will refer to later on (for a detailed discussion of the statistics of collocation, see Evert 2005).

5.4.1 Mutual Information

As is the case for the analysis of keyness, collocational significance can be measured using a variety of statistical tests. And providing that the corpus software you are using has a collocates function, you will not need to carry out such tests yourself; as with keyness analysis, the software will do this for you. As ever, though, it helps to understand the basis of the calculation that the software carries out. To this end, we will consider one of the most commonly used tests of collocational significance, the Mutual Information test. The process for calculating Mutual Information is as follows (this description is based on Barnbrook et al. 2013: 55–68; see also Barnbrook 1996: 87–106):

- First of all, we need to establish a span, sometimes referred to as a window of collocation. This is a predefined distance from the node word. Any word that falls within this span counts as a collocate. A 9 word window is a commonly used span (Sinclair 1991: 175; Sinclair et al. 2004) and equates to four words either side of the node, though as we explained in Chapter 2, other spans may be used.

- Once a span has been determined, we can generate a concordance of our node word to ascertain its collocates.
- We then need to establish the observed frequency of each collocate of the node word. This involves counting how many times each collocate appears within the window of collocation for each of the concordance lines we have generated.
- In order to determine the strength of the collocations we have identified, we next need to compare the observed frequency of each collocate with its *expected* frequency, that is, the number of times we would expect to see it in the window of collocation if its frequency of occurrence in the span were proportionate to its frequency of occurrence in the corpus as a whole. (N.B. Barnbrook 1996: 93 notes that we can also derive an expected frequency by considering the frequency of occurrence of the collocate in question in a large reference corpus.)
- To determine the expected frequency of a collocate, we first need to know how frequent it is in the corpus as a whole (i.e. not just in the span). We then need to calculate its *relative* frequency. This is done by dividing its overall frequency by the size of the corpus as a whole. The resulting figure tells us what proportion of the corpus is made up of the collocate in question.
- Next we multiply this figure by what is known as the environment size. This is the number of concordance lines for our original node word, multiplied by the span (including the node; for example, if our node word *car* generates 500 concordance lines, and we are using a 9 word window, then the environment size is 500 × 9 = 4,500). The result of multiplying relative frequency by environment size gives us the expected frequency, which is essentially an estimation of the number of times the collocate would appear in proximity to the node word if it were distributed evenly throughout the corpus.
- We have now obtained the observed and expected frequencies for each of our collocates. The expected frequency for each collocate then needs to be compared with its observed frequency. To do this, we calculate a Mutual Information score by dividing the observed frequency by the expected frequency and determining the base 2 logarithm of the result. The formula for this is:

$$MI = log_2 \frac{O}{E}$$

(Barnbrook 1996: 98; see also Oakes 1998: 63 and Fujimura and Aoki 2015: 275)

What this equation means is that the Mutual Information score is calculated by determining the number of times that the base number 2 needs to be multiplied by itself in order to arrive at whatever the observed frequency divided by the expected frequency happens to be.

- The number resulting from this calculation is the MI score. Conventionally, if this is higher than 3, then this can be taken as indicative of strong collocation (Barnbrook 1996: 99; Hunston 2002: 71).

5.4.2 T-score

Mutual Information is not the only test of collocation available. Other measures of collocational significance are often used, since different tests take account of different factors. For instance, any word will collocate more often with high frequency words in a language than it will with low frequency ones. One problem with the MI test is that it does not work well with words of low frequency, which can end up with deceptively high MI scores. This is because the MI test primarily takes account of collocational strength. For example, a node word might appear in a corpus very rarely but if in each instance it collocates with the same other word, then it will receive a high MI score. Another measure of collocation, however, is not just how strong the collocation is but how frequently it occurs in a corpus. This can be determined using a t-score (see Barnbrook 1996: 97–8 for details of how this differs from an MI test). Under this measure, a collocation may score much lower than it does in an MI test. Conventionally, t-scores of 2 or above are considered to be noteworthy. (N.B. We have deliberately avoided the term *significant* here as Barnbrook 1996: 98 notes that absolute statistical significance is difficult to assess using a t-score.)

In addition to MI and t-score, there is a range of other tests available, such as z-score (Berry-Roghe 1973), log-likelihood (Dunning 1993), MI3 (Oakes 1998) and log-log (Kilgarrif and Tugwell 2001). And as Baker (2006: 102) points out, each test favours particular categories of word. Log-likelihood and MI3 tend to favour grammatical words, for instance, while log-log favours lexical words but does not attach as much importance to low frequency items as MI does (see Baker 2006: 102 for a comparison of collocates derived using six different statistical tests).

To summarise, then, MI measures the strength of cohesion, interdependence or association between words (see Manning and Schütze 1999: 182; Clear 1993: 280), while t-score measures 'the confidence with which we can claim that there is an association' (Clear 1993: 281). MI can overestimate the attraction between low frequency collocates and therefore the importance of potentially chance co-occurrences, while t-score tends to favour items which co-occur very frequently because this offers a means of being confident that such collocates are not co-occurring by chance. Because of this, Church et al. (1991) suggest using MI first to identify collocates, and then t-score to check the probability that the association is not a chance happening. If you are relying on a particular piece of corpus linguistic software, of course, then your choice of test may be determined by what is available to you. AntConc, for instance, offers a choice of MI or t-score, while WordSmith Tools offers a range of others, including MI3 and z-score. GraphColl, a tool specifically for collocation analysis and a component of the #LancsBox software package (Brezina et al. 2015), offers 14 collocation measures. It is, then, worth being clear about the advantages and disadvantages of the various tests. In the next section, we implement keyness and collocation in a case study of David Peace's novel *1974*.

5.5 Case study: salience and foregrounding in David Peace's *1974*

One of the inherent problems with analysing prose fiction is summed up by Leech and Short as follows:

> the sheer bulk of prose writing is intimidating; [...] In prose, the problem of how to select – what sample passages, what features to study – is more acute, and the incompleteness of even the most detailed analysis more apparent. (Leech and Short 2007: 2)

There are, in fact, two issues here. One is the simple fact that it is impossible to analyse a whole novel qualitatively at the level of detail required by stylistics. The second is that, because of this, it may be necessary to select one or more short extracts from the novel in question to subject to qualitative analysis. In this case study we show how keyness can be used to select an extract for analysis. This is of particular value in cases where the research is not driven by a specific hypothesis (cf. the case study in Chapter 4). We then analyse this extract qualitatively, using the concept of foregrounding as an analytical framework. In so doing, we demonstrate the difference between statistical salience and linguistic foregrounding, arguing that keyness does not in and of itself equate to interpretative significance.

5.5.1 *1974*

1974 (Peace 1999) is the first book in the British writer David Peace's *Red Riding Quartet*, which focuses on police corruption set against a fictionalised account of the Yorkshire Ripper murders that were carried out in Leeds, Bradford, Manchester and Huddersfield, in the UK, between 1975 and 1980. *1974* is narrated in the first-person by Eddie Dunford, Crime Correspondent for a local newspaper, *The Yorkshire Post*. The story takes place in West Yorkshire and begins with the discovery of the body of a girl who has been brutally murdered. As Eddie investigates the crime, he discovers potential connections between the young girl's murder and a series of other child murders in the recent past. However, his investigation is hampered by the utter corruption of the police force.

The story is bleak, realistic and powerfully told. Peace is widely acknowledged to be a distinctive writer stylistically (Shaw 2010, 2011) and our aim here is to show how a corpus-based analysis of an extract from the novel can be of value in identifying the source of particular literary effects in Peace's writing. In particular, we discuss what a corpus-driven stylistic analysis of the novel, in conjunction with a qualitative analysis of an extract from it, can reveal about atmosphere and character.

5.5.2 Keyness for text selection

We used Wmatrix to generate a list of keywords for *1974*, using the BNC Written Imaginative Sampler as a reference corpus.[9] We decided on 15.13 as a threshold for significance and required a log ratio of at least 4 (i.e. the keyword occurs at least 12 times more frequently in *1974* than in the reference corpus). We made a decision to ignore proper nouns on the basis that character names will always be key in a target text.[10] We also decided to select for the purpose of concordancing the first lexical word to appear in the keyword list that met the criteria for log-likelihood value and log ratio score, which produced the list shown in Table 5.8. (N.B. We show only the top ten items, since our selection criteria for concordancing is met within this frame.)

The first keyword to meet our selection criteria is *fucking*. It is also noteworthy that the related form *fuck* is the next lexical word in the list. With regard to the other items in the list whose meanings are perhaps not transparent, *s* is a possessive form and *t*, *d*, *m*, *re* and *ll* are contractions of *not*, *would*, *am*, *you're* and *I'll*. There is perhaps an indication here that the narrative style is more akin to spoken language

Table 5.8 Keywords in *1974* compared with BNC Written Imaginative Sampler

Word	O1	%1	O2	%2	LL	Log ratio
s	814	1.00	2	0	2,113.59	10.11
t	550	0.67	8	0	1,367.40	7.55
fucking	312	0.38	16	0.01	702.54	5.73
don	204	0.25	3	0	506.93	7.53
d	201	0.25	3	0	499.13	7.51
m	186	0.23	0	0	489.08	9.98
i	2,929	3.58	4,734	2.13	468.55	0.75
fuck	196	0.24	8	0	452.88	6.06
re	147	0.18	0	0	386.53	9.65
ll	132	0.16	0	0	347.09	9.49
...	...	...	...	...	...	...

and this would form the basis of an interesting research question for another project (again, what is demonstrated here is the capacity of corpus-driven stylistics for identifying potential research questions).

Having decided to examine the first lexical word, though, the next issue was to determine (1) which sections of the novel contain instances of that keyword, and (2) which of the sections where the keyword is found are candidates for qualitative analysis. The concordance plot function in AntConc can be used to help narrow down this search. Concordance plots (sometimes called dispersal plots) indicate the position of a chosen search word in the corpus file. For example, the concordance plot for *fucking* in a file comprising the whole novel (see Figure 5.2) shows that the keyword is spread fairly evenly across the whole text (single black lines indicate the presence of the keyword; thicker lines indicate conglomerations of keywords).

Figure 5.2 clearly shows the keyword is not concentrated in a particular part of the novel but is instead fairly evenly dispersed. This in itself is an interesting result but is not particularly helpful for determining an area to focus on for qualitative analysis.

To this end, we then separated the novel into chapter files in order to generate concordance plots for each chapter. We decided to focus on the first instance of a clustering of our chosen keyword. This occurs in chapter 2. The plots for the first two chapters are shown in Figure 5.3.

HIT FILE: 1   FILE: 1974.txt

No. of Hits = 315
File Length (in chars) = 453973

Figure 5.2 Concordance plot of *fucking* in *1974* (single file)

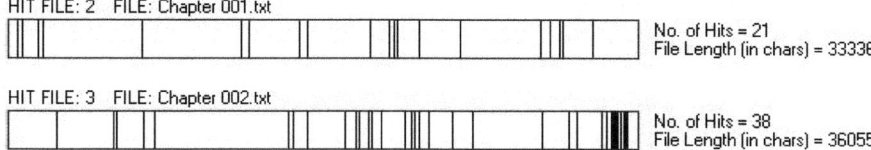

Figure 5.3 Concordance plot of *fucking* in chapters 1 and 2 of *1974*

Examining concordance plots for single chapters is similar to zooming in on a particular area of a street map. The result is a clearer picture of what a particular area looks like. Figure 5.3 shows that *fucking* is present in both chapters 1 and 2 and that there is a particular clustering of keywords towards the end of the second chapter (indicated by the thicker black lines).

The question of why the keyword should cluster at this point in the chapter is an interesting starting point for a stylistic analysis. For this reason, we decided to focus on the end of chapter 2 for qualitative analysis. Clicking on the thick black line in AntConc takes you to the second paragraph in the extract below. To contextualise this, we have included the preceding and subsequent paragraphs in the selection (instances of the keyword are marked in bold and sentences are numbered for ease of reference):

> If it bleeds, it leads. (1)
>
> 'How'd it go with Hadden?' Kathryn was standing over my desk. (2)
>
> 'How do you **fucking** think,' I spat, rubbing my eyes, looking for someone easy. (3)
>
> Kathryn fought back tears. (4) 'Barry says to tell you he'll pick you up at ten tomorrow. At your mother's.' (5)
>
> 'Tomorrow's bloody Sunday.' (6)
>
> 'Well why don't you go and ask Barry. I'm not your bloody secretary. I'm a **fucking** journalist too.' (7)
>
> I stood up and left the office, afraid someone would come in. (8)
>
> In the front room, my father's Beethoven as loud as I dared. (9)
>
> My mother in the back room, the TV louder still: ballroom dancing and show jumping. (10)
>
> **Fucking** horses. (11)
>
> Next door's barking through the Fifth. (12)
>
> **Fucking** dogs. (13)
>
> I poured the rest of the Scotch into the glass and remembered

the time when I'd actually wanted to be a **fucking** policeman, but was too scared shitless to even try. (14)

Fucking pigs. (15)

I drank half the glass and remembered all the novels I wanted to write, but was too scared shitless to even try. (16)

Fucking bookworm. (17)

I flicked a cat hair off my trousers, trousers my father had made, trousers that would outlast us all. I picked off another hair. (18)

Fucking cats. (19)

I swallowed the last of the Scotch from my glass, unlaced my shoes and stood up. (20) I took off my trousers and then my shirt. (21) I screwed the clothes up into a ball and threw them across the room at **fucking** Ludwig. (22)

I sat back down in my white underpants and vest and closed my eyes, too scared shitless to face Jack **fucking** Whitehead. (23)

Too scared shitless to fight for my own story. (24)

Too scared shitless to even try. (25)

Fucking chicken. (26)

I didn't hear my mother come in. (27)

'There's someone on the phone for you love,' she said, drawing the front room curtains. (28)

'Edward Dunford speaking,' I said into the hall phone, doing up my trousers and looking at my father's watch:

11.35 p.m. (29)

A man: 'Saturday night all right for fighting?' (30)

'Who's this?' (31)

Silence. (32)

'Who is it?' (33)

A stifled laugh and then, 'You don't need to know.' (34)

'What do you want?' (35)

'You interested in the Romany Way?' (36)

'What?' (37)

'White vans and gyppos?' (38)

'Where?' (39)

'Hunslet Beeston exit of the M1.' (40)

'When?' (41)

'You're late.' (42)

The line went dead. (43)

(Peace 1999: 43–4)

The above example demonstrates how the combination of keyword analysis and concordance plots can be a useful means of determining a short section of a text to subject to qualitative analysis. In the next section, we provide a qualitative analysis focused on uncovering elements of foregrounding in the passage.

5.5.3 Foregrounding in *1974*

As we discussed in Chapter 4, an alternative approach to hypothesis testing in stylistic analysis is to follow Spitzer's (1948) technique of beginning with an intuitive response to the text in question and then attempting to validate (or invalidate) this impression through linguistic analysis. As part of an initial response to *1974* we might note an overwhelmingly negative atmosphere described by a narrator who appears to be volatile and almost irrationally angry. As a character he gives the impression of being instinctive rather than contemplative, with a tendency towards plain speaking, the latter quality perhaps being indicative of a fairly basic level of education. And given the method we used for selecting this extract, we might also ask: what is the function of the keyword *fucking* in this extract?

First of all, we can observe that the nine instances of *fucking* from the concordance plot occur in the second paragraph and are part of the first-person narration of Eddie Dunford. The other two examples in the selection above occur in direct speech in the preceding paragraph. Furthermore, seven of the examples from the second paragraph occur in instances of free direct thought presentation, in which Eddie apparently addresses himself (for details of a stylistic model of speech and thought presentation, see Leech and Short 2007: ch. 10; we discuss speech and thought presentation and the investigation of this through corpus methods in more detail in Chapter 8). These instances constitute a stylistically interesting pattern. Each instance of *fucking* is followed by reference to an animal:

> Fucking horses. (11)
> Fucking dogs. (13)
> Fucking pigs. (15)
> Fucking bookworm. (17)
> Fucking cats. (19)
> Fucking chicken. (26)

The first two examples of this (*horses* and *dogs*) express Eddie's annoyance at, respectively, the show jumping programme which he can hear on the television in the next room and the barking of the dog in the adjoining house. There is something comic in the fact that Eddie's annoyance is directed at the animals generally rather than the noise which is the actual locus of his irritation. Following this, the next reference is to 'fucking pigs', which deviates from the previous two structures in that the animal reference is metaphorical, *pigs* being a slang term for police. The lexical and syntactic parallelism of the three examples, with the semantic deviation in the third example, generates the effect of Eddie viewing the police as being on the same level as animals which cause him annoyance. The next phrase in the series, 'fucking bookworm', is an instance of Eddie turning his ire against himself by referring scornfully to his literary ambitions. This metaphorical use of an animal term has the further effect of characterising Eddie as small and insignificant, especially when contrasted against the 'pigs' of the police force. There is a return to a literal animal term in the next phrase, and the switch from introspective self-loathing to general irritation at cats seems blackly comic. The final phrase in the sequence again constitutes self-assessment, with *chicken* being a common colloquialism for *coward*. The general function of this sequence is to convey the emotions of irritation, self-loathing and anger that Eddie feels, thereby aiding the characterisation process. The repeated use of *fucking*, appended equally to referents which generate both mild irritation (e.g. cats) and extreme loathing (e.g. pigs) characterises Eddie as extremely tense, angered as he is by both serious and minor issues. This anxiety is reinforced by the parallelism of the sentences that intersperse the free direct thought presentation (14, 16, 18, 20). Dynamic verbs indicate a series of small-scale actions ('I poured ...', 'I drank ...', 'I flicked ...', 'I swallowed . . .') which may be seen as suggestive of restlessness and nervous tension.

The nature of the Spitzerian (1948) approach to stylistic analysis is that one analytical insight leads to another. In the case of *1974*, the fact that the keyword *fucking* occurs primarily in short bursts of free direct thought presentation leads naturally to a consideration of the general functions and effects of discourse presentation in the extract. What is clear is that all speech presentation is either direct speech or free direct speech (for the model of discourse presentation employed here, see Leech and Short 2007: 256–8 and ch. 10 generally). That is, speech is presented using the maximal presentation option; there is no narrator interference. Thought, on the other hand, is presented in a variety of forms: free direct thought (e.g. 'Fucking cats'), the presentation of thought acts (akin to speech acts; e.g. 'remembered all the novels I wanted to write') and the presentation of internal states (e.g. 'Too scared shitless to even try'; see Short 2007 for more on this category).

The distinction between speech presentation and introspective thought is emphasised by the lack of narrator interference in the former. There is consequently a distinct change in atmosphere between the first and second paragraphs of the extract, as Eddie moves from an external presentation of speech with no narrator interference to a highly introspective presentation of thought.

What is also interesting in relation to speech and thought presentation in the extract is the presentation of narration (the Narrator's Report of Action, as Short 1996a terms it in relation to discourse presentation). While the narration in paragraph one is conveyed in full sentences, paragraph two has some marked differences. Sentences (9), (10) and (12) are all minor sentences, lacking a main verb. In this respect, they have more in common with dramatic stage directions than conventional past tense prose narration. This sparse narration has a tendency to occur when Eddie is alone (see McIntyre 2011 for further commentary on this issue) and appears to belie a lack of concern on the part of the narrator for descriptive minutiae. The effect that this generates is the suggestion that Eddie has little regard for anything beyond his immediate concerns; the narration is the bare minimum needed to establish the sense of time, place and action that Eddie needs in order to relate what he considers to be the important elements of the story. Further evidence of this can be seen in the minimal use of reporting clauses for direct speech and the preponderance of free direct forms. This also creates something of a cinematic effect, in the sense that the emphasis here is on mimesis rather than diegesis (see McIntyre 2006: 33).

With regard to the narrator's lexical choice, we can observe a tendency towards direct and concrete expression. Of the 64 nouns (excluding proper nouns), just five are abstract (*story, silence, laugh, tomorrow, time*). The dominance of concrete nouns seems appropriate for a direct and plain-speaking narrator. Similarly, of the 29 adjectives there are just ten types, four of which relate to fear (*shitless, scared, afraid*) and anger (*fucking*), and three of which are strongly negative in connotation (*stifled, dead, bloody*). The lack of adjectival variation is also indicative of a limited vocabulary on the part of the narrator, which functions as a characterisation device. Of the 18 past tense verbs in the passage whose subject is Eddie (via the first-person pronoun *I*), we can observe that the majority are transitive verbs, all of which relate to minor actions (e.g. 'I flicked a cat hair off my trousers', 'I swallowed the last of the Scotch'). Eddie is purposeful but his actions are small-scale. This is perhaps emblematic of a wider theme in the novel which might be summarised by noting that Eddie's capacity to effect major change is limited by his lack of personal and institutional power. Adverbs in the extract are primarily emphatic (*still, actually, even, too*), which, in combination with the other lexical and grammatical features discussed, further contributes to the characterisation of Eddie as volatile and highly strung.

Our analysis so far begins to explain the source of some of our impressionistic responses to the *1974* extract. For example, the impression of volatility on the part of the narrator arises in some measure from his tendency to express the same level of anger towards minor and major issues. His plain-speaking nature is conveyed via his limited vocabulary, by the predominance of concrete rather than abstract nouns, and by the lack of concern for descriptive detail in narrative sentences. Maximal speech presentation forms and a lack of reporting clauses also contribute to this straightforward and sparse narrative style.

Having established all of this through qualitative analysis, we might now return to keyness analysis to seek further support for some of the claims being made. Table 5.9 shows key semantic domains in the novel.

The two highest ranked domains, LIGHT and DARKNESS, are conventional opposites, and the connotational significance of these domains may well seem appropriate thematically for a novel that is about uncovering corruption. However, this opposition is undermined somewhat when we examine the contents of the LIGHT domain. Of the 146 items in the LIGHT category, 60 of these are the word *light*. Table 5.10 shows those collocates of *light* in the novel which are generated by both MI and t-score.

Light as a collocate of *light* refers to a traffic light, as does *red*. Neither of these collocates conveys the thematic and metaphorical notion of light as a force for good (i.e. light in opposition to darkness). This is also the case when we examine many of the other collocates. Figure 5.4, for example, shows a concordance of the collocate *through*, and what we can observe here is that the wider context for *through* incorporates lexical items with negative connotations (e.g. *unlit, grey, little, low, tears, disgusting*).

Table 5.9 Key semantic domains in *1974* compared with BNC Written Imaginative Sampler (log-likelihood > 15.13; log ratio > 4; arranged by log ratio score)

Tag	O1	%1	O2	%2	LL	Log ratio	Semantic domain
W2	146	0.18	0	0	383.9	9.64	LIGHT
W2-	52	0.06	0	0	136.73	8.15	DARKNESS
A13	25	0.03	0	0	65.74	7.09	DEGREE
T1.1	32	0.04	4	0	61.53	4.45	TIME: GENERAL

Table 5.10 Collocates of *light* in *1974*
determined by both MI and t-score
(9 word window; minimum frequency = 3;
MI > 3; t-score > 2)

Collocate	MI	t-score
light	7.07337	2.43130
red	5.89559	2.19851
through	5.38352	2.18250
from	4.86456	2.55493
on	4.69765	3.96422
into	4.56117	2.14135
the	3.87591	7.03559
in	3.66961	2.91377
a	3.66872	3.56844
and	3.40960	4.05129
up	3.37039	2.01985

car procession crawled down the Dewsbury Cutting,	**through**	the unlit Christmas lights in the centre o
I rubbed my eyes free and drove off	**through**	the grey light, everywhere the browns and
the same as Mrs Sheard's. A little light coming	**through**	the glass front door at the
if they were. 'Kathryn's eyes were shining	**through**	the low light, on the verge of tears.
burning yellow in the windows. I was walking	**through**	the wood, light snow underfoot, heading ho
.' Why did they think you did it, Jimmy? '	**Through**	the Christmas lights of Leeds City Centre,
Rover's engine went dead as I approached	**through**	the grey light. I tapped on the glass
hem both. Disgusting, that's what they are.'	**Through**	the Christmas lights and the first spits o

Figure 5.4 Concordance of the collocate *through* in *1974*

cold on the floor. Each time the moon light seeping	**into**	the room, shadows making the
religious rite and not something to be entered	**into**	lightly. This film creates a totally false im
be back. Sorry,' smiled Scotch Clare, squinting	**into**	the light. 'No she's not back yet,
stone shaft with a metal ladder leading down	**into**	a faint light some fifty odd feet below.
mouth of the hole. I pulled myself up	**into**	the light and crawled on to the shelf.
the blanket of feathers towards him. He turned	**into**	the light, his eyes holes, his mouth open
up and walked out of the living room,	**into**	a cold and light expensive kitchen. A tap

Figure 5.5 Concordance of the collocate *into* in *1974*

The same can be seen in concordances of the other collocates too. Figure 5.5, for instance, shows a concordance for the collocate *into*.

As with *through*, we can observe in the surrounding context a number of lexical items with conventionally negative connotations. These include *seeping, false, squinting, faint, crawled* and *cold*. In effect, what we are seeing here is a collocational network (Baker 2006: 116) that functions to associate *light* with negativity. This undermines the stereotypical thematic opposition of good and evil connoted by the semantic domains LIGHT and DARK. This, then, would begin to account for the sense of bleakness that pervades the story as a whole; in both literal and metaphorical terms, even light does not illuminate the darkness.

There is, of course, more that could be said about the other semantic domains in Table 5.9 and the collocates in Table 5.10. In addition, there are other noteworthy stylistic features in the extract which we selected for qualitative analysis (see McIntyre 2013b for a discussion of the interpretative significance of sentence length and n-grams, for example). Nonetheless, the above analysis reveals at least some of the sources of our intuitive response to the text, such as the atmosphere of desolation in the novel and the sense of the narrator as tense, nervous and hopeless. What the case study as a whole also demonstrates is the value of using keyness for text selection, as well as how keyness and collocation can facilitate a Spitzerian analysis that takes us from corpus to text and back again.

5.6 Conclusion

Our aim in this chapter has been to explain the principles that underpin some of the most common inferential statistical tests used in off-the-shelf corpus software such as WordSmith Tools, AntConc and Wmatrix. In particular, we discussed the calculations that underlie log-likelihood tests of keyness (as well as the log ratio measure of effect size), and the various statistical tests used in the calculation of collocational frequency and strength. It is important to understand at least the principles of such statistical tests if we are to make sensible interpretations of the results arising from them. In addition, an understanding of the principles behind common statistical tests is important for making an informed choice about which test to use in any given analysis. The results of a collocational analysis, for instance, will be dependent on whether a Mutual Information test is used in preference to, say, t-score or log-log.

Having introduced various tests of keyness and collocation, we then demonstrated how such tests can be used (a) in the selection of an extract from a larger corpus for qualitative analysis and (b) to reduce keyness and collocation lists to a manageable size for manual analysis. We illustrated this through an analysis of David Peace's novel *1974*. What the case study of *1974* also aimed to show is that statistical significance does not necessarily equate to foregrounding in the stylistic sense of the term. A lexical item may be salient as a result of its frequency in a corpus, but salience is primarily a quantitative concept whereas foregrounding is primarily a qualitative concept. To ascertain whether or not a linguistic item is foregrounded in stylistic terms, we need to identify deviation or parallelism in relation to a predefined linguistic norm. Salience, by contrast, is determined only by comparing an observed frequency against what we might take to be a frequency norm. Of course, a salient item might also turn out to be foregrounded in functional terms, though this will not always be the case.

Finally, while inferential statistical tests are essentially used to determine whether or not to reject a null hypothesis, what we also aim to have demonstrated in this chapter is that tests of keyness can also be used to support corpus-driven stylistic analysis, that is, stylistic analysis which is not primarily aimed at hypothesis testing. For example, we have shown how keyness analysis can be used to generate candidate research questions, as well as how keyness and collocation analysis can be used to facilitate a Spitzerian approach to stylistics. The next chapter builds on this by discussing how insights from cognitive stylistics might be integrated into corpus stylistic studies.

Notes

1. Of course, it is important to be clear about potential issues with comparing texts. Here we compare Dickens's prose against nineteenth-century fiction generally. This kind of comparison is common in corpus linguistics and, indeed, in corpus stylistics (see, for example, McEnery's 2009 comparison of the writings of Mary Whitehouse against the LOB and FLOB corpora, and Mahlberg's 2013b study of Dickens's novels in comparison with nineteenth-century novels generally). However, in the case of vocabulary comparison, we might wish to argue that this is not a fair comparison to make, on the grounds that the combined vocabularies of multiple authors are likely to outclass the vocabulary of a single author in terms of size.

2. 'Student' was the pseudonym of William Sealy Gosset, who invented the t-test. The 't' in t-test doesn't actually stand for anything. Rather, it was introduced by Fisher (1924) as a short way of referring to Gosset's method for testing hypotheses based on the mean of the normal distribution (see Student 1908).

3. Welch's t-test does assume a normal distribution of data, however, which in itself can be problematic for reasons discussed in section 5.3.1.

4. Excel will need to have the Analysis ToolPak loaded and activated. Instructions on how to do this are available on the Microsoft Support website at <https://bit.ly/2EEdE47> (last accessed 20 August 2018).

5. SPSS stands for Statistical Package for the Social Sciences and is available at <https://www.ibm.com/products/spss-statistics> (last accessed 20 August 2018).

6. A Type II error occurs when you fail to reject a null hypothesis that is actually false. Increasing sample size reduces the chance of a Type II error occurring.

7. Even then, some corpus linguists argue that neither χ^2 *nor* log-likelihood are appropriate tests. For example, Bestgen (2017) points out that for such tests to be valid, the unit of analysis must be the same as the sampling unit; but in corpus linguistics this is often not the case, as the unit of analysis is the word while the sampling unit is a text. Bestgen (2017) points out how this problem can lead to skewed results, such as a word being identified as key even if it appears in only one of the constituent texts of a corpus (see also Paquot and Bestgen 2009 for a comparison of different statistical tests). Kilgarriff (2005) identifies a different problem with keyness tests. He points out that language is never random (i.e. we do not produce words or sentences randomly but for some specific purpose) and so, because of this, the null hypothesis that there is no difference between two corpora can never be true (see Gries 2005 for a response). It will be clear from these arguments that there are complex issues surrounding the use of inferential statistical tests. This is not a reason for dispensing with them, however. Rather, it is important to be aware of the potential limitations of particular tests and to consider (and report) the impact that these might have on your results.

8. To convert N to $\log_2$ using a scientific calculator, first find the *ln* (= natural logarithm) of N. Do this by typing N, pressing the *ln* key and saving the result. Now find the *ln* of 2 by typing *ln* 2. Save the result. Now divide the *ln* of N by the *ln* of 2. For the example of *said* in Hemingway, $N = 7.65$, *ln* = 2.03 and the *ln* of 2 = 0.69. Hence, the $\log_2$ of 7.65 = 2.93. Numerous log base calculators can be found online.

9. This consists of 222,541 words of twentieth-century prose fiction.

10. N.B. This is not to suggest that ignoring proper nouns is always recommended; research questions pertaining to address and reference forms, for example, would require proper nouns to be considered.

6

Cognition, character and corpus stylistics

6.1 Introduction

In Chapters 2 to 5 we outlined the methodological principles and primary analytical methods of corpus linguistics, explaining how these can be applied in the service of stylistic analysis. The next four chapters illustrate how corpus methods can be employed in particular areas and sub-fields of stylistics. To this end, this chapter considers how corpus-based stylistics can be used to support the cognitive stylistic analysis of characterisation in TV and film drama. In particular, we explore how corpus methods can be used to investigate the impact on characterisation of intralingual subtitling. Intralingual subtitling refers to the practice of providing subtitles in the same language as the original dialogue in a film or TV programme (cf. interlingual subtitling, which is the process of translating dialogue into a different language). Since the primary purpose of intralingual subtitling is to make TV and film accessible for deaf and hard-of-hearing viewers, it is important to ensure that the viewing experience for subtitle users is as close to that of hearing viewers as possible. And since characterisation is partly a linguistic process, this inevitably necessitates some consideration of how linguistic indicators of characterisation in dialogue are transferred to the corresponding subtitles. The case study in this chapter shows how corpus methods can be used to study the extent to which this happens. We argue that using corpus stylistic techniques for this purpose has a potential practical value, in that insights arising from such analyses can be used to inform the improvement of subtitling practices. We illustrate this through a case study of characterisation triggers in the 1979 BBC

TV series *Tinker Tailor Soldier Spy* (Hopcraft 1979; our reasons behind this choice of text are explained in full in section 6.4). In particular, we discuss how to deal with low frequency items in a corpus analysis, stressing the importance of qualitative stylistic analyses of samples from the corpus. Consequently, our analysis combines quantitative and qualitative methods and is informed by an influential cognitive stylistic model of the characterisation process.

What this chapter also does is demonstrate a different analytical approach to null hypothesis significance testing. In the case of *Tinker Tailor Soldier Spy*, we know from the outset that there are differences between the dialogue and the subtitles. And we know that these differences are the result of decisions made by the subtitler. What we concentrate on in our case study is effect size, in order to determine the scale of such differences. Our case study demonstrates one aspect in particular of corpus stylistic research, namely the application of stylistic frameworks in the qualitative analysis of corpus-derived data.

We begin by outlining the cognitive stylistic model of characterisation that we utilise in our case study. We then discuss the subtitling process in general terms and explain the constraints on subtitling that necessitate modifications being made to the original dialogue. These include reading speed, software restrictions and pragmatic issues. In particular we consider the stylistic effects of any such changes on characterisation. Having done this, we then move on to our case study, explaining first the reasons behind our choice of data before summarising some of the literary critical commentary on character in the TV version of *Tinker Tailor Soldier Spy*. We then explain the process of data preparation and the analytical method we employ to compare subtitles with dialogue. Ultimately, we argue that corpus stylistic analysis is a useful supplement in the design of subtitles, offering as it does a means of evaluating the likely impact of particular subtitling decisions.

6.2 A cognitive stylistic approach to characterisation

The prevailing view within stylistics is that characterisation (the process by which we comprehend and conceptualise characters as we read) is best explained by reference to how we perceive real people. This assumption is at the heart of all cognitive stylistic theories of characterisation (e.g. Culpeper 2001; Schneider 2001; Stockwell and Mahlberg 2015). We will focus here on Culpeper's (2001) model of characterisation, since in our view the nature of its composition makes it particularly open to being used in conjunction with corpus methods. (In fact, Schneider 2001 offers a very similar model, developed independently of

Culpeper's.) We will describe the model first before considering some of the criticisms that have been levelled against it.

Culpeper (2001) argues that characterisation is a result of both top-down and bottom-up processing. Top-down processing in this case refers to the practice of using schematic knowledge to formulate an impression of character. The concept of a schema originates in the work of Bartlett (1932), which was later developed by, among others, Minsky (1975), Schank and Abelson (1977) and Rumelhart (1984). Essentially, a schema is a structured element of world knowledge, derived from experience and stored initially as episodic memory before being abstracted into semantic memory. Schemas can pertain to places, events, actions and, crucially for characterisation, people (see Eysenck and Keane 2010 for a general summary of schema theory, and Jeffries and McIntyre 2010 for stylistic applications). Culpeper explains that our 'knowledge of real life people is our primary source of knowledge used in understanding characters' (2001: 87) and that, consequently, the schematic information on which we draw to comprehend characters has often been gained through real-life experiences. For example, important social knowledge in the creation of impressions of characters includes (1) the social categories to which people belong, such as their social role and social group (sex, class, age), and (2) the social schemata associated with membership of social categories (Culpeper 2001: 75–9). Though it is true that much characterisation is based on our encounters with real people, it is important to note that not all schemas are based on direct personal experience or on real-life encounters. Indeed, our prior experience of fiction is key to the formulation of schematic knowledge about character types. For example, *Tinker Tailor Soldier Spy* (Le Carré 1974) is, as the title suggests, a spy novel. Anyone sitting down to read the novel for the first time will be aware of this and, as a consequence of the back cover blurb, will know that the central character, Smiley, is himself a spy. Most readers, then, will draw on their existing schema for a spy as they begin to read, in order to formulate an impression of the character of Smiley. However, as most readers are unlikely to have had personal encounters with spies, these schemas will most likely have been developed as a consequence of reading books and watching films. Depending on what this fictional experience has been, a reader's schema for a spy may constitute anything from the chauvinistic alpha male of Ian Fleming's James Bond stories to the down-at-heel deadbeat protagonist of Le Carré's *The Spy Who Came in from the Cold* (1963). The reader who expects a spy in the mould of Bond, however, will quickly realise that Smiley's character is entirely at odds with that of Fleming's suave secret agent. At this point, the reader's schema for a spy will need to be adapted ('tuned', in Rumelhart and Norman's 1976 term). This tuning happens as a result of bottom-up processing.

Bottom-up processing refers to the procedure of taking information about character from linguistic cues in the text itself. These cues may come from the author or the character and, in the case of the latter, may be explicit or implicit. Authorial cues are found most obviously in character names (and, in the case of scripts, in stage/screen directions that describe characters). For example, we might observe an aptronymic element to the surname *Bland* (Roy Bland is one of Smiley's ex-colleagues in *Tinker Tailor Soldier Spy*). Conversely, we might note that the surname *Smiley* is at odds with Smiley's quiet and studious character, and that consequently there is a degree of irony attached to the name which functions as a further characterising device.

Character cues, on the other hand, are linguistic triggers of characterisation that appear to come from the characters themselves. Such characterisation information may be explicit and self-directed, as when a character explains something intrinsic to their personality in a direct fashion. Alternatively, it may be explicit and directed at other characters, as when Smiley mutters to himself of one of his compatriots, 'Roddy's such a windbag' (Le Carré 1974: 24). Of course, as Culpeper notes, 'the validity of presentation may be affected by strategic considerations' (2001: 168). That is to say, characters might have ulterior motives for saying what they say about themselves or other characters in certain situations, and this might well lead the reader to interpret such cues with a degree of scepticism or even to discount them altogether. Culpeper explains, though, that in the case of other-presentation, we have a tendency to 'underestimate the impact of contextual factors' (2001: 171), preferring to take at face value what is said about others. This is known as the fundamental attribution error (Ross 1977, cited in Culpeper 2001: 171). ⟶ Sirius Black

Unlike explicit cues, implicit characterisation triggers convey character information by a combination of association, connotation and implicature. Culpeper (2001) provides the following list of linguistic, paralinguistic and non-linguistic features which can serve as characterising devices:

- conversational structure
- conversational implicature
- (im)politeness
- lexis (e.g. Germanic vs Latinate; lexical richness; surge features; social markers; keywords)
- syntactic features

- accent and dialect
- verse and prose
- paralinguistic features
- visual features (kinesics, appearance)
- context.

Conversational structure takes into account phenomena such as turn-taking, the distribution of turns in a conversation, and topic control, and can be indicative of power and status. Conversational implicature (Grice 1975) refers to the conveying of implied meaning by flouts of the maxims of quality, quantity, relation and manner. A character who constantly flouts the maxim of manner may, for instance, be seen as pompous and self-important, in contrast to characters who observe this maxim (though there is no straightforward fit between breaking conversational maxims and particular characterising effects; rather, such effects arise as a consequence of a complex interplay of behaviours). How characters deal with face-threatening acts (Brown and Levinson 1987) through linguistic (im)politeness can also have clear ramifications for characterisation.

Features of accent and dialect may be conveyed through voice quality in performance or orthography in the case of texts, with consequent importance for the portrayal of particular identities. The same is true of verse and prose (consider, for example, how verse is often associated with upper-class characters in Shakespearean drama, while prose is spoken by the lower-class characters). Paralinguistic elements, such as non-fluency features, loudness and voice quality (which can be indicated textually via stage directions, for example), can lead to impressions about emotional states and personality, as can visual features. And context shapes the particular impression of a character that may be gained from the manipulation of any or all of the above features.

Of the above list of characterising features, perhaps the most applicable to a corpus study is lexis. The characterising effects of lexical choice arise from a range of sources, including etymology (e.g. whether a word-form is Germanic or Latinate, the latter perhaps seen as more complex and therefore evocative of a particular educational level), lexical richness (which can be indicated by, for example, type-token ratio), and terms of address (which can be indicative of power and status). Also considered by Culpeper are lexical items that relate to emotions, feelings and moods (and that are indicators of what Culpeper terms personal affect). These are what Taavitsainen (1999: 219–20) calls 'surge features', which she glosses as 'outbursts of emotions'. These include 'exclamations, swearing, and pragmatic particles' (Taavitsainen 1999:

219–20). Exclamations might signal emotions such as regret, disdain or surprise, while swearing may signal anger or frustration. Pragmatic particles (also known as pragmatic markers, discourse markers, or implicit modifiers) include such word-forms as *well, why* and *what* (Culpeper 2001: 192) and may express, for example, surprise or indignation.

Culpeper's (2001) model of the characterisation process suggests that it is a cyclical combination of top-down and bottom-up processing. Schematic knowledge and textual cues (drawn from both the surface structure of the text and the textbase, i.e. the text's propositional content) are combined to form a situation model, in which is located our impressions of character. This is a necessarily brief summary of the model; see McIntyre (2014) for a more detailed outline, and Culpeper and McIntyre (2010) and McIntyre and Culpeper (2010) for stylistic applications of it.

While Culpeper's model of characterisation has been influential within stylistics, it has not been without its critics. Stockwell and Mahlberg (2015: 131), for example, note that it idealises the reading process by presuming some kind of model reader. We would argue against this view on the grounds that the cyclical nature of the model is such that it is adaptable to a broad range of readers and reading experiences. Nonetheless, we would agree with Stockwell and Mahlberg's (2015: 131) point that the top-down element of the model suffers from the same problems associated with schema theory itself, including definitional vagueness and a lack of empirical evidence to support the concept as it currently stands (see Sadoski et al. 1991 for a summary of these issues). Additionally, we have ourselves noted elsewhere (McIntyre 2014) that Culpeper's (2001) distinction between authorial and character cues skews the model towards a humanising approach to characterisation, despite the fact that Culpeper's intention is to avoid the worst excesses of both the humanising and de-humanising approaches to character (Culpeper 2001: 9). Despite these problems, the value of the model for our purposes is that the list of textual indicators of characterisation essentially works as a checklist of characterising devices. We explain how this is useful to the study of characterisation via subtitles in the next section.

6.3 Constraints on subtitles

In recent years, intralingual subtitling for the deaf and hard of hearing has increased exponentially (Díaz-Cintas and Remael 2007: 15). Subtitles for the deaf and hard of hearing (SDH), or closed captions as they are also known, are now particularly common in the television industry. This increase in popularity is in many cases the result of legislative requirements. In the UK, for example, the BBC is required to subtitle 100 per cent of its programme content, with other commercial channels having only a slightly lower target (90 per cent for ITV1 and Channel 4, and 80 per cent for Five; Ofcom 2015: 11).

One of the difficulties with subtitles of all kinds (i.e. intralingual and interlingual) is that in translating from one medium into another (i.e. from speech into writing), certain elements of the original dialogue inevitably have to be altered. The restrictions of the written form, not to mention technical limitations, thus have the potential to affect both pragmatic and semantic meaning as speech is rendered into subtitles. Pérez-González summarises the difficulties associated with what is, in effect, multimodal translation:

> Commercial subtitling conventions do not allow mediators to spatialize, localize or give depth to diegetic voice. Speech is subtitled uniformly throughout a whole film or television drama, with translators making no attempt to recreate in their subtitles the occasional changes in the volume of utterances or in the physical distance between the speaking character and fellow diegetic characters or viewers – as realized through the use of close-up or long shots. Although '[s]ound-based prosodic features such as variations in tone of voice, pitch (intonation), loudness (stress), rhythm and speed, will modulate words and in certain cases even change their meaning to degrees that might imply irony and contradiction' (Neves 2005: 221), they are routinely ignored by commercial subtitlers, on the grounds that viewers have direct access to the relevant prosodic features in the original soundtrack (Díaz-Cintas and Remael 2007). By contrast, when subtitling for Deaf [sic] viewers, mediating these para-verbal means of speech is crucial. The semiotic contribution of prosodic features, conveyed exclusively along the acoustic channel, must then be acknowledged through the insertion of bracketed annotations in the subtitles – which amounts to an inter-modal transfer of acoustic information into visual cues assisting Deaf [sic] viewers to successfully interpret audiovisual texts. (Pérez-González 2014: 202–3)

While some advances have been made in the area of creative subtitling (McClarty 2014), it is indeed the case that most subtitlers disregard the multimodal elements of communication. Undoubtedly, the key reasons for this are the time pressures that subtitlers work under and the limited financial remuneration they receive. As Pérez-González (2014) points out, though, the problem of multimodal translation is particularly acute in SDH, where it is not only the dialogue that has to be subtitled but other meaningful acoustic features too, including sound effects. Aside from the linguistic difficulties associated with this task, what exacerbates these problems is a series of practical issues that act as constraints on what can feasibly be handled in a subtitle. In essence, these are spatial restrictions and temporal restrictions.

While spatial restrictions were originally a consequence of software limitations, nowadays most subtitling software allows for subtitles of any length and font size (notwithstanding practical constraints such as screen width). Spatial restrictions, then, are no longer primarily a consequence of technical constraints but are instead tied closely to temporal restrictions. Here, the primary issue is reading speed. The average for adults is generally taken to be somewhere between 150 and 180 words per minute (wpm; Wallot et al. 2014 report an average of 174.3 wpm with a standard deviation of 34.3 for silent reading). According to de Linde and Kay (1999: 11), this is approximately 66 per cent of the average speaking speed, meaning that each subtitle must be reduced by around one third compared with its counterpart dialogue. In practice, it is difficult to determine a precise number of characters per line for subtitles since, as Díaz-Cintas and Remael (2007: 23–4) point out, some letters take up more space on a line than others (compare, for instance, *l* and *w*). Nonetheless, taking into account reading speed, common practice in subtitling is to use around 35–40 characters per line. These spatio-temporal constraints necessitate some reduction in the original dialogue, especially in the case of SDH where it is also necessary to incorporate non-linguistic elements of sound. The question, then, is what elements of the original dialogue can be dispensed with.

Advice in the literature on audiovisual translation is relatively sparse, and that which does exist is often not supported by empirical evidence, as Díaz-Cintas and Remael (2007: 149) admit (see McIntyre and Lugea 2015 for a critique of such advice). What has been observed in numerous studies, however, is that linguistic elements that convey what Halliday and Matthiessen (2004) term ideational meaning have a tendency to be preserved at the expense of those linguistic features which convey interpersonal and textual meaning (de Linde 1995; Gottlieb 1992). The problem here is that it is interpersonal meaning that is often key to character development, and if these elements of dialogue are deleted, then their associated characterising effects are likely to be lost. This is a problem that has not received a great deal of attention in the literature on subtitling. Indicative of this is the fact that Pérez-González's (2014: 202–3) lengthy critique of the failings of commercial subtitling makes no mention of the issue of translating stylistic features of dialogue into corresponding subtitles. Luyken (1991), however, is clear that methodological techniques from linguistics are needed in order to assess the effects on plot and characterisation of cuts in the dialogue.

Perhaps in response to this, in recent years the use of corpora in audiovisual translation studies has become more popular. Nonetheless, such corpus linguistic studies have tended to be focused primarily on interlingual translation (e.g. Balirano 2013; Freddi 2013; Calzada Pérez 2018), with particular attention paid to dubbed dialogue rather than subtitling. Where subtitle corpora have been constructed, this is often in pursuit of the development of training data for machine translation (e.g. Bywood et al. 2013). Corpus studies that aim to tackle primarily stylistic issues in intralingual subtitling are rare. It is this lack that is the impetus for the case study in the next section.

6.4 Case study: subtitling and characterisation in *Tinker Tailor Soldier Spy*

Tinker Tailor Soldier Spy began life as a novel by the British author John Le Carré. Published in 1974, the book was critically acclaimed (see, for example, the review by Locke 1974), leading in 1979 to a seven-part BBC television adaptation by the well-known British screenwriter, Arthur Hopcraft. Our analysis is of the dialogue from Hopcraft's scripts and the associated subtitles found on the DVD of the BBC series (*Tinker Tailor Soldier Spy* 2003). Our choice of this series as an object of study stems in part from its critical acclaim, specifically the recognition by critics of the importance of character to the drama. Given that characterisation has been acknowledged as a significant element of the success of the series, we wanted to see to what extent characterisation triggers were also present in the subtitles. Our analysis focuses in particular on the central character, the retired spymaster George Smiley. We begin with a plot synopsis and summary of Smiley as a character. We then consider critical commentary on the performance of Alec Guinness, the celebrated British actor who portrayed Smiley in the BBC series. Following this, we explain how we created corpora of dialogue and subtitles, before going on to demonstrate what a corpus stylistic analysis reveals about differences in characterisation between the two datasets. Finally, we consider what our case study suggests about the potential for integrating cognitive and corpus stylistics.

6.4.1 Plot, character and critical plaudits

The British secret service, known informally as 'the Circus', has a Russian mole – a double agent – right at the heart of its operations. The head of the Circus (known as Control) is sure of this but does not know who the mole is. However, he has narrowed his search down to five suspects: Percy Alleline, Bill Haydon, Roy Bland, Toby Esterhase and George Smiley. Control gives these suspects the codenames Tinker, Tailor, Soldier, Poorman and Beggarman respectively. Control believes that Stevcek, a Czech artillery general (codename Testify), is ready to reveal the identity of the mole (codename Gerald). Consequently, he dispatches his most trusted operative, Jim Prideaux, to Czechoslovakia to meet Stevcek. However, the meeting is a trap and Prideaux is shot and captured by the Russians. Within a few months of the operation, Control is dead from natural causes, having been forcibly retired; Smiley and others have also been 'retired', and Percy Alleline is the new head of the service.

At this point, Ricki Tarr, a British agent thought by the service to have vanished, makes contact with his handler, Peter Guillam, a protégé of Smiley's. Tarr claims to have evidence of a double agent currently operating within the Circus. Guillam informs Oliver Lacon, government under-secretary with responsibility for intelligence, of Tarr's claim. Lacon, who had previously dismissed Control's fear of a mole, now comes to believe that Control was right all along. Smiley, having retired, is now above suspicion, and so Lacon tasks him with identifying the double agent. Smiley carries out his operation in secret and after a painstaking investigation is finally able to uncover the identity of the mole.

Like its source novel, the 1979 BBC adaptation of *Tinker Tailor Soldier Spy* attracted considerable acclaim. It was nominated for ten BAFTA (British Academy of Film and Television Arts) awards, winning two.[1] One of these was for Alec Guinness, who was awarded the 1980 Best Actor BAFTA for his role as George Smiley. Guinness's performance is widely acknowledged to be a masterclass in screen acting. Denby (2012), for example, notes that '[h]is performance is one of the great literary-cinematic creations of the post-war era, an actor's masterpiece', while Le Carré himself said, 'we could not have had a better Smiley'.[2] What Denby and other critics have pointed to in particular is Guinness's capacity for conveying the defining characteristics of Smiley. Commenting on this, Denby says:

> Guinness's Smiley is circumspect yet fearless. As Guinness plays him, shading his rounded, musical baritone into infinite tonal

varieties, Smiley is bland and quizzical, except when he has to be direct and masterful; silent, except when he absolutely needs to speak; vague about what he believes, except when he's roused by some expression of cynicism to defend patriotism and loyalty. (Denby 2012)

Further summarising Guinness's portrayal of Smiley's character, Denby explains that '[h]e seems the ultimate in equanimity, purpose, and effectiveness [...] He's so mild and polite – never getting excited, never rushing – that it takes even us, his intimates, quite a while to realize how driving and single-minded he is' (Denby 2012). In our analysis in section 6.4.3, we explore the extent to which these characteristics are realised linguistically in both the dialogue and the subtitles.

6.4.2 Data preparation

Our data comprises the seven episodes of the original BBC series of *Tinker Tailor Soldier Spy* in DVD format. To convert these into a corpus we first extracted the subtitles from the DVDs using the freeware package SubRip.[3] We then converted the subtitles into .txt files. Next, we compared the subtitles with the actual dialogue, by closely watching each of the seven episodes and manually recording the differences (in .doc files) between the subtitles and the words spoken by the actors. We created three files for each episode: file #1 was a .txt file containing the ripped subtitles; file #2 was a .doc file recording the additions and deletions using Word formatting; and file #3 was a .txt file containing the final version of the dialogue.

In addition to analysing the dialogue and subtitles for the whole series, we also wanted to be able to examine Smiley's dialogue in particular. To extract this from the files we had prepared, we inserted mark-up to indicate character identity into both the subtitle and dialogue files, as in the example in Figure 6.1.

We consulted the original scripts for the series in order to speed up the process of identifying Smiley's lines of dialogue.[4] Figure 6.2 shows a page from the original script. It will be clear from the formatting, the handwritten additions, and the poor type quality why ripping the subtitles and revising these to reconstruct the spoken dialogue was a preferable option to OCR-scanning.

<Smiley> I'll slip out that way, if you don't mind. </Smiley>

Figure 6.1 Example mark-up of character names in the subtitle and dialogue files for *Tinker Tailor Soldier Spy*

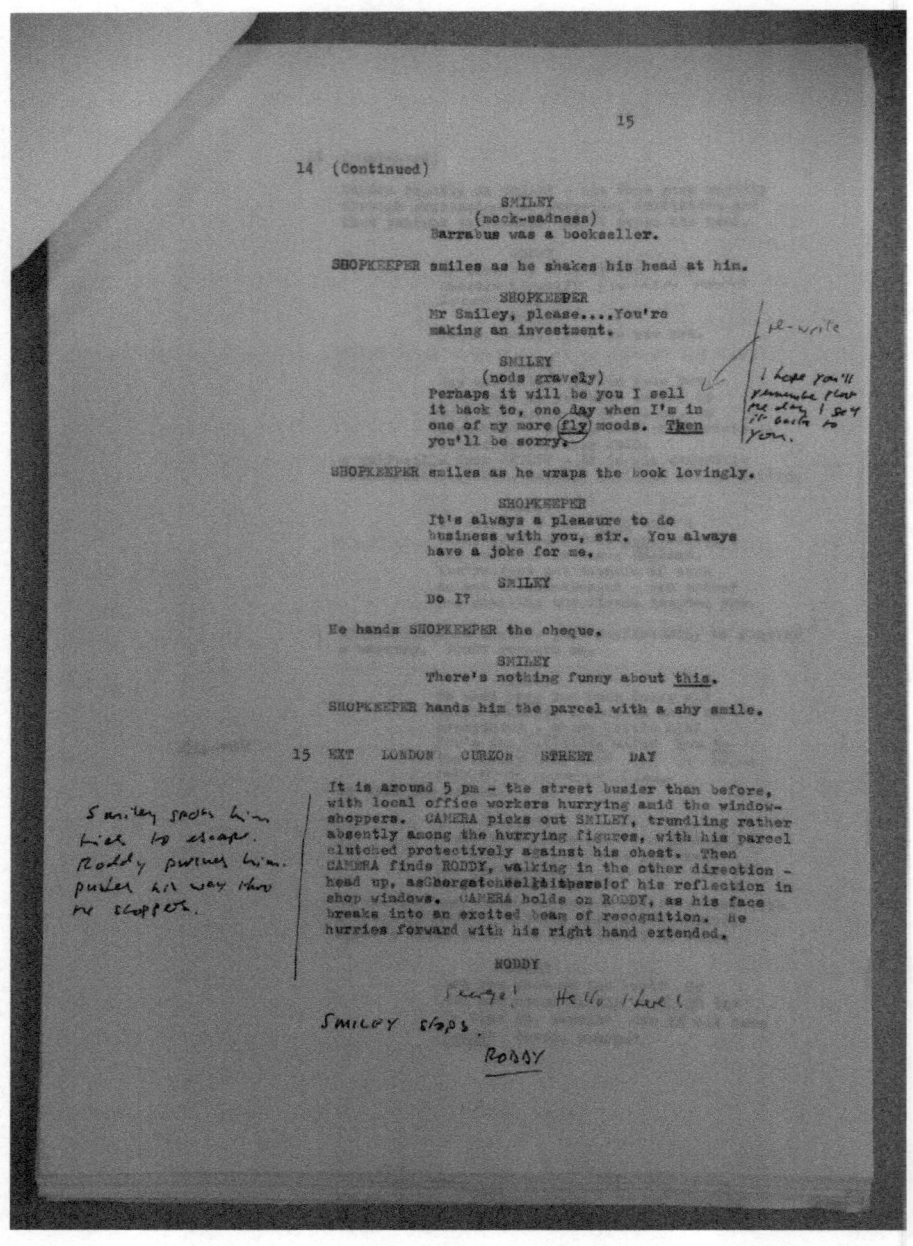

Figure 6.2 Page from Arthur Hopcraft's draft script for *Tinker Tailor Soldier Spy*

Having inserted character mark-up, we then used Multilingual Corpus Toolkit (Piao et al. 2002), a freeware package for corpus analysis, to extract Smiley's dialogue into a separate .txt file, from which we then removed the mark-up (see Box 6.1).

Ultimately, we produced four corpora in total:

1. TTSS-Di (original dialogue for the whole series).
2. TTSS-Sub (subtitles for the whole series).
3. TTSS-Di-Smiley (original dialogue for Smiley).
4. TTSS-Sub-Smiley (subtitles for Smiley).

We then used Wmatrix to analyse the corpora, paying particularly attention to those features that are present in the dialogue but absent from the subtitles.

Box 6.1 Using Multilingual Corpus Toolkit to manipulate annotated data

Multilingual Corpus Toolkit (MLCT) can be downloaded from <https://sites.google.com/site/scottpiaosite/software/mlct>.   MLCT   provides similar analytical functions to most other off-the-shelf corpus analysis software but in addition offers useful mechanisms for compiling corpora (e.g. web scraping) and for text manipulation (which we used to extract Smiley's dialogue and subtitles from our whole corpora). The software requires some knowledge of regular expressions (see Friedl 2006), which are essentially complex wildcards for defining specific search patterns. While we cannot make our *Tinker Tailor Soldier Spy* corpora publicly available, here are the steps we took to extract Smiley's dialogue from the TTSS-Di corpus as a whole.

1. Open MLCT and upload the TTSS-Di corpus by clicking **File** and **Open in Left Window**.

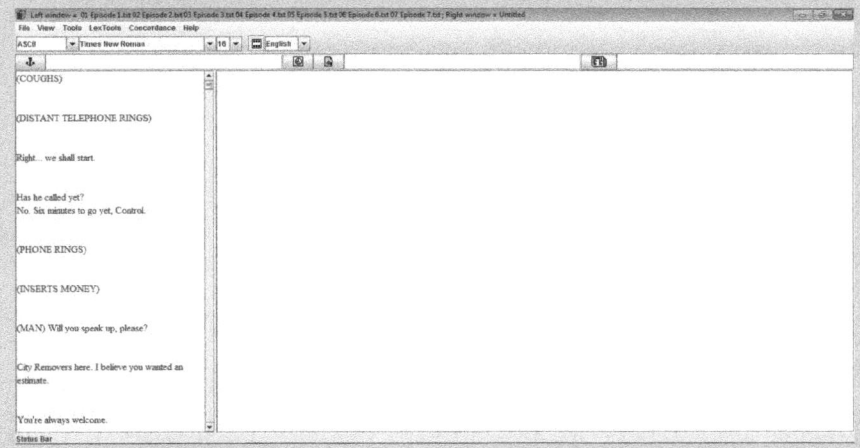

2. Insert <Smiley>.*?</Smiley> into the search bar above the left window. The characters between the tags constitute a regular expression that

essentially tells MLCT to extract every character that occurs between the angle bracket mark-up.

3. Click the anchor icon to the left of the search bar. MLCT will extract all the text between the predetermined tags to the right window, from which they can be copied and saved as a separate .txt file.

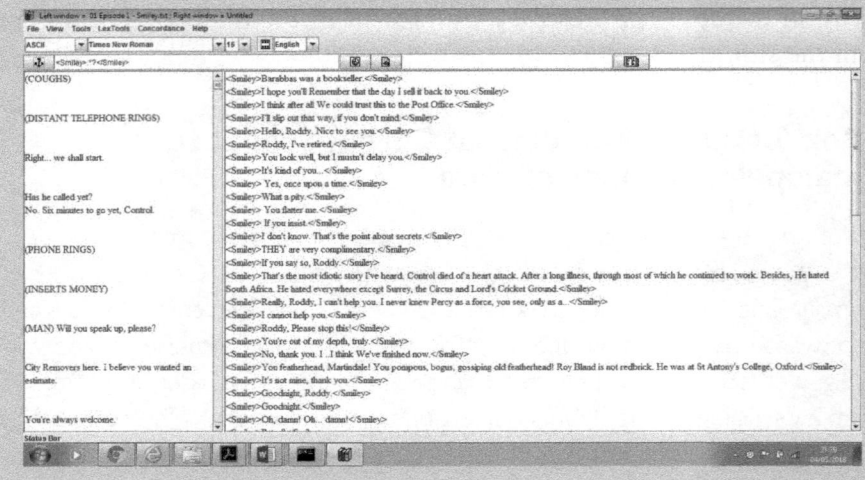

6.4.3 Quantitative and qualitative corpus stylistic analysis

The first stage of our analysis was to work out how much difference there is between the subtitles and the actual dialogue. Using Microsoft Word, we counted the number of alphanumeric characters in the corpus containing just the subtitles (TTSS-Sub), and in the corpus containing the actual dialogue (TTSS-Di). Comparisons at the character level (rather than the word level) were made between these two corpora. We opted to count characters in order to account for all the changes we made. That is to say that counting characters captures changes in situations where, for example, the subtitles show a character saying *Czech*, but the character actually says *Czechoslovakian*. If word counts were used, this sort of difference would not be captured. Furthermore, changes to

Table 6.1 Character counts for subtitles and actual dialogue in *Tinker Tailor Soldier Spy*

	Part 1	Part 2	Part 3	Part 4	Part 5	Part 6	Part 7
Subtitles	14,368	16,487	17,910	14,548	14,406	14,004	12,291
Actual dialogue	15,502	17,974	18,987	15,728	15,424	14,841	12,504
Difference	1,134	1,487	1,077	1,180	1,018	837	213
% change	7.89	9.02	6.01	8.11	7.07	5.98	1.73

punctuation are also captured using character counts. Table 6.1 shows the numbers of characters in the subtitle files, and the numbers of characters in the files containing the actual dialogue. It also shows the difference in character counts between the two files.

As per the constraints on subtitling discussed in section 6.3, it is no surprise that the character counts for dialogue are higher than those for subtitles. It is also fairly clear from the figures in Table 6.1 that Part 7 of the drama is unusual when compared with the other episodes because there are very few differences between the subtitles and the actual dialogue. Possible reasons for this include the fact that this episode has substantially less dialogue than the others.

The character counts make clear that there is, as expected, a difference between the dialogue and subtitle corpora. Our next step was to carry out a keyness analysis to ascertain which lexical items were being used less in Smiley's subtitles than in his actual dialogue. To do this we used Wmatrix to compare the subtitle file against the dialogue file and generate a list of negative keywords. However, contrary to the conventional way of using a keyness list, here we are not primarily concerned with log-likelihood values. The reasons for this are (1) the number of items for comparison is very small and therefore a log-likelihood test is potentially unreliable, and (2) we are chiefly concerned with the interpretative significance of characterising cues. That is, what we wanted to know at this stage was whether those lexical features in the dialogue corpus deemed by Culpeper (2001) to have a characterising function are present or absent in the subtitle corpus. In order to limit the amount of data for analysis, we used log ratio to sift our results. We required a frequency in the subtitle corpus of more than 1 and a log ratio (LR) score of 1. This generated two results, shown in Table 6.2.

Figure 6.3 shows a concordance for *oh* in TTSS-Di (the dialogue corpus) while Figure 6.4 shows a concordance for *oh* in TTSS-Sub (the subtitle corpus).

What we can observe from Table 6.2 is that *oh* is used twice as much in the dialogue corpus as it is in the subtitle corpus. The next step is to consider the functional effects of *oh* in order to determine the potential impact of its lower level of use in the subtitles.

Table 6.2 Negative keywords in TTSS-Sub (frequency in subtitle file >1; log ratio >1)

Item	01	%1	02	%2	LL	LR
oh	7	0.11	14	0.22	2.31	−0.99
i_suppose	2	0.03	4	0.06	0.66	−0.99

not mine, thank you. Goodnight, Roddy. Goodnight.	Oh, damn! Oh... damn! Peter? Well, you're not me,
thank you. Goodnight, Roddy. Goodnight. Oh, damn!	Oh... damn! Peter? Well, you're not me, Peter. And
r. Does Lacon have any particular title nowadays?	Oh, I think I manage very well, thank you. Yes,
I do. And you? All goes well with you?	Oh, very good. Very bonny, thank you. Of course I
and, Toby Esterhase. Three of them. And Alleline.	Oh I quite understand your dilemma. With Bill Hayd
of people who've been cleared in that way?	Oh, Are you off? You won't forget Prideaux, will
Got all you need? Yes. Well, why not, Peter?	Oh, yes. I told you he'd been clever. A
? And That's why they sacked you? For fibbing?	Oh, I couldn't convince them I wasn't involved.
he say how he came by it? Anything else?	Oh Come on, Jim, I'm not going to weaken
Esterhase. It wasn't. Thank you, Jerry. But good.	oh Come on, Jerry, out with it. Did Toby say
senior men walks in. We'll call him Gerald.	oh It's just a name. Gerald says, ?Percy, I'
month into a Swiss bank, according to the file.	Oh Yes, Toby, this is official. There came the day
magic circle. There are two of them and Alleline.	Oh, yes. Karla really did bring off the perfect fi
be a matter of a day or two now.	Oh... Why? When? How? What medals? Quite a lot to

Figure 6.3 Concordance of *oh* in TTSS-Di

not mine, thank you. Goodnight, Roddy. Goodnight.	Oh, damn! Oh... damn! Peter? Well, you're not me,
thank you. Goodnight, Roddy. Goodnight. Oh, damn!	Oh... damn! Peter? Well, you're not me, Peter. And
r. Does Lacon have any particular title nowadays?	Oh, I think I manage very well, thank you. Yes,
I do. And you? All goes well with you?	Oh, very good. Very bonny, thank you. Of course I
Got all you need? Yes. Well, why not, Peter?	Oh, yes. I told you he'd been clever. A
magic circle. There are two of them and Alleline.	Oh, yes. Karla really did bring off the perfect fi
be a matter of a day or two now.	Oh... Why? When? How? What medals? Quite a lot to

Figure 6.4 Concordance of *oh* in TTSS-Sub

The first point to note is that *oh* is a discourse marker and therefore constitutes what Culpeper (2001) terms a surge feature. It is, then, a potential characterising element of language. Schiffrin (1987) defines discourse markers as indicating sequentially dependent units of discourse. Fraser explains that 'they signal a relationship between the interpretation of the segment they introduce [...] and the prior segment' and goes on to note that they have 'a core meaning, which is procedural, not conceptual, and their more specific interpretation is "negotiated" by the context, both linguistic and conceptual' (1999: 931). In this respect, discourse markers have an interpersonal metafunction which, as McIntyre and Lugea (2015) point out, makes them potentially significant as characterising devices.

Corpus studies of *oh* have shown it to have a wide range of meanings. For example, Aijmer's (1987) study of the London-Lund Corpus of Spoken British English identifies the following as just some of the functions associated with *oh*:

- To signal surprise.
- To indicate that what the speaker has just heard is new information to them.
- To express disappointment, annoyance and frustration.
- To indicate the speaker's doubt in something they have just heard.

- To introduce a vague or partial answer.
- To indicate that the speaker disputes something they have just heard.
- To acknowledge a correction issued by an interlocutor.
- To indicate that no importance should be attached to the speaker's answer.
- To signal evaluation.
- To signal acceptance.
- To signal endorsement.
- To signal a qualification.
- To convey politeness.

The concordance of *oh* in Figure 6.3 suggests Smiley's use of the discourse marker to fulfil a range of these functions. For example, in response to his colleague Peter Guillam's incredulous question, 'And that's why they sacked you? For fibbing?', Smiley replies, 'Oh, I couldn't convince them I wasn't involved.' The function of *oh* in this example would seem to be to indicate an unwillingness to give a full explanation, that is, to introduce a deliberately vague answer (note how this is consistent with Smiley's status as a spymaster). And in response to a barbed question about whether he is enjoying retirement (from someone instrumental in forcing him out of a job), Smiley says, 'Oh, I think I manage very well, thank you.' The *oh* in this case would seem to be a politeness marker, demonstrating a refusal to be needled by the question.

Despite the value of corpus studies such as Aijmer's (see also Erman 1987; Jucker 1993), they are inherently descriptive in nature. Tests of how listeners actually interpret discourse markers are, as Fox Tree and Schrock (1999) point out, rare. Furthermore, the problem with enumerating the potential functions of discourse markers through corpus studies is that it becomes difficult to determine an underlying pattern to their usage. For this reason, Fox Tree and Schrock (1999) adopt Heritage's (1984) suggestion that what binds the above list of functions together is that *oh* indicates that the communicative exchange is undergoing a change of state. For example, using *oh* to acknowledge a correction made by your interlocutor indicates that you have registered and understood that the situation is in fact different from what they initially suggested. Fox Tree and Schrock (1999) use Heritage's (1984) proposal as a hypothesis which they test through a series of experiments. One such experiment involves playing participants a series of recordings of naturally occurring conversation in which the discourse marker *oh* occurs numerous times. One such example was the following:

> And they started talking about – *oh* he asks her about um her
> having bought a house. (Fox Tree and Schrock 1999: 285)

For each conversation, one of the *oh*s was preselected by the researchers
for study. However, some of the recordings were then edited to remove
the *oh* in question. Prior to hearing a recording, participants were given
a target word to listen out for in the recorded conversation. This was
the first content word appearing after the selected discourse marker
which did not also appear before the *oh*. Participants then listened to
the recording and were asked to press a response button if and when
they heard the target word. The results of the experiment showed that
participants were roughly 62 ms faster at identifying a target word
when it followed a discourse marker than when it didn't. Fox Tree
and Schrock (1999: 288) argue that the results of this and their other
experiments confirm the claims in the literature that the use of *oh*
reduces the capacity for confusion with regard to the following discourse. Additionally, they claim that this faster response time supports
the notion that listeners recognise *oh* as an indicator of a change of state
and therefore listen more carefully to what comes after it.

If we now consider the use of *oh* in the corpus of Smiley's subtitles,
what we can observe is that its absence from some of the subtitles is
potentially problematic. Here, for instance, is an example of how the
omission of *oh* affects the pragmatic effect of Smiley's reply (in the
examples that follow, square brackets indicate omissions in the subtitles while underlining indicates additions):

> (Context: Oliver Lacon is explaining the circumstances that led
> ultimately to Smiley's forced retirement.)

> **Lacon**   My Minister and I felt there had been [gross]
>   incompetence on the part of Control. [We wanted a
>   new broom.] A view which the Foreign Office shared[,
>   to put it mildly].
> **Smiley** [Oh] I quite understand your dilemma.
>   (*Tinker Tailor Soldier Spy*, Episode 2)

In the dialogue, Smiley's *oh* functions to indicate acceptance. In this
respect, it also functions as a politeness marker, since this is a response
to someone who had previously forced Smiley out of his job, therefore
there are plenty of contextual reasons for Smiley not to respond so
politely. Smiley gives the impression of being a rather mild character,
though this outward appearance belies the tenacity that has enabled

him to be so effective as a spymaster. The use of *oh* works to convey Smiley's meek exterior, which is in contrast to his shrewd and persistent actions. Omitting it from the subtitles results in this aspect of his character no longer being conveyed. This is also an example of a case where there are no spatio-temporal constraints that require the line of dialogue to be shortened.

We can see similar effects in the use of *oh* in the other concordance lines in Figure 6.3. Fox Tree and Schrock's (1999) study also points to the fact that *oh* indicates a disjunct between the information that precedes the *oh* and that which comes after it. This again is in accordance with the notion of *oh* as signalling a change of state. In the following example, for instance, Smiley is talking to another ex-colleague, Jerry Westerby.

> **Westerby** You won't forget to give my love to Ann[, will you]? One of the great marriages, always said so.
> **Smiley** [Oh] come on, Jerry, out with it. Did Toby say something about Ann?
> *(Tinker Tailor Soldier Spy*, Episode 5)

Smiley's wife is widely known to have had a series of extramarital affairs, suggesting that Westerby's comment has an implicature of insincerity. Smiley's use of *oh* signals to Westerby that Smiley has changed direction in the conversation and is no longer content to exchange social niceties. Following Fox Tree and Schrock's (1999) findings, without the discourse marker, this meaning would be less likely to be picked up on by Smiley's interlocutor (and possibly, then, by the viewing audience). The same effects can be observed in the lines '[Oh] Come on.[, Jim, I'm not going to weaken] I'll not buckle just because a Russian hood's made a joke about me' and '[Oh] Yes, Toby, this is official.'

Our analysis so far has centred on the interpretative significance of *oh* in Smiley's dialogue, and the likely effects of its omission on audience perceptions of his character. What we have shown is that the omission of *oh* from the subtitles, while seemingly insignificant in propositional terms, is likely to be highly significant in terms of its effect on the conveyance of interpersonal characterisation. There is an additional consideration to be made, though, of the significance of *oh*, and this is its effect on the comprehensibility of Smiley's subtitles to the viewing audience. What Fox Tree and Schrock's (1999) findings also suggest is that the use of *oh* serves to assist hearers in interpreting the discourse in question. What we need also to consider, then, is that omitting *oh* from the subtitles might well make the subtitles harder to interpret than if the discourse marker were included. Given that spatio-temporal constraints on subtitling would still allow for the inclusion of *oh* in most instances, it would seem that a better course of action would be to include it in the subtitles.

The second item identified in Table 6.2 as underused (though not to a statistically significant level) in the subtitle corpus is *I suppose*. Given the cumulative effect of characterisation triggers, we might observe that this example is of lesser significance than *oh*, since it occurs only four times in the dialogue corpus. Omitting two of these instances in the subtitles may not, then, seem particularly important. And given that there are so few instances, we will not consider them here, particularly since *I suppose* is not obviously a characterisation trigger according to Culpeper's checklist of bottom-up cues. However, this does raise the question for corpus stylistic analysis of how to handle low frequency items. It is, of course, important to remember that corpus stylistic analysis is not a purely quantitative pursuit. Statistical significance can point to interpretative significance though there is no necessary correlation between these two elements. Moreover, the results of a corpus search should in most cases be used to motivate a qualitative analysis of a sample of the corpus in question. In the case of low frequency items in particular, it is important to look at their functions in context in order to determine their potential stylistic significance. What we can observe about *I suppose* is that it functions as a hedge and a possible politeness marker. And while the difference in frequency of this utterance between the dialogue and subtitle corpora is small, it points towards the interpretative significance of hedges as characterising devices. To investigate this, we will consider a low frequency item from Episode 1 of *Tinker Tailor Soldier Spy* that has a similar function to *I suppose* but whose log ratio score indicates a larger effect size. A keyness comparison of the dialogue and subtitle files for Episode 1 reveals *think* to be comparatively underused in the latter. As with *oh*, this difference is not statistically significant though there is an associated log ratio value of 1.47, indicating that *think* is used more than twice as often in the dialogue as in the subtitles. Figures 6.5 and 6.6 show the concordances for *think* in both files.

While there are only a few instances of *think* in the dialogue, and even fewer in the subtitles, we cannot assume that this is therefore indicative of a lack of interpretative significance. Certain elements of character may indeed be fleeting as opposed to long-term, but this does not mean that low frequency items are necessarily indicative only of transitory features. Nor does it mean they are unimportant in characterisation terms. To illustrate this, we will now consider the wider context surrounding

h , truly . No , thank you . I ...I	**think**	We 've finished now . You featherhead
tal millionaire . Which He seems to	**think**	explains everything . I 'm so out of
particular title nowadays ? Oh , I	**think**	I manage very well , thank you . Yes
at the day I sell it back to you . I	**think**	after all We could trust this to th
t of my sopping shoes . And , also I	**think**	, make a pot of coffee . Me , Peter
buy a cottage , in the Cotswolds , I	**think.**	Steeple Aston sounds about right

Figure 6.5 Concordance of *think* in TTSS-Di

particular title nowadays ? Oh , I	**think**	I manage very well , thank you.
buy a cottage , in the Cotswolds , I	**think**	. Steeple Aston sounds about right

Figure 6.6 Concordance of *think* in TTSS-Sub

just one of the instances of *think*, providing a qualitative stylistic analysis of the impact on characterisation of omissions in the subtitles. While *think* is not key statistically, it functions as a politeness marker and, as a result, as a potential trigger for characterisation. Furthermore, its use is in the context of a number of other potential characterising devices. We have chosen an extract from Episode 1 because we can assume that, this being the first episode of the drama, it has a particularly important function in conveying the key characteristics of the principal characters. The extract is also the first introduction to Smiley:

> (Context: Smiley is in an antiquarian bookshop, in the process of purchasing a book, when he notices an ex-colleague, Peter Guillam, loitering outside.)

> 1. **Smiley** Barabbas was a bookseller.
> 2. **Bookseller** Mr Smiley, please. You're making an investment.
> 3. **Smiley** [I hope you'll] [r]Remember that <u>when</u> [the day] I sell it back to you.
> 4. **Bookseller** [Always] [a]<u>A</u> pleasure to do business with you, sir. You always have a joke for me.
> 5. **Smiley** [I think after all] [w]<u>W</u>e could trust this to the Post Office.
> 6. **Bookseller** [Yes sir,] I'll send it on.
> 7. **Smiley** I'll slip out that way, if you don't mind.
> 8. **Bookseller** Not at all, sir.

> *(Tinker Tailor Soldier Spy*, Episode 1)

In this scene, the viewer meets Smiley for the first time in what seems to be an antiquarian bookshop, where he is writing a cheque. Turn 1 contains the first words uttered by Smiley in the drama, and even though the extract begins *in medias res* they appear to flout Grice's

(1975) maxim of relation. The implicature generated by the biblical reference to Barabbas (the thief freed instead of Jesus before his crucifixion) is that Smiley thinks the bookseller is a thief, that is, that he is charging too much for the book. This is a face-threatening act (FTA; Brown and Levinson 1987) towards the bookseller's positive face, but is mitigated by the accusation being off-record and made via biblical allusion. Smiley goes on to threaten the bookseller's negative face in turn 3. Here, however, there is a difference between the subtitles and what Smiley actually says. In the subtitles, the FTA is not mitigated but is issued in the form of an imperative. In the dialogue, Smiley mitigates this negative face threat by saying that he *hopes* that the bookseller will remember. In the dialogue, then, Smiley's utterance does not have the speech act force of a command. In turn 5, Smiley asks the bookseller to post the book to him, which is another threat to the bookseller's negative face, albeit relatively minor. In both the subtitles and the dialogue the face threat is mitigated by the request being made off-record. In the dialogue, however, Smiley's use of 'I think' mitigates the threat further by increasing the indirectness of the request. Moreover, 'after all' implies that the bookseller has already offered this service to Smiley, prior to the point at which the scene begins. This implication is lost in the subtitles as a result of the dialogue reduction. What we can observe in this short extract, then, is that Smiley's dialogue presents him as being more polite and attentive to his interlocutor's face than the subtitles do. And as Culpeper (2001: 261) notes, (im)politeness demonstrates the dynamics of the social relationship that exists between characters. This in itself is indicative of character traits. Consequently, the omission of politeness features in subtitles can be deleterious to the viewer's experience of character, even if the omitted linguistic cues are not particularly frequent across the course of the drama.

After slipping out of the back door of the bookshop to avoid Peter Guillam, Smiley is almost immediately noticed and accosted by his old acquaintance, Roddy Martindale. Smiley initially pretends not to notice him. When he does acknowledge his presence, he pretends to be happy to see him. That Smiley is not pleased to see Roddy is shown in his facial expressions and general demeanour: he attempts to hide himself from Roddy by raising his shoulders and burying his chin in his chest. However, this apparent displeasure is not obvious from his greeting.

    1. Smiley   Hello, Roddy. [Nice to see you.]
    2. Roddy   How marvellous to run into you.
(Tinker Tailor Soldier Spy, Episode 1)

'Nice to see you' is not included in the subtitles and, consequently, neither Smiley's continued social politeness nor his disingenuousness is apparent. Smiley's behaviour in this particular scene is thus distorted. This is significant because part of what makes Smiley engaging as a character is the extent to which his mild-mannered linguistic behaviour contrasts with the callous streak that enables him to operate so effectively as a spymaster. Moreover, this contrast is important to the generation of dramatic tension across the series as a whole, therefore its absence from the subtitles has a damaging effect that goes beyond characterisation.

After saying hello, Smiley attempts to take his leave. However, Roddy does not allow this and persuades the reluctant Smiley to go to dinner with him. The scene then changes to a gentlemen's club where Smiley and Roddy have reached the final course of their meal. Throughout this scene, Roddy bombards Smiley with questions about the current state of the secret service they are both no longer a part of. Smiley does not answer most of the questions; indeed, Roddy often provides his own answers. Many of the mismatches between the subtitles and the dialogue lie in what Roddy Martindale says. For the hearing viewer, he is persistent and annoying. However, some of the features that make him annoying (e.g. the tag questions and the repeated use of Smiley's first name) are not present in the subtitles:

(a) Place him in the batting order[, George].
(b) [Of course] [i]It wasn't a secret to you[, was it George?]
(c) but we know his REAL name[, don't we?]
(d) but power sits poorly on those we've grown up with[, doesn't it?]
(e) What's his knack[, George]? Living off the wits of his subordinates[, am I right]?
(f) So who's doing the business for him? [Eh George?]
(g) draws them like bees to a honey pot[, doesn't he, our Bill?]

The tag questions make the over-dinner chat seem even more like an interrogation, and are markers of Roddy's persistence. Some of this persistence is lost in the subtitles. Eventually Smiley implores Roddy to stop:

Smiley [Roddy,] [p]Please stop this!
(*Tinker Tailor Soldier Spy*, Episode 1)

What is apparent in this turn is that even when driven to distraction by Roddy's incessant questioning, Smiley still avoids marked impoliteness by mitigating his face threat with a conventional politeness marker. This, we would argue, is suggestive of a persistent character trait: that of maintaining politeness even when provoked. But because the subtitles fail to communicate the annoying tenacity of Roddy, Smiley's outburst could potentially be interpreted as an over-reaction, thereby further distorting his character. And since this is the only time that Smiley seems to temporarily lose control of his emotions in the whole drama, it is important to convey the cause of this behaviour.

The analysis above also highlights another potential area for investigation: terms of address. While these are not revealed in our keyness analysis, the qualitative analysis which that provoked has shown them to be potentially important in interpretative terms. Culpeper notes that '[t]erms of address, including vocatives and pronouns, can be an important means of signalling social information' since they enable characters to be 'rapidly placed within particular social groups, and their social relations with other characters [...] indicated' (2001: 193). Smiley's superiors (Lacon and Control) and his close colleagues (Peter Guillam, Roy Bland and Bill Haydon) address him as *George*, whereas more junior members of the service (Ricki Tarr and Fawn) address him as *Mr Smiley* or *sir*. Indeed, when Guillam introduces Smiley to Ricki Tarr, he refers to him as *Mr Smiley*, thereby taking account of Tarr's hierarchical position relative to Smiley. Ricki Tarr continues to use this mode of address, perhaps to excess, leading to the impression that he is being sardonic and gently mocking Smiley's authority. This can be seen in the following extract:

> (Context: Ricki Tarr, one of the Circus's 'scalphunters' [Circus terminology for field agents] is holed up in a safe house, having acquired potentially explosive information about the presence of a mole at the very top of the service hierarchy.)

1. Guillam	I think you know Mr Smiley, don't you?
2. Tarr	[Yes] 'Course I do. You once gave me a job[, Mr. Smiley]. [Don't] [y]You remember? Tarr, sir. Ricki Tarr. The lawyer's boy from Marseilles. You changed my first nappies[, as we used to say]. They were very tough interviews you [used to give] gave us tender young recruits. Of course, 12 years ago. It's that long[, Mr Smiley]. You don't look any different to me, sir. No, 12 years ago nobody, but nobody, got taken on unless we got past you. Not even scalphunters, who aren't quite

	your type. We all had to get the nod from Mr Smiley.
3. Guillam	Tarr.
4. Smiley	Of course I remember you. Your father was an Australian, I recall. A solicitor and a Nonconformist lay preacher. Altogether a most unusual chap to pop up in Marseilles. Just such odd circumstances do seem to provide us with ... suitable personnel.
5. Tarr	Bad boys like Ricki. Daddy thought he could beat the sin out of me, but you knew better[, didn't you Mr. Smiley]. He only beat it further in ... and that's what scalphunters are made of. Isn't that right, Mr Guillam?
6. Guillam	We're waiting [for you], Tarr.

(*Tinker Tailor Soldier Spy*, Episode 2)

The importance of vocatives and address terms is that they trigger schematic information about social hierarchies (i.e. they cue top-down processing of character by activating social category schemas). The importance of this to characterisation in *Tinker Tailor Soldier Spy* is that the range of terms by which Smiley is addressed indicates where particular characters fit in relation to Smiley with the social hierarchy of the Circus. In a drama whose plot has considerable complexities, being able to ascertain how characters relate to each other is particularly important. The fact that many of these vocative and address terms are omitted from the subtitles could well mean that hard-of-hearing viewers place Smiley within the social hierarchy of the service less rapidly, thereby missing key information about the social relations that exist within the Circus.

6.5 Conclusion

In this chapter we have argued that corpus stylistics can be used to supplement the cognitive stylistic analysis of character. While our analysis has been of a corpus of TV scripts, the underlying analytical principles are equally applicable to other text-types such as prose fiction (e.g. Mahlberg and McIntyre 2011) and poetry, as well as non-fiction texts (note that the concept of a character is still applicable to non-fiction representations of real people, though sometimes a difference in terminology is used to overcome the association of characters with fictionality; Emmott 1992, for instance, introduces the term *enactor*). In particular, we have aimed to show how corpus stylistic analysis of dialogue and subtitles can shed light on the potential interpretative effects of subtitling decisions. To this end, the case study in this chapter has demonstrated the stylistic impact of particular characterisation triggers, using Culpeper's (2001) cognitive model of characterisation to support a quantitative and qualitative analysis of the seven episodes of *Tinker Tailor Soldier Spy* (BBC 1979). We have shown how the omission of particular linguistic elements from the subtitles has a potentially serious impact on the process of characterisation. By so doing, we have demonstrated the importance to characterisation of the interpersonal metafunction of language, information that we argue has the potential to improve subtitling practice. We should be clear that we are not arguing that all linguistic markers of interpersonal relationships should be retained in subtitles (in some cases, spatio-temporal constraints will mean this is not practical), only that in those cases where such constraints are not in operation, greater consideration should be given to the effects of deleting potential character cues (see McIntyre and Lugea 2015 for a purely qualitative case study examining the effects of subtitling decisions on characterisation, as well as a critique of subtitling guidance that advises on the removal of markers of personal affect).

What the case study in this chapter has also demonstrated is that it is important not to ignore low frequency items in a keyness analysis. As we noted in Chapter 5, statistical significance does not necessarily equate to interpretative significance, and concentrating only on items that are statistically key is likely to mean that some items of interpretative importance will be missed. Our way of dealing with this dilemma in this chapter has been to use a keyness analysis as a means of identifying potentially important items for qualitative analysis, and then to use that qualitative analysis to determine other important items. In this respect, our practice has been one of analytical diffusion, moving from keyness results to a text sample for qualitative analysis, and from there to further text samples and further qualitative analysis. For example, the concordance of *think* led us to the first scene in which Smiley appears, which then highlighted additional characterising devices that were also missing from the subtitles. Our process then was to use Culpeper's (2001) model of characterisation to inform a stylistic analysis of our chosen samples, paying particular attention to those linguistic items in the surface structure of the text identified by Culpeper as having the potential to act as character cues. Additionally, we considered the possibility that the lack of such cues could lead to particular schemas not being activated for the viewer, and the potential effects on the characterisation process that this might then lead to.

What we aim to have shown here is the importance of qualitative stylistic analysis to the corpus stylistics enterprise. An over-reliance on numerical data at the expense of qualitative insight will only ever result in an impoverished analysis. Corpus stylistics at its optimum should be a blend of quantitative and qualitative analysis, informed by stylistic theories, models and frameworks, and guided by Spitzerian principles (see Chapter 4). In the next chapter we illustrate this further through an exploration of the concept of historical corpus stylistics.

Notes

1. See <http://awards.bafta.org/keyword-search?keywords=Tinker+Ta ilor+Soldier+Spy+> (last accessed 20 August 2018).
2. Letter from David Cornwell (a.k.a. John Le Carré) to Arthur Hopcraft, 31 July 1979 (AHP/1/18, Arthur Hopcraft Papers, University of Salford Archives and Special Collections).
3. See <https://sourceforge.net/projects/subrip/> (last accessed 20 August 2018).
4. The original BBC scripts can be found in the Arthur Hopcraft Papers (AHP/1/18), part of the University of Salford's Archives and Special Collections. Included are Hopcraft's original drafts, rehearsal and shooting scripts, and ephemera concerning critical reaction to the series.

7

Pedagogical corpus stylistics

7.1 Introduction

In this chapter we turn our attention to what has become known as pedagogical stylistics (Burke 2010; Clark and Zyngier 2003), which involves the application of stylistic techniques in teaching generally, but in particular in second language English language teaching. McIntyre (2011, 2012) differentiates between pedagogical stylistics and the pedagogy of stylistics, where the latter investigates best practices for teaching stylistics (see, for example, Alderson and McIntyre 2006; Bellard-Thomson 2010; Crisp 2006; McIntyre 2003; Plummer and Busse 2006; Poole 2006; Short 2006), though in this chapter our focus is on the former. Drawing on research into first language (L1) and second language (L2) or foreign language (FL) teaching contexts, we consider what stylistics can offer pedagogically to both students and teachers, before going on to examine how corpus techniques can be used in corpus-based language teaching activities. We also consider the teaching of English stylistics in countries where English is not a first language, which is something that is not addressed as often as it ought to be by stylisticians, especially considering the popularity of stylistics outside the UK (see Shen 2012 and Teranishi et al. 2012 for discussions of Chinese and Japanese contexts respectively). We conclude the chapter with an illustrative case study investigating how a corpus-informed stylistic analysis of Adrian Henri's poem 'Tonight at Noon' can be used to explore language norms in Standard English. The case study suggests how corpus linguistic methods used for language teaching and stylistics can be combined in a pedagogical corpus stylistic approach.

7.2 Stylistics in the L2/FL classroom

According to Clark and Zyngier (2003), the roots of pedagogical stylistics can be traced back to the language teaching classrooms of the 1950s, where stylistic methods were applied in particular to the teaching of literature to ESL/EFL language students.[1] They go on to say that stylistics is used extensively in the language teaching context, and state that 'the principal aim of stylistics in the classroom is to sensitize students to language use within the texts chosen for study' (Clark and Zyngier 2003: 241). They explain that while there is an assumption that this can lead to an improvement in certain language skills, any improvements are a 'by-product' and not 'the main aim or reason for teaching stylistics' (Clark and Zyngier 2003: 241). According to Clark and Zyngier's view, therefore, stylistics is a tool to raise language awareness in L2 students and aid engagement with difficult texts, but not by or in itself a tool for facilitating language acquisition. However, without the assumption of the 'by-product' of increased language proficiency, the benefits of stylistics in L2 teaching become doubtful. This point is taken up by Hall who questions 'whether awareness raising stylistic activities [...] can be shown to translate into enhanced ability for learners', arguing that even where benefits can be identified, there is 'little empirical evidence that they result from stylistic approaches' (2007: 4–5). Similarly, Paran states that 'the usefulness of stylistics [for pedagogical purposes] has still to be demonstrated', adding that 'what we now need is research that will back up the intuitive endorsement of these techniques for language learning' (2008: 487). Fogal's (2015) review of publications that concern pedagogical stylistics found that, since 1997, just 13 reported findings concerning 'stylistics as a language learning tool in L2 contexts based on some form of observation' (2015: 58). Fogal concludes from his review that pedagogical stylistics is lacking 'a more rigorous research agenda aimed at demonstrating via verifiable conclusions the benefits of stylistics in classroom-based L2 learning contexts' (2015: 67). Fogal points out, however, that some studies do hint at 'the potential usefulness of stylistics for developing L2 linguistic competency' (2015: 62; he cites, for example, Paesani 2006; Timucin 2001; Yañez Prieto 2010), while others demonstrate that 'using stylistics in L2 contexts encouraged learning that went beyond L2 acquisition, such as analytical skills' (as exemplars, Fogal cites Al-Jarf 2007; Badran 2012; Saugera 2011; Warner 2012). Regardless of these glimmers of empirical support for using stylistics in language teaching, Paran, in an extensive review of existing research on using literature in the language teaching classroom, suggests that stylisticians need to 'engage less in conversation among themselves, and more with language teachers' (2008: 487). This comment fails to acknowledge, however, that many stylisticians are themselves language teachers and are actively engaged in language teaching in the classroom, and use stylistics as part of that enterprise. For example, based on her own language teaching experiences, Zerkowitz notes that pedagogical stylistics provides 'a practical way of bridging meaning and form' (2012: 208) and offers a framework for the systematic study of texts. Furthermore, Teranishi et al., in their report on the importance of stylistics in Japan, both in L1 and L2 contexts, note that stylistics has an 'undeniable' effect on learners' reading skills, and 'makes English texts accessible to Japanese readers' (2012: 232). Shen (2012: 100) also reports the extensive use of stylistics in a language teaching context in China, particularly in intensive reading courses which focus on close reading of texts. Shen notes that stylistics helps students to understand the effects of language choices, and can be beneficial in improving listening awareness and the ability to process pragmatic information.

Pedagogical stylistics is often discussed in connection with the practice of using literary texts (i.e. prose fiction, poetry and plays) in the L2 classroom (see, for example, Hall 2005, 2007). Using literary texts allows students to interact with authentic texts, where authentic is taken to mean examples of language produced for/by L1 speakers (Breen 1985; Tomlinson 2001: 67; Harmer 2001: 204–5).[2] The use of authentic texts requires great care since language learners can easily become demotivated if presented with texts that are beyond their capabilities (Harmer 2001: 205). While this is a particular danger with literary texts, since their inherent creativity might easily pose too much of a challenge to L2 learners, their use is 'often advocated as a means to enhance proficiency in reading, vocabulary growth and cultural knowledge' (Hall 2007: 4). Indeed, numerous language teaching practitioners have stressed the importance of literary texts in language teaching (see, for example, Teranishi et al. 2012). On this matter, though, Edmondson, in his often cited assessment and discussion of the use of literary texts in language learning, dismisses their use on the grounds that arguments in support of literary texts 'are either false, dishonest, invalid, or they merely establish that literary texts can be used as can other types of text' (1997: 52–3). Edmondson therefore concludes that 'there are no valid arguments whatever for the special status of literature', and that the 'educational rationale' for using literary texts in language teaching is merely 'tied up with an historical tradition' (1997: 53). While we tend to agree that no one genre should necessarily have 'special status' in language teaching, and that other genres might be equally as useful, in his review of the use of literature in language teaching, Paran notes that 'principled evidence is emerging showing the benefits of using literature' (2008: 489). However, empirical evidence as to the impact on L2 acquisition of using literary texts is still thin on the ground and, as Paran (2008) points out, more research is needed that focuses on particular aspects of using literary texts to improve L2 language skills, including the role of the teacher, the type and aim of the task, and the role of the student.

Pedagogical stylistics, therefore, seems to have rather an uncertain status and track record of empirical success. Nevertheless, as we have noted, there are numerous stylisticians operating in language teaching environments for whom stylistics is part of their language teaching repertoire. And, there is continued developing interest and research in this sub-category of stylistics (see, for example, Viana and Zyngier 2017). Stylistics by its nature pays close attention to linguistic forms and their function. The benefits of such activities would, as Hall notes, 'seem self-evident' (2007: 5). This is especially true if we see stylistics fitting in to established teaching methods and frameworks. For example, stylistics can be seen as a way of operationalising inductive approaches to language learning such as consciousness raising/developing language awareness, which is defined by Rutherford and Sharwood Smith as the 'deliberate attempt to draw the learner's attention to the formal properties of the target language' (1985: 274, cited in Johnson 2008: 251), something that stylistics seems eminently suitable for. Another possibility is that stylistic analysis can be part of a Task Based Teaching/Learning (TBT/L) approach, which was first introduced in the 1970s by Prabhu (Johnson 2008: 181) and has undergone several reworkings (see, for example, Willis 1996). Within such an approach stylistic analysis becomes part of a task cycle that specifically aims to improve a particular aspect of learner language competence. In our case study in this chapter, we present ideas for incorporating stylistics into consciousness-raising exercises using a number of tasks which utilise a highly linguistically deviant poem. Our case study guides students and teachers through a corpus-informed analysis of the poem, thereby taking a corpus stylistic approach to a learning task. Before that, though, we assess the uses of corpora and corpus linguistics in the language teaching classroom.

7.3 Using corpora in the classroom

It is widely recognised that corpus linguistics has had an important impact on English language teaching (ELT) (see Aarts and Smith-Dennis

2018 for further discussion). Corpora are being used increasingly in language teaching classrooms (Warren 2016), either indirectly (Leech 1997), via corpus-derived dictionaries and learning materials such as the Collin *COBUILD* series, or directly (Leech 1997) through the 'hands-on' use of corpora by students and teachers. It is the latter approach that we will focus on for the rest of this section.

A key approach in the direct, classroom usage of corpora is what is usually referred to as data-driven learning (DDL), which stems from the ground-breaking work of Tim Johns (see, for example, Johns 1991, 1994). DDL is where students use corpus outputs, such as concordance lines, provided by corpus tools or web-based interfaces, to interact with corpora. The corpus data might be in the form of paper hand-outs (Johns 1991) or now, more usually, accessed using corpus tools and web interfaces. The general idea with DDL is that students interact with real examples of language to make discoveries or answer questions about language. Johns summarises the approach thus:

> What distinguishes the DDL approach is the attempt to cut out the middleman as far as possible and to give direct access to the data so that the learner can take part in building up his or her own profiles of meaning and uses. The assumption that under-lines this approach is that effective language learning is itself a form of linguistic research, and that the concordance printout offers a unique resource for the stimulation of inductive learning strategies – in particular, the strategies of perceiving similarities and differences and of hypothesis formation and testing. (Johns 1994: 297)

With DDL, then, language learners become language researchers, and use authentic language data to discover rules about language. DDL is therefore an inductive (as opposed to deductive) type of learning, where the corpus data raises awareness/consciousness of language patterns that can be generalised to rules. As we mentioned in the previous section, consciousness-raising is an established approach in language teaching, and DDL offers a practical route to achieve this.

Johns (1991: 4) suggests that DDL involves a three-stage process, which he summarises as *identification, classification, generalisation,* which refers to identifying and classifying differences in patterns in concordances, and then generalising the findings into a rule. Carter and McCarthy (1995), following Johns, propose *illustration, interaction, induction,* which in a similar way involves first looking at examples from the data, then discussing the examples with other students and then coming up with a rule. Flowerdew (2009: 407), however, observes that some students have difficulties making the inductive leap, and proposes an optional fourth stage of *intervention*, which allows for extra teacher guidance when needed. Through these three (or four) stages, DDL incorporates (and students encounter) a number of different types of learning (Baker et al. 1997), which can be summarised as follows:

- Discovery learning – where students make their own discoveries about language.
- Divergent learning – where different students take different routes through the corpus outputs.
- Mediated learning – where interaction with the corpus facilitates language learning.
- Directed learning – where teachers direct rather than lead the learning, and the students work more independently.

(Summarised from Baker et al. 1997)

Boulton and Cobb (2017: 350) suggest that the stages involved with DDL of identifying and classifying patterns and then making generalisations, stimulate cognitive skills and encourage student autonomy. They go on to say that DDL reflects current thinking in psycholinguistic and learning theory, both of which suggest that detecting patterns comes naturally to humans. Boulton and Cobb also note that many learners already use computing technology (such as internet search engines) to search for answers to various questions (some concerning language), and DDL activities draw on these 'existing behaviours'.

According to Gilquin and Granger (2010: 359), there is some agreement about the advantages of DDL. This conclusion is, in general, supported by Boulton and Cobb (2017) who completed a survey of 64 publications from between 1989 and 2014 that provided empirical research into DDL. Boulton and Cobb came to the 'surprising and possibly encouraging conclusion that DDL works pretty well in almost any context where it has been extensively tried' (2017: 386). More specifically, they found that, overall, DDL provided good results for first year undergraduate intermediate level students, with medium to large effect sizes for vocabulary and lexico-grammar learning. As for the use of concordances and other CL tools, they found that, overall, the studies they assessed showed DDL works best when students get to use a concordance hands-on rather than using printed materials and worksheets, and that students are able to use the concordances effectively to perceive language patterns (even though the concordance lines are necessarily limited).

DDL has not been without some criticism, however, and as Flowerdew (2009) points out, inductive learning might not be for everyone, with some teachers, in particular, reporting that the processes involved in DDL were too time-consuming to be practical in a class (see Flowerdew 2009 for a fuller discussion of some of the issues that have been raised concerning DDL). Additionally, many students (and teachers) are simply not comfortable using computer tools, and Gotz (2012, cited in Timmis 2015: 141) found that, in general, learners did better when the tasks were guided by the teacher. Boulton and Cobb (2017) also point out that for some the concordance lines can be off-putting, and provide too much data and/or difficult examples that learners are unable to cope with. Furthermore, some concordances might include examples that are confusing and contain errors, which may be counterproductive in the learning process. Clearly, no learning strategy will suit all learners. If classroom activities are to include direct use of corpora, then the chances of these activities being successful will be improved with careful management and judicious consideration of the students who will be involved, with the role of the teacher and the learner being clearly defined and explained (Timmis 2015: 141).

In the next section we discuss some of the ways in which corpora have been and can be directly integrated into language teaching.

7.4 Corpus activities in the classroom

Incorporating corpus activities into the language learning classroom requires not only careful planning, but also access to resources, such as ready-made corpora and corpus tools. Some corpora are freely available, and can be accessed via web front-ends (see, for example, the range of corpora available on Andrew Hardie's CQPWeb website,[3] and Mark Davies's BYU corpora website[4]). Corpus interfaces and tools will provide concordances as well as frequency lists and collocates. Additionally, if the corpora are encoded grammatically, as is the British National Corpus (BNC), then they can also be used to show grammatical patterns. There are numerous methodological possibilities and an associated meta-language, which can be off-putting for some teachers and learners. This perhaps helps to explain an apparent 'resistance' to using corpora (Romer 2006: 124) that has resulted in comparatively few language teachers using DDL in the classroom (Frankenberg-Garcia 2012). DDL, therefore, also requires both students and teachers to be trained to use corpus tools, and associated corpus linguistic concepts such as collocation. As Gavioli comments, 'introducing students to corpus methodology [...] also involves, in many sense, introducing them to corpus theory' (2005: 35). Language learners are therefore presented with the same learning objectives as an L1 learner of corpus linguistics, but with the added challenge of being in an L2 context, and they must look to their teacher for guidance. Frankenberg-Garcia (2010) explains, therefore, that a crucial first step in bringing corpus activities into the classroom is for language teachers to learn how to use corpus tools and interfaces in order to exploit corpora for language teaching. This echoes Leech (1997), who points out that 'exploiting' corpora in order 'to teach' language 'implies teaching' how 'to exploit' corpora, in the first place. Frankenberg-Garcia (2010) suggests three topics that language teachers should be instructed on:

1. Knowing about the different corpora available and the type of language (spoken/written), language variety (e.g. British English; American English) and the genre(s) (e.g. academic writing) they contain.
2. Querying the corpus using single word, multiple word and wild-card search terms.
3. Interpreting corpus output.

For each of these topics Frankenberg-Garcia (2010) proposes a set of consciousness-raising exercises that aim to demonstrate in general terms the possibilities and consequences of different choices. For example, choosing a general corpus (such as the BNC) to search for technical terms specific to a particular domain is unlikely to provide enough, if any, results to discern a pattern. Similarly, searching for phrases rather than single words will drastically reduce the number of results from any corpus and make identifying patterns more difficult.

Students could also be trained on how to exploit corpora using the corpus awareness exercises Frankenberg-Garcia proposes for teachers, and one way to achieve this would be to incorporate the training into a lesson that has both language and corpus learning objectives. In this way, through addressing the task of learning about corpora, students also learn about language. Another option for teaching students about corpus linguistics and associated tools is to invite them to build their own mini corpora of whatever language variety they choose. This approach is advocated by Cheng et al. (2003) and Charles (2017), who also introduces the students to AntConc (Anthony 2018) so that they can interrogate their corpora. An additional advantage of a corpus building task is that students have the opportunity to create a resource that they can use for their own research outside the class.

Once students and teachers are able to explore corpora confidently, then such resources can be used for a variety of purposes. By and large, DDL involves interacting with concordance lines of a corpus for some specific learning purpose. Concordance lines retrieved from corpora using the interfaces provided can supply students with multiple examples of words and phrases with sufficient surrounding co-text for them to be able to discern patterns. Such patterns can be used to explore word meanings. Johns (1991), for example, uses concordances to help students discover for themselves the difference between the near synonyms *convince* and *persuade*, and different uses of the modal verb *should*. Johns explains that the choice of synonyms to investigate was prompted by student enquiries, and so represented a real problem faced by language learners. The lesson proceeded along Johns's three stages, *identify*, *classify*, *generalise*, where the task was clearly defined (i.e. the question: 'what is the difference between ...?' was asked), introduced and guided by the teacher, and students were able to work independently on completing the task in class. In this way, students were able to answer questions about the target language.

An example of a more open-ended, out-of-class task is described by Gilmore (2008), in which he instructs his students on using concordances so that they can self-correct lexical and grammatical problems in their own essays. Gilmore found that 90 minutes of training on a front-end to the BNC provided his second year undergraduate Japanese English Language students with sufficient skill to be able to use concordance data to correct problems highlighted in first drafts of their essays. Here, students were working independently and at their own pace. Gilmore (2008: 369) reports that around 61 per cent of changes made by students resulted in more natural language, suggesting that students are able to make corrections based on corpus data when prompted towards a particular language issue. Frankenberg-Garcia also uses DDL to enable students to make their own corrections in written work, and found that 'multiple concordances helped [...] as much as dictionary definitions', with the additional advantage that concordances 'made a big difference when it came to helping them [the students] to correct the use of words that they understood but frequently misused' (2012: 289).

Whatever corpus activity is used, it makes sense for it to be part of a wider teaching strategy that involves a number of approaches in order, at the very least, to cater for the different learning needs of students. Doing this addresses one of the problems highlighted by Flowerdew (2009) that corpus approaches are not for everyone (reported above). Corpus activities could also be incorporated into established teaching frameworks/methodologies, especially those that have an 'explicit focus on language structure and use' and 'reserve a role for noticing or awareness/consciousness-raising' (Gabrielatos 2005: 18), such as, for example presentation-practice-production (PPP) and Task Based Teaching/Learning (TBT/L) frameworks.

In our case study in the next section, we demonstrate the use of DDL in a task that asks students to focus on deviant language in a poem in order to help them reach conclusions about the meaning of the poem, as well as to understand better the notion of linguistic norms in Standard British English. Through the case study, we explore the possibilities of combining pedagogical stylistics and data-driven learning.

7.5 Case study: from internal deviation to external norms via Adrian Henri's 'Tonight at Noon'

In this section we illustrate some of the possibilities of incorporating corpus-based stylistics (which we introduced in Chapter 2) in an English teaching classroom via a corpus assisted analysis of a poem. Poems can be useful in the language teaching classroom because, as Hanauer notes, they 'involve language input which is foregrounded, unusual, and likely to draw attention to itself' (2001: 298), and this can potentially direct students to focus on particular forms, from which they then have to derive meaning. Our case study therefore uses a poem to focus students' attention on particular foregrounded forms. Importantly, it then demonstrates how meanings can be investigated through a series of directed corpus-based tasks aimed at encouraging discovery learning. Our case study therefore combines pedagogical stylistics with data-driven learning and in doing so offers a practical way to raise language awareness.

7.5.1 Stylistics inside out

In 1988, Mick Short and Mike Breen published two articles (Breen and Short 1988; Short and Breen 1988) which detailed the construction of a (then) new course on stylistics that Short and Breen had devised together. The course, which became known as *Language and Style*, was subsequently taught by Short at Lancaster University for many years. What made *Language and Style* different from other courses that had gone before it was the fact that it turned on its head the traditional way of teaching stylistics. Instead of beginning by teaching linguistic theory (grammar, phonology, semantics, etc.) and then applying this to literature, Short and Breen made literary texts the focus of their course and drip-fed requisite elements of linguistic theory to students as and when they needed it to supplement their analyses of the texts they were studying. This proved to be a very successful way of teaching stylistics, as evidenced by the continued success of the original course (McIntyre 2003) and the electronic developments of it in later years (for details of which, see Alderson and McIntyre 2006; Crisp 2006; Plummer and Busse 2006; Poole 2006; Short 2006; Short and Archer 2003).

In addition to the structural changes that were implemented in the *Language and Style* course, a philosophical change was also ushered in with regard to what stylistics is actually for. Short describes this as follows:

> stylistic analysis, which until now has largely been thought of as an analytical tool to support or test interpretative hypotheses already arrived at by sophisticated interpreters of literary texts, can also be used by less sophisticated readers who happen to have been trained in the methodology to help them puzzle out meaning when they get stuck. (Short 1996b: 41)

Short (1996b) describes this practice of teaching stylistics as stylistics 'upside down', that is, stylistics used to help students interpret texts rather than stylistics used to test interpretative hypotheses.

In this case study, we suggest that if stylistics can be taught upside down, as proposed by Short and Breen, it can also be taught 'inside out'. By this we mean that it is possible to move outwards from the analysis of a highly deviant text in linguistic terms to an understanding of what constitute linguistic norms in Standard English. That is, rather than beginning by teaching students what counts as normal in English and then examining texts that deviate from such norms, it is possible to do this the other way round and use an abnormal text to help students discover for themselves the norms from which linguistic creativity deviates. The deviant text drives the direction that the lesson takes and the forms that the students investigate (using a large reference corpus) but the lesson is nevertheless constrained and focused by the stylistic theory of foregrounding.

We propose, therefore, that corpus-based stylistics can be used as a means to teach English as a foreign language in a way that reduces the need for didactic information transfer and empowers students to discover the norms of Standard English (or, at least, naturally occurring English) for themselves. In addition, we contend that such language learning can be used to introduce cultural knowledge. In support of our argument, in this case study we analyse the poem 'Tonight at Noon' by Adrian Henri. Following this we discuss how the poem could be taught to non-native speakers of English in order to bring out the issues of norms, deviation and specific cultural knowledge that are necessary for a reasonable interpretation. Before that, we introduce the poet and the poem.

7.5.2 'Tonight at Noon' by Adrian Henri

Adrian Henri was born in Liverpool, England, in 1932 and is widely associated with a loose grouping of writers known as the Liverpool poets. Like his fellow Liverpool poets Roger McGough and Brian Patten, Henri was influenced by the American Beat poets of the 1950s: writers such as Allen Ginsberg, Lawrence Ferlinghetti and Gary Snyder. The work of the Liverpool poets was concerned with expressing the everyday in language that was accessible to ordinary people who might not normally think of poetry as being for them. Henri's poem, 'Tonight at Noon', is a prime example of his work and appears in the anthology, *The Mersey Sound* (Henri et al. 1967), a collection of poems by the Liverpool poets:

> *Tonight at Noon*
> Tonight at noon   [1]
> Supermarkets will advertise 3d extra on everything
> Tonight at noon
> Children from happy families will be sent to live in a
>   home
> Elephants will tell each other human jokes   [5]
> America will declare peace on Russia
> World War I generals will sell poppies on the street on
>   November 11th
> The first daffodils of autumn will appear
> When the leaves fall upwards to the trees
>
> Tonight at noon   [10]
> Pigeons will hunt cats through city backyards
> Hitler will tell us to fight on the beaches and on the
>   landing fields
> A tunnel full of water will be built under Liverpool
> Pigs will be sighted flying in formation over Woolton
> And Nelson will not only get his eye back but his
>   arm as well   [15]
> White Americans will demonstrate for equal rights
> In front of the Black house
> And the monster has just created Dr. Frankenstein

Girls in bikinis are moonbathing
Folksongs are being sung by real folk [20]
Art galleries are closed to people over 21
Poets get their poems in the Top 20
There's jobs for everybody and nobody wants them
In back alleys everywhere teenage lovers are kissing
 in broad daylight
In forgotten graveyards everywhere the dead will
 quietly bury the living [25]
and
You will tell me you love me
Tonight at noon

(Adrian Henri 1967[5])

In the next section we present a brief stylistic analysis of the poem before going on to consider how best to use the poem in a language teaching classroom.

7.5.3 A stylistic analysis of 'Tonight at Noon'

'Tonight at Noon' is a love poem. When we discuss this poem with our own students we always start by asking them the question: 'is the addressee of the poem in love with the speaker of the poem?' Without exception, students always answer 'no'. This is because we as readers do not take at face value the statement in line 27 ('You will tell me you love me') due to the effects of a pattern of semantic deviation that runs throughout the poem. Interpreting 'Tonight at Noon', therefore, relies on understanding the significance of a large number of semantic deviations, of which the most prominent is the title itself.

As a phrase, 'Tonight at Noon' is, of course, paradoxical because noon is a point of time during the day, so 'tonight' can never occur at noon. In stylistic terms, this is a semantic deviation. The title is further foregrounded as a result of 'Tonight at Noon' occurring at the beginning of the first two stanzas of the poem, each of which is nine lines long. This sets up a pattern which is then broken through internal deviation in the final stanza, where the title phrase occurs as the last line. This final line is itself further foregrounded as a result of it occurring in a stanza that is one line longer than the other two and being the second part of a couplet that occurs after the graphological foregrounding (via its positioning on a separate line) of *and* in line 26. Such 'congruence of foregrounding' (Leech 2008: 65) is likely to focus our attention on the title phrase as being the key to understanding the meaning of the poem.

As well as the repetition of the phrase 'tonight at noon', stanzas 1 and 2 follow a pattern whereby each line describes a future situation that is impossible, unlikely or which is in some sense incongruous to our expectations. Some of the impossible situations include the following: elephants do not have the ability to tell jokes (5), the laws of physics prevent leaves from falling upwards (9) and pigeons do not hunt cats (11). Unlikely situations include: supermarkets do not tend to advertise the fact that prices have gone up (2), children from happy families are not usually taken away from their parents (4) and countries do not usually declare peace on another country, since peace is the default situation which we assume to exist (6).

Stanza 3, as we have already mentioned, does not repeat the phrase 'tonight at noon' but it does continue the pattern of describing situations that are obviously incongruous. At line 27, though, this pattern is broken because at this point in the poem a situation is described that is not in and of itself unlikely or impossible. A lack of incongruity therefore makes this line internally deviant and consequently foregrounded because it is the only line in the poem that does not depict a situation that by any normal standards is impossible or unlikely. However, the semantic parallelism throughout the rest of the poem leads us to interpret the hypothetical speech event depicted in this line as being as nonsensical as all the others described in the poem. This is compounded in the final line which repeats once more the paradoxical title. Ultimately then, we interpret line 27 as meaning that the addressee is likely to say that he/she does *not* love the speaker of the poem. This leads to a general interpretation of the poem as being an introspective acceptance of unrequited love.

7.5.4 Teaching the poem to learners of English as a foreign language

The students with whom we have discussed this poem are primarily from the UK and most speak English as their first language. Without exception, their general interpretation of the poem matches that which we described in the previous section (even if they are unable to articulate in stylistic terms where this interpretation stems from). However, there are a number of lines in the poem that are likely to be interpretatively difficult for non-native speakers of English. This is because some rely on cultural knowledge while some rely on an understanding of the norms of Standard English or naturally occurring spoken English. These may well get in the way of such students being able to interpret the poem as a whole. In this section, we discuss some possibilities for teaching the poem to non-native speakers of English and, in so doing, how such students might be introduced to both aspects of British culture and some of the norms of Standard English.

The difficulties of interpreting 'Tonight at Noon' are exacerbated by the fact that not all of the semantic deviations in the poem work in the same way. For example, 'When the leaves fall upwards to the trees' is a straightforward reversal of the normal state of affairs, since leaves (and things generally) fall downwards to the ground. Indeed, 'fall' semantically encodes downwards movement. However, the statement in line 12 that 'Hitler will tell us to fight on the beaches and on the landing fields' has no conventional opposite. Instead, with enough cultural knowledge we are likely to interpret this line as positioning Hitler as the constructed opposite (see Davies 2012; Jeffries 2010a: ch. 4; Jeffries 2010b) of Churchill (whose famous wartime speech included the declaration that 'We will fight on the beaches and on the landing grounds'). The statement also potentially constructs a histori- cally opposite scenario whereby Germany stood ready to defend itself from invasion by Britain.

We suggest that unravelling these semantic deviations would be a profitable task for language learners since it would mean discovering rules concerning the norms of English, as well as finding out about British (historical) culture. Because of the complexities of the semantic deviations in the poem, we suggest that a practical way forwards is for teachers to guide students through the least difficult of these and, following this, for students to attempt to apply the analytical principles they have learned to make sense of the more complex deviations for themselves. We suggest the following stages offer one way of guiding students through an analysis of the poem.

7.5.5 Guided analysis

Our guided analysis uses the stylistic principle of foregrounding as its basis and focuses on graphological deviation within the text in the first instance before moving on to semantic deviation. At this stage we invite students to use the BNC to assess language norms in standard British English, thus adopting DDL methods to encourage discovery learning. The lesson, in general, follows the stylistic analysis in the section above, but it will depend largely on the ability and needs of the students whether meta-language associated with language components and fore- grounding theory is introduced or not, or rephrased less technically (e.g. graphology = visual aspects of the text; semantics = lexical/phrasal meanings and meaning relations).

Identifying graphological parallelism

First of all, before considering the complex semantics of the poem, we suggest asking students to look for patterns in the poem's appearance on the page. To start with, ask students to identify the title of the poem, count the number of stanzas and establish how many lines there are in each stanza. Then ask students to decide whether all the stanzas are the same graphologically and to explain what makes one of the stanzas different from the other two in this respect. Students should then be asked to look more closely at the title and to establish where the title phrase appears in the poem. A discussion could then follow about whether or not the graphological differences that have been identified and the positioning of the title phrase are important, and about the effects they might have on how readers treat the final stanza.

Identifying simple semantic deviation

Moving on from graphological to semantic deviation, we propose that the next directed task should be for the teacher to establish with the students the paradoxical nature of the title phrase, because this is key to interpreting the poem. Students could look at dictionary definitions of the word *noon* if they are unsure as to its meaning. Once they have done that, they should find it easier to see that 'tonight at noon' is paradoxical and therefore whatever follows cannot logically happen. This point can be made by asking students to consider whether the situations described in the following lines are likely:

> When the leaves fall upwards to the trees [9]
> Pigeons will hunt cats through city backyards [11]
> In forgotten graveyards everywhere the dead will quietly bury
>   the living [25]

The deviations in the lines above relate to globally recognised laws of physics or nature: the Earth's gravitational pull makes falling upwards impossible; the dead cannot *do* anything; pigeons do not have a hunting instinct, and are not physically equipped to hunt (and kill) cats. At this point, the term *semantic deviation* could be introduced.

Exploring complex semantic deviation through corpus analysis

Having established that the poem, starting from the title, describes paradoxical or illogical situations, more complex semantic deviation can be explored, and it is at this point in the lesson that a corpus of British English, and therefore DDL, would come into play. We suggest using the BYU interface[6] (developed by Mark Davies) to the British National Corpus (BNC) of 100 million words of British English from the 1990s, since this offers a fairly uncomplicated way to perform searches within the BNC corpus. Before logging into the interface, users need to register, which is a straightforward procedure that takes very little time (see Box 7.1).

Once students have registered and logged into BYU-BNC, they should return to stanza 1 of the poem and consider line 6: 'America will declare peace on Russia'. Their focus here should be directed to the word form *declare* and the fact that it is followed by *peace*. The goal here is for students to understand more about the meaning of *declare*.

As we saw in Chapter 2, concordances of words are one way in which we can use corpora to examine word meanings, so students could be directed to search for *declare* in the BNC to see how it is used normally. Students can scroll through the resulting concordance lines and will be able to make some observations about how the word *declare* is used in the BNC data, and whether, for example, it has obviously positive or negative meanings. While the teacher might support this activity, students could be left to work as independently as possible.

Box 7.1 Registering and logging on to BYU-BNC

1. Go to <http://corpus.byu.edu/bnc/>.

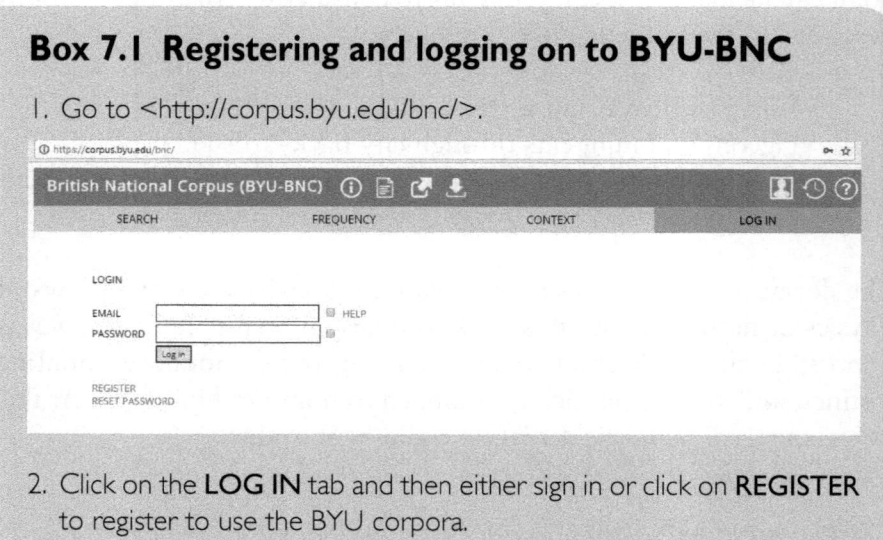

2. Click on the **LOG IN** tab and then either sign in or click on **REGISTER** to register to use the BYU corpora.

Box 7.2 Generating a concordance of the word *declare*

Generate a concordance of the word *declare* by typing the word into the search box and then clicking **Find matching strings**.

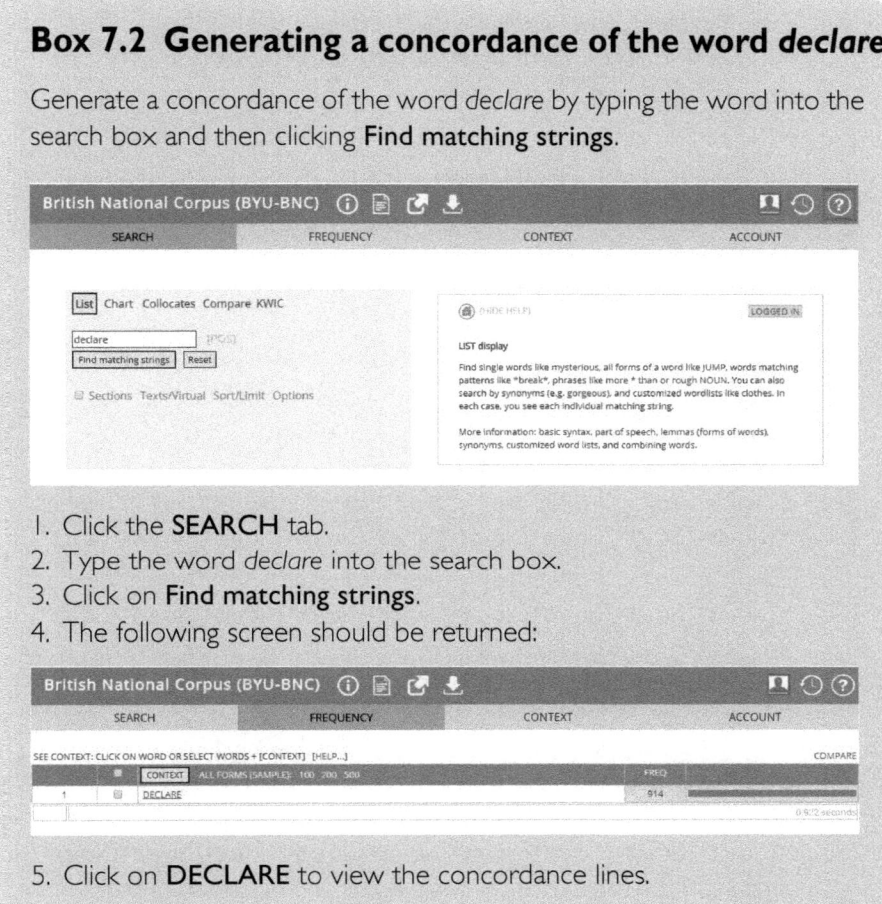

1. Click the **SEARCH** tab.
2. Type the word *declare* into the search box.
3. Click on **Find matching strings**.
4. The following screen should be returned:

5. Click on **DECLARE** to view the concordance lines.

Simply reading concordance lines is just one way of investigating word meaning. As we discussed in Chapter 2, we can also improve our understanding of the meaning of the word *declare* by examining a list of its collocates. The procedure for generating collocates can be found in Box 7.3. The results that should be obtained can be found in Table 7.1.

Box 7.3 Generating a list of collocates for *declare*

1. Click on the **Collocates** tab.
2. Type *declare* into the **Word/phrase** box.
3. Click in the **POS** box to the right of the word **Collocates** and from the dropdown menu select **noun.ALL**. The code _nn* will appear in the box to the left of the word **Collocates**.

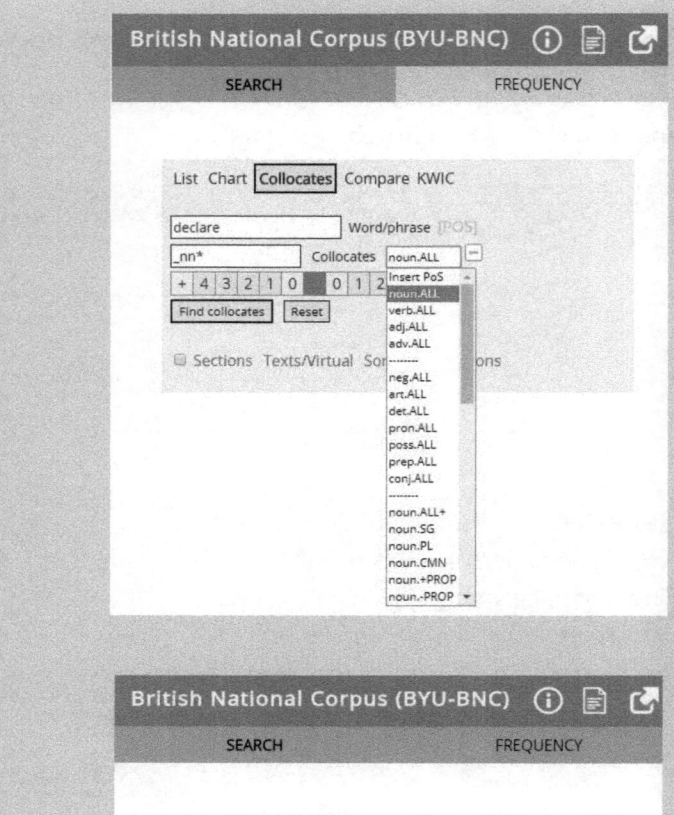

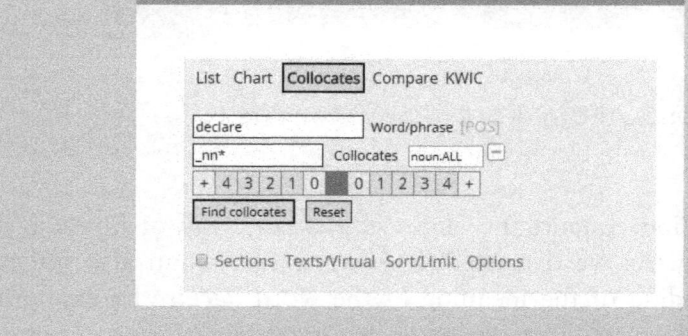

4. Click on both 4s to set the window size to 9 words (4 words to the left and to the right, plus the search word).
5. Click on **Find collocates**.

What is apparent from Table 7.1 is that *peace* is not a strong collocate of *declare*. As a result, using it in the poem deviates from the norms of everyday English as represented by the BNC. This unusualness can be related to foregrounding, a concept that can be introduced to students at this point. Students can then be asked about the likelihood

Table 7.1 Strong noun collocates of *declare* (using a 9 word window and [nn*])

No.	Collocate	Frequency	All	%	MI
1	interest	38	26,773	0.14	4.22
2	war	34	26,881	0.13	4.06
3	state	27	37,764	0.07	3.23
4	law	24	26,256	0.09	3.59
5	dividend	15	1,438	1.04	7.10
6	resolution	14	3,534	0.40	5.70
7	emergency	14	3,785	0.37	5.61
8	independence	11	4,262	0.26	5.09
9	intention	9	4,607	0.20	4.68
10	income	8	11,862	0.07	3.15

of what is described in line 6 actually happening. This exploration of line 6 might also include students constructing more usual phrases that include *declare* based on their corpus findings. It might also help for the instructor to introduce the global historical context of the Cold War and to provide students with some contextual information about when the poem was written.

We turn now to line 4: 'Children from happy families will be sent to live in a home'. This is a more complex line interpretatively since EFL learners may well be unaware of the possible connotations of *a home* to a native speaker. *Home* has many meanings, and students could use a dictionary to explore them. Perhaps the primary meaning is that of a dwelling, or place of residence, that can sometimes go beyond the structure of the building (as in the phrase *turn a house into a home*). The students might also be made aware of *home* relating to a sense of belonging (as in the phrase *feeling at home*). These (rather positive) meanings could be discussed before returning to the use of *home* in the poem, and students could be asked whether the positive meanings they have so far discussed are reflected in the poem. At this point, the semantic importance of *home* being preceded by the indefinite article should be introduced. To help them explore this, students should generate collocates of the phrase *in a home*, using a 9 word window (see Box 7.4). The results that should be obtained are shown in Table 7.2. From this table it becomes clear that particular types of people (children, the elderly, the handicapped) are associated with the word *home*, particularly when it is preceded by the indefinite article (although not always); in this sense, *home* would appear to be a shortened term for *care home*.

Table 7.2 Strong collocates of *in a home* (using a 9 word window)

No.	Collocates	Frequency	All	%	MI
1	put	13	57,050	0.02	4.38
2	children	6	45,334	0.01	3.59
3	elderly	5	4,877	0.10	6.55
4	live	5	16,595	0.03	4.78
5	handicapped	4	1,541	0.26	7.89
6	residents	4	3,365	0.12	6.76
7	living	4	15,414	0.03	4.56
8	care	4	24,178	0.02	3.91
9	mentally	3	1,938	0.15	7.14
10	lives	3	10,092	0.03	4.76

Box 7.4 Searching for *in a home* in the fiction section of the BNC

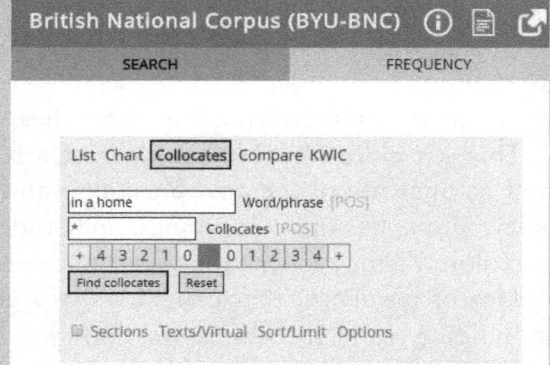

1. Click on the **Collocates** tab.
2. In the **Word/phrase** box, type *in a home*.
3. In the **Collocates** box type in an asterisk (this is the automatic default for this box and means that no part of speech has been specified).
4. Click on both 4s to set the window size to 9 words.
5. Click on **Find collocates**.

The semantic paradox in line 6 can be explored further by asking students to generate a concordance of the phrase *be sent to*. In order to limit the number of results and to increase the coherence of the concordances, we suggest using the fiction section of the BNC. Instructors will need to explain that the BNC is constructed of both spoken and written texts from a number of different genres, including prose fiction. The concordance that should be obtained can be found in Figure 7.1. What becomes apparent from the concordance is that the phrase *be sent to* tends to co-occur with events and occurrences that have unpleasant connotations; collocates include, for example, *prison*, *forgotten*, *war* and *punishment*. We can reasonably assume that no child (whether from a happy family or otherwise) likes to be on the receiving end of bad things, hence being sent to live in a home is something that most children would be upset by.

The class could discuss the kinds of circumstances that might lead to children being sent to live in a home, and the kinds of families that such children might come from. What ought to become apparent from this discussion is that these are not necessarily the conventional opposite of *happy* families. From this, students can be made aware that not all of the lines in the poem describe straightforwardly oppositional situations, and that, consequently, students should bear this in mind when interpreting other lines.

Investigating culturally specific references

By now, students are likely to have picked up on the fact that most lines in the poem describe situations that are in some sense the opposite to the norm. However, the cultural specificity of some of the lines means that students may well struggle to determine exactly which aspects of a particular line are semantically deviant. For example, in line 7 ('World War I generals will sell poppies on the street on November 11th') it may well be unclear whether it is 'World War I', 'generals', 'poppies', 'on the street' or 'on November 11th' that is the unusual element of the line. Ask students to carry out an internet search for the significance of November 11th in British culture. From this it should become clear that the only possible candidate for deviation is 'generals', since Remembrance Day originated from the World War I armistice and poppies are sold on the street to raise money for ex-servicemen and women. Students can then be asked what the possibilities are for a constructed opposite to 'generals', that is, who would normally sell poppies and why is it incongruous for generals to sell them?

Initially, this activity of actively seeking out cultural information would seem to run counter to Toolan's (2011) argument that, in many cases, students do not need the amount of cultural knowledge they might imagine they do in order to understand what appear to be specific cultural references. Toolan analyses the opening paragraphs of George Eliot's *Middlemarch* to demonstrate that knowledge of allusions and

	be sent to	
the details of at least one refuge. Was young Donald sound enough to	be sent to	contact other families?' Donald and Jean,' he said, and
, wiping himself clean with a handkerchief.' Kip quiet or you'll	be sent to	prison and fed on bread and wayter. Kip quiet whatever else thou's
raine shouted at him and Mr Jotter said any more slacking and he would	be sent to	he Headmaster. # You sleep all lesson and do not care, #
Christabel's desk when she died -- she expressed a wish that they should	be sent to	one of her nieces, May Bailey,' in the hope that she
set to turn the quern to grind the oatmeal, and then she'd	be sent to	fetch hay, peats, water. She often brought in mussels, gritty
. But no, Jessie had to be something else; Jessie had to	be sent to	the Secretarial School: no getting her hands sticky from the toffee ham
Luke.' Bull O'Malley stared at him dumbfounded.' Luke had to	be sent to	the infirmary in Castlebar,' the sergeant went on.' The lad
on for the daughter of Jack Malone and Sarah Westward. Now she would	be sent to	a convent of the same order in Dublin where she would do a secretarial
. If you fail to do what is required of you, prints will	be sent to	the KGB, to Major Tzann and one of your co-pilots at the base
they were born, children had to wait for six years before they could	be sent to	school and forgotten for most of the day. The ladies had several methods
and summoned Eileen. He came to see her father and advised that she	be sent to	relatives in Cork and kept there till the danger to her immortal soul was
his way to the office he had asked for a thermos of coffee to	be sent to	him and two mugs and a bowl of sugar and some milk. When
report that to the police. My guess is a quite different couple will	be sent to	track you down." They found me here quickly enough,'
line Wendy Willow and Nicholas Peter Willow -- only with no address to	be sent to	.None of them, not even the teachers, knew where they were
'd have my passport confiscated. I'd be fined. I might even	be sent to	prison. And you'd have an
she had been the lucky one. The one of the three sisters to	be sent to	Italy, before the war. She was the eldest, my mother the
eaming casserole. Thomas, his voice light, asked for his compliments to	be sent to	Cook, asked for a little more wine. He was biding his time
has turned to our Government for assistance. That means that arms will	be sent to	the Baltic -- more work for us all. Another war... it's
'd die. And so they all agreed. In three days Reldresal will	be sent to	explain your punishment to you. He'll inform you that the King has
him. He would keep her for himself. On no account would she	be sent to	the Avenue Foch. She and Madeleine would make a fine pair of concubin
ge signs in some villages warned him that anyone caught begging would	be sent to	prison. Travellers on the road refused to give him money; they said
not return to Bristol by the end of August, a rescue ship will	be sent to	look for us.' So we made a plan to get ourselves off
a pipe of port. Arthur told the lordly one that it was to	be sent to	Mr and Mrs Stokes, but Fred knew whom it was tacitly meant for
given to her brother. In the accompanying letter, Beatrix said it would	be sent to	me by a friend in the event of her death. She also implored
'It is our will -- the Will of Heaven -- that an embassy	be sent to	the lands across the Great Sea --' He waved a hand.'
form of licence is prescribed in this section. List of licence holders to	be sent to	Customs and Excise 22. # GENERAL NOTE Repealed 1983, c.28, 5.9,
wer Hamlets. Harry Chiltern had died, and asked that all his possessions	be sent to	Charles. It was depressing to think that he was the closest friend that
Each article was laid out on a polythene bag, labelled, ready to	be sent to	the laboratory. Wycliffe worked through the items. A dark-brown rainco
and I are not very close -- I'm not a son who could	be sent to	sea. 'She said this, I thought, rather bitterly. And
Place well at one time. A transcript of the questions and answers would	be sent to	all interested parties. All in the TAS would receive one. A senior
with nervous reaction.' How did you know that letter was going to	be sent to	me?" I'd rather not go into that right now.
month. Even if such a licence is issued, a copy may not	be sent to	me.' Corbett scratched his head and grinned sheepishly.' I have

Figure 7.1 Concordance of *be sent to* (BNC Fiction)

	be sent to	her home address, and she was humming softly when he came in.
ion. Before Luke arrived back she had arranged for details and menus to	be sent to	her room and hear them going on about how if it wasn't for
eyes and wiped her brow with a hanky soaked in cologne. She'd	be sent to	the Tower. Of course, Henry was playing games. He wanted more
beat Cromwell, telling him he was a caitiff and a knave and would	be sent to	me, and the newspaper will have to be cancelled,' he added
'll arrange for her to collect Bertha's mail. Bills will have to	be sent to	gaol for being a whore. Anyway, he wouldn't even be arrested
Melody's short laugh.' He'd likely walk free and she'd	be sent to	join the Bishop at Kinrimund, where the King would be pleased to def
Siward, and a request that Bishop Malduin's wife and household should	be sent to	the house immediately, a policeman said. Loretta got back into her car
just seen two men acting suspiciously in the garden. A patrol car would	be sent to	a concentration camp. He argued as best he could. The final agreement
hadn't met the others. He had a choice. To join or	be sent to	the Mixed Courts, where the law was different from that in the ordinary
Egyptian national was involved as well as a foreigner, the case had to	be sent to	prison immediately!' she added forcefully.' Yeah -- that's what
drugs is disgusting. Anyone who sells them is thoroughly evil and should	be sent to	her, and dismissed her on the spot. She was still in shock
his son's weaknesses, told her that a month's severance pay would	be sent to	finishing school. Oh, yes, I was only a girl, and
-- we came back for about six years, until I was ready to		

Figure 7.1 Continued

inter-textual references are often secondary in importance to a grasp of the relations between participants, processes and circumstances in a sentence. However, what is different with regard to the analysis of 'Tonight at Noon' is that students are using a key piece of cultural information to determine the constructed oppositional element of the line; that cultural knowledge does not, in and of itself, allow them to make sense of the line without applying the stylistic patterns they have identified in their analysis up to this point.

7.5.6 Round-up of the analysis so far

At this point in the lesson, the students could be asked to report back on what they have discovered so far about the poem. The discussion could be focused by the students being asked first about the graphological structure of the poem and any patterns they have noticed, and then about the semantic deviations in stanza 1. Based on this, the teacher could then ask the students what they expect to see in stanzas 2 and 3. The students are likely to expect the same pattern of semantic deviations, but regardless of their answers they can now be asked to carry on their investigation of the other stanzas for themselves independently of the teacher in order to find out what happens semantically. In the next section we outline how that investigation might proceed and provide a list of lines from the poem to be investigated along with a set of study questions.

Independent analysis: stanzas 2 and 3

Stanzas 2 and 3 have a number of cultural references that students will need to make sense of (e.g. reference to 'Woolton', 'Nelson', the 'Top 20'). As with the example of line 7, cultural knowledge is essential to determine the element of each line that is in some way deviant. In making sense of stanzas 2 and 3, students are moving towards an interpretation of the poem (doing stylistics 'upside down', as Short 1996b puts it). They are also adding to their knowledge of British (perhaps specifically English) culture. This is in addition to the knowledge of norms of Standard English determined through their analysis of stanza 1 (stylistics 'inside out', as we term it). The following is a list of semantically deviant lines from the poem, which warrant further investigation, along with study questions aimed at guiding student enquiry:

1. Line 5: 'Elephants will tell each other human jokes'
   What is an elephant joke? Look this up on the internet.

2. Line 2: 'Supermarkets will advertise 3d extra on everything'
   What kind of advertisements do you usually see in supermarkets?
   What does 3d refer to? (Hint: what was the currency in Britain
   at the time the poem was written?)

3. Line 11: 'Pigeons will hunt cats through city backyards'
   Pigeons don't hunt and they certainly don't hunt cats. Test the
   unusualness of line 11 by using BYU-BNC to look for **verb
   forms** that collocate with *pigeons*. In the **Word/phrase** box,
   type *pigeons*; in the **Collocates** box select **verb.ALL**.

   The results should include (in order of frequency):
   > *racing, homing, fly, kept, shown, fed, flying, roosting,
   > shooting.*

   Using these findings, discuss what actions pigeons *normally*
   perform.

   Rewrite line 11 using one of these actions.

4. Line 14: 'Pigs will be sighted flying in formation over Woolton'
   In BYU-BNC, search for **pigs * fly**. The concordance that should
   be obtained can be found in Figure 7.2. Can you identify a
   phrasal pattern(s)? Discuss the meaning of any such pattern(s).

Making sense of internal deviation in stanza 3

Finally, students can be asked to discuss their independent analyses of
stanzas 2 and 3, and could be asked whether they found similar patterns
to those they discovered in stanza 1. At this stage, even if they have been
unable to fully interpret some of the specific cultural references, they
are likely to have a sense that the pattern from stanza 1 is continued in
stanza 2 and the first part of stanza 3. The focus should now be on what
is different about stanza 3 compared with their expectations. Students
can be guided towards this by returning to their initial comments about
graphological deviation, that is, the positioning on a separate line of
and in line 26 draws attention to line 27, which is further foregrounded
by virtue of being the only line in the poem that is not unusual at the
surface level. Students can then be asked whether they think this line
describes a likely situation.

7.5.7 Analysis: case study summary and conclusions

In this case study we have shown how using a highly deviant poem
in the language classroom can introduce English language learners to
certain language norms in English as well as to specific aspects of British
(English) culture. In doing so we have introduced the potential of

	pigs might fly	
area could have been driving through and seen something." Yeah, and	pigs might fly	' Kate's voice was bitter. Caitlin took another puff on
I'll do what's necessary.' She gave a disbelieving sniff.'	Pigs might fly	. And I fail to see why someone with such an inventive,
Steiner out and safely in France in no time at all." And	pigs might fly	, General. Not only would you need a suitable plane. You
embarrassment than satisfaction. She took refuge in sarcasm.' And	pigs might fly	!' She gibed, and found her attention unwillingly
but it's still there. Perhaps the artery's just compressed."	Pigs might fly	', the paramedic muttered, and fastened the collar at last.
love it. But trampolining won't be catching on with the other animals.	Pigs might fly	– but Crackle the pot-bellied Vietnamese will have none of
symptoms, see your GP straight away. # YOU'LL NEVER BELIEVE IT #	Pigs might fly	? Some do... # Jockeying for position, these racing pigs took
would have emerged to take their place. But this is like suggesting that	pigs might fly	. They might, but they don't. Far too much scholarly
next ten years as a successor to Sir Malcolm Sargeant. Well, I know	pigs might fly	, but hope springs eternal and Bob was eternally hopeful that

Figure 7.2 Concordance of *pigs * fly* (BNC)

stylistics to be taught 'inside out'; that is, we have shown how the stylistic analysis of unusual texts can be carried out to uncover more general language phenomena. The idea we have described with this approach to language learning is that students start to discover language patterns for themselves using different methods including corpus searches. After initial guidance from the teacher the lesson would develop into a series of independent discovery tasks for the student, which could fit into a Task Based Teaching framework such as that proposed by Willis (1996). The tasks involve dictionary searches, web investigations using a search engine, and a series of corpus enquiries using a web front-end to the BNC. Each of these tasks alone requires the student to think very carefully about language, moving from a focus on form to a focus on meaning. Consequently, simply completing these tasks (preferably in pairs or small groups) tests their knowledge and helps to develop their understanding of English. Clearly, this sort of lesson would be unsuitable for beginner learners. However, as a lesson for upper intermediate or advanced level learners it introduces sophisticated concepts relating to semantics and helps to demonstrate that not attending to minor details in language can have major consequences for meaning. The lesson also has the potential to encourage the development of understanding of complex semantic meanings in texts, which is achieved in part by students discovering and making sense of language patterns in a corpus of British English, thus incorporating inductive methods from DDL.

7.6 Conclusion

Pedagogical stylistics is still very much a developing sub-discipline of stylistics. Despite criticisms of pedagogical stylistics that question its contribution to language learning there is, nevertheless, a growing body of work in the field demonstrating some of its benefits. Part of the issue is that stylistics is not in and of itself a teaching framework or theory, and therefore pedagogical stylistics should be seen and used within the context of established approaches to language teaching. Our case study demonstrates that pedagogical stylistics can be part of a consciousness-raising exercise whereby students are encouraged to notice language and draw conclusions about meaning. The case study also demonstrated some of the possibilities of combining DDL with stylistics. DDL has been criticised for only addressing bottom-up processing and not top-down (Flowerdew 2009). The combination of stylistics and DDL in our case study offers a way to address this issue. The poem we used in the task presents a number of language conundrums which students could solve using patterns from a corpus, and in doing so notice different language features. The combination of task, stylistics and DDL encourages top-down processing by asking students to consider an overall meaning of the poem, and bottom-up processing by asking students to focus on individual forms that will help them to draw conclusions about the meaning. Additionally, the use of a poem offers a window onto language and English culture that might not have emerged from other texts or teaching materials.

Notes

1. ESL stands for English as a Second Language. ESL teaching describes English language teaching in countries where English is the dominant language. EFL stands for English as a Foreign Language. EFL teaching refers to English language teaching in countries where English is not the dominant language.
2. The notion of authenticity is not uncontroversial; see Widdowson (1990: 45–7) for further discussion.
3. See <https://cqpweb.lancs.ac.uk/> (last accessed 20 August 2018).
4. See <https://corpus.byu.edu/> (last accessed 30 August 2018).
5. We are grateful to the author's estate for granting permission for us to use the poem in this chapter.
6. The BNCweb interface developed at Lancaster University could also be used for this exercise and is available at <http://corpora.lancs. ac.uk/BNCweb/> (last accessed 20 August 2018). User registration is straightforward and quick, and details can be found at <http:// bncweb.lancs.ac.uk/bncwebSignup/user/login.php> (last accessed 20 August 2018). Note that the search tools of Lancaster BNCweb are different from the BYU interface.

8

Historical corpus stylistics

8.1 Introduction

At the beginning of Chapter 2 we pointed out the extent to which corpus linguistic methodologies have revolutionised historical linguistics (see, for example, Herce 2017; Jenset and McGillivray 2017; Viola 2017). But beyond the investigation of formal elements of language such as syntax and morphology, corpus methods also open up the possibility of studying the diachronic development of aspects of style (see, for example, Adamson 1994; Rissanen et al. 1997; Studer 2008; Evans 2013). Indeed, investigating functional as well as formal elements of language is essential if we are to record what Watts and Trudgill (2001) term 'alternative' (i.e. non-formal) histories of English (Watts and Trudgill's focus is on English specifically, though what they advocate is applicable to all languages). Stylistics is, of course, well placed to make a contribution to such an endeavour, and over recent years there has been an ongoing and steadily growing interest in the corpus stylistic study of texts from earlier historical periods. This chapter demonstrates how the concepts discussed in Chapters 2–5 can be used to explore diachronic developments in style. We discuss such practical matters as how to choose appropriate corpora for historical stylistic analysis, the extent to which representativeness is an issue in historical corpora, and how to deal with issues particular to historical language varieties, such as spelling variation. In so doing, we discuss the particular difficulties of researching style and meaning-making in historical texts and corpora. We use two case studies to illustrate the possibilities of this kind of analysis. The first examines discourse presentation techniques in Early Modern English texts. The second examines the stylistic effects of modality in Early Modern English journalistic writing. In both these case studies we move our focus away from text style (discussed in Chapter 4) and turn our attention to style developments within genres. We begin by considering the principles that underpin the diachronic and synchronic study of style.

8.2 Studying style diachronically and synchronically

A primary concern of historical stylistics is diachronic variation in style, that is, the study of how language features that relate to style may vary over time. For example, we might investigate how markers of genre style change over a 100-year period. Also essential, as Wales (2011: 112) points out, is examining style synchronically if we are to gain a historical perspective on language and style. This means being clear about how particular linguistic features function at any given moment in time, and how these functions might be influenced by such non-linguistic variables as geographical region, genre or author, to name but a few. According to Bray (2014; see also Busse 2015), a further important aspect of historical stylistics is contextualising (or situating) any analysis within the time period in which the text was written, so that diachronic/synchronic variation is seen (and perhaps explained) through a historical perspective, as well as connected to social, economic and political events and change. It is important that interpretations or explanations of how historical texts make meaning are made in the light of those historical contexts (see Auer et al. 2016: 1).

Rather obviously, historical stylistics focuses on historical texts, which in the case of most published research in the field means those written in older varieties of English – though, of course, there is no reason why other languages should not also be studied from a historical stylistic perspective. With regard to English specifically, there are generally agreed to be three main stages in its development prior to the advent of contemporary English: Old English (OE; approximately 450–1100), Middle English (ME; approximately 1100–1500) and Early Modern English (EModE; approximately 1500–1750), and it is easy to see how notions of what counts as historical can be mapped onto these stages. English as it developed beyond the Early Modern period and into the nineteenth century (usually referred to as Late Modern English [LModE]; approximately 1750–1900) has also been studied from a historical perspective and has recently received renewed attention (see, for example, Tieken-Boon van Ostade 2009). In a special issue of *English Language and Linguistics* (2012) devoted to LModE, Beal et al. (2012: 201) suggest that one reason why interest in this particular variety of English has increased is that, since the start of the new millennium, the temporal distance between contemporary English and LModE is perceived to be sufficient to enable the identification of linguistic change. Beal et al.'s reasoning suggests that what counts as enough temporal space, and therefore what counts as historical, is debatable and that, arguably, diachronic change within Present Day English (PDE) can be seen from a historical perspective (see, for example, Leech 2003, 2004).[1] If we take this view, then the diachronic comparison of a comic strip from 1977 and 2003 we presented in Chapter 3 might also be seen as a historical corpus stylistic study, since time is the central variable in the data and there is enough temporal space between the data sets for the text-type to potentially evolve. Also, in order to make sense of some of the results of that study, we need to appreciate the socio-cultural and technological differences between 1970s and new millennium Britain.

Regardless of the time period being researched, it is important in historical linguistic studies to be clear about whether the investigation concerns writing or speech. While this may sound an obvious point to make, because of the paucity of data from some earlier periods of history it is important to be clear about the extent of the claims that can be made on the basis of the data studied. For example, a historical corpus stylistic study of Old English will tell us nothing about speech in the Anglo-Saxon period because the only data we have is textual in nature. Any claims about the nature of Old English, then, need to be qualified as being about Old English writing specifically.[2] Also important is distinguishing which changes in linguistic features relate to changes in genre and which relate more generally to changes in the language code associated with that time period. That is, any claims about language change need to come with caveats that consider whether the claims are about writing or speech or both, and whether the change is one that has affected all domains or just one.

8.3 Historical corpora and tools

Historical corpus stylistic research that deals with archaic language varieties, particularly those from earlier periods of English, is made feasible by the considerable online resources now available for the study of historical data. These include online digital archives and ready-made corpora, some of which are free to use while others require subscription or a one off-payment. These electronic resources and corpora represent an enormous amount of effort from various groups of people who scanned and copy-typed data from archives of old texts. Some of the most well-known corpora and collections are listed in Appendix 1, while the list of corpus software in Appendix 2 includes tools specifically for historical analysis. While two case studies in this chapter each make use of specially constructed corpora, in both cases we drew in part on material already available in other collections.

Two notable corpora of historical English are the Zurich English Newspaper (ZEN) Corpus (Fries et al. 2004) and the Helsinki Corpus (HC),[3] both of which have been the subject of considerable research into diachronic variation across past varieties of English.

The HC contains 1.5 million words from 400 samples of texts, ranging from 2,000 to around 20,000 words, dating from the eighth to the eighteenth centuries. The corpus is thus a diachronic corpus that spans 1,000 years of English language development from Old English to the beginning of Modern English (early 1700s). Although the HC aims to represent 1,000 years with just 1.5 million words of data, it lends itself to certain types of study. As Rissanen explains, 'it gives reliable and useful diagnostic information on structural and lexical developments, particularly of high-frequency items' (2000: 8). Emerging from this corpus is a large body of work that explores numerous aspects of diachronic variation, some of which relate to style (see, for example, Meurman-Solin 1999; Taavitsainen 1994).

The ZEN Corpus is more narrowly constrained in terms of both time period and genre, containing 1.6 million words from 349 complete newspaper editions published between 1661 and 1791 (see Lehmann et al. 2006). Approximately half the corpus is made up of issues of *The London Gazette*, with the rest being made up of other major newspapers from the seventeenth and eighteenth centuries, including *The London Post*, *The English Post*, *The Post Man* and *The Daily Courant*. The corpus was built by manually copy-typing facsimiles of newspapers obtained from the Burney Collection (of early English newspapers) held at the British Library in London, and is marked-up using TEI conformant XML to encode year of publication, newspaper issue and an indication of the type of text within each edition of the newspaper (e.g. foreign news, home news, advertisement). There have been numerous publications based on analyses of the data in the ZEN Corpus, including Fries and Lehmann (2006) and Studer's (2008) book-length study of style in newspapers.

Building and analysing historical corpora that contain archaic language varieties can involve overcoming a number of problems. For example, we noted in Chapter 3 that a corpus is a sample of a language population and that part of the process of constructing a corpus involves identifying a sampling frame from which to sample texts. In effect, the sampling frame indicates the reality of what can possibly be sampled. With historical varieties, the number of texts that are available to be sampled can be small, since in some circumstances very few texts have survived. This is the case with Old English, where the number of texts from this historical period amounts to just 3,124. The Old English Corpus (OEC) at the University of Toronto contains at least one copy of every known surviving OE text, and this amounts to just over three million words of Old English. The OEC therefore contains all that survives of an unknown population of written texts, and can thus only represent written OE as it is presented in those texts. However, given that there are no more texts that can be sampled, researchers are forced to formulate hypotheses about OE based on the available data. While there are considerably more surviving examples of the language varieties that immediately followed OE (i.e. Middle English and Early Modern English), we still cannot be sure how representative these texts are of the actual population. So here too representativeness is less easy to realise. Instead, corpora can only contain texts sampled from what is known to remain and what is accessible (through, for example, publicly available collections). As Studer notes:

> While research is ideally guided by historical and stylistic considerations, it is the hard-copy version that finally determines the viability of a project idea. [...] historical research is determined by a body of texts that has been preserved and handed down to us. (Studer 2008: 27)

Another problem with historical texts, which we noted in Chapter 3, is that in order to create machine readable versions they must be manually typed in. This, of course, can be a time-consuming exercise. There might also be difficulties with reading degraded (copies or scans of) originals.

A further difficulty with historical data is that archaic texts that were written before a standard system of spelling was in place contain spelling variants of the same word (we will see examples of this in our second case study). Such variation in spelling can be a problem for corpus analyses that use, for example, keywords and concordances, since variants of the same lemma will not be collected and assessed together. This problem can be alleviated by using software that corrects spelling variants in a corpus to standard forms, before proceeding with any further analysis. For example, Variation Detector (VARD) 2 (Baron 2013) is software designed to normalise spelling in texts where there is variation. The program was designed initially for Early Modern English but has also been used to normalise spelling in texts in other English language varieties (including text messaging language). The idea is that texts are processed first by VARD2, which normalises spelling variation, before being processed by other corpus tools such as AntConc (Anthony 2018) or Wordsmith (Scott 2016). The preprocessing and spelling standardisation means that any results from other tools are more accurate (see Baron et al. 2009).

There are, therefore, a number of obstacles to negotiate when designing and building corpora that aim to represent in some way archaic varieties of languages. Despite the difficulties with carrying out historical corpus stylistic research, it is a growing area of study with increasing numbers of resources becoming available. In the case studies that follow we explore the potential for using corpus approaches when analysing historical data, and put into practice some of the methods that we have discussed in previous chapters.

8.4 Case study: discourse presentation in Early Modern English

Our first case study in this chapter is a diachronic investigation of discourse presentation (DP). Our aim is to compare discourse presentation in Early Modern English (EModE) writing with equivalent phenomena in Present Day English (PDE) writing. To do that, we compiled a small corpus of EModE texts, annotated it for categories of DP using a model set out in Semino and Short (2004) and later modified by Short (2007), and then used the annotation to quantify the different types of DP in our data. We then compared our quantitative results with those from Semino and Short's (2004) study of DP in PDE writing. By doing this, we were also able to test whether a discourse presentation model that was developed through work on PDE writing can be applied to an older variety of English. We decided that if we found instances of DP in the EModE data that was not described by the model, then a secondary objective would be to propose amendments to the model in light of such difficulties. These aims can be summarised as a series of research questions:

RQ1   Can we apply a model of discourse presentation designed for PDE to EModE? (By this we mean, can the Semino and Short 2004/Short 2007 model of discourse presentation adequately account for all speech, writing and thought presentation in a corpus of EModE texts?)

RQ1.1 If we can't, then what modifications/additions do we need to make to the model in order for it to account for the EModE data?

RQ2   Based on the results from a small corpus of EModE texts and the results reported by Semino and Short (2004), do the proportional frequencies of DP in a corpus of EModE writing match equivalent frequencies reported by Semino and Short (2004) for a corpus of PDE?

RQ2.1 Are any differences in frequencies statistically significant?

We chose the early modern period because at this stage in the development of English a standard form of the language was becoming more prevalent and there was an increase in printed texts and literacy (van Gelderen 2014). The Early Modern period was therefore an era of considerable linguistic development, and we hypothesised that discourse presentation as a stylistic technique might operate differently from how it does in PDE. As a first step towards investigating this, a general working hypothesis for this study is that DP in EModE is found in the same quantities as in PDE. In effect, this is a null hypothesis of there being no difference between the quantities of DP found in EModE and PDE. To summarise:

$$H_0 \text{ DP in EModE} = \text{DP in PDE}$$
$$H_1 \text{ DP in EModE} \neq \text{DP in PDE}$$

Of course, the simple observation of quantities will not tell us about the functions of DP in our corpus. Qualitative analysis is necessary to ascertain these. Nonetheless, as we have seen throughout this book, quantitative analysis can offer an objective method of determining results that are potentially of interest in qualitative terms and offer a focus for further analysis.

8.4.1 Discourse presentation

Prototypically, discourse presentation (DP), also known as speech, writing and thought presentation (SW&TP), refers to the presentation of speech, writing or thought from an anterior discourse in a posterior discourse. Discourse can be presented using a variety of different forms. The framework we use for this study is based on that described by Short (2007), which is a development of a framework first proposed by Leech and Short (1981) and later expanded by Semino and Short (2004). The categories of discourse presentation in the framework are summarised in Table 8.1.

The discourse presentation framework presents a cline of presentational forms that range from (apparent) verbatim renderings of the

Table 8.1 Speech, writing and thought presentation categories (based on Short 2007)

Speech presentation		Writing presentation		Thought presentation	
(F)DS	(Free) Direct Speech	(F)DW	Free Direct Writing	(F)DT	Free Direct Thought
FIS	Free Indirect Speech	FIW	Free Indirect Writing	FIT	Free Indirect Thought
IS	Indirect Speech	IW	Indirect Writing	IT	Indirect Thought
NPSA	Narrator's Presentation of a Speech Act	NPWA	Narrator's Presentation of a Writing Act	NPTA	Narrator's Presentation of a Thought Act
NPV	Narrator's Presentation of Voice	NPW	Narrator's Presentation of Writing	NPT	Narrator's Presentation of Thought

original discourse, to minimal forms that indicate merely that speech, writing or thought occurred. As one moves down the categories set out in Table 8.1 there is an increase in what Leech and Short (1981, 2007) call narrator interference, and a consequent decrease in claims that can be made about faithfulness to the purported original discourse. Direct forms (DS/DW/DT) express the exact words of the original discourse enclosed in quotation marks and include a reporting clause. Free Direct forms express the same but exclude reporting clauses and/or other indicators of a narrator's presence (such as quotation marks). Indirect forms (IS/IW/IT) present the propositional content of the original but with (1) the original words subjected to a backshift in tense, and contained within a subordinate clause, and (2) any pronouns changed to be appropriate to the presenter rather than the original speaker/writer/ thinker. Free Indirect forms (FIS/FIW/FIT) typically blend aspects of the indirect form (e.g. backshift in tense; changed pronouns) with a flavour of the original words (e.g. sequencing of information; lexis; punctuation). The Narrator's Presentation of a Speech/Writing/Thought Act (NPSA/NPWA/NPTA) category presents the illocutionary force of the original and optionally an indication of the topic, but none of the propositional content, so that typically the anterior discourse cannot be reconstructed. Finally, the Narrator's Presentation of Voice/Writing/ Thought (NPV/NPW/NPT) indicates only that speech, writing or thought occurred; that is, it gives no indication of propositional content or original form.

While there has been some work on DP from a historical perspective (see Busse 2010; Jucker 2006; Moore 2002; Włodarcyzk 2007), only

Busse's (2010) study of nineteenth-century narrative fiction uses the analytical framework we employ here. Busse (2010) found that direct speech presentation is the most frequent type of discourse presentation in her corpus (which matches Semino and Short's 2004 findings for twentieth-century fiction) but also discovered differences in how characters' mental states and thought processes are presented. Jucker (2006) also adopts a corpus-based approach to investigate DP in news discourse, though he uses an unannotated corpus, which means that his findings are limited to the structural forms of DP that it is possible to search for. For example, Jucker does not analyse free indirect discourse because this is only apparent by its context, not by its linguistic form. Our technique of first annotating our data means that we are able to retrieve all instances of all the categories of discourse presentation outlined in Table 8.1.

8.4.2 Building the corpus

When building our corpus of EModE texts, our first concern was to decide the time frame from which to collect data. The date boundaries between earlier language varieties cannot be fixed absolutely, and are not agreed. For example, Burchfield ([1985] 2006) decides on 1476–1776, while Johnson (2016) uses a similar starting point but draws a line at 1700. We opted for a 250-year frame from 1500 to 1750, these dates being roughly synonymous with, respectively, Caxton's printing press revolution taking effect and the publication of Samuel Johnson's dictionary. This is not to suggest that these two events had an equal impact on all varieties of English, only that they are important milestones in the development of English and are likely to have had at least some effect on the written standard. They mark convenient points (and events) where (1) English started to become more standardised, and (2) standardisation was well on its way.

Our second concern was which texts to put into our corpus. Because our aim was to eventually compare the results from our research with those from Semino and Short's (2004) project, the data profile for our corpus needed to match that of Semino and Short's corpus. The Lancaster SW&TP Written Corpus, as it is known, contains a total of 260,000 words made up of equal numbers of 2,000-word samples of serious and popular prose fiction (broadly akin to 'high' and 'low' literature), tabloid and broadsheet news journalism, and biography and autobiography. Due to time constraints and the labour-intensive nature of SW&TP annotation, we were unable to construct a corpus of equivalent size and scope. We restricted our corpus to just prose fiction and news reports and we did not distinguish between serious and popular fiction or broadsheet and tabloid news, since these distinctions did not exist in the Early Modern period in quite the same way. Furthermore, because our corpus was already rather small, sub-dividing our data in this way would have generated raw figures too small to draw reliable conclusions from.

In order to collect a selection of texts spread across our chosen period, we divided the 250-year frame into 50-year segments and collected four texts (two prose fiction and two news) for each segment. In a similar way to the compilation of the Lancaster Corpus, we collected 2,000-word samples of each text-type, giving us ten samples, and around 20,000 words of each text-type (prose fiction and news).

Tables 8.2 and 8.3 outline the content of the fiction and news sections of our corpus. It is worth noting that our earliest examples of news journalism are somewhat different from PDE newspapers. The newspaper (as we would recognise it today) did not exist at the beginning of our time frame, and news was often in the form of letters containing personal accounts (Brownlees 2014: 13 uses the term 'epistolary news'), which were printed and distributed on a fairly limited basis. Our earliest samples of news journalism are therefore of the contents of letters describing newsworthy events (e.g. J1.2 'Hevy newes of an earthquake'). While our data is not absolutely equivalent to the Lancaster

Table 8.2 The composition of the fiction section of the EModE corpus

EModE Corpus – Prose Fiction sub-section					
Extract no.	Time period	Title	Word count	Author	Pubn date
PF1.1	1500–49	The Noble History of King Ponthus	2,072	Henry Watson	1511
PF1.2		The Mad Men of Gotham	2,002	William Tyndale	1547
PF2.1	1550–99	The Carde of Fancie	2,154	Robert Greene	1584
PF2.2		Arcadia	2,022	Philip Sydney	1590
PF3.1	1600–49	The Blacke Booke	2,057	attr. Thomas Middleton	1604
PF3.2		Cloria and Narcissus	2,047	attr. Percy Herbert	1653
PF4.1	1650–99	The blazing-world	2,097	Margaret Cavendish	1668
PF4.2		Oroonoko	2,073	Aphra Behn	1688
PF5.1	1700–50	Moll Flanders	1,993	Daniel Defoe	1722
PF5.2		Tom Jones	2,079	Henry Fielding	1751
		Total words	20,596		

Table 8.3 The composition of the news section of the EModE corpus

		EModE Corpus – News Report sub-section			
Extract no.	Time period	Title	Word count	Author	Pubn date
J1.1	1500–49	An account of the Battle of Flodden	2,200	Not Known	1513
J1.2		Hevy newes of an earthquake	825	Not Known	1542
J1.3		A copy of a letter containing certayne newes	1,017	Not Known	1549
J2.1	1550–99	The Spoyle of Antwerpe	2,122	George Gascoigne	1576
J2.2		The English Mercurie	1,391	Not Known	1588
J3.1	1600–49	The weekely Newes	1,079	Not Known	1606
J3.2		The courant of newes	1,386	Not Known	1620
J3.3		The marchings of Two Regiments	2,101	Henry Foster	1643
J4.1	1650–99	Every Day's Intelligence 1	1,019		1653
J4.2		Every Day's Intelligence 2	1,013	Heneage Finch	1653
J4.3		A true designe of the Late Eruption of Mt Etna	2,170		1669
J5.1	1700–50	The Flying Post	1,107	Not Known	1700
J5.2		London Post	1,184	Not Known	1700
J5.3		Country Journal	1,876	Not Known	1736
		Total words	20,490		

news data, it does afford an opportunity to gain an insight into how the genre develops across the period.

We collected texts for our corpus from a variety of data sources, including: Early English Books Online (EEBO); the Oxford Text Archive (OTA); Renascence Editions (University of Oregon); Project Gutenberg; the Lampeter Corpus; the Lancaster Newsbook Corpus; the Corpus of Early English Dialogues 1560–1760; and the Burney Collection. In order to save time, where possible we avoided manually typing in texts from digital facsimiles and collected data that were already in machine readable format.

8.4.3 Annotating the corpus

We manually annotated the corpus using XML-style tags made up of an element, *dptag*, and an attribute, *cat*. The *cat* attribute is where we specified the category of discourse presentation using predesignated

Element	Attribute	Attribute Value
<dptag	cat	= "x x x x x x x x x x">
		fields 1–10

Figure 8.1 Annotation scheme used to tag the EModE corpus for speech, writing and thought presentation categories

alpha-numeric codes, which are based on those described by McIntyre et al. (2004). We entered the codes into the *cat* attribute using a strategy whereby we divided the attribute into ten (imaginary) fields or place-holders (see Figure 8.1).

Each field could contain one of a small number of predesignated constituent codes that provided details about the type of discourse presentation. We used *x* as a placeholder for empty field positions in the *cat* attribute but did not mark empty positions following the final attribute value. So, in practice, NT is marked <dptag cat="NxT"> rather than <dptag cat="NxTxxxxxxx">.

This tagging strategy meant that the same codes would always be in the same position within the attribute throughout the corpus. This makes subsequent searches for types of discourse presentation using corpus tools more straightforward. The codes and their positions within the *cat* attribute are set out in Table 8.4.

The possible constituents designated to the first four fields relate to the major DP categories (outlined in Table 8.1) and are always upper-case letters. The constituents designated to the remaining fields relate to DP sub-categories and provide further details about the DP. These are generally lower-case letters, but numbers and the hash symbol (#) are also possible in fields 9 and 10 respectively. The following example shows how the annotation scheme works in practice:

Table 8.4 Constituents of the fields of the *cat* attribute in the EModE Corpus

Field	Possible constituents	Definition of constituent
1	x N F	Narrator's; Free
2	x P I D	Presentation; Indirect; Direct
3	x S T W V I	Speech; Thought; Writing; Voice; Internal state
4	x A	Act
5	x p	Topic
6	x h	hypothetical
7	x i	inferred
8	x y	discourse summary
9	x 1 2 3 4	DP split into sections
10	x #	# = odd/interesting cases

<dptag cat="N"> But though that general has taken the crown from a head that was not worthy to wear it, and placed it on his own for good of the publick, and the honour of that mighty empire, </dptag>

<dptag cat="xIWxxxxx1"> he has, </dptag>

<dptag cat="NRW"> as they write from Vienna, </dptag>

<dptag cat="xIWxxxxx2"> settled the succession </dptag>

<dptag cat="N"> so, that after his death the crown shall return to the family again in the person of the young prince and deposed Sophi's son, of whose education he takes particular care. </dptag>

Notice that an instance of DP can be split into more than one part by, for example, a reporting clause. This situation is indicated in attribute 9 of a tag. We also mark all instances of narration and the clausal and non-clausal structures that introduce (or 'signal' [Thompson 1996: 524]) discourse presentation. In this way all text is enclosed in tags which mark function.

Once we had annotated the corpus, we calculated the numbers of occurrences of each DP category using Multilingual Corpus Toolkit (MLCT) (Piao et al. 2002), which we introduced in Chapter 6. We did that using regular expressions (see Friedl 2006) to search for individual DP categories using our tagging format (see Box 8.1). Using MLCT, it is also possible to extract the words in-between particular tags into separate files (see Box 8.2). In this way we were able to extract all instances of, say, IT into a file for further analysis using, for example, AntConc (Anthony 2018). Furthermore, by creating files for every DP category we were able to check that the sum of the words in the individual files matched the sum of the words in the whole corpus, which assured us that all our data had been accounted for.

8.4.4 Quantitative results

Figure 8.2 shows the overall distribution of speech, writing and thought presentation in both the EModE and PDE data.

From Figure 8.2 we can see that the overall patterns of distribution of discourse presentation in the EModE data and the PDE corpus are similar, with speech presentation being the dominant category, followed by thought and writing presentation. While the bar chart indicates that there is more thought and writing presentation in the EModE data than in PDE, log-likelihood tests show that these differences are not significant. Initially then, on the basis that the distribution of SW&TP

Box 8.1 Using Multilingual Corpus Toolkit to count DP tags

The software requires some knowledge of regular expressions, which are essentially complex wildcards for defining specific search patterns. In this box we will assume that we are interested in searching for tags that mark indirect thought (IT) in the EModE corpus.

1. Start MLCT and open the corpus under investigation by clicking **File > Open in left window**.

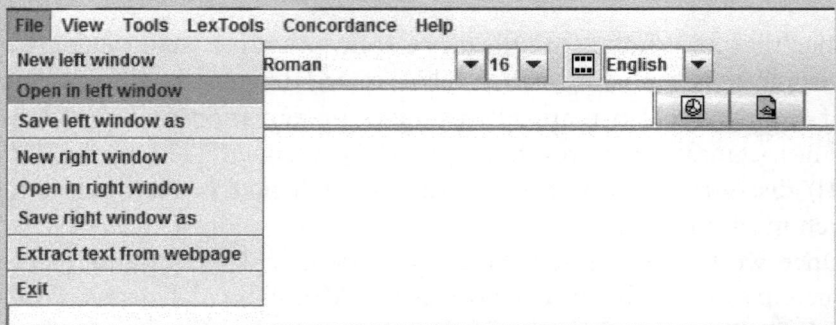

2. In the search bar next to the anchor symbol, type in the following search pattern:
   <dptag cat=" xIT.*?">

3. The characters describe a search pattern that tells MLCT to look for a dptag that contains xIT (so a tag for indirect thought) followed by any number of characters that fall within the rest of the tag. This is to capture IT tags that include any of the sub-category codes that might occur in any of the tag placeholders, for example, an *h* for hypothetical. The search pattern contains the following meta-characters, which are characters with special meaning:

   . (full stop) any character except a line break
   * (asterisk) zero or more times
   ? (question mark) once or none

Essentially, the special characters tell MLCT to find any number (including zero) of any characters (except a line break) occurring within the dptag after IT and before the closing quotation mark and angle bracket. The question mark instructs MLCT to stop searching once the pattern is satisfied for the first time (this is known as a non-greedy search). Without a question mark, the search would match as much data as possible, stopping only when the first line break was encountered.

4. Click the anchor icon to the left of the search bar. MLCT will extract all tags to the right window.

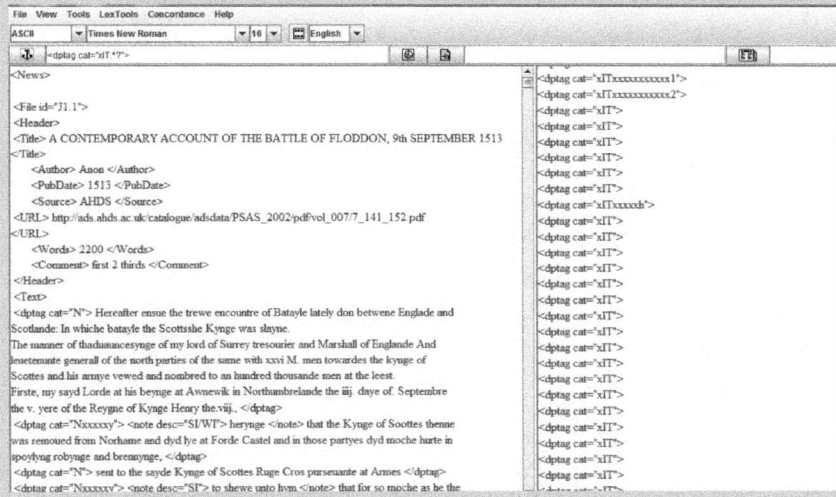

5. Click on **Tools > Count Lines**, and right window, and this will count the number of instances of the IT tag extract from the corpus.

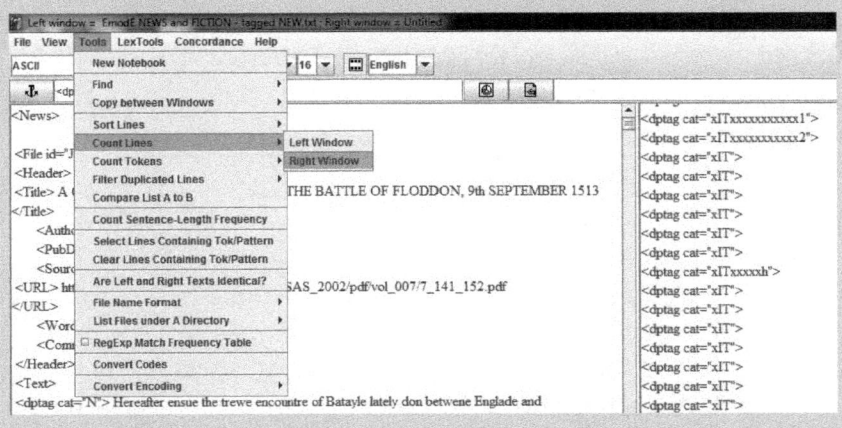

Box 8.2 Using Multilingual Corpus Toolkit to extract words in-between tags

In this box, we will again use indirect thought (IT) as our example to demonstrate the procedure for extracting text that occurs in-between tags.

1. Start MLCT and open the corpus under investigation by clicking **File > Open in left window**.
2. In the search bar next to the anchor symbol, type in the following search pattern:

<dptag cat=" xIT.*?">.*?</dptag>

The search pattern tells MLCT to look for any characters that fall between start and end tags for IT. As in Box 8.1, the opening tag in the search specifies that the tag contains xIT followed by any number of characters that fall within the rest of the tag in order to capture tags that contain sub-category codes.
3. Click the anchor icon to the left of the search bar. MLCT will extract all tags to the right window. Notice that this time, the right window contains tags, and text in-between tags.

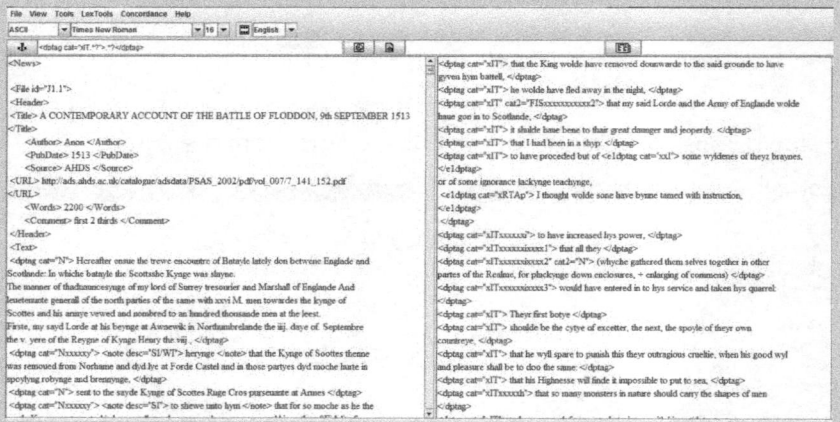

4. If we want just text with no tags, then we need to carry out a further stage of processing using MLCT. First, copy the results from the first search (in the right window) across to the left window by clicking on **Tools > Copy between Windows > Copy right window to left window**.

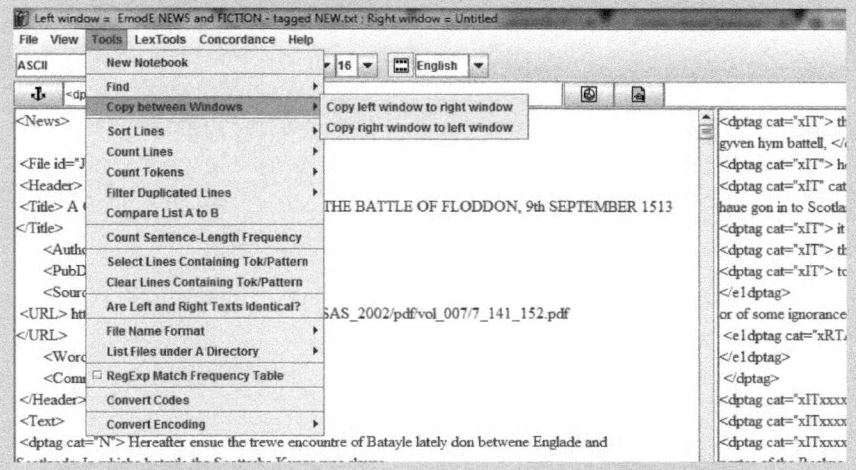

5. Now type in the following pattern in the search box

   <.*?>

   This pattern looks for any number of any characters that occur in-between angle brackets (i.e. tags) and stops once the pattern has been found (because the question mark makes it non-greedy).

6. Now click on the pie-chart icon to the right of the search box. The results of the search will appear in the right window, and will contain all the text that was tagged as indirect thought, but without the tags.

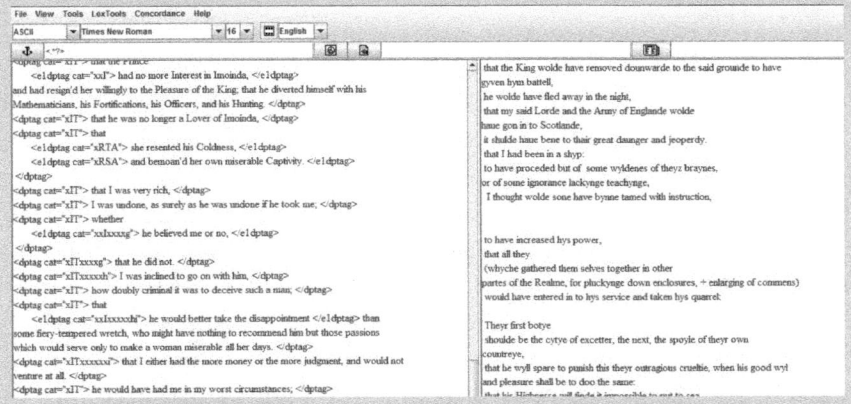

7. Notice that if you click on the anchor icon, this will extract all the tags, and ignore the text.

8. To save the results of the search (in the right window) as a plain text file, click on **File > Save right window as**. A dialogue box will open, within which you must select a location to save the file, and specify a name. When you type in the file name, remember to include the .txt suffix. If you miss this off, then MLCT will save the file in a format that may not be recognised by some software.

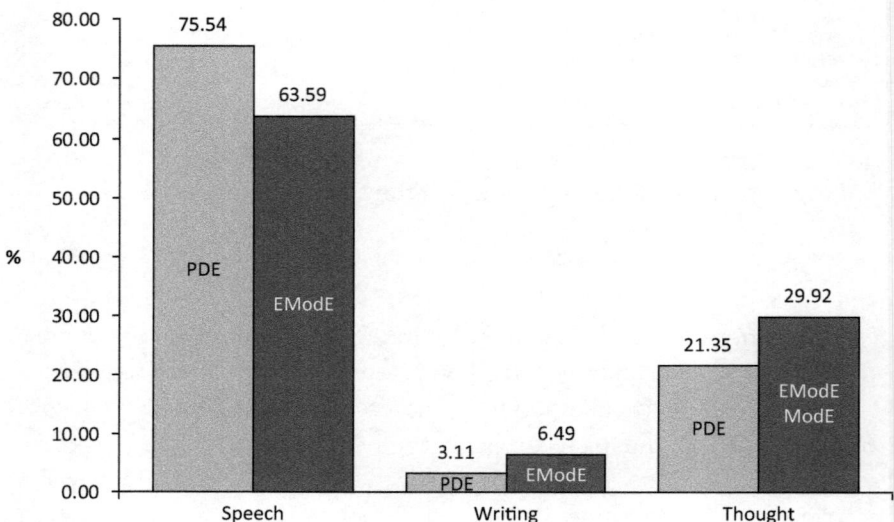

Figure 8.2 Overall distribution of speech, writing and thought presentation in the EModE and PDE corpora

in EModE is the same as for PDE, our alternative hypothesis (H_1: DP in EModE ≠ DP in PDE) is rejected and our null hypothesis (H_0: DP in EModE = DP in PDE) is upheld.

However, when we consider the frequencies of individual categories on the speech, writing and thought presentation clines (see Tables 8.5, 8.6 and 8.7) we find that some of differences between EModE and PDE are statistically significant. Tables 8.5, 8.6 and 8.7 show, respectively, the frequency of categories of speech, writing and thought presentation in the EModE corpus compared against the PDE data. The totals and percentages are based on the number of tags. We used log-likelihood to test the significance of differences, and figures in bold indicate those which are statistically significant.

Table 8.5 Frequencies of speech presentation categories

Category	PDE			EModE			LL
	Tag freq.	% of all DP	% of cline	Tag freq.	% of all DP	% of cline	
(F)DS	2,339	40.38	53.45	275	27.89	43.87	**37.12**
FIS	90	1.55	2.06	11	1.12	1.75	1.17
IS	784	13.53	17.92	120	12.17	19.14	1.20
NPSA	918	15.85	20.98	109	11.05	17.38	13.89
NPV	245	4.23	5.60	112	11.36	17.86	**64.73**
Totals	4,376	75.54	100.00	627	63.59	100.00	5.79

Table 8.6 Frequencies of writing presentation categories

Category	PDE			EModE Corpus			LL
	Tag freq.	% of all DP	% of cline	Tag freq.	% of all DP	% of cline	
(F)DW	43	0.74	23.89	17	1.72	26.56	6.96
FIW	12	0.21	6.67	0	0.00	0.00	6.96
IW	30	0.52	16.67	36	2.64	40.63	**19.68**
NPWA	82	1.42	45.56	10	1.01	15.63	10.38
NPW	13	0.22	7.22	11	1.12	17.19	5.26
Totals	180	3.11	100.00	74	6.49	100.00	0.59

Table 8.7 Frequencies of thought presentation categories

Category	PDE			EModE Corpus			LL
	No. of tags	% of all DP	% of cline	Tag freq.	% of all DP	% of cline	
(F)DT	84	1.45	6.79	5	0.51	1.70	15.00
FIT	230	3.97	18.59	1	0.10	0.34	**51.08**
IT	119	2.05	9.62	66	6.69	22.37	**45.13**
NPTA	71	1.23	5.74	39	3.96	13.22	**28.39**
NPT				11	1.12	3.73	4.38
NI	733	12.65	59.26	173	17.55	58.64	1.69
Totals	1,237	21.35	100.00	295	29.92	100.00	12.34

8.4.5 Discussion

In this section we use the results from our quantitative analysis to guide a qualitative examination of our data.

Starting with speech presentation, Table 8.5 shows that NPV, the most minimal speech presentation option for a writer, is over-represented in

EModE writing when compared with PDE. Conversely, the table shows that (F)DS, the category that apparently presents the original discourse verbatim, is over-represented in the PDE data. That the opposite ends of the cline are used proportionally more in the two corpora suggest that a stylistic feature of EModE writing is that it is more diegetic than PDE writing, which in turn is more mimetic by comparison. In the fiction section of the corpus, this suggests that we hear more from narrators and less from characters. This reflects the early development of the then new literary form (John Lyly's *Euphues* published in 1573 is regarded as the first novel), wherein writers were uncertain about 'what prose should be' (Baker 1936: 13). Initially, fiction was a means of lecturing or discussing morals which contained 'blundering mixtures of narration and reflection' (Baker 1936: 1).

The over-representation of NPV in EModE news can be related to the practice of news gathering in the early days of newspapers. This was done by word-of-mouth, via rumours and gossip, or by collecting stories told by people returning from overseas (Clarke 2004: 42). Certainly, recording (by transcription) what people were saying was difficult, and getting an audience with a high-ranking dignitary in order to conduct an interview was hardly likely. NPV therefore reflects the socio-historical context, and allows the news writer to be vague or to make generalisations about the information received (as well as to censor speech deemed to be politically sensitive).

Looking now at writing presentation in EModE, Table 8.6 shows that Indirect Writing is statistically over-used in the EModE data when compared with the PDE data. The majority of the Indirect Writing presentation in the EModE corpus (34 out of 36 examples) occurs in the news journalism data. In each case, there are reporting clauses that introduce the indirect writing. For example: as 'it is written', 'the port-letters say', 'they tell us from Stetin', 'we have advice from Lubeck' and 'they write from Lynn'. Considerable emphasis is placed on identifying the source of the report that follows. It appears, then, that there is a concern among EModE writers of news reports to make clear that the report of news is taken from an identifiable source, rather than being, say, conjecture on the part of the writer. The indirect category makes it clear that the news report is a *re*-presentation of an original source, as opposed to, say, a summary report. This choice of presentational mode might have been adopted in order to raise the standing of the news. Alternatively, it might be a consequence of the news writer/ editor deciding against the interjection of personal opinion in favour of letting the news speak for itself. This would accord with the relative absence of press freedom in the period, and the necessity of avoiding overtly critical comment in news writing. Taking care to indicate that a report is based on information from another source, and presenting that source in such a way that the original discourse is recoverable, is one way of implicitly claiming no responsibility for the content of the report. We can also note that, in contrast, the quantitative norm of NPWA (Narrator's Presentation of Writing) for PDE news report has the function of summarising more than reporting. Indirect Writing, on the other hand, is the closest we can get to the original discourse while still allowing the reporting of this from a different viewpoint. This, we suggest, may be indicative of the developing nature of the news report genre from report to summary; in effect, a move towards the narrator end of the discourse presentation cline.

Finally, the statistically significant results from the thought presentation cline given in Table 8.7 highlight an over-representation of IT and NPTA in the EModE data, and an under-representation of FIT. The relative proportional prevalence of these two types of thought presentation in the fiction section of the corpus, along with an under-representation of FIT (we found only one instance), suggests that the presentation options for character thoughts were still developing and that IT in particular was the default option. However, this requires further careful investigation using more data, especially from the earlier part of the period. As for the news section, some of the thought presentation was due to earlier forms of news being personal accounts which contained the thought presentation of the person recalling the newsworthy incident (or even, in one story, the presentation of the thoughts of the devil!). Other instances of IT occur later in the time period and relate to an apparent process of summarising generalised or collected opinion (see Short 2012 for a discussion of speech and writing summary). So, unlike IW, which provides a re-presentation of news, IT provides non-verifiable summary (for more insight into discourse presentation in EModE, see McIntyre and Walker 2011; Walker and McIntyre 2015).

8.4.6 Summary remarks

In this case study we used a corpus to represent a single historical variety of written English from a particular time period (EModE). This corpus was built to match a corpus containing texts from a different period of time (PDE). We analysed the data in our EModE corpus for discourse presentation using the same model used to analyse the PDE corpus. The results of our analysis were recorded in the data in our corpus using XML tags, and using these tags we calculated frequencies for different types of discourse presentation. Therefore, unlike the keyword comparisons we have made in previous chapters, our comparison here was between frequencies that resulted from a stylistic analysis of the data. We tested any differences resulting from these comparisons using the log-likelihood test (which we introduced in detail in Chapter 5) to determine statistical significance. We then used the results of the significance testing to provide a focus for further analysis of the tagged data via concordances. This more detailed analysis suggested possibilities for further data collection, amendments to tagging, and further analysis. Indeed, Walker and McIntyre (2015), in one particular line of enquiry stemming from this initial research, used patterns identified in the annotated data to search a larger, untagged corpus of EModE. Our investigation, therefore, proceeded in cycles of qualitative and quantitative analysis, which was guided to some extent by the use of relevant statistical testing.

8.5 Case study: Frequencies and functions of modal auxiliary verbs in Early Modern English journalism

For our second case study, we stay in the Early Modern period and focus on print news media in an effort to determine some of the linguistic features of this evolving genre. However, rather than making comparisons between the past and the present, as we did in section 8.4, here we aim to track changes across a 100-year time period. We focus on the Early Modern period because during this time there were significant developments in the evolution of the newspaper as a text-type which are widely acknowledged (Raymond 1996, 1999; Brownlees 2006a; Jucker 2009). Our investigation concentrates on just one linguistic feature in news journalism – modal auxiliary verbs – and we plot the frequencies of this finite set of linguistic forms between 1620 and 1719.[4] One reason we look at modal auxiliary verbs is because, as McEnery and Hardie note, grammatical features such as modal auxiliary verbs 'may be responsive to relatively short-term sociohistorical pressures' (2012: 103). We hypothesised that modal auxiliary verb usage would change over this period in response to developments in laws concerning press freedom. Specifically, at those points in the period when journalists were allowed free expression, we expected to see a rise in the use of those modal auxiliary verbs whose function is to indicate the likelihood of the truth of a proposition, effectively acting as indicators of journalistic opinion, attitude and stance.

To investigate this, we constructed a corpus of EModE news texts drawn from the period 1620–1719. We chose this 100-year time period on the basis that 1620 is generally recognised as the beginning of regular publishing of news sheets and pamphlets (Brownlees 2015: 6), and by 1720 news publishing was firmly established with daily newspapers in circulation. Over two million copies of newspapers were being published annually (Goff 2007) and press freedom was becoming recognised.

Our research question for this case study asks whether frequencies of modal auxiliary verbs, in terms of both their forms and their function, change significantly over the 100-year period. We also wanted to know if any changes coincided with important historical events, such as the relaxing of restrictions on the press.

8.5.1 Building a corpus of Early Modern English news texts

To answer our research questions, we constructed a corpus of approximately 500,000 words of EModE news journalism spanning 100 years (1620–1719). We manually transcribed facsimiles of news publications drawn from the online Burney Collection of English newspapers and also reused files from other news corpora such as ZEN (see Appendix 1 for details). We divided our 100-year period into decades (1620–9, 1630–9, and so on), within which we collected approximately 50,000 words of newspaper text (around 5,000 words per year). We acknowledge that these ten-year divisions and associated data boundaries are artificial but they are necessary given the size of our corpus and the amount of data. As Millar points out, 'changes in the frequency of language features over time cannot be assumed *a priori* to be smooth' and, as a result, 'data from multiple chronological points appear to be essential to obtain a clear overview of any trend and to allow for accurate statistical modelling' (2009: 208).

To help make our corpus as representative as possible of EModE news journalism generally, we sampled from a wide spread of newspapers. We restricted the sample size to between 1,000 and 2,000 words per text. We chose this range to ensure our texts were long enough to give an indication of the style of a particular newspaper (see Biber 1993: 248–52) but not so long that a single text might skew the corpus and any results we obtained from it. Whenever possible we collected complete texts (i.e. complete articles/new stories). We included data from at least three and at most five newspapers for each year, although there are some years for which this was not possible due to a lack of available data. Advertisements were not included in our data; we collected only news reports.

In his study of diachronic changes in modal auxiliaries in the twentieth century, Millar (2009) criticises Leech's (2003) study of this topic for using small corpora (Leech uses the Brown family of one million word corpora; see Appendix 2). Compared with the corpora used by both Leech (2003) and Millar (2009), our corpus is relatively small. This is a result of (1) a relative scarcity of textual material, and (2) the labour-intensive nature of turning our data into machine-readable text and then annotating it. Since many of our texts were considerably degraded, OCR scanning was not practical and texts therefore had to be typed by hand. Nonetheless, our corpus contains a broad range of news publications in order to be representative of EModE news journalism generally and it has the requisite multiple chronological points to allow reasonable statistical measurements. As we shall see, though, our corpus presents us with issues that are not just related to size.

8.5.2 Annotating the corpus

We identified and marked-up, using XML tags, all the modal auxiliary forms and their functions in our corpus. We achieved the formal annotation by first compiling a list of possible modal auxiliary forms and variants using descriptions of PDE and EModE grammar. According to Depraetere and Reed (2006: 272), a distinction is commonly made between central and peripheral (or marginal) modal auxiliary verbs. For PDE the central modals are *can, could, may, might, shall, should, will, would* and *must*, while the peripheral modals are *dare, need* and *ought*. For EModE, Barber (1976: 177) suggests that at the start of the Early Modern period (which for Barber spans 1500–1700) there were 12 central modal auxiliaries (*can, couth, dare, durst, may, might, mote, must, shall, should, will* and *would*) and two peripheral modals (*ought* and *need*). Barber notes that there were numerous variant spelling of the forms; for example, *couth* could be spelled *coud* or *coude*, with *could* appearing part way through the sixteenth century. Additionally, the auxiliary *might* had the alternative form *mought*, and *will* also occurred as *woll* and *wull*. All these PDE and EModE forms and variants above were included in our list, along with (1) all regular contracted forms, such as *'ll* and *'d*; (2) variant contracted forms, such as *cu'd, cou'd, shou'd, wou'd*; (3) irregular forms that occur with markers of negation, such as *cannot, shan't, won't*; (4) regular negated forms, such as *wouldn't*; and (5) other variants identified during the transcription process, such as *heel, shal, wil*.

   We created a Visual Basic (VB) macro that contained a series of find and replace routines for every modal form in our list.[5] For example, the set of commands shown in Figure 8.3 uses the *find* and *replacement* VB

```
Selection.Find.Replacement.ClearFormatting
   With Selection.Find
        .Text = "can"
        .Replacement.Text = "<mod type=" "e" ">can</mod> "
        .Forward = True
        .Wrap = wdFindContinue
        .Format = False
        .MatchCase = False
        .MatchWholeWord = True
        .MatchWildcards = False
        .MatchSoundsLike = False
        .MatchAllWordForms = False
   End With
Selection.Find.Execute Replace:=wdReplaceAll
```

Figure 8.3 An example of the Visual Basic commands used to place XML tags round modal verbs in the EModE corpus

objects to find the modal form *can* and replace it with *can* plus some XML annotation.

The macro, which contained a similar set of commands for every modal form in our list, searched through the whole corpus and placed tags around each instance that it found. The tags are in the format:

<mod type="e"> mmmm </mod>

where *mmmm* represents the modal auxiliary verb form found by the macro. The type attribute, which has a default setting of *e*, encodes the function of the modal auxiliary, which is explained below. It is worth mentioning here that not all variants reported by Barber (1976) occurred in our data (the forms *coude, couth, couthe, mote, mought, woll* and *wull* did not appear in our data) but we found a number of additional spelling variants that were *not* reported by Barber (1976) – for example, *shal* and *cu'd*. This serves as a reminder that the process of annotating a corpus is itself a form of analysis and can bring to light revealing insights.

The model of modal function we applied to our data is based on Quirk et al. (1985) and Biber et al. (1999), who divide modality into two types: extrinsic and intrinsic. According to Biber et al., extrinsic modality refers to the 'logical status of events or states, usually relating to assessments of likelihood: possibility, necessity, or prediction' (1999: 485). This type of modality combines what other grammars (e.g. Depraetere and Reed 2006) refer to as epistemic modality, which

Table 8.8 Modal functional categories, meanings and prototypical forms

Intrinsic	Extrinsic	Prototypical modal forms
permission	possibility and ability	*can, could, may, might*
obligation	necessity	*must, should*
volition (intention)	prediction	*will, would, shall*

relates to 'the necessity or possibility of the truth [...] of proposi-
tions [...]' (Depraetere and Reed 2006: 274), and root modality, which
relates to 'the necessity or possibility of the actualization of situations'
(Depraetere and Reed 2006: 274). Intrinsic modality relates to 'actions
and events that humans (or other agents) directly control [...]' (Biber et
al. 1999: 485) and includes meanings relating to permission, obligation
and volition (or intention). The former two meanings are often classified as deontic modality (see Huddleston 1976; Lyons 1978; Palmer
2001), while the latter is classed by some linguists as a type of dynamic
modality (see Palmer 2001). With regard to ability, Quirk et al. suggest
that it 'is best considered a special case of possibility [...]' (1985: 221)
and is therefore extrinsic.

Table 8.8 shows the PDE modal forms prototypically associated with
particular modal function. For example, it is possible for *can* to be used
to grant permission (intrinsic), suggest possibility (extrinsic), or state
someone's ability (also extrinsic in the model used for this study).

We manually analysed each instance of the tagged modal forms to
ascertain their function using the above framework. If the function was
intrinsic, the type attribute in the tag was changed from the default
setting of *e* to *i*. If the modality was epistemic, then the type indicator
remained unchanged. It was during this process that we disambig-
uated the tagged modal forms. That is to say, instances of tagged
forms that were not used as modal verbs (e.g. when *may* denoted
the fifth month, or *will* denoted a legal document) were untagged,
and therefore not included in our quantification. We also untagged
any instances of *need, dare* and *ought* that were not used as modal
auxiliaries. The modal auxiliary verbs were initially analysed (and the
type attributes changed accordingly) by one of us and then checked
by the other. Where we disagreed, revisions were made in light of our
discussions.

8.5.3 Quantification and results

Once the corpus was tagged, making accurate counts of different modal
verb forms and functions was a straightforward process. Table 8.9

Table 8.9 Raw frequencies of modal forms with per thousand frequencies in brackets

Modal	1620–9 No. (‰)	1630–9 No. (‰)	1640–9 No. (‰)	1650–9 No. (‰)	1660–9 No. (‰)	1670–9 No. (‰)	1680–9 No. (‰)	1690–9 No. (‰)	1700–9 No. (‰)	1710–19 No. (‰)
CAN	30 (0.65)	32 (1.1)	41 (0.86)	43 (0.9)	39 (0.76)	22 (0.53)	26 (0.58)	60 (0.91)	28 (0.5)	24 (0.55)
COULD	25 (0.54)	19 (0.65)	23 (0.48)	28 (0.58)	17 (0.33)	20 (0.48)	21 (0.47)	55 (0.83)	11 (0.2)	21 (0.48)
MAY	45 (0.97)	22 (0.75)	77 (1.62)	57 (1.19)	59 (1.15)	57 (1.37)	48 (1.06)	55 (0.83)	57 (1.02)	38 (0.87)
SHALL	103 (2.22)	59 (2.02)	75 (1.58)	60 (1.25)	74 (1.44)	23 (0.55)	49 (1.09)	73 (1.1)	79 (1.41)	50 (1.15)
SHOULD	42 (0.9)	36 (1.23)	89 (1.87)	57 (1.19)	44 (0.85)	21 (0.51)	44 (0.98)	66 (1)	34 (0.61)	38 (0.87)
WILL	73 (1.57)	77 (2.64)	134 (2.81)	124 (2.59)	125 (2.43)	146 (3.52)	124 (2.75)	209 (3.16)	207 (3.7)	161 (3.7)
WOULD	43 (0.93)	33 (1.13)	57 (1.2)	72 (1.5)	32 (0.62)	39 (0.94)	64 (1.42)	130 (1.97)	45 (0.8)	39 (0.9)
DARE	1 (0.02)	1 (0.03)	4 (0.08)	2 (0.04)	1 (0.02)	0 (0)	0 (0)	1 (0.02)	1 (0.02)	0 (0)
DURST	1 (0.02)	2 (0.07)	1 (0.02)	2 (0.04)	0 (0)	0 (0)	1 (0.02)	0 (0)	0 (0)	0 (0)
MIGHT	16 (0.34)	10 (0.34)	48 (1.01)	33 (0.69)	28 (0.54)	20 (0.48)	32 (0.71)	23 (0.35)	7 (0.12)	12 (0.28)
OUGHT	0 (0)	0 (0)	9 (0.19)	9 (0.19)	2 (0.04)	4 (0.1)	5 (0.11)	16 (0.24)	4 (0.07)	6 (0.14)
MUST	15 (0.32)	9 (0.31)	15 (0.32)	23 (0.48)	15 (0.29)	10 (0.24)	10 (0.22)	19 (0.29)	7 (0.12)	10 (0.23)
Total	394 (8.49)	300 (10.29)	573 (12.03)	510 (10.64)	436 (8.46)	362 (8.72)	424 (9.4)	707 (10.69)	480 (8.57)	399 (9.17)

shows the raw totals (with per thousand totals in brackets) for the modal verbs forms for each decade represented by our corpus.

The modal forms in column one of the table (under the heading *Modal*) represent groupings which include all negated, contracted and irregular variants of the form. So, for example, the numbers shown for COULD include totals for *could, couth, couthe, coud, coude, cu'd, cou'd* and *coulde* (we use small caps to indicate these grouped forms). The bottom row of Table 8.9 shows the raw totals (and per thousand totals in brackets) for all modal auxiliary verbs for a whole decade. In 1620–9, for example, there are 394 instances of modal verbs, which equates to 8.49 words per thousand in that section of the corpus. Figure 8.4 presents the per thousand totals for each decade in the form of a graph, and this shows that there is a distinctive peak in the total number of modals in 1640–9 and a minor peak in 1690–9.

An additional result observable from this data is that there is a slight rise in per thousand frequency when the start of the period is compared with the end of the period represented by our corpus (8.49 versus 9.17). To some extent, this result seems to match the findings from Biber's (2004) work using the ARCHER Corpus (see Appendix 1), which plots modal frequencies from 1650 to 1990. Biber (2004: 200) shows, albeit via a line graph only, what looks to be a slight rise in modal frequencies across three sample points: 1650–99, 1700–99 and 1800–99. These comparable findings from different datasets and sample points begin to provide a body of evidence that suggests an increased tendency towards modal usage in news discourse between the 1600s and the 1800s.

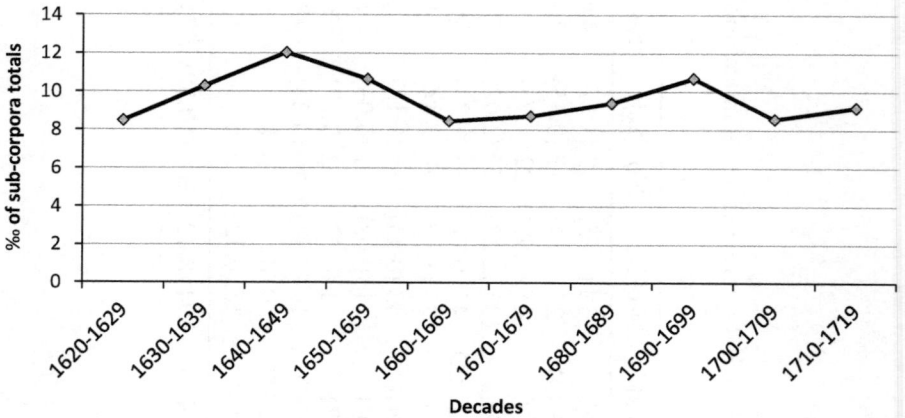

Figure 8.4 Per thousand totals of modal forms for each decade

8.5.4 Statistical analysis

We wanted to assess whether the peaks and troughs that can be seen in Figure 8.3 were unusually high or low compared with the rest of our data. One option for checking this is to use standard deviation, which we briefly mentioned in Chapter 5. Standard deviation measures the variance from the mean value of a set of numbers, and is calculated using the formula shown in Figure 8.5.

We calculated the mean of the decade totals of all modal verb usage using per thousand frequencies (these are shown in the *Total* rows of Tables 8.8 and 8.9). The mean value, which came to 9.65, was subtracted from each of the decade totals (referred to as the observed frequencies in the formula) and the product of each subtraction squared. The sum of all these values is then divided by the number of values in the set minus one (i.e. 10 − 1) and the standard deviation is the square root of this value, which for our data was 1.21. We assessed whether a decade total was unusually high if it was more than one standard deviation (i.e. 1.21) above the mean frequency of 9.65 (i.e. above 10.86), and unusually low if it was less than one standard deviation below the mean frequency (i.e. below 8.44). From this we were able to see which totals were higher and lower than a normal distribution. Using this method, the only unusually high value in our data is for the 1640s with a value of 12.03, which we can show more clearly by plotting the figures shown in Figure 8.3 again, but this time with trend lines indicating the mean, SD high and SD low (see Figure 8.6).

One of the other statistical tests we discussed in Chapter 5 is log likelihood (LL), and we used it here as a further check of whether differences observed in decade totals were real as opposed to chance happenings. We did this by comparing individual decade totals against the sum of the remaining decade totals. So, for example, the total number of modal verbs found in the 1620–9 section of the corpus was assessed against the total number of modal verbs found in the rest of the corpus (1630–1719). Likewise, the modal usage in 1630–9 was assessed against the combined modal usage in 1620–9 and 1640–1719. We refer to the ten-year portion of the corpus being assessed as the target and

$$\sigma = \sqrt{\frac{\Sigma\left(observed\ frequency - mean\right)^2}{\left(number\ of\ observed\ values - 1\right)}}$$

Figure 8.5 Formula for standard deviation (where σ = standard deviation and Σ = the sum of)

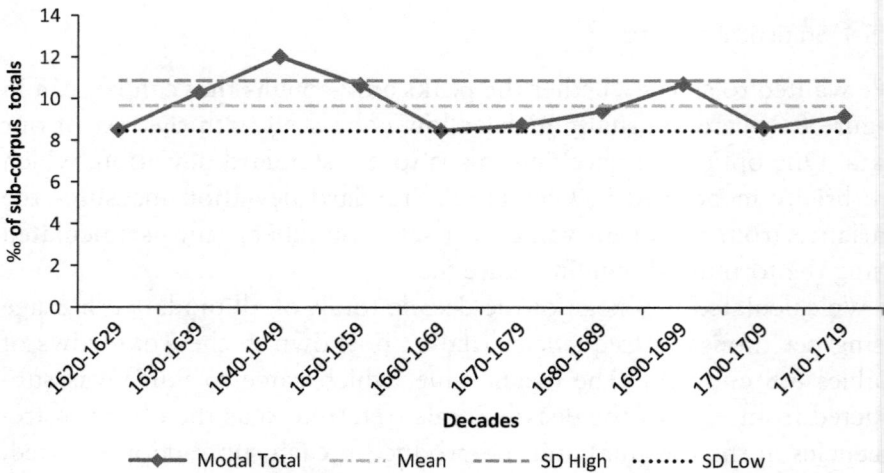

Figure 8.6 Per thousand totals of modal forms for each decade with standard deviation trend lines

the remaining portion of the corpus as the comparator. Therefore, in the latter example, 1630–9 is the target, and (1620–9) + (1640–1719) is the comparator. The size of the target and the comparator changes with each comparison. We calculated the log-likelihood using an online tool,[6] and the resulting figures are shown in Table 8.10.

The final column of the table is the log-likelihood value, which represents a rating of the confidence that the difference between the target and comparator totals is not occurring by chance. These values suggest whether modal verbs are under-represented (indicated by minus signs)

Table 8.10 Log-likelihood figures for total modal usage within each ten-year period compared with the rest of the corpus

Decade	Target: total no. of words	Target: total no. of modal forms	Comparator: total no. of words	Comparator: total no. of modal forms	LL
1620–9	46,418	394	428,504	4,191	−7.52
1630–9	29,155	300	445,767	4,285	+1.27
1640–9	47,613	573	427,309	4,012	+29.03
1650–9	47,922	510	427,000	4,075	+5.23
1660–9	51,526	436	423,396	4,149	−8.84
1670–9	41,509	362	433,413	4,223	−4.23
1680–9	45,124	424	429,798	4,161	−0.35
1690–9	66,115	707	408,807	3,878	+8.35
1700–9	56,007	480	418,915	4,105	−7.99
1710–19	43,533	399	431,389	4,186	−1.20

or over-represented (indicated by plus signs[7]) within a particular ten-year period when compared with the rest of the corpus. The higher the log-likelihood score, the more likely it is that the difference is not the result of chance. The highest value is 29.03 for the 1640–9 decade, which suggests that there is a less than 0.01 per cent probability that this over-representation is by chance.

Both the tests applied to our data indicate that, on a statistical basis, the 1640–9 data is worth further investigation. Nonetheless, as we have made clear before, statistical significance does not equate to interpretive significance, and further qualitative analysis is required to investigate the implications of these results. One fairly obvious observation, though, is that the dataset reflects part of the time period during which the English Civil War (1642–51) took place. This unsettled period in English history is important with regard to English news reporting, not least because of the abolishment in July 1641 of the Star Chamber and the High Commission, the two most powerful courts in England, which during the reign of Charles I became instruments of oppression. As Clarke notes, '[w]ithout the authority of the Star Chamber [...] the press was free' (2004: 17). Brownlees (2006a: 9) suggests that during the years of the Civil War (1642–8) newspapers took on a 'highly personalized' style before reverting to a less fanatical form of reporting in response to governmental wishes after the conflict. Our data suggests that one possible linguistic manifestation of that changing style is an increase in the use of modal auxiliary verbs. We explore this further in the following sections.

8.5.5 Further analysis and discussion

We turn our attention now to the function of the modal verbs, which were classified as either extrinsic (possibility, ability, prediction) or intrinsic (volition, obligation, permission). Table 8.11 shows the frequencies per thousand of extrinsic and intrinsic modals across our corpus. These figures are also shown in the form of a graph in Figure 8.7. The dashed line in Figure 8.7 represents total modal verbs in the period, so this line is exactly the same as that in Figures 8.3 and 8.5. The separate lines for extrinsic modality (i.e. that associated with probability and ability) and intrinsic modality (i.e. that associated with obligation and permission) plot the changes in the function of modality over the period and show that, generally, there is more extrinsic modality in our corpus than intrinsic. The solid grey line indicates that there is a dip in extrinsic modality in the 1640–9 portion of the corpus, while the dashed-dotted line indicates an opposite trend for intrinsic modality, which rises in the 1640–9 period.

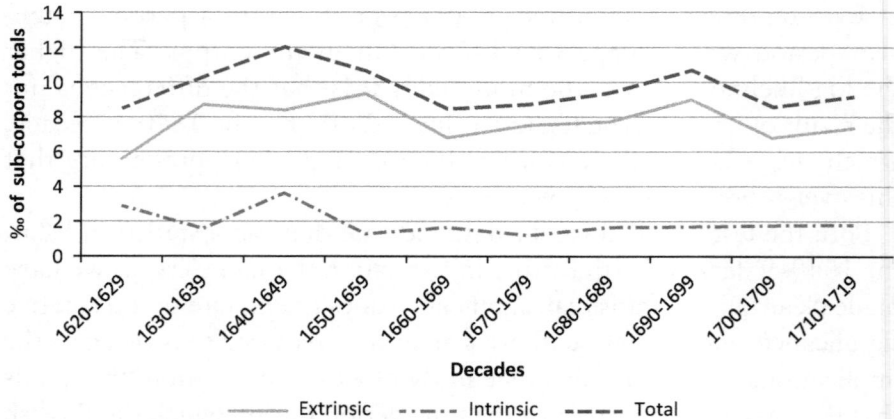

Figure 8.7 Modal function in the EModE News Corpus

Using standard deviation again, and plotting it on the chart that shows intrinsic and extrinsic totals (Figure 8.8), we can see which totals are higher or lower than average across the 100-year period and that intrinsic modality in the 1640–9 portion of the corpus is unusually frequent.

We calculated the log likelihood for the difference between the totals for intrinsic modality in the 1640–9 portion of the corpus and the rest of the corpus, and obtained a score of 65.27, showing that we could be confident that the difference was not a chance happening ($p = 0.0001$). The effect size for the difference was calculated, using log ratio, to be 1.07, which shows (in line with our standard deviation calculations) that intrinsic modality is about twice as common in the 1640s as it is in the rest of the corpus. So, while this shows that there is a difference, it is classed as small. Nevertheless, the result offers an obvious focus for further analysis.

Turning our attention, then, to the 1640–9 portion of our corpus, we again used standard deviation to assess which particular modal auxiliary verbs had an unusually high usage during this period. In this way, we were able to find a focus for further, more detailed analysis of *may*, *should* and *might*. The individual graphs for the frequencies of these verb-forms, for the whole period, are shown in Figure 8.9.

We looked more closely at the functional distributions of these modal verbs and noted an increase in intrinsic usage for each of them. In particular, as Figure 8.10 shows, for *should* the frequency of intrinsic modality exceeds that of extrinsic modality, which, in fact, decreases. This seemed a noteworthy difference, so we investigated *should* in more detail.

In the 1640s there are 30 instances of *should* used extrinsically and 59 instances of intrinsic usage. We analysed the concordance lines for

Table 8.11 Per thousand frequencies for modal functions in the EModE News Corpus

Function	1620–9		1630–9		1640–9		1650–9		1660–9		1670–9		1680–9		1690–9		1700–9		1710–19	
	Freq. ‰		Freq. ‰		Freq. ‰		Freq. ‰		Freq. ‰		Freq. ‰		Freq. ‰		Freq. ‰		Freq. ‰		Freq. ‰	
Extrinsic	5.6		8.71		8.4		9.35		6.81		7.51		7.73		9		6.8		7.36	
Intrinsic	2.89		1.58		3.63		1.29		1.65		1.2		1.66		1.69		1.77		1.81	
Total	8.49		10.29		12.03		10.64		8.46		8.71		9.39		10.69		8.57		9.17	

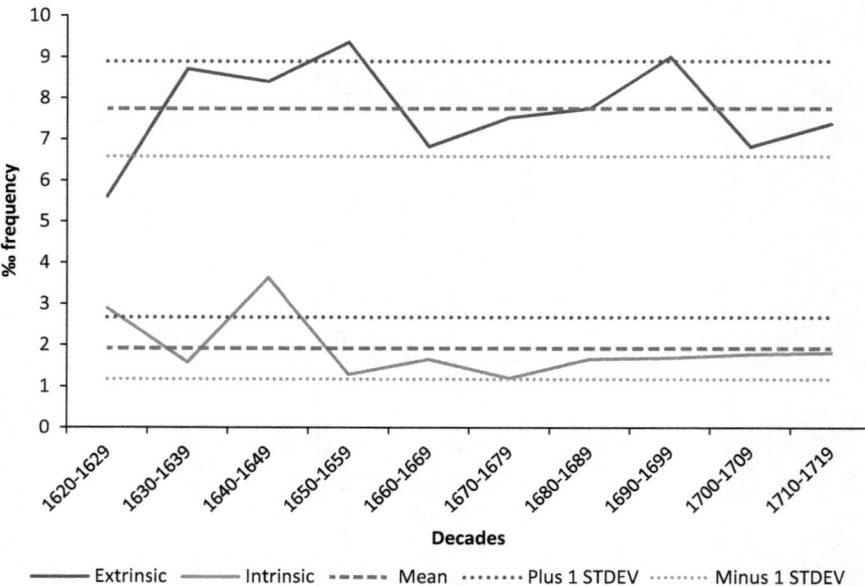

Figure 8.8 Extrinsic and intrinsic modality in the EModE News Corpus

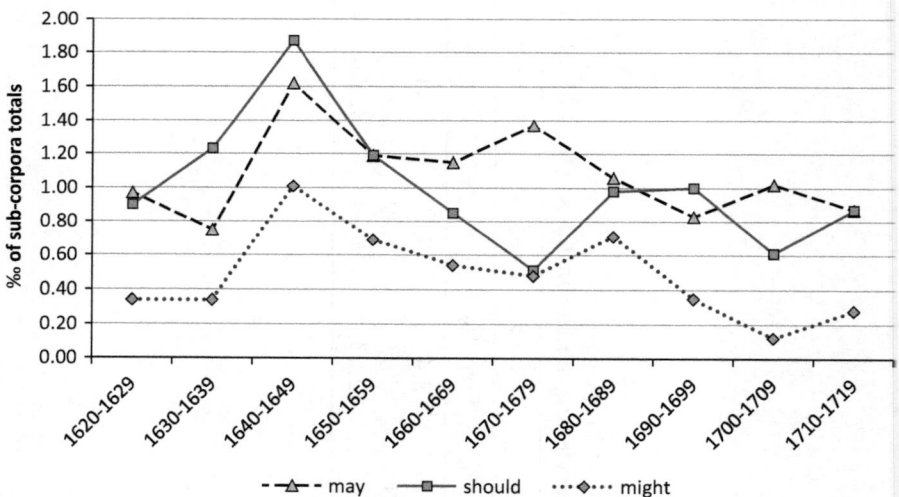

Figure 8.9 Frequencies of *may*, *should* and *might* in the EModE
News Corpus

the intrinsic uses (i.e. those associated with obligation and permission) and found that none of the instances expressed editorial opinion, but instead they reported speech or writing relating to parliamentary proceedings (see Figure 8.11). The abolition of the Star Chamber was an important event for freedom of the press in this period because, amongst other things, it allowed the press to report parliamentary

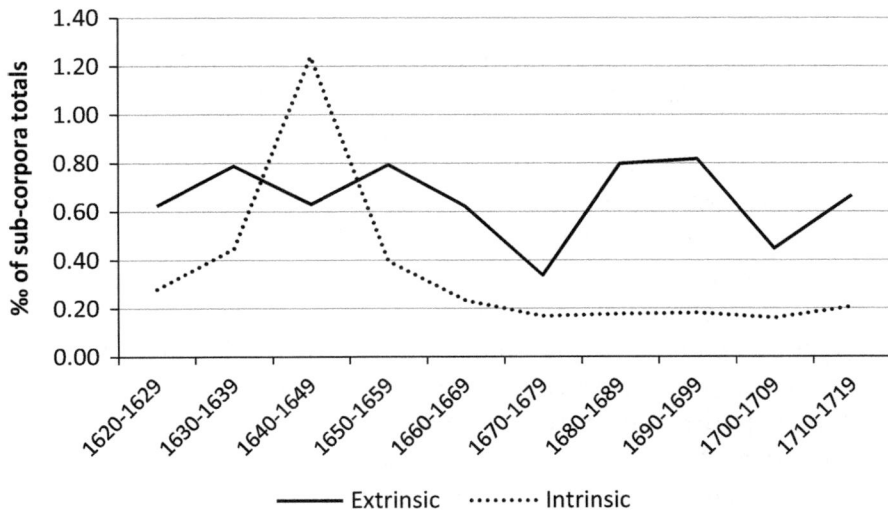

Figure 8.10 Frequencies of extrinsic and intrinsic *should* in the EModE News Corpus

	should	
s near the King (as Privy Counsellors, &c.)	should	be placed without consent of Parliament, so a
without consent of Parliament, so also none	should	be displaced without like consent. We appoint
It was ordered that Captaine Legge	should	bee sent for up to the Commons house, and a
a Conference, wherein the foresaid letters	should	be read, purporting that the Earle of Ne
mittee of the Comments ordered that the same	should	be reported on Monday to the Commons house.
ven against Captaine Hide , that he	should	say, himselfe was the man who drew a swords a
reed that eight companies of the Traine Band	should	be raised for the safety of the King and Par
xt day, and that Captaine Skipwith	should	be appointed Sarjant Major for the City of
hat none besides his Majestie and the Lords	should	passe through the Court of guard to the house
nd that after that they had so searched they	should	appoint a watch that none shou
should appoint a watch that none	should	enter thereinto that night. The Lievetenant r
an Order to the Lieutenant that the Bishops	should	have no more then two men a peece to attend t
th the Lords, and it was agreed that letters	should	be sent into all parts of the Kingdome, to p
ds, and that a list of all the Lievetenants	should	be brought in, and that all criminall persons
brought in, and that all criminall persons	should	be put out of office &c. Ma4ter Speaker
was found there, and it was decreed that it	should	be brought to the City of London . S
ason. And it was ordered that a Declaration	should	be publisht of his Majesties severall breach
upon it was ordered, that the Lord Admirall	should	be desired to be carefull to take the said s
uth; and it was ordered that others of them	should	be sent to Windsor Castle, and other prisons
n order that no shipping going to New-Castle	should	carry any Corne thither, nor bring any Coale
they agreed that an ordinance of Parliament	should	be drawne up to that purpose. It was also ag
ns that the Collectors of the Custome-house	should	be removed from their places for some complain

Figure 8.11 Sample concordance lines of intrinsic *should* in the EModE News Corpus

proceedings. This change is reflected in our data since it contains reports from Parliament.

The sharp increase in intrinsic *should* is therefore attributable to an incursion of language features from one genre or register (parliamentary proclamations) into another (news report). While this is not evidence of a change in reporting language or style in the way that we envisaged, it is nevertheless a distinct way of reporting. That is to say, the increase in *should* suggests that news writers are reporting fairly faithfully what happened in Parliament by *re*-presenting the proclamations. This is of interest when we consider the alternative ways in which happenings in Parliament could have been reported. Faithful representation could be seen as a style of report, marked by inter-discursivity and indicative, to some extent, of a lack of personal style in this type of news reporting. So while the abolition of the Star Chamber meant that news from Parliament was allowed, the evidence from our corpus suggests that it was reported in a neutral, non-inflammatory way. Of course, given the size of our corpus, these results are to be viewed with caution, but offer working hypotheses for future research.

One issue, of course, is that our results represent only the data in our corpus. During the latter stages of the Civil War period a number of newspapers were published that contained more biased reports. As Clarke notes:

> So far the newsbooks purported to give strictly factual accounts of events, albeit one-sided. They avoided comment. Even the London parliamentary presses had refrained from being too critical of the other side in case a reconciliation between King and Parliament took place leaving them isolated and vulnerable to the accusation of alienating Parliament from the Crown. Neutrality ended with the advent of the mercuries. The mercuries added another factor to the development of English journalism – the attempt to influence public opinion by providing a partisan commentary on the news. (Clarke 2004: 20)

Issues of some of these newspapers are in our corpus (*Mercurius Aulicus*, which was first published in 1643, supported the King, while *Mercurius Britanicus*, which was also published from 1643, supported Parliament) but these do not appear to affect our results. This is, of course, what we should want from a balanced corpus, that is, no single publication skewing results. But it does raise questions concerning how these mercuries attempted to influence opinion linguistically. It could be that our corpus is not as balanced as we thought it was, and so revisiting its design in the light of this initial study is a possible next step. This reminds us again of the Spitzerian principles that should guide corpus stylistics (see Chapter 4). Additionally, if the mercuries were an unusual type of newspaper, then a comparative study wherein a corpus of mercuries is compared against other contemporary newspapers would help to expose any linguistic differences in their news writing. Our historical perspective would shift in this case from being diachronic to synchronic. Nevertheless, this would continue to build a picture of the development of print news media and how external social/economic/political events were triggers for linguistic variation within the genre.

8.6 Conclusion

Our aim in this chapter has been to demonstrate the value of corpora for the study of the diachronic development of aspects of style. As we have shown in the case studies in this chapter, corpus stylistics offers a means of gaining a perspective on the diachronic development of text-types and genres, as well as on particular literacy practices. Indeed, it is only through a corpus stylistic approach that such insights can be gained. The importance of this for stylistics is that corpus techniques allow for generalisable claims about the nature of long-term stylistic development. And for historical linguistics more broadly, stylistic techniques of analysis offer a means of exploring the alternative histories of English advocated by Watts and Trudgill (2001). There is, then, a mutually beneficial element to the combination of corpora and stylistics.

What this chapter has also shown is the capacity of corpus techniques for expanding the range of texts and periods amenable to stylistic analysis. In the next chapter, we develop these analytical practices further through an exploration of how corpus stylistics can be used in the solution of real-world problems.

Notes

1. Present Day English (PDE) relies on a shared temporal perspective as well as some mutual understanding of the variety of English being discussed, since there are, of course, numerous present day Englishes (see McIntyre 2009: 113) – for example, Australian English (AuE) and American English (AmE). For this reason, the variety of PDE being discussed should be made clear. However, it is also worth bearing in mind that labelling international varieties of English in this way propagates a view of languages as belonging to nation states. Needless to say, this view is no longer tenable – if, indeed, it ever was.
2. In some cases, it may be possible to make inferences about the nature of speech in earlier historical periods on the basis of the presentation of direct speech in texts (see Culpeper and Kytö 2010).
3. The Helsinki Corpus of English Texts (1991). Department of Modern Languages, University of Helsinki. Compiled by Matti

Rissanen (Project leader), Merja Kytö (Project secretary); Leena Kahlas-Tarkka, Matti Kilpiö (Old English); Saara Nevanlinna, Irma Taavitsainen (Middle English); Terttu Nevalainen, Helena Raumolin-Brunberg (Early Modern English).
4. See Studer (2008: 194–230) for an alternative approach to studying modality in EModE news.
5. Another possibility is to use Notepad++ which allows for complex find and replace searches across many texts simultaneously.
6. See <http://ucrel.lancs.ac.uk/llwizard.html> (last accessed 20 August 2018).
7. The minus signs indicate under-representation, not a negative number.

9

Real-world applications for corpus stylistics

9.1 Introduction

This chapter looks outwards to examine the possibility of using corpus stylistic techniques to examine and potentially solve real-world problems. This will be of particular interest to students looking for the practical value of stylistics and for academics interested in demonstrating the impact of research in corpus stylistics. Demonstrating the impact of academic research generally is currently a significant topic in academia, particularly in the UK, although other countries such as Australia and the Netherlands are also experimenting with using impact as a measure of value in the distribution of research funding (see McIntyre and Price 2018b for a critique of this approach). In our final chapter of this book we therefore concentrate on the analysis of contemporary non-literary texts, a practice which is seeing a resurgence of popularity within stylistics, and explore the possibilities of using corpus stylistics for practical purposes. In so doing, we discuss the language consultancy that we operate at the University of Huddersfield (Language Unlocked) and, in our final case study, which is the main part of this chapter, describe some of the consultancy work we have done for the UK Green Party. The case study begins with a more detailed introduction to Wmatrix (Rayson 2009), a corpus tool we have referred to throughout this book, and puts into practice some of the statistical testing we introduced in Chapter 5. Whereas the case study in that chapter used the results from significance and effect size tests as a way to select sections of a novel to analyse in more detail, in this chapter we use the output from Wmatrix, along with the concordance function provided by AntConc (Anthony

2018; see Appendix 2), to identify salient patterns in a collection of texts that relate to style.

9.2 The impact of applied stylistics

Throughout this book we have examined how stylistics can be combined with corpus linguistic approaches, methods and tools in order to investigate style and meaning-making in texts and collections of texts. Some of our focus has been on fictional prose and authors, though we have also examined non-fiction (early news texts) and looked at how social events can influence language use in texts (which in turn might have influenced the opinions or point of view of the people reading those texts). We also examined the ways in which corpus stylistics can be used as a tool for classroom teaching of English. These different applications of corpus stylistics, and the focus on different text-types, begin to demonstrate how corpus stylistics is not just an insular academic activity, the results of which are intended only for other academics. Rather, it can be applied in a variety of 'real-world' situations in ways that are beneficial to practitioners, institutions and organisations (see, for example, Jeffries et al. 2018 for a discussion of the role of applied critical stylistics in conflict resolution). In such cases, the language insights offered by corpus stylistic research might inform and improve professional practice (see, for example, McIntyre and Lugea 2015 for a discussion of the stylistics of subtitling, and Bruti and Zanotti forthcoming for a review of the impact of linguistics in audiovisual translation more generally; for a critical appraisal of the concept of the *real world* in relation to academia, see Price 2018). This might be to do with understanding more about language output from a particular organisation, language use directed towards or about an organisation, or methodologies for data handling and research within an organisation (such as listener/viewer responses to TV programmes). All such work falls within the remit of applied linguistics (Bex 1999; Widdowson 1984), which has long since developed beyond its initial focus on the use of linguistics for pedagogical purposes. Nowadays, applied linguistics may be understood more widely as encompassing the identification and solution of problems in society generally using linguistic theories and methods.

The idea that academic research should have wider implications is now a more commonplace notion within academia, certainly within the UK. Since 2014 and the advent of the UK's Research Excellence Framework (REF), what was previously a sometimes desirable possibility has now become a necessary requirement. The REF now asks academics to demonstrate the impact of their research on society in general. So while linguistics has made a substantial impact on various areas of society (for exemplars, see McIntyre and Price 2018: 8), there is now increased pressure to show impact that matches the requirements of the REF more closely. Consequently, in those countries where impact is high on government agendas, the impact of linguistic research now has to be spelled out in the language of the REF and its counterpart assessment exercises, and research shown to have direct impact on end-users.

A direct consequence of the REF and similar schemes is that linguists are increasingly seeking research partners from areas outside academia to work with on projects where linguistics can help to identify problems and offer recommendations to resolve them. In our final case study in this book, we present some research resulting from one such research partnership. We use the case study in this chapter to show the possibilities for applying corpus stylistics to answering research questions developed in collaboration with non-academic partners, as well as to demonstrate further some of the tools and techniques we have used throughout this book.

9.3 Language Unlocked

Language Unlocked is a consultancy based in the Institute for Applied Linguistics at the University of Huddersfield that uses the combined methods and frameworks offered by corpus linguistics and stylistics to produce objective analyses of how organisations are represented in texts. The aim of such analyses is to reveal textual meanings which may not be immediately obvious but which influence how people perceive and respond to organisations and their concerns. The purpose of providing such analytical insights to organisations is to improve the focus and effectiveness of their communication, to understand how their enterprise is perceived by stakeholders, and to enable them to respond effectively to exterior representations of their organisation's concerns. In the following sections we describe a study carried out for (and with) the UK Green Party. Before that, though, we discuss Wmatrix, the corpus tool which we used for this project, drawing particularly on its capacity to automatically tag corpus data.

9.4 Wmatrix

We introduced Wmatrix (Rayson 2009) in Chapter 4, and drew on it again in the case studies in Chapters 5 and 6. What we focus on in this section, then, is providing more detail about its development and operation.

Wmatrix, unlike many other off-the-shelf software packages, is able to automatically add grammatical and semantic tags to the words in a corpus. The grammatical tagging is carried out by CLAWS (the Constituent Likelihood Automatic Word-tagging System, introduced in Chapter 3), which assigns every word in a text (or corpus) a tag denoting its grammatical category or part-of-speech (POS; see Garside 1987; Leech et al. 1994; Garside 1996; Garside and Smith 1997). The system uses a predefined set of tags, with each tag denoting a particular grammatical category. Over the years there have been a number of different tagsets, each offering different amounts of grammatical distinction within broad grammatical categories (noun, pronoun, verb, adjective, and so on). So, for the broad grammatical category of noun, several tags are possible. For example, a non-count noun would receive the tag NN, whereas a singular count noun would be tagged NN1, and a plural noun NN2. Wmatrix currently uses what is called the C7 tagset, made up of 137 tags. Information about the different tagsets can be found on the CLAWS website.[1]

The semantic tagging is carried out by the UCREL Semantic Analysis System (USAS; also described briefly in Chapter 3), which assigns semantic tags to each word in the text or corpus based on a scheme developed from McArthur's (1981) *Longman Lexicon of Contemporary English*. The semantic tags consist of an upper-case letter, which indicates one of 21 general semantic fields, which are shown in Table 9.1. So, for example, W indicates the semantic field of WORLD AND ENVIRONMENT (we use small capitals for semantic domains throughout this chapter). The first upper-case letter is followed by a number, which indicates the first (and in some cases only) sub-division of that field. For example, WORLD AND ENVIRONMENT has five sub-divisions: W1 (THE UNIVERSE); W2 (LIGHT); W3 (GEOGRAPHICAL TERMS); W4 (WEATHER); and W5 (GREEN ISSUES). Some fields have more than one sub-division, which is indicated by a decimal point and another number. For example, GOVERNMENT & PUBLIC, which is designated by the letter G (see Table 9.1), is first divided into: G1 (GOVERNMENT, POLITICS AND ELECTIONS); G2 (CRIME LAW AND ORDER); and G3 (WARFARE, DEFENCE AND THE ARMY). The first sub-field G1 (GOVERNMENT, POLITICS AND ELECTIONS) is further divided into: GOVERNMENT ETC., which has the tag G1.1; and POLITICS, which has the tag G1.2. Some tags can also include either a plus or a minus sign to indicate positive or negative positioning within the semantic field. For example, G.2.2 (GENERAL ETHICS) is divided into G2.2+ (ETHICAL) and G2.2- (UNETHICAL). Through these types of

Table 9.1 The 21 top level categories of the USAS tagset

A GENERAL & ABSTRACT TERMS	B THE BODY & THE INDIVIDUAL	C ARTS & CRAFTS	E EMOTION	F FOOD & FARMING
G GOVERNMENT & PUBLIC	H ARCHITECTURE, HOUSING & THE HOME	I MONEY & COMMERCE (IN INDUSTRY)	K ENTERTAINMENT	L LIFE & LIVING THINGS
M MOVEMENT, LOCATION, TRAVEL, TRANSPORT	N NUMBERS & MEASUREMENT	O SUBSTANCES, MATERIALS, OBJECTS, EQUIPMENT	P EDUCATION	Q LANGUAGE & COMMUNICATION
S SOCIAL ACTIONS, STATES & PROCESSES	T TIME	W WORLD & ENVIRONMENT	X PSYCHOLOGICAL ACTIONS, STATES & PROCESSES	Y SCIENCE & TECHNOLOGY
Z NAMES & GRAMMAR				

sub-division, 21 major semantic fields expand to 232 finer semantic categories.

Wmatrix is a web-based tool, hence electronic versions of texts (in plain, unformatted .txt files) are uploaded, via the internet and using a web interface, to a server at Lancaster University. During the upload process, the words in the text are tagged, quantified and organised lexically, grammatically and semantically, and frequency lists based on all the words in a text and their grammatical and semantic groupings are generated. This process involves Wmatrix creating multiple versions of whatever text or corpus is being analysed, in order to accommodate the different tags and to preserve the original data.

The tagging abilities of Wmatrix mean that it can perform keyness comparisons not only at the word level, but also on a grammatical and semantic basis, a capability we have already demonstrated in Chapters 4 and 5. Wmatrix is therefore able to identify keywords, key grammatical categories (key POS) and key semantic domains (key concepts). Nonetheless, the grammatical and semantic quantifications performed by Wmatrix are still essentially word-based because the software counts the word-forms within each grammatical or semantic grouping based on the tags it automatically assigns. It is therefore the number of words within a group that decides the group's ranking.

9.4.1 Checking key concepts and key POS categories

It is worth pointing out that the CLAWS and USAS taggers are 96–7 per cent and 91 per cent accurate respectively (Rayson 2008: 529), so some errors do occur, mostly (as the percentages suggest) in the allocation of semantic categories. An important first step, therefore, when investigating key POS or key concepts, is making sure that Wmatrix has correctly tagged individual lexical items. This can be done using the 'list' function to check that all the words have been assigned correctly. If an error is detected, the totals need to be adjusted and the log-likelihoods recalculated. When doing this, both the target text or corpus and the comparison text or corpus need to be considered. It is also important to consider the category that the erroneous tags could be assigned to and whether doing this would affect the category's significance levels. Recalculations can be performed with the help of the log-likelihood calculator available at <http://ucrel.lancs.ac.uk/llwizard.html>. This is an online utility which returns log-likelihood values once the relevant (adjusted) word frequencies and corpus sizes have been entered.

9.5 Case study: the self-presentational style of the UK Green Party

In 2013 we were tasked by the UK Green Party to investigate the likely impact of its policy documents on voters and explore how the party was represented in the press more widely. In the remaining sections of this chapter we describe our investigation and show how we used Wmatrix to help us carry out a corpus stylistic analysis of Green Party policy documents. Through our discussion of the results we will demonstrate how corpus stylistic techniques can be used to assess the likely impact of particular stylistic choices.

9.5.1 Establishing research questions

As we saw in Chapter 4, a crucial first step in any research is developing research questions, and this applies equally when research extends beyond academia. Research questions become particularly important when working with other organisations because they help to set out precisely the scope of the work that is to be carried out. It is therefore important that research questions are developed and agreed upon through discussion with the external partner about their particular needs.

The research questions that framed our consultancy work with the UK Green Party developed from dialogue with representatives from the organisation. The general frame for the research suggested by the party was to investigate how it was represented in the UK press and how it presented itself in its own publicity texts. Looking towards the general election in 2015, the Green Party wanted to know how to position itself in its literature as an alternative to the Labour and Conservative parties, the two main political parties in the UK. The Green Party was working with an advertising agency, and part of the aim of our research was to help support these advertising consultants by providing evidence-based language insights as they planned their campaign. From these discussions we designed a series of research objectives. In this chapter we focus on just the following general research question:

RQ1 Does the UK Green Party use language in any way that might undermine its self-representation and policy messages in its 2010 policy documents and manifesto?

RQ1 relates to the notion of style in that we were not so much interested in *what* the Green Party said in its policy documents as in *how* it said it.

That is, we were interested in (patterns of) lexical choices that together represent the Green Party and whether these choices might somehow be unappealing to the electorate.

9.5.2 Methods and data

To answer our research question we constructed two corpora of policy documents and manifestos drawn from the various party websites. There were noticeable differences in the amounts of policy information available from the different parties, with the Green Party (henceforth GP) offering the most policy material, much of which was in downloadable PDF format,[2] and the Conservatives offering the least. These differences are reflected in the corpus sizes, which are shown in Table 9.2. The GP corpus (GP-POL-2010) contains around 187,000 words, while the Labour and Conservative party corpus (LAB-CON-POL-2010) contains around 173,000 words, with just over 62,000 words (around 35 per cent) coming from the Conservative Party website. The Labour Party was similar to the GP in that it made available several downloadable PDF documents detailing its stance in various areas (e.g. defence, education, health).

The two corpora represent everything that we could collect for each party that was either a manifesto or policy document. As far as we could ascertain at the time, they are complete datasets within the specification and scope of the data to be collected. That is we defined our language population by political party, genre (policy documents and manifestos) and location of the data (party political websites), and collected everything we could find relating to that definition. Therefore, in this situation we did not sample from the population; instead, we aimed to collect the whole population as we had defined it. Clearly, our definition of the language population could have included other written outputs, such as paper pamphlets and leaflets, but this presented considerable practical issues.

The difference in size between the two corpora, and hence the written outputs stored on political party websites, is inevitable, since it would be highly unlikely to find exactly the same amount of data for each

Table 9.2 Word totals for the Green Party and Labour/Conservative policy document corpora

	GP-POL-2010	LAB-CON-POL-2010
Tokens	187,718	173,580

party. It was, however, unexpected that the GP should have more than both the Labour and Conservative parties combined.[3] The differences might suggest different approaches to informing the electorate, with the Conservatives apparently adopting a less-is-more style.

We compared GP-POL-2010 with LAB-CON-POL-2010 using Wmatrix, and made keyword and key semantic domain comparisons to determine which words and semantic domains were over- or under-represented in our target corpus. In this comparison neither of the corpora represents a norm; rather, they aim to represent the written style of the GP, and the Labour and Conservative parties combined, based on their use of language in policy documents and manifestos. We used Wmatrix to identify differences at the word and semantic level, which we investigated further in order to identify qualitative variances in the way different parties use language which related to style, and thereby answer our research question.

9.5.3 Positive key semantic domains in GP-POL-2010

Using Wmatrix, we investigated the key semantic domains in GP policy documents by comparing the policy documents of the Green Party with the policy documents of the Labour and Conservative parties combined. We decided on an alpha level of 0.0001 for our significance threshold, which equates to a log-likelihood (LL) critical value of 15.13, and the log ratio threshold of 1. The comparison process produced 34 key semantic categories, or key concepts, which are shown in Table 9.3.

The semantic analysis provided by Wmatrix shows which semantic domains are used more often in the GP texts when compared with the Labour and Conservative party texts. Each key item can be considered a potential starting point for further, more detailed analysis. However, even with the statistical cut-offs applied, there are still 34 key concepts, which is a considerable amount of data to analyse qualitatively. Therefore, a crucial next step when dealing with lists of key items (keywords, key grammatical categories or key concepts) is working out which ones, if any, help most to answer your research questions. In order to be rigorous, every key item needs to be considered systematically.

These semantic groupings, especially those with descriptors that seem self-explanatory and which appear to straightforwardly connect with discourse topics in the text, readily invite general observations about the data. Some, however, are more opaque. In order to show more clearly what each key item relates to in both corpora, Table 9.4

Table 9.3 Positive key concepts in the Green Party manifesto and policy documents

Semantic domain (USAS code)	GP frequency (%)	LAB-CON frequency (%)	LL	Log ratio
SUBSTANCES AND MATERIALS: GAS (o1.3)	244 (0.14)	6 (0.01)	192.38	4.67
LIFE AND LIVING THINGS (l1)	145 (0.08)	5 (0)	106.86	4.18
ANTI-WAR (g3-)	24 (0.01)	1 (0)	16.87	3.91
SUBSTANCES AND MATERIALS: LIQUID (o1.2)	284 (0.16)	13 (0.01)	194.51	3.78
SMOKING AND NON-MEDICAL DRUGS (f3)	67 (0.04)	5 (0)	38.45	3.07
FARMING & HORTICULTURE (f4)	835 (0.47)	71 (0.06)	450.44	2.88
GREEN ISSUES (w5)	1,043 (0.59)	94 (0.08)	546	2.8
MONEY: LACK (i1.1--)	42 (0.02)	4 (0)	21.34	2.72
SUBSTANCES AND MATERIALS GENERALLY (o1)	396 (0.22)	44 (0.04)	183.36	2.5
LIKE (e2++)	69 (0.04)	9 (0.01)	28.55	2.27
GENERAL ETHICS (g2.2)	115 (0.06)	16 (0.01)	45.22	2.17
GEOGRAPHICAL TERMS (w3)	978 (0.55)	137 (0.12)	382.47	2.16
SUITABLE (a1.2+)	340 (0.19)	52 (0.05)	123.31	2.04
LIVING CREATURES: ANIMALS, BIRDS, ETC. (l2)	409 (0.23)	70 (0.06)	133.19	1.87
NOT ALLOWED (s7.4-)	140 (0.08)	25 (0.02)	43.61	1.81
TIME PERIOD: SHORT (t1.3-)	95 (0.05)	17 (0.02)	29.53	1.81
TEMPERATURE: HOT/ON FIRE (o4.6+)	93 (0.05)	18 (0.02)	26.47	1.7
DISTANCE: FAR (n3.3+)	83 (0.05)	16 (0.01)	23.73	1.7
USING (a1.5.1)	1,042 (0.59)	203 (0.18)	294.26	1.69
RELIGION AND THE SUPERNATURAL (s9)	96 (0.05)	20 (0.02)	24.95	1.59
COMPARING: VARIED (a6.3+)	200 (0.11)	43 (0.04)	49.87	1.54
FLYING AND AIRCRAFT (m5)	163 (0.09)	38 (0.03)	36.24	1.43
VEHICLES AND TRANSPORT ON LAND (m3)	1,072 (0.6)	255 (0.23)	231.2	1.4
SCIENCE AND TECHNOLOGY IN GENERAL (y1)	349 (0.2)	85 (0.08)	72.55	1.36
CALM (e3+)	84 (0.05)	21 (0.02)	16.74	1.33
SAILING, SWIMMING, ETC. (m4)	223 (0.13)	57 (0.05)	42.82	1.29
SENSORY: SIGHT (x3.4)	503 (0.28)	130 (0.12)	94.78	1.28
MEDICINES AND MEDICAL TREATMENT (b3)	644 (0.36)	167 (0.15)	120.64	1.27
INDUSTRY (i4)	283 (0.16)	74 (0.07)	52.25	1.26
PLANTS (l3)	150 (0.08)	44 (0.04)	22.21	1.1

Table 9.3 Continued

Semantic domain (USAS code)	GP frequency (%)	LAB-CON frequency (%)	LL	Log ratio
SUBSTANCES AND MATERIALS: SOLID (o1.1)	281 (0.16)	84 (0.08)	39.96	1.07
OTHER PROPER NAMES (z3)	1,931 (1.09)	586 (0.53)	265.67	1.05
COMPARING: SIMILAR (a6.1+++)	148 (0.08)	46 (0.04)	19.29	1.01
DECIDED (x6+)	290 (0.16)	91 (0.08)	36.96	1

shows the key semantic domains again, but this time along with up to the five most frequent lexical items in the semantic domain (fewer if the category contains fewer than five items). This table helps to show what these key domains relate to in terms of their textual content. We can see from the table that many of the key domains equate to key political issues, such as the environment (SUBSTANCES AND MATERIALS: GAS; LIFE AND LIVING THINGS; GREEN ISSUES; SUBSTANCES AND MATERIALS: SOLID), rural affairs including farming (FARMING & HORTICULTURE), people on lower incomes and poverty (MONEY: LACK), the health service (MEDICINES AND MEDICAL TREATMENT), transport (VEHICLES AND TRANSPORT ON LAND; SAILING, SWIMMING, ETC.; FLYING AND AIRCRAFT) and industry (INDUSTRY), all of which we would expect to see in a political party's policy documents and manifesto. We can see that both corpora talk about these issues, and often use the same terms, but the GP talks about them more. Some of the semantic categories less obviously relate to political issues, such as DECIDED, which reflects the discussion of different types of decisions (economic, planning, financial) and where they are taken (locally, nationally, internationally).

These results are not surprising; they are no doubt what most people would expect of GP texts. In this respect, they indicate at least that the software is working. Moreover, these domains help us to ascertain what the GP policy documents cover in what might be described as topics. The domains equate to important political issues and from this we can say that the GP covers these issues so it is not (as some maintain) a one-policy party. However, although these key concepts help us to see what the GP discusses more than the Labour and Conservative parties, most are not especially helpful as regards our research question since they relate mainly to the content of the policy documents, which, by and large, is as expected. Only two offer any sort of help with our research question. These are SUITABLE and LIKE.

Table 9.4 Key concepts in the Green Party manifesto and policy documents and up to the top five most frequent words forms in the GP-POL-2010 and LAB-CON-POL-2010 corpora

Semantic domain	GP	LAB-CON
SUBSTANCES AND MATERIALS: GAS	gas, air, co2, gases, carbon dioxide	gas, air, gases
LIFE AND LIVING THINGS	organic, biodiversity, wild, biological, biologically	biodiversity, organic
ANTI-WAR	civilian, disarmament, civilians, unarmed	civilian
SUBSTANCES AND MATERIALS: LIQUID	oil, water, waters, waterways, sewage	water, water companies, oil, oil markets
SMOKING AND NON-MEDICAL DRUGS	tobacco, trafficked, cannabis, smoking, heroin	smoking, rehabilitation programmes, trafficked, drug pushers
FARMING & HORTICULTURE	rural, farming, agricultural, crops, farmers	rural, farming, farmers, farms, fisheries
GREEN ISSUES	environmental, environment, pollution, ecological, nature	environment, nature, environmental, energy policy, conservation
MONEY: LACK	poorer, worse off, lower-paid	poorer, worse off
SUBSTANCES AND MATERIALS GENERALLY	fuel, fuels, materials, material, pesticides	fuel, fuels, material, fat, sugar levels
LIKE	favour, preference, preferably, prefer, preferred	homophobia, preferred, prefer, bias, favours
GENERAL ETHICS	principles, objectives, ethos, animal rights, objective	principles, objectives, ethos, morally, verifiable
GEOGRAPHICAL TERMS	land, global, countryside, sea, natural resources	global, universal, countryside, land, bedrock
SUITABLE	appropriate, relevant, suitable, qualifies, accordingly	fit, appropriate, eligible, relevant, qualify
LIVING CREATURES: ANIMALS, BIRDS, ETC.	animal, animals, wildlife, fish, organisms	animal, animals, wildlife, fish, bovine
NOT ALLOWED	ban, banned, prohibit, prohibited, banning	ban, veto, unlicensed, ban, banned
TIME PERIOD: SHORT	short term, short, in the short term, transitory, part time basis	short, short term, brief, save time, provisional

TEMPERATURE: HOT / ON FIRE	warming, heat, burning, heating, incineration	heat, warm, fire, lit, incubation
DISTANCE: FAR	distance, far, distances, remote, distant	far, remote, distant, deepen, deepening
USING	use, used, consumption, using, users	use, used, using, exploitation, users
RELIGION AND THE SUPERNATURAL	religious, religion, spiritual, parish, religions	myths, religious, spirit, new age, sacrifices
COMPARING: VARIED	diversity, diverse, various, variety, mixed	diverse, various, variety, mixed, diversity
FLYING AND AIRCRAFT	aircraft, airports, aviation, air transport, flying	aviation, aircraft, flights, runway, aerospace
VEHICLES AND TRANSPORT ON LAND	transport, public transport, road, vehicles, roads	transport, street, drive, roads, streets
SCIENCE AND TECHNOLOGY IN GENERAL	technology, nuclear, technologies, scientific, gm	technology, technologies, technical, nuclear, science
CALM	peace, peaceful, peacekeeping, calming, tranquil	peace, peacetime
SAILING, SWIMMING, ETC.	marine, ships, ports, port, vessels	launched, marine, ports, launch, flow
SENSORY: SIGHT	see, seen, sees, observe, look at	see, look at, seen, looking at, saw
MEDICINES AND MEDICAL TREATMENT	drugs, drug, treatment, treatments, healthcare	drugs, doctors, clinical, nurses, hospitals
INDUSTRY	industrial, industry, industries, industrialised, factory	industry, industrial, industries, water industry, workshops
PLANTS	plants, plant, woodland, trees, seed	trees, clearing, rooted, tree planting, woodland
SUBSTANCES AND MATERIALS: SOLID	carbon, soil, coal, woods, timber	carbon, silicon, timber, coal, soil
OTHER PROPER NAMES	green party, eu, european, nhs, un	nhs, eu, european, women's aid, home office
COMPARING: SIMILAR	same, equal, replicated, on an equal basis, identical	same, equal, replicate
DECIDED	decisions, decision making, decision, decide, decided	decisions, decision, down to, concluded, resolution

The key concept SUITABLE suggests a possible linguistic trait in the GP policy documents that indicates an over-reliance on the word *appropriate*, which is used 205 times across the GP-POL-2010 corpus. Some examples of usage of *appropriate* are shown below:

(1) Policies to promote reduced consumption and assist in appropriate consumer choices include ensuring openness in the workings of all ...

(2) Issues currently decided at the EU level should be dealt with at a more appropriate level for effective action, which might be local, national or global ...

The word has limited meaning unless what counts as appropriate is explained. In (1) one wonders what 'appropriate consumer choices' are, and whether these are the same for all consumers. In (2) there is some attempt to clarify what *appropriate* refers to, but the force is weakened by the modal *might*, and the options are so diverse that they offer no real clue as to what would be appropriate.

The key concept LIKE highlights the use of *favour*, as shown in the following examples:

(3) We favour a Robin Hood Tax

(4) In the long run we favour moving to a system of Land Value Tax

(5) we favour electoral systems with a regional basis

The minor issue suggested by the examples above is that favouring something does not equate to action, or promise of action, so this seems an odd way to state political preferences in documents that can potentially be read by the electorate.

So far, our investigation of key semantic domains in GP-POL-2010 has offered us limited but nonetheless useful information about Green Party style that would have been difficult to find without corpus methods. In the next section, where we discuss the key concepts that are under-represented in the GP data (negative key concepts), we find differences in the way that the Labour and the Conservative parties present ideas and discuss topics that could be related to the persuasive power of their policy documents and manifestos. These findings also assist in our understanding of the Green Party's linguistic style.

9.5.4 Negative key semantic domains in GP-POL-2010

We also looked at the negative key concepts generated by the comparison described above. These are the key concepts that are under-represented in Green policy documents when compared with the Labour and Conservative policy documents combined. These are, in effect, the key concepts that are over-represented in the Labour and Conservative documents in comparison with the Green documents. The 27 negative key concepts with a log-likelihood of 15.13 or more and a log ratio of at least 1 are shown in Table 9.5. Where these key concepts relate to important political issues within the data, they indicate which issues are discussed more by the Labour and Conservative parties in the policy documents, compared with the GP.

We worked through each negative key concept in much the same way as we did with the positive key concepts. That is, we looked at the lexical content of each domain, and the associated concordances, in order to understand more clearly what the concept related to in the data, as well as to establish whether it could be connected to differences in style. Table 9.6 shows the list of negative key concepts again but with the top five most frequent lexical items for each category (or as many items as the category contains if fewer than five) for both corpora. This is to indicate more precisely what was being discussed, although in some cases, which we examine in due course, this strategy is not completely successful since some categories relate (sometimes rather obliquely) to more than one issue or topic.

There are a small number of issues that, from the evidence in Tables 9.5 and 9.6, are discussed more by the Labour and Conservative parties in comparison with the GP, which we will summarise. The PEOPLE: FEMALE semantic domain relates to discussion of women in relation to equality, sexual harassment and domestic violence. These issues also account in part for the prominence of VIOLENT/ANGRY, NO KNOWLEDGE, RELATIONSHIP: INTIMACY AND SEX and SENSORY: TOUCH. Other lexical items in the latter category refer to 'sleeping rough' and relate to the bigger issue of homelessness, which also largely accounts for NON-RESIDENT. The category PEOPLE: MALE is connected to PEOPLE: FEMALE and is prominent largely because men are discussed in comparison with women across various issues. The categories THE MEDIA: BOOKS and TEMPERATURE: COLD relate to spending cuts (libraries are often an emotive theme in such discussions) and council tax freezes. The issues of refugees and safe havens are captured by the domain SAFE,

Table 9.5 Key concepts in Labour and Conservative party policy documents

Semantic domain	GP frequency (%)	LAB-CON frequency (%)	LL	Log ratio
PEOPLE: FEMALE	75 (0.04)	729 (0.65)	964.62	−3.95
SENSORY: TOUCH	3 (0)	23 (0.02)	28.18	−3.61
NO KNOWLEDGE	2 (0)	14 (0.01)	16.59	−3.48
PEOPLE: MALE	15 (0.01)	82 (0.07)	87.43	−3.12
THE MEDIA: BOOKS	35 (0.02)	158 (0.14)	152.63	−2.85
TEMPERATURE: COLD	5 (0)	19 (0.02)	16.54	−2.6
PARTICIPATION	9 (0.01)	30 (0.03)	23.84	−2.41
DECIDING	10 (0.01)	25 (0.02)	15.53	−2
VIOLENT/ANGRY	273 (0.15)	662 (0.59)	398.88	−1.95
KNOWLEDGE	26 (0.01)	57 (0.05)	30.81	−1.81
NON-RESIDENT	34 (0.02)	63 (0.06)	27.57	−1.56
PERSONAL NAMES	168 (0.09)	308 (0.28)	132.82	−1.55
TIME: EARLY	30 (0.02)	53 (0.05)	21.67	−1.49
EVALUATION: TRUE	126 (0.07)	213 (0.19)	81.48	−1.43
THE MEDIA: NEWSPAPERS ETC.	39 (0.02)	65 (0.06)	24.32	−1.41
TIME: MOMENTARY	45 (0.03)	73 (0.07)	26.14	−1.37
SIZE: BIG	40 (0.02)	61 (0.05)	19.65	−1.28
TIME: OLD, NEW AND YOUNG; AGE	110 (0.06)	157 (0.14)	44.66	−1.19
RELATIONSHIP: INTIMACY AND SEX	91 (0.05)	130 (0.12)	37.05	−1.19
INFORMATION TECHNOLOGY AND COMPUTING	80 (0.05)	114 (0.1)	32.33	−1.18
SAFE	130 (0.07)	184 (0.17)	51.48	−1.17
KIN	253 (0.14)	349 (0.31)	92.67	−1.14
TIME: PERIOD	536 (0.3)	713 (0.64)	175.19	−1.09
TIME: NEW AND YOUNG	544 (0.31)	722 (0.65)	176.51	−1.08
SPEECH: COMMUNICATIVE	320 (0.18)	413 (0.37)	94.8	−1.04
ATTENTIVE	82 (0.05)	106 (0.1)	24.42	−1.04
WORRY	139 (0.08)	178 (0.16)	40.12	−1.03

and the discussion of issues surrounding families and children and the elderly accounts for the semantic domains KIN and TIME: OLD, NEW AND YOUNG; AGE.

The remaining negative key concepts are less indicative of the issues that appear more in the LAB-CON-POL-2010 corpus. Instead, some of them highlight differences in rhetorical style between the Labour and Conservative parties and the GP. For example, SIZE: BIG indicates that

Table 9.6 Negative key concepts in the Green Party manifesto and policy documents and up to the top five most frequent words forms in the GP-POL-2010 and LAB-CON-POL-2010 corpora

SEMANTIC DOMAIN	GP	LAB-CON
PEOPLE: FEMALE	women, woman, female, girls, girl	women, girls, woman, female, girl
SENSORY: TOUCH	smooth, rough, smoothly	rough, smoothly, groped, touch, stroke
NO KNOWLEDGE	forgotten, ignorance	in the dark, strangers, forgotten, out of touch with, undiagnosed
PEOPLE: MALE	men	men, boys, male, lads, man
THE MEDIA: BOOKS	chapter, libraries,	libraries, library, chapter, book, books
TEMPERATURE: COLD	cooling, freeze, extinguish, refrigerators	freeze, frozen, freezing, frosties, cold
PARTICIPATION	participants, under-represented, participant	participant, participants, under-represented
DECIDING	estimated, estimates, estimate, judges	estimated, estimates, estimate, adjudicator, estimating
VIOLENT/ANGRY	abuse, threat, violence, toxic, threats	violence, abuse, violent, threat, force
KNOWLEDGE	data, database, informative	data, database, informants, databases, informative
NON-RESIDENT	homeless, homelessness, vacant, vagrancy, unoccupied	homelessness, homeless, walk the streets, vacant, non-resident
PERSONAL NAMES	european union, jim killock, caroline lucas, english, mayor	english, david cameron, shadow, ed miliband, sylvia
TIME: EARLY	early, in advance, premature	early, in advance, late at night, premature
EVALUATION: TRUE	evidence, true, fact, openness, valid	evidence, fact, credible, proved, in fact
THE MEDIA: NEWSPAPERS ETC.	article, press, newspapers, subscriptions, journals	papers, newspapers, headline, magazines, journalists
TIME: MOMENTARY	at the point of, stage, stages, date, timely	stage, midnight, date, occasions, brink
SIZE: BIG	huge, largest, biggest, enormous, giant	biggest, huge, largest, enormous
TIME: OLD, NEW AND YOUNG; AGE	age, one, life expectancy, aged, ageism	age, one, aged, 16 years old

(Continued)

Table 9.6 Continued

SEMANTIC DOMAIN	GP	LAB-CON
RELATIONSHIP: INTIMACY AND SEX	sexual, couples, gay, bisexual, sexually, brothels	sexual, sexual harassment, prostitution, couples
INFORMATION TECHNOLOGY AND COMPUTING	internet, digital, website, processors, software	online, website, digital, internet, hi-tech
SAFE	safety, safe, safeguards, refugees, safely	safety, safe, refuge, refugees, safeguards
KIN	parents, families, family, foster, parent	families, parents, family, households, marriage
TIME: PERIOD	years, year, hours, period, week	years, year, session, generation, night
TIME: NEW AND YOUNG	new, renewable, young, recent, modern	new, young, recent, renewable, youth
SPEECH: COMMUNICATIVE	representatives, outlined, point, content, points	told, said, consultation, argued, response
ATTENTIVE	focus, concentration, attention, concentrate, concentrations	focus, attention, highlighted, focused, focusing
WORRY	concerned, concerns, concern, stress, care	concerns, concern, concerned, worrying, care

the Labour and Conservative texts contain more hyperbole than those of the GP. For example:

(6) We have set up the biggest welfare to work scheme

(7) That is why we have delivered the biggest ever rise in the basic state pension

(8) We are delivering the biggest expansion in railways in over 150 years

(9) Although we inherited the biggest deficit in our peacetime history

(10) Britain faces huge problems that demand radical change

(11) This will allow a huge increase in renewable power

Also of interest are PARTICIPATION, WORRY and SPEECH: COMMUNICA-TIVE, all of which indicate a particular strategy used more in the Labour and Conservative data. The most frequent lexical items in PARTICIPA-TION in the LAB-CON-POL-2010 corpus are *participant* (frequency 17) and *participants* (frequency 12) and each occurrence is part of reporting what participants have said in focus groups and meetings. This semantic domain indicates the inclusion of other public voices in the political documents. For example:

(12) One participant suggested that when the percentage of women rose beyond 30% 'men would say there were a lot of women'

Similarly, WORRY relates to the reporting of concerns of the public. For example:

(13) Concerns have been raised about the high number of young people between the ages of 16 and 19 who gain little or no value from the education system.

(14) Some organisations in the Midlands, expressed concerns that there should be a review of how domestic violence work is funded,

(15) We understand people's concerns about immigration – about whether it will undermine their wages or job prospects,

These examples show that the noun *concerns* reifies people's worries. In examples (13) and (14) these worries might have been expressed either by spoken or written discourse; it is not altogether clear. In (13)

the use of a passive construction makes a general claim about some form of discourse that happened without any hint of the source. In the case of (14) the concerns appear to exist just as a state of mind in people.

This rhetorical strategy of bringing other people's voices (real or otherwise) into the discussion of political topics is also highlighted by SPEECH: COMMUNICATIVE (which includes the word-forms *told*, *said*, *consultation* and *argued*). The semantic domain reflects the inclusion of voices of others through different forms of speech presentation. We can illustrate this by looking at the most frequent lexical item in the semantics grouping, which is *told* with a frequency of 50. Using AntConc (Anthony 2018) to provide a sorted concordance of *told* (see Box 9.1), because Wmatrix does not have a sorting facility, we assessed the patterns (if any) that the word is involved in. We found that the majority of the occurrences are part of the following phrases (frequencies are shown in brackets):

(i) *we were told that* (17)
(ii) *we were told* (1)
(iii) X *told us that* (22; X is a group or organisation)
(iv) X *told us* (3; X is a group or organisation)
(v) *who told us* (2)

The phrases in (ii) and (iv) introduce direct speech (of which there are four instances), and the rest introduce indirect speech (IS). The beginning sections of the four occurrences of direct speech (DS) are shown below (word counts for the quoted speech are in square brackets):

(16) For instance, Platform 51 (formerly YWCA), who we were pleased to have at several of our events, told us: "Increasing numbers of women we deal with are reoffending because ... ." [41]

(17) Eaves Housing told us: "In the past it was rare that we could not find a refuge or hostel place for women calling us – ...". [197]

(18) Describing the crisis in funding they are facing, staff working for domestic abuse organisations told us: "We have already had to make redundancies ..." [28]

(19) We found a similar message in Coventry where we were told: "there are many contracts to fill but Commissioners don't know much about this sector." [14]

These quotations bring other voices into the manifestos and policy documents that make up the LAB-CON-POL-2010 corpus, and present the 'real-life' views and experiences of people. It is noticeable in the examples above that some of the quotations are quite long, and one wonders to what extent the words quoted present summaries of conversations (see Short 2012). The summary nature of the speech presentation is probably more pronounced with the indirect speech, especially since the reporting verb is part of a passive construction. For example:

(20) In Northumbria, we were told that cuts to the SDVC mean there is low attendance at oversight meetings on operational issues.

(21) For example, we were told that between September 2009 and 2010, 267 people were referred by police to Ashram Housing,

Nevertheless, the presence of the speech presentation in the data demonstrates that dialogue occurs between politicians and people/groups, and that what people/groups say is noted, which suggests that they have been listened to. There are no such occurrences in the GP-POL-2010 corpus, although the fact that they are in dialogue with voters might be communicated in different ways not reflected in the key concepts.

These differences suggest ways in which the GP might want to engage with voters and present different ideas. Of course, that is not to say that one way of presenting policies is right and one is wrong, but it is useful to observe the differences since they offer one possible starting point for attending to the business of persuading the electorate to rethink the status quo and consider voting differently. In the next section, we turn our attention to keywords in the GP-POL-2010 corpus and notice further linguistic tendencies in the GP documents that might have important effects on their readers.

Box 9.1 Using the concordance facility in AntConc

In this box we demonstrate the AntConc concordance facility using the LAB-CON-POL-2010 corpus. You can follow the same steps using any corpus data that you might have.

1. Navigate to the AntConc webpage at <http://www.laurenceanthony. net/software/antconc/> and download the latest version of AntConc (versions are available for Windows, Mac OS and Linux).

2. Start up AntConc on your computer, and open the corpus under investigation by clicking **File > Open File(s)**. A dialogue box will open; use that to locate your file. If you need to open more than one file, then simply repeat this procedure, or select multiple files.

3. Select the concordance utility by clicking the concordance tab.

AntConc 3.5.6 (Windows) 2018	
File Global Settings Tool Preferences Help	
Corpus Files	Concordance	Concordance Plot	File View	Clusters/N-Grams	Collocates	Word List	Keyword List
ConManPolALL.txt	**Concordance Hits** 50
LabourManPolALL.txt	Hit KWIC

4. Type in the required search term in the search box at the bottom of the screen. Click **start**. A concordance will appear on your screen for the search term.

Search Term ☑ Words ☐ Case ☐ Regex			Search Window Size
told		Advanced	50
Start	Stop	Sort	Show Every Nth Row 1
Kwic Sort			
☑ Level 1 1R ☐ ☑ Level 2 2R ☐ ☑ Level 3 3R ☐			Clone Results

5. By default, concordance will be sorted alphabetically by the words that occur to the right of the search term. There are three levels of alphabetical sorting, with the default being that the concordances are first sorted by the first word to the right of the search term, followed by the second word to the right, followed by the third word to the right. These levels of sorting are colour coded on the concordance red, green and purple, respectively. The different levels of sorting force the concordances into groups, which can be useful to show patterns of usage.

```
                 be in their area. Women's organisations told us that a further issue is that
                  the heart of the Specialist Court process, told us that few courts are now able
                       a grim picture. All the refuge providers told us that financial pressure had already forced
             to have represented at our evidence session, told us that in research last year on
                        across two local authorities. But its CEO told us that she was fearful for the
       women who gave evidence to the commission told us that socialising at home with friends
              in Bristol which supports street sex workers told us that "sofa surfing" was a very
                          legal aid for social welfare law. They told us that the telephone gateway, which is
                    income than men. Yet, women in London told us that the cost of travelling by
         Refugee Council, along with WAST in Manchester, told us that the same was the case
                      work with women street sex workers and told us that the beneficial effects of giving
       h particular needs are already closing. Mumsnet told us that their website was inundated when
                       in the last four years.36 Women also told us that their use of public transport
          sed sparingly, AVA ( Against Violence and Abuse) told us that they are used by the
                 was a concern: women across the country told us that they often preferred to park
             heard evidence from the One25 Project, who told us that they had been forced because
           one evidence session, a women's organisation told us the a London local authority had
                 the victims of domestic violence. Some centres told us they were set to lose half
       exual Assault Referral Centre in Manchester, who told us they were being asked to divide
```

6. The way in which the concordances are sorted can be changed by altering the sorting levels at the bottom of the screen using the clickable up and down arrows.

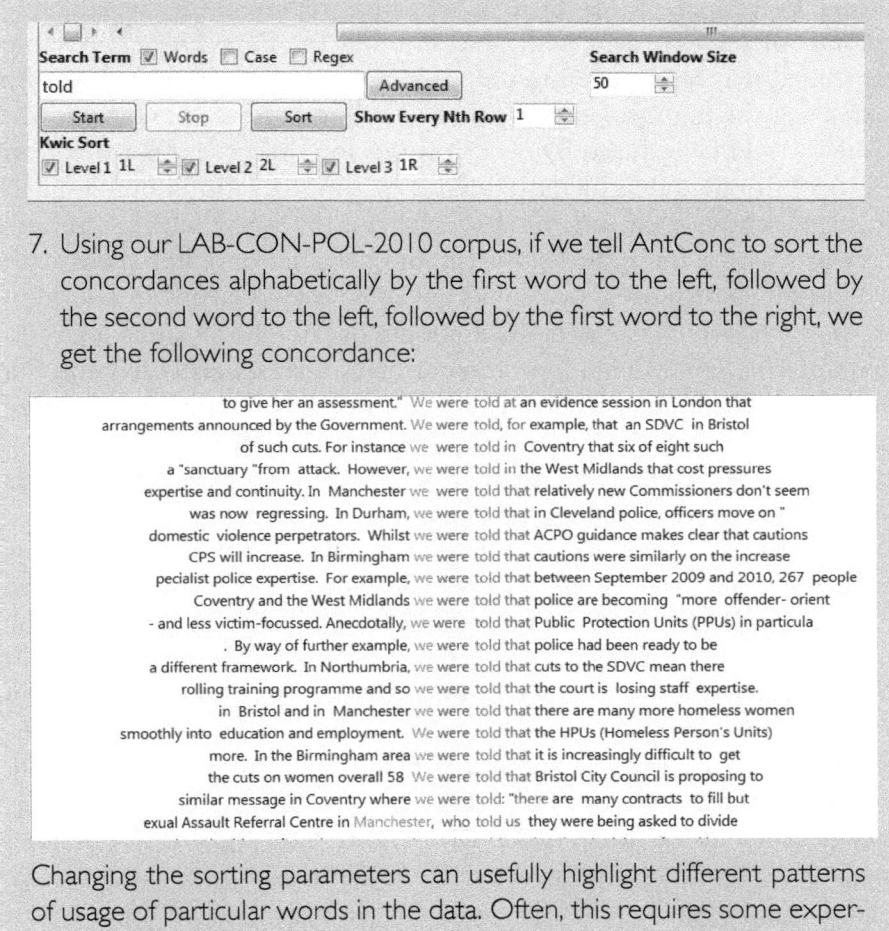

7. Using our LAB-CON-POL-2010 corpus, if we tell AntConc to sort the concordances alphabetically by the first word to the left, followed by the second word to the left, followed by the first word to the right, we get the following concordance:

Changing the sorting parameters can usefully highlight different patterns of usage of particular words in the data. Often, this requires some experimentation with the parameter settings.

9.5.5 Keywords in GP-POL-2010

We used Wmatrix to work out which words were key in the GP-POL-2010 corpus compared with the LAB-CON-POL-2010 corpus. These are the words whose frequencies we can confidently say are different in one corpus when compared with another. We limited our results again by specifying an alpha level of 0.0001, which equates to a log-likelihood score of 15.13, and a minimum log ratio of 1, which indicates that a word is twice as frequent in one corpus compared with the other. Using these criteria we generated 291 positive keywords all with a log-likelihood of at least 15.13. Recall that positive keywords are those words that appear more than you would expect by chance in a corpus, whereas negative keywords are those that appear less than you would expect by chance. A list of 291 keywords represents a considerable amount of data to deal with, and limiting the data further in some principled way was therefore desirable. One way to achieve this is by increasing the log ratio cut-off value. Table 9.3 shows how much our results would be reduced by using various log ratio cut-offs from 1 up to 10.99 (a range that includes the maximum log ratio in our results). So, if we chose a cut-off of 10 (which means we would ignore any keyword with a log ratio below 10, and consider only keywords with a score of 10 or more), we would have just one keyword to consider: *green_party*[4] which has a log-likelihood score of 898.58 and a log ratio score of 10.18. This high log ratio cut-off is not especially helpful. On the basis of the information in Table 9.3, a possible optimum effect size cut-off would be 5 since this would result in 25 keywords, whereas a log ratio of 4 increases the number of keywords to 119. These figures can be found in the 'running total' column in Table 9.7.

A total of 25 keywords is a more manageable amount of data for further analysis. The list of 25 keywords with a log-likelihood of above 15.13 and a log ratio of 5 or more can be found in Table 9.8, sorted by log ratio. Looking at the 25 keywords, we can see that the corresponding frequencies in the LAB-CON-POL-2010 corpus are all either zero or 1. So, the most statistically significant keywords in the GP-POL-2010 corpus with the largest effect size are either not present or hardly present in the LAB-CON-POL-2010 corpus. On the one hand, this is a potential issue because keywords that have very low observed frequencies in either corpus are generally less useful for comparative analysis (although in Chapter 6 we saw an exception to this), which

Table 9.7 Log ratio ranges with associated numbers of keywords, and running totals of accumulated keywords

Log ratio	Number of keywords	Running total of keywords
10.00–10.99	1	1
9.00–9.99	0	1
8.00–8.99	0	1
7.00–7.99	2	3
6.00–6.99	1	4
5.00–5.99	21	25
4.00–4.99	94	119
3.00–3.99	46	165
2.00–2.99	69	234
1.00–1.99	57	291

usually involves using concordances in the first instance. Certainly, low frequencies make the notion of patterns in the data either less convincing or null and void. On the other hand, however, this is a result that might offer some analytical purchase because it informs us about the lexical items that the Labour and Conservative parties do not use in their policy documents and manifestos. For example, *shall*, which is the third keyword in Table 9.8, is not used at all in the Conservative and Labour policy documents but is used 121 times in the Green Party corpus. This result has a bearing on style since the modal *shall* sounds archaic and has legal or biblical connotations (Williams 2007: 182). The research carried out by Leech (2003, 2004) on modal auxiliary verbs indicates that this particular modal is in decline. However, in the Green Party corpus, it is used comparatively frequently. So regardless of the frequency in the LAB-CON-POL-2010 corpus, *shall* marks some of the GP-POL-2010 data as having a particular formal, legal or archaic style. In fact, it could be argued that the complete lack of use in the comparison data makes the GP's usage more noteworthy.

Another unusual word that is not used at all by the Labour or Conservative parties is *peoples*, which appears to be used by the Green Party as a shorthand for groups of people. For example:

(22) Raging local conflicts have risen up the international agenda and attempts to address the conflict between peoples have varied in efficacy and moral justification

(23) providing creative alternatives to IMF austerity measures imposed on the world's already most impoverished peoples;

The possible issue with this word is that it could be seen as an in-group marker, which could alienate readers of the GP documents who are not acquainted with that plural use of *people*. These keywords bring into question the intended audience of the documents. If they are for GP members, then they are essentially preaching to the converted. As these documents are publicly available, there might be a problem with how some of the language that marks a particular overly formal style is received by readers.

If we look at the rest of the keywords shown in Table 9.8, a number of them suggest the topical preoccupations of the Green Party policy documents. Such keywords indicate what Scott and Tribble (2006; see also Scott 2000, 2010) refer to as 'aboutness' (after Phillips 1989 and as opposed to those keywords that relate to style or are proper nouns). 'Aboutness' keywords tend to be content-words, while style keywords

Table 9.8 The first 25 keywords in the GP-POL-2010 corpus

Keyword	GP-POL-2010 frequency (%)	LAB-CON-POL-2010 frequency (%)	LL	Log ratio
green_party	923 (0.52)	0 (0)	898.58	10.18
pollution	130 (0.07)	0 (0)	126.56	7.35
shall	121 (0.07)	0 (0)	117.8	7.25
oil	107 (0.06)	1 (0)	94.72	6.07
waterlow_road	48 (0.03)	0 (0)	46.73	5.91
co-operation	47 (0.03)	0 (0)	45.76	5.88
species	45 (0.03)	0 (0)	43.81	5.82
ecological	84 (0.05)	1 (0)	72.81	5.72
nationality	38 (0.02)	0 (0)	36.99	5.57
sea	37 (0.02)	0 (0)	36.02	5.54
self-reliance	35 (0.02)	0 (0)	34.07	5.46
peak	33 (0.02)	0 (0)	32.13	5.37
buildings	65 (0.04)	1 (0)	54.82	5.35
cycling	32 (0.02)	0 (0)	31.15	5.33
quotas	31 (0.02)	0 (0)	30.18	5.28
peoples	31 (0.02)	0 (0)	30.18	5.28
greens	30 (0.02)	0 (0)	29.21	5.23
co2	30 (0.02)	0 (0)	29.21	5.23
tncs	29 (0.02)	0 (0)	28.23	5.18
ecologically	28 (0.02)	0 (0)	27.26	5.13
freight	54 (0.03)	1 (0)	44.48	5.08
small-scale	27 (0.02)	0 (0)	26.29	5.08
carbon_dioxide	27 (0.02)	0 (0)	26.29	5.08
air	53 (0.03)	1 (0)	43.55	5.05
currency	26 (0.01)	0 (0)	25.31	5.03

are those with less semantic content.[5] In the context of political policy documents, the aboutness of the keywords relates to political topics of discussion and political issues. So, for example, we can see that *pollution*, *oil*, CO_2 and *carbon dioxide* are all mentioned in the GP-POL-2010 corpus. The keyword *oil* reflects extended discussions of our current over-reliance on that substance and of the notion of 'peak oil' (*peak* is another keyword), which is when oil production reaches its peak and then goes into decline due to dwindling recoverable reserves. Similarly, *pollution* reflects discussion of various types of pollution (suggested by collocates such as *plastic, marine, air*) and ways to reduce or eliminate

it. Occurrences of both CO_2 and *carbon dioxide* relate to discussion
of levels of the gas in the atmosphere, with 9 instances of CO_2 and
11 of *carbon dioxide* co-occurring with *emissions*. That these word-
forms occur in the Green Party data is probably unsurprising, since
they reference concepts that are of environmental importance and are
usually associated with the Green Party. Perhaps more surprising is that,
aside from one use of *oil*, these words do not occur in the LAB-CON-
POL-2010 data. Given that these keywords relate to what are not just
Green Party issues but global issues that are discussed at an international
level, we might have expected some mention of them in pre-election
policy documents, especially in an election manifesto. However, the
point here is that while these and other keywords (such as *sea*, *freight*,
air and *currency*) tell us about the content of the policy documents,
they are not as helpful when it comes to discerning style (which can be
indicated by what Enkvist 1964, 1973 refers to as style markers).

An alternative possibility for constraining our original list of 291
keywords that we have not yet discussed is to simply specify a raw frequency cut-off in Wmatrix. This eliminates keywords from the list that
have an observed frequency below a predesignated amount in either
one of the corpora, and can be used to avoid keywords that have a low
frequency in either corpus. Specifying a cut-off of 1, for example, would
remove all the keywords from the list that have a frequency of zero in
the comparison corpus. The effects that various frequency cut-offs have
on the number of keywords, when combined with log-likelihood and
log ratio cut-offs of 15.13 and 1 respectively, are shown in Table 9.9.
So, with no observed frequency restriction (i.e. a cut-off of zero) but a
minimum log-likelihood of 15.13 and a log ratio of at least 1, we have
291 keywords. If we impose a frequency cut-off of 50, then we are left
with just 11 keywords.

Table 9.9 Frequency cut-offs with associated numbers of keywords
(log-likelihood = 15.13; log ratio = 1 or more)

Observed frequency	Number of keywords
50 or more	11
40 or more	20
30 or more	25
20 or more	42
10 or more	78
1 or more	209
0 or more	291

If we opt for a cut-off of an observed frequency of 30 or more, we are left with 25 keywords, which are shown in Table 9.10. The keywords are arranged in order of effect size.

This selection of keywords, constrained by various quantitative measures, provides what appears to be an optimal selection of words, some of which appear potentially to constitute style markers. What counts as optimal is highly dependent on the project and the research needs, as any selection, however principled, reduces the number of keywords,

Table 9.10 Keywords in the GP-POL-2010 corpus (log-likelihood = 15.13; log ratio at least 1; minimum frequency = 30)

Keyword	GP-POL-2010 frequency (%)	LAB-CON-POL-2010 frequency (%)	LL	Log ratio
see	443 (0.25)	48 (0.04)	208.45	2.53
would	1,047 (0.59)	115 (0.1)	488.4	2.51
sustainable	272 (0.15)	34 (0.03)	116.16	2.33
international	273 (0.15)	38 (0.03)	107.32	2.17
rights	248 (0.14)	40 (0.04)	85.62	1.96
use	505 (0.28)	82 (0.07)	173.24	1.95
food	348 (0.2)	62 (0.06)	108.67	1.82
within	234 (0.13)	42 (0.04)	72.5	1.8
should	1,139 (0.64)	207 (0.19)	348.14	1.79
countries	293 (0.16)	54 (0.05)	88.19	1.77
include	169 (0.1)	31 (0.03)	51.13	1.77
encourage	246 (0.14)	47 (0.04)	71.08	1.71
and_other	164 (0.09)	32 (0.03)	46.23	1.68
eu	247 (0.14)	52 (0.05)	63.33	1.57
existing	157 (0.09)	35 (0.03)	37.25	1.49
global	198 (0.11)	45 (0.04)	45.7	1.46
environment	196 (0.11)	45 (0.04)	44.58	1.45
be	3,075 (1.73)	740 (0.66)	651.39	1.38
must	374 (0.21)	95 (0.09)	72.58	1.3
levels	166 (0.09)	43 (0.04)	31.16	1.28
workers	153 (0.09)	40 (0.04)	28.26	1.26
all	861 (0.48)	241 (0.22)	140.16	1.16
such_as	250 (0.14)	70 (0.06)	40.67	1.16
given	142 (0.08)	41 (0.04)	21.73	1.12
areas	235 (0.13)	72 (0.06)	31.65	1.03

and might mean that we miss some that are important. For instance, we noticed above the use of *shall* and *peoples*, which we would have missed if we had opted only to look at the keywords presented in Table 9.10. This suggests that we need to exercise caution when reducing numbers of keywords. However, the alternative to applying frequency and effect size cut-offs is to go back to our list of 291 (or more if we lower the LL cut-off to 10.83, or 6.63) and work through them all. In most cases, this will not be practical. As with other lists of key items, each keyword in Table 9.10 needs to be assessed for its usefulness in answering our research question, which relates to style. A number of the keywords fall into this category; for example, *include, and other* and *such as* mark the start and ends of short lists indicating a particular way in which the Green Party introduces examples, and suggestive of a particular (potentially academic) style. Additionally, the modal auxiliaries *would, must* and *should* present potentially fruitful avenues for further analysis. By way of illustration of the kind of analysis that is possible (and for reasons of space), for the remainder of this section we focus on just one of those keywords: *should*.

The modal auxiliary *should* is over-represented in the GP-POL-2010 corpus when compared with the LAB-CON-POL-2010 corpus. Given that *should* is typically associated with strong obligation (deontic modality), we hypothesised that this might be due to the GP making statements about what the other political parties should have done or should be doing but are not. We further hypothesised that this language choice would represent the GP as a strong voice of opposition. To test out our hypothesis, we used AntConc (Anthony 2018) to look more closely at how *should* is used in both corpora. Unlike Wmatrix, AntConc is able to provide sorted concordances, which are extremely useful for discerning patterns in the data. We first looked at the sorted concordances of *should* in GP-POL-2010, and found a frequent pattern was *should + be*. The pattern suggests the textual construction of alternative possibilities (or worlds) through statements of desire rather than of intent, and raises the possibility of an alternative outcome (Ninan 2005 notes that deontic *should* can be cancelled: 'we should, but ...'). In such cases, *should* presents an ideal that is unlikely to happen. In order to quantify this pattern and determine whether the GP uses *should be* more frequently, we exported the sorted concordance to a .txt file, which we then opened in Excel. From there, we were able to manually separate out the concordances that contained *should + be* by cutting and pasting from one worksheet into another.

We found that in the GP-POL-2010 corpus the *should + be* pattern made up 65 per cent of the total occurrences of *should*. We followed the same process for the LAB-CON-POL-2010 corpus, and found that *should* + *be* made up 45 per cent of the occurrences of *should* in the LAB-CON-POL-2010 corpus. The results indicate, therefore, that the GP engages in more hypothesising about 'what should be' than the Labour and Conservative parties combined. The Labour and Conservative parties use these constructions considerably less in the data, indicating that they hypothesise less about possible ideal situations.

Looking in more detail at *should* + *be*, we noticed that many instances were followed by a past tense verb (i.e. were passive constructions). We again exported the concordances to Excel to help carry out our analysis, and we found that of the 1,137 occurrences of *should* in the GP-POL-2010 corpus, 46 per cent were part of passive constructions, while in the LAB-CON-POL-201 corpus we found that the figure was less than half that, at 19 per cent. As the following examples from GP-POL-2010 demonstrate, passive constructions can remove, hide or not acknowledge agency:

(24) An import ban should also be imposed on products linked directly or indirectly to deforestation

(25) Permission should also be required to increase the power of existing masts.

(26) WTO, International Monetary Fund, World Bank and similar bodies should also be reformed, democratised, or replaced.

This is a potential issue for the Green Party because it means that on numerous occasions when it talks about policy it is not making itself the agent of the action. For example, (24) could be rephrased as 'we/ the Green Party would impose a ban ...', which would make the party's position clearer and make the GP an active participant in that process and policy. In example (25) the agent of the verb process is not the GP but the owners of 'existing masts'. Here the action that the GP seems to be proposing is introducing legislation to require owners of masts to apply for permission to increase power. This could have been stated more clearly by making the GP an active participant in the text. Similarly, in (26) it is highly unlikely the GP would be able to reform the institutions mentioned, but if the GP's intention is to press for these reforms, this too could be stated more clearly. While this pattern also exists in the LAB-CON-POL-2010 corpus, it is considerably less frequent, which means that not being active participants in clauses is less of an issue for the Labour and Conservative parties.

As for the rest of the occurrences of *should be*, in both corpora a minority are followed by an -ing participle (five occurrences in GP-POL-2010; six in LAB-CON-POL-2010), while the majority are modalised relational processes (in Hallidayan terms) with the pattern of NP + *should* + *be* + complement. For example, here are two instances of *should be* followed by -ing participles:

> (27) Under Labour, our aid funding is not used in a focused way, and is sometimes spent in countries that should be looking after their own poor citizens.
>
> (28) Hazardous waste production should be reaching zero levels by 2020.

Example (27) shows the modal use of *should* to be more clearly deontic since it imposes or suggests an obligation for other countries. In (28) the modality relates to probability and certainty, or obligation based on desire; it is more ambiguous. It may come as no surprise, based on our discussion of *should* so far in the GP data, that example (27) is from the LAB-CON-POL-2010 corpus, while (28) is from the GP-POL-2010 corpus.

The following examples are all from the GP data and show *should* + *be* + complement:

> (29) The supply of fossil fuels is already tightly controlled for the purposes of collecting tax so there should be no insurmountable problems in ensuring that carbon units are paid.
>
> (30) Fares should be cheaper, including subsidies where necessary,
>
> (31) Information on the allocation of quotas should be open and transparent.
>
> (32) There should be no restriction on an asylum seeker taking work.

In example (29) mentioning problems raises the spectre of difficulties, which could cause doubts in a reader's mind. The statement could be paraphrased as 'we don't foresee any problems', which sounds rather uncertain because that does not mean that there are *no* problems. The statement could, instead, be rewritten along the lines of 'carbon units will be paid using the existing tax payment mechanism'. Using *will* instead of *should* suggests a greater degree of certainty, that a viable mechanism for collecting carbon units is already in place, and avoids the mention of problems.

While the modal auxiliary *should* can suggest strong obligation, in the GP data we analysed this is not the case. Our findings and discussion of *should be* show that it is used to encode the wishes or desires of the Green Party (i.e. it conveys boulomaic modality; see Simpson 1993) or the writer's certainty about states of affairs (epistemic modality).

9.6 Implications of the research

The analysis of the policy documents that we present here suggests that the rhetoric used by the Labour and Conservative parties is different to that used by the Green Party. While our aim was not to tell the Green Party how to write political documents, this information could help it to appreciate the different ways in which to communicate ideas to the electorate, and suggest discourse strategies for it to explore. An important finding was the use of *should* in the Green Party documents, which highlighted that *should* does not always encode strong obligation but can sometimes create ambiguity and weaken ideas. Highlighting this to the Green Party made it aware of a particular language trait in its documents that presented it in an unfavourable way to the electorate. Again, it was not our intention to prescribe but simply to raise awareness so that the Green Party could make informed decisions about the use of modality and the use of categorical statements.

An important part of our research was to report back our findings to the Green Party and provide answers to our research questions. We did this through a written report and via a presentation and language awareness training session at the Green Party headquarters in London. The idea behind the training was to raise awareness of key language issues, using our findings as a focus, to Green Party Members responsible for producing publicity materials. This stage in the project was useful because we were able to assess what the Green Party representatives knew about their party's language use and whether our results told them something that they already knew or not. From the responses we received during the training session it appeared that the representatives were unaware of the language traits we reported to them from the policy document data, meaning that a corpus stylistic approach was able to expose patterns in their language use that they would have otherwise not noticed. These insights subsequently found their way into the party political broadcast that the GP commissioned.

9.7 Conclusion

This chapter discussed the use of stylistics in the solution of a real-world problem, before going on to present a case study that demonstrated some of the possibilities for engaging in projects with non-academic research partners in order to help them address language-related issues. Our case study also provided a further demonstration of the use of keywords and key semantic domains in a stylistic analysis where we used the corpus outputs to assess patterns of usage across a range of texts (rather than one text, as in Chapter 5). We also explored different ways of organising and restricting keyword lists using different statistical measures including effect size, and showed the quantitative consequences of applying different statistical thresholds. This demonstrated that different thresholds can highlight different key items, which may have consequences for the focus of qualitative strands of analysis. We suggested that no one approach for restricting results statistically is suitable for all research projects and that if key items need to be constrained, then decisions about cut-off points should be informed by the aims of the research. We also showed that while there are various ways of producing a list of keywords, in the end, once a list has been established, each keyword needs to be analysed in more detail using, in the first instance, concordance lines. Such analyses are helped by using sorted concordances, since these can help to identify patterns. Once patterns have been established, then a further phase of analysis is required that quantifies the patterns and then establishes their interpretative significance through further analysis that is itself informed by a stylistic framework.[6] Key items therefore offer ways in to the data that may then go on to reveal further interpretatively useful patterns.

Notes

1. See <http://ucrel.lancs.ac.uk/claws/> (last accessed 20 August 2018).
2. PDFs needed to be converted to plain text format. Laurence Anthony's AntFileConverter (Anthony 2018) is one possible way to do this. The resulting .txt files might need further editing before they are used in a corpus.
3. Since collecting the data, the websites for these three parties have changed considerably. In particular, the Green Party no longer seems to be offering any downloadable policy documents.
4. Note that Wmatrix sometimes groups words into multi-word units (MWUs). Such groupings represent one lexical item in the word lists it generates. In the GP corpus there are 923 instances where 'green'

and 'party' co-occur. There are a further 203 instances of 'green' when it does not co-occur with 'party'.

5. A potential problem with 'aboutness' is determining precisely what it relates to. Part of the issue is that aboutness is a complex notion that is concerned with the macrostructure of texts, determined via collocational associations and distributions (Phillips 1989); it is not simply a synonym for topic.

6. For an extended example of this kind of keyword analysis, see Jeffries and Walker (2018).

10

The scope of corpus stylistics

10.1 Introduction

We began this book by noting that the term *corpus stylistics* is relatively new. While this is certainly true, work that has taken a computational approach to the analysis of literary texts has been around for almost as long as corpus linguistics itself. The corpus analysis of literature, of course, does not necessarily equate to stylistics. Corpus stylistic research, according to the argument we have made throughout this book, necessitates a focus on linguistic style and the use of stylistic theories and analytical frameworks. Moreover, the object of study for stylistics is style in all text types, not just literature. Nonetheless, we can see in some of the early corpus analysis of literature the beginnings of the kind of work that now underpins contemporary corpus stylistics. Wisbey (1971), for example, is an edited volume of papers from a symposium held at the University of Cambridge on 23 March 1970, entitled *The Computer in Literary and Linguistic Research*. What is perhaps surprising in Wisbey's introduction to the book is his claim that 'there can be few readers today for whom this concatenation [i.e. computers in literary research] will evoke quite the *frisson* of surprise (and possibly mortification) which would have been their reaction only ten years ago' (Wisbey 1971: vii). Given Wisbey's claim in 1971 of a positive change in attitude towards using computational methods in stylistics, we might have expected the number of stylisticians using computational techniques to have increased exponentially over the past decades, and for corpus-based stylistics to be much more central to the discipline of stylistics than it currently is. It has, however, taken a long time for stylisticians to adopt corpus linguistic approaches.

There are, perhaps, a number of reasons for this. Until the advent of desktop computing, carrying out corpus-based research in stylistics was complex, time-consuming and expensive. The difficulties involved in generating even a simple concordance are likely to have been off-putting to most literary scholars (see, for example, Porter's 1971 description of the labour-intensive process of developing a programming language for concordancing, and Leighton's 1971 account of the difficulties involved in using punched cards to count clause types in sonnets[1]). The introduction of personal computers made such techniques easier, though it was not until the development of user-friendly software packages such as WordSmith Tools, AntConc and Wmatrix that the computational analysis of aspects of style was made relatively easy. Even then, corpus stylistics remained the niche interest of a relatively small number of stylisticians. The two most likely reasons for this are (1) that stylisticians could not see the value of using corpora in stylistic analysis, and (2) that doing corpus stylistics appeared to be difficult, and the knowledge and skills needed for such analysis time-consuming to acquire. This book has aimed to address both of these views by (1) demonstrating the worth of corpora in stylistic analysis and (2) explaining how to go about doing corpus stylistics. We hope that this book will encourage greater numbers of stylisticians to adopt corpus methods in their own research, and that by so doing the discipline of stylistics will be enriched and pushed forwards into new and interesting areas.

In this final chapter we reflect on the insights arising from the corpus stylistic analyses we have presented in this book. We argue that it is no longer tenable for stylisticians to view the use of corpus methods as a niche practice on the fringes of stylistics. So easy is it to access corpus analytical software nowadays that there is no longer any reason for viewing corpus stylistics as a specialist sub-field of stylistics practised only by those who are particularly interested in it. Rather, where corpus methods can contribute to a stylistic analysis, it is important that they be employed. In this respect, corpus stylistics should be seen as intrinsic to stylistic analysis generally and corpus stylistic methods fully integrated into the mainstream.

We begin this chapter by returning to the issue of a definition of corpus stylistics. We argue that this goes beyond claims that corpus stylistics is simply the use of corpus linguistic techniques in the study of literature. Having discussed existing definitions of corpus stylistics, we then go on to summarise the value of corpus linguistics to stylistics. Here we also consider what stylistics has to offer to corpus linguistics. On the basis of the above discussion, we then offer our own definition of corpus stylistics, based on the arguments presented in the previous chapters. Finally, we discuss the scope of corpus stylistics and consider what the future might hold for this approach to text analysis.

10.2 The problem of definition

Discussing the relationship between corpus linguistics and stylistics, Widdowson observes that:

> Stylistics claims to provide linguistic substantiation for the interpretation of literary texts. Since corpus analysis is par excellence a means of revealing textual features in precise detail, it seems reasonable to suppose that it must be relevant to the stylistic enterprise. (Widdowson 2008: 293)

While Widdowson's reasoning cannot be faulted, his observation includes the erroneous suggestion that stylistics is aimed at the analysis of literary texts only. While it is true that most stylisticians are primarily interested in 'literature' (the scare quotes are necessary to indicate that even such a category is contested), the analytical methods of stylistics are equally applicable to non-literary texts. Indeed, as Carter and Nash (1990) convincingly explain, literariness is not necessarily a property of fiction alone but should instead be viewed as a point on a cline on which *all* texts feature. It is particularly important that this be acknowledged, as the Russian Formalist school of literary criticism (the direct forerunner of modern stylistics; see Lemon and Reiss [1917] 1965) very quickly discovered that the forms of literary language are no different to those found in non-literary texts. It would seem odd, then, to claim that literary texts are the sole object of study of stylistics. Moreover, despite the reputation of stylistics as something of a magpie discipline, taking analytical approaches from other areas of language studies, it is also the case that it has developed theories, models and analytical methods of its own; for example, foregrounding theory (van Peer 1986), models of speech and thought presentation (Leech and Short 1981) and text world theory (Werth 1999). In this respect, stylistics has progressed considerably and can no longer be thought of as simply an eclectic mix of methods borrowed from other sub-disciplines of linguistics. Any definition of corpus stylistics, then, needs to take account of these issues.

In her own definition of corpus stylistics, Mahlberg acknowledges that stylistics is not simply about the analysis of literature:

Corpus linguistics + (literary) stylistics = corpus stylistics?

(Mahlberg 2007a: 219)

What is interesting about this definition is the question mark at the end, which appears to suggest that there is more to the corpus stylistic enterprise than the simple use of corpus approaches in stylistic analysis (*pace* Fischer-Starcke 2010). Mahlberg (2007a) goes on to explain that the value of corpus linguistics to stylistics goes beyond its capacity to generate quantitative findings. She suggests that, in addition, corpus stylistics can 'help with the analysis of an individual text by providing various options for the comparison of one text with groups of other texts to identify tendencies, intertextual relationships, or reflections of social and cultural contexts' (Mahlberg 2007a: 221).

We agree that it is important to acknowledge that statistics form just one possible aspect of a corpus stylistic analysis. One element that will always be present to some degree, however, is intuition. We explained in Chapter 4 the importance of intuition to stylistic analysis. We also pointed out the value of intuition in corpus linguistics generally. Stubbs, for instance, acknowledges 'the essential role of intuition in formulating hypotheses and analysing data' (2007: 234). Intuition also forms part of Carter's definition of corpus stylistics, which is as follows:

Corpus stylistic analysis is a relatively objective methodological procedure that at its best is guided by a relatively subjective process of interpretation. (Carter 2010: 67)

While we do not disagree with this definition, the problem with this and all such descriptions is that they are essentially macro-level summaries of corpus stylistics. They do not themselves offer *practical* insight into what corpus stylistics is. By contrast, this is what we have aimed to do in this book, that is, to demonstrate how the theories, models, frameworks and analytical insights of stylistics can be employed in the analysis of linguistic style in corpus data. This forms part of our own definition of corpus stylistics, which we present in section 10.4. Before we do this, however, it will be useful to summarise the value of corpus linguistic methods and theories for stylistics, as well as consider the reciprocal value of stylistics to corpus linguistics.

10.3 Corpus linguistics and stylistics: a symbiotic relationship

As we have shown throughout this book, corpus linguistics offers a wide range of analytical methods and theoretical insights which have value for stylistics. This is where the significance of our book lies for stylistics. By the same token, insights from stylistics have substantial value for corpus linguistics, and this is where the significance of our book lies for corpus linguists. In Chapter 2, for example, we showed how it is possible to use the concept of collocation to determine the locus of irony in a short extract from a theatre script. Our analysis of 'Aftermyth of war' from *Beyond the Fringe* also showed that a qualitative analysis of the text, informed by pragmatic insights, was able to demonstrate that the semantic prosody which is key to an ironic interpretation is not the sole trigger for irony. Rather, it is the clash of semantic prosodies that is responsible for the ironic effects. In this way, we have shown stylistic and corpus linguistic analytical methods to be mutually beneficial.

This symbiotic relationship between stylistics and corpus linguistics can be seen throughout the book. In Chapter 3 we showed how tagging corpus data using a stylistic framework can be used to investigate diachronic changes in text style. Our analysis of the 'Judge Dredd' comic strip revealed an increase in the use of free indirect thought over time, a finding only accessible through the process of corpus annotation. By the same token, the model of speech and thought presentation that we use provides a systematic means of analysing the range of textual data in our corpora. In Chapter 4, we showed how corpus analytical methods can be employed to test hypotheses about the linguistic style of a single author. At the same time, we explained how intuition born of a familiarity with Hemingway's writing was necessary to formulate such hypotheses in the first place. The case study in Chapter 5 focused on the use of statistics to determine text samples for qualitative stylistic analysis. The stylistic concept of foregrounding was then used to interpret the data and determine the interpretative significance of particular stylistic patterns in the text. Similarly, Chapter 6 showed how a cognitive stylistic model of characterisation could be used to determine interpretatively significant elements of a screenplay that are likely to have an impact on the characterisation process. In this chapter we also made the point that a quantitatively focused corpus analysis is just one aspect of corpus stylistics and that equally important is the qualitative stylistic analysis of representative samples of the corpus data. Chapter 7 explained the value of corpus linguistic techniques for pedagogical stylistics, arguing that corpus analysis can be used to teach the linguistic and cultural knowledge that is necessary for the interpretation of foregrounding in poetry. Here again, however, it is qualitative stylistic analysis that reveals the interpretative significance of deviations from such norms. Chapter 8 illustrated the importance of statistical analysis for the identification of diachronic changes in style. But the identification of diachronic stylistic change was only made possible by the application of stylistic frameworks in the annotation and interpretation of the corpus data. Finally, Chapter 9 showed how corpus linguistic and stylistic approaches can be combined to address problems outside of academia, thereby demonstrating the value of a combined approach in the solution of real-world challenges.

In relation to the above summary, then, what makes corpus analytical techniques particularly valuable in stylistics is that they can be used to:

- identify patterns in texts
- determine norms
- validate or invalidate intuitions
- test literary critical claims
- increase the potential for the falsification of claims about style and its effects
- improve analytical standards and the reporting of results.

In addition, we might note that in cases where copyright law allows for the distribution of stylistic corpora, the availability of such datasets (particularly those that are annotated) aids the process of replication and falsification, as well as increasing the possibilities for collaborative working. All of this is in line with the move towards open data (see Kitchin 2014) that is becoming ever more prevalent in the social and natural sciences. Furthermore, it also seems likely that the practices of corpus linguistics are having a washback effect on stylistics in general terms. The manual annotation of data for the analysis of stylistic function is now much more common than it was, even in non-corpus stylistic work (see, for example, Tilney 2018). In some cases, we might even want to term such work *corpus-inspired*; see, for example, Wang et al.'s (2016) development of a web-based tool for annotation and visualisation of data based on text world theory (the annotation scheme for which is described in Ho et al. forthcoming). We would also claim (although our evidence for this view is anecdotal only) that greater attention is currently being paid to data sampling for representativeness than was previously the case in qualitative stylistics.

10.4 Conclusion

Having outlined the reciprocal importance of corpus linguistics and stylistics to the corpus stylistics enterprise, we can now turn to a summary
definition of corpus stylistics itself. In our view, corpus stylistics is best
used to describe a particular focus of corpus linguistics, one in which the
research questions being investigated and/or the analytical frameworks
used are primarily concerned with issues of style. What this definition
suggests is that corpus stylistics is scalar in nature, with some corpus
stylistic projects including a greater corpus stylistic element than others.
First, we need to acknowledge that in corpus stylistics it is common to
deviate from conventional definitions of what a corpus is. Much corpus
stylistic work focuses on single texts or small corpora that by the terms
of corpus linguistics may not in fact be thought of as corpora at all. We
have argued that this is not a major issue, providing that this is acknowledged in such studies and the analytical ramifications of this made clear.
Second, to clarify the claim that corpus stylistics is a scalar enterprise,
we can note that there are degrees of corpus stylistics. At one end of the
scale, we might use corpus linguistic tools and analytical techniques to
test a literary critical claim. Such an investigation may be deemed stylistic in terms of its overall focus, though the analytical aspect of the work
may owe more to corpus linguistics than stylistics (see, for example,
our discussion of the 'strolling with intent' example in section 2.2).
At the opposite end of the scale we can consider research that uses a
stylistic model to inform an annotation scheme and which then analyses
the results of the corpus analysis using a stylistic framework (see, for
example, the case study in section 8.5). While we can make a distinction
between corpus-based and corpus-informed stylistics, this distinction
is not in itself responsible for where a corpus stylistic project may sit
on the cline of corpus stylistics. Finally, we would argue that corpus
stylistics rests on the basis of a symbiotic relationship between stylistics
and corpus linguistics. What corpus linguistics offers to stylistics is a
set of theories and analytical methods for exploring large quantities
of language data. What stylistics offers to corpus linguistics is a set of
theories, models and analytical frameworks that may be deployed in the
interpretation of corpus data and corpus-derived results.

What we hope to have shown in this book is that corpus methods
have a significant contribution to make to stylistics. Moreover, such
is the ubiquity of corpus linguistic software now that in cases where
corpus evidence would be of substantial value to a stylistic analysis,
there is really no excuse not to provide this. While some aspects of
corpus linguistics may seem initially alien to the qualitatively minded

stylistician, none is beyond the abilities of those willing to put in some time and effort to acquire the necessary skills to apply them stylistically. We should also be clear that stylistics should not be viewed as the poor relation in the corpus stylistics partnership. As Buse writes:

> The real problem in, for example, stylistics is not the secondary one of counting and analysing large masses of data: the primary difficulty is knowing what to count and what to analyse. Such knowledge comes only from an intuitive perception of those features which are stylistically important in a given text, married to an adequate theory about the nature, structure, and use of language. (Buse 1974: 274)

What we would add to this is that corpus methods offer the potential for testing such intuitions, strengthening such insight through the realisation of a Spitzerian method of analysis. What we hope to see in the future, then, is stylistics engaging to a much greater extent with corpus linguistics, and using the insights it can provide to develop stylistics in new and exciting areas. There is, for example, much to explore in relation to how corpus methods might be used to develop cognitive stylistics (see, for instance, the pioneering work of Mahlberg et al. 2016). The current interest in stylistics in multimodality is also amenable to corpus analysis, and the potential to develop insights into common patterns in multimodal expression should encourage work in this area. As stylistics expands the repertoire of text-types that it is interested in, we would also be keen to see more work on style in naturally occurring spoken language. In its early days, stylistics was closely aligned with sociolinguistics (see, for example, Crystal and Davy 1969), and while there has been some recent work in this area (e.g. Coupland 2007), there is scope for much more. In all respects, there are encouraging signs. Since its first appearance in 1992, *Language and Literature* (the journal of the Poetics and Linguistics Association, the foremost international organisation for stylistics) has seen a steady rise in articles referencing the term *corpus*. We would like to see this trend continue and our hope is that this book will encourage such work.

Note

1. Though to some degree at least, Leighton's difficulties are still shared by corpus stylisticians today; he notes that '[i]t is perhaps worth mentioning that the collection of material is almost more problematic than the processing of it' (Leighton 1971: 149).

Appendix 1 Corpora for corpus stylistics

The following is a list of corpora likely to be of particular interest for research in corpus stylistics.

Useful commercially available corpora

ARCHER (A Representative Corpus of Historical English Registers)

A historical corpus of British and American English containing numerous genres from 1600 to 1999. Access, via a web interface, is granted after filling in a user agreement form.

BNC (British National Corpus)

100m words of written and spoken British English from the 1960s to the early 1990s.
Freely available with restrictions via BYU Corpora (see Appendix 2 for details).

Brown

1m words of 1960s written American English.
Available to purchase as part of the ICAME Corpus Collection at: <http://clu.uni.no/icame/newcd.htm>.
Freely available with restrictions via CQPWeb (see Appendix 2 for details).

Burney Collection

A searchable digital archive of nearly 1m pages from around 1,270 different newspapers and pamphlets published between the early seventeenth and the early nineteenth centuries.

Available under licence at: <https://www.bl.uk/collection-guides/burney-collection>.

COCA (Corpus of Contemporary American English)

560m words of written American English from 1990 to 2017.

Freely available via BYU Corpora (see Appendix 2 for details).

COHA (Corpus of Historical American English)

400m words of written American English from 1810 to 2009.

Freely available via BYU Corpora (see Appendix 2 for details).

Corpus of American Soap Operas

100m words from 22,000 transcripts of American soap operas from the early 2000s.

Freely available via BYU Corpora (see Appendix 2 for details).

Dictionary of Old English Web Corpus

3m words of Old English; contains a copy of every known surviving OE text (3,124 texts in total).

Freely available at: <https://tapor.library.utoronto.ca/doecorpus/>.

FLOB (Freiburg-LOB)

1m words of 1990s written British English.

Available to purchase as part of the ICAME Corpus Collection at: <http://clu.uni.no/icame/newcd.htm>.

Freely available with restrictions via CQPWeb (see Appendix 2 for details).

FROWN (Freiburg-Brown)

1m words of 1990s written American English.

Available to purchase as part of the ICAME Corpus Collection at: <http://clu.uni.no/icame/newcd.htm>.

Freely available with restrictions via CQPWeb (see Appendix 2 for details).

GloWbE (Global Web-Based English)

1.9bn words of textual varieties of English from 20 different countries.

Freely available via BYU Corpora (see Appendix 2 for details).

Helsinki Corpus

1.5m words from 400 samples of English texts dating from the eighth to the eighteenth centuries (i.e. Old English to Early Modern English).

Freely available via the Oxford Text Archive: <https://ota.ox.ac.uk/>.

Lancaster Speech, Writing and Thought Presentation Spoken Corpus

250k words of twentieth-century spoken British English; annotated for categories of speech, writing and thought presentation.

Freely available via the Oxford Text Archive: <https://ota.ox.ac.uk/>.

Lancaster Speech, Writing and Thought Presentation Written Corpus

260k words of twentieth-century British English fiction, journalism and (auto)biography; annotated for categories of speech, writing and thought presentation.

Freely available via the Oxford Text Archive: <https://ota.ox.ac.uk/>.

LOB (Lancaster-Oslo-Bergen)

1m words of 1960s written British English.

Available to purchase as part of the ICAME Corpus Collection: <http://clu.uni.no/icame/newcd.htm>.

Freely available with restrictions via CQPWeb (see Appendix 2 for details) and with no restrictions via the Oxford Text Archive: <https://ota.ox.ac.uk/>.

NOW (News on the Web)

Monitor corpus of 6bn words of web-based newspapers and magazines from 2010 to the present time; updated daily.

Freely available via BYU Corpora (see Appendix 2 for details).

Spoken BNC2014

10m words of spoken British English, recorded between 2012 and 2016.

Freely available at: <http://corpora.lancs.ac.uk/bnc2014>.

ZEN (Zurich English Newspaper)

1.6m words of Early Modern English from 349 complete newspaper editions published between 1661 and 1791.

Freely available from: hmlehman@es.uzh.ch.

Specialist corpora used in this book

N.B. Due to copyright restrictions, we are unable to make most of these corpora publicly available. Those that are copyright-free are marked with an asterisk and copies may be obtained from the authors.

1974

Full text of the novel *1974* by David Peace.

EModE Modality*

500k words of Early Modern English news texts; annotated for modal auxiliary verb functions.

EModE SW&TP*

60k words of Early Modern English fiction and news texts; annotated for categories of speech, writing and thought presentation using the same framework as applied in the Lancaster Speech, Writing and Thought Presentation Written Corpus.

GP-POL-2010

187,718 words of UK Green Party policy documents from 2010.

Hemingway

783,551 words comprising eight novels by Ernest Hemingway.

HUM (Huddersfield-Utrecht-Middelburg)*

13m words of nineteenth-century British fiction.

JD77C

11,674 words of 'Judge Dredd' comic strips from 1977; taken from the comic *2000AD* and annotated for categories of speech, writing and thought presentation.

JD02C

11,276 words of 'Judge Dredd' comic strips from 2002; taken from the comic *2000AD* and annotated for categories of speech, writing and thought presentation.

LAB-CON-POL-2010

173,580 words of Labour Party and Conservative Party policy documents from 2010.

TTSS-Di

26,661 words of dialogue from the 1979 BBC TV series *Tinker Tailor Soldier Spy*.

TTSS-Sub

25,247 words of subtitles from the 1979 BBC TV series *Tinker Tailor Soldier Spy*.

Appendix 2 Software for corpus stylistics

AntConc

Widely used software for corpus analysis.

Freely available along with a range of related software at: <http://www.laurenceanthony.net/software.html>.

BYU Corpora

Web front-end to a wide variety of corpora, including the BNC, COCA, COHA and many more.

Freely available at: <https://corpus.byu.edu/>.

CLiC (Corpus Linguistics in Context)

Web-based software for the corpus stylistic analysis of literary texts; includes various nineteenth-century novels, including the complete works of Dickens, as well as a reference corpus of nineteenth-century fiction.

Freely available at: <http://clic.bham.ac.uk/?>.

CQPWeb

Web-based corpus query processor providing access to a wide range of corpora.

Freely available at: <https://cqpweb.lancs.ac.uk>.

#LancsBox

Web-based software for the corpus linguistic analysis of commercial and home-made corpora. Incorporates a POS-tagger and GraphColl for visualising collocational networks.

Freely available at: <http://corpora.lancs.ac.uk/lancsbox/>.

MLCT (Multilingual Corpus Toolkit)

Useful software package for corpus building and processing; requires some knowledge of regular expressions.

Freely available at: <https://sites.google.com/site/scottpiaosite/software/mlct>.

Sketch Engine

Web-based corpus analysis tool containing 500 large (in some cases, multibillion-word) corpora in over 90 languages. Can also be used with your own purpose-built corpora; licence required (free trial available).

Available at: <https://www.sketchengine.eu/#blue>.

VARD 2 (Variant Detector)

Software designed to normalise spelling in (particularly historical) texts where there is variation. Designed initially for Early Modern English, but has been used to normalise spelling in texts in other language varieties (including text messaging).

Freely available at: <http://ucrel.lancs.ac.uk/vard/availability/>.

Wmatrix

Web-based software for corpus analysis, incorporating automatic POS and semantic tagging; licence required.

Available from: p.rayson@lancaster.ac.uk.

WordSmith Tools

Widely used software for corpus analysis; licence required.

Available at: <http://www.lexically.net/wordsmith/>.

References

Aarts, B. and Smith-Dennis, E. (2018) 'Using corpora for English language teaching and learning', in McIntyre, D. and Price, H. (eds) *Applying Linguistics: Language and the Impact Agenda*, pp. 163–76. Abingdon: Routledge.

Adamson, S. (1994) 'From empathetic deixis to empathetic narrative: stylisation and (de)subjectivisation as processes of language change', *Transactions of the Philological Society* 92(1): 55–88.

Adolphs, S. (2006) *Introducing Electronic Text Analysis: A Practical Guide for Language and Literary Studies*. Abingdon: Routledge.

Adolphs, S. and Carter, R. (2013) *Spoken Corpus Linguistics: From Monomodal to Multimodal*. Abingdon: Routledge.

Ai, H. and Lu, X. (2013) 'A corpus-based comparison of syntactic complexity in NNS and NS university students' writing', in Díaz-Negrillo, A., Ballier, N. and Thompson, P. (eds) *Automatic Treatment and Analysis of Learner Corpus Data*, pp. 249–64. Amsterdam: John Benjamins.

Aijmer, K. (1987) '*Oh* and *ah* in English conversation', in Meijs, W. (ed.) *Corpus Linguistics and Beyond*, pp. 61–86. Amsterdam: Rodopi.

Alderson, J. C. and McIntyre, D. (2006) 'Implementing and evaluating a self-assessment mechanism for the web-based *Language and Style* course', *Language and Literature* 15(3): 291–307.

Al-Jarf, R. S. (2007) 'Processing of advertisements by EFL college students', *The Reading Matrix* 7(1): 132–40.

Alsuweed, M. (2015) 'Accessing Dickens's Style as an EFL Learner: A Corpus Stylistic Approach to Lexical Style'. Unpublished PhD thesis. University of Huddersfield.

Anthony, L. (2018) *AntConc* (Version 3.5.6) [Computer Software]. Tokyo: Waseda University. <http://www.laurenceanthony.net/software> (last accessed 6 July 2018).

Anthony, L. (2017a) *AntFileConverter* (Version 1.2.1) [Computer Software]. Tokyo: Waseda University. <http://www.laurenceanthony.net/software> (last accessed 6 July 2018).

Anthony, L. (2017b) *AntFileSplitter* (Version 1.0.0) [Computer Software]. Tokyo, Japan: Waseda University. <http://www.laurenceanthony.net/software> (last accessed 6 July 2018).

Aston, G. (2011) 'Applied Corpus Linguistics and the learning experience', in Viana, V., Zyngier, S. and Barnbrook, G. (eds) *Perspectives on Corpus Linguistics*, pp. 1–16. Amsterdam: John Benjamins.

Auer, A., González-Díaz, V., Hodson, J. and Sotirova, V. (eds) (2016) *Linguistics and Literary History: In Honour of Sylvia Adamson*. Amsterdam and Philadelphia: John Benjamins.

Badran, D. (2012) 'Metaphor as argument: a stylistic genre-based approach', in *Language and Literature* 21(2): 119–35.

Baker, E. A. (1936) *The History of the English Novel Volume 2: The Elizabethan Age and After*. New York: Barnes and Noble.

Baker, P. (2004) 'Querying keywords: questions of difference, frequency and sense in keyword analysis', *Journal of English Linguistics* 32(4): 346–59.

Baker, P. (2006) *Using Corpora in Discourse Analysis*. London: Continuum.

Baker, P. (2010) *Sociolinguistics and Corpus Linguistics*. Edinburgh: Edinburgh University Press.

Baker, P. and Egbert, J. (eds) (2016) *Triangulating Methodological Approaches in Corpus-Linguistic Research*. Abingdon: Routledge.

Baker, P., Wilson, A. and McEnery, T. (1997) 'Teaching grammar again after twenty years: corpus based help for grammar teaching', *ReCALL* 9(2): 8–16.

Balaev, M. (2014) 'Language's limits and a doubtful nature: Ernest Hemingway's "Big Two-Hearted River" and Friedrich Nietzsche's foreign language', *The Hemingway Review* 33(2): 107–18.

Balirano, G. (2013) 'The strange case of *The Big Bang Theory* and its extra-ordinary Italian audiovisual translation: a multimodal corpus-based analysis', *Perspectives: Studies in Translation Theory and Practice* 21(4): 563–76.

Barber, C. (1976) *Early Modern English*. London: Deutsch.

Barnbrook, G. (1996) *Language and Computers: A Practical Introduction to the Computer Analysis of Language*. Edinburgh: Edinburgh University Press.

Barnbrook, G., Mason, O. and Krishnamurthy, R. (2013) *Collocation: Applications and Implications*. Basingstoke: Palgrave.

Baron, A. (2013) *VARD2*. <http://ucrel.lancs.ac.uk/vard/about/> (last accessed 1 July 2018).

Baron, A., Rayson, P. and Archer, D. (2009) 'Word frequency and key word statistics in historical corpus linguistics', in Ahrens, R. and Antor, H. (eds) *Anglistik: International Journal of English Studies* 20(1): 41–67.

Bartlett, F. C. (1932) *Remembering: A Study in Experimental and Social Psychology*. Cambridge: Cambridge University Press.

Bateson, F. W. (1967) 'Literature and linguistics', *Essays in Criticism* 17: 322–47.

Bateson, F. W. (1968) 'Language and literature', *Essays in Criticism* 18: 164–82.

Beal, J. C., Fitzmaurice, S. and Hodson, J. (2012) 'Special issue: selected papers from the fourth International Conference on Late Modern English', *English Language and Linguistics* 16(2): 201–7.

Bellard-Thomson, C. (2010) 'How students learn stylistics: constructing an empirical study', *Language and Literature* 19(1): 35–57.

Bennett, A., Cook, P., Miller, J. and Moore, D. (1987) 'Aftermyth of war' (1963), in *The Complete Beyond the Fringe*, pp. 72–8. London: Methuen.

Berry-Roghe, G. (1973) 'The computation of collocations and their relevance to lexical studies', in Aitken, A. J., Bailey, R. W. and Hamilton-Smith, N. (eds) *The Computer and Literary Studies*, pp. 103–12. Edinburgh: Edinburgh University Press.

Bestgen, Y. (2017) 'Getting rid of the chi-square and log-likelihood tests for analysing vocabulary differences between corpora', *Quaderns de Filologia: Estudis Lingüístics* 22: 33–56.

Bex, T. (1999) *Standard English: The Widening Debate*. London: Routledge

Biber, D. (1988) *Variation Across Speech and Writing*. Cambridge: Cambridge University Press.

Biber, D. (1993) 'Representativeness in corpus design', *Literary and Linguistic Computing* 8(4): 243–57.

Biber, D. (2004) 'Modal use across registers and time', in Curzan, A. and Emmons, K. (eds) *Studies in the History of the English Language II: Unfolding Conversations*, pp. 189–216. Berlin: Mouton de Gruyter.

Biber, D. (2006) *University Language: A Corpus-Based Study of Spoken and Written Registers*. Amsterdam: John Benjamins.

may be interesting to read

Biber, D., Johansson, S., Leech, G., Conrad, S. and Finegan, E. (1999) *Longman Grammar of Spoken and Written English*. London: Longman.

Bloch, B. (1953) 'Linguistic structure and linguistic analysis', in Hill, A. A. (ed.) *Report of the Fourth Annual Round Table Meeting on Linguistics and Language Study*. Monograph Series on Language and Linguistics, IV. Washington, DC: Georgetown University Press.

Boas, F. (1917) 'Introduction', *International Journal of American Linguistics* 1(1): 1–8. [Reprinted in Boas, D. (1940) *Race, Language and Culture*, pp. 199–210. New York: The Free Press.]

Boulton, A. and Cobb, T. (2017) 'Corpus use in language learning: a meta-analysis', *Language Learning* 67(2): 348–93.

Bray, J. (2014) 'A portrait of historical stylistics', in Stockwell, P. and Whiteley, S. (eds) *The Cambridge Handbook of Stylistics*, pp. 485–500. Cambridge: Cambridge University Press.

Breen, M. P. (1985) 'Authenticity in the language classroom', *Applied Linguistics* 6(1): 60–70.

Breen, M. P. and Short, M. (1988) 'Alternative approaches in teaching stylistics to beginners', *Parlance* 1(2): 29–48.

Brezina, V., McEnery, T. and Wattam, S. (2015) 'Collocations in context: a new perspective on collocation networks', *International Journal of Corpus Linguistics* 20(2): 139–73.

British Association for Applied Linguistics (BAAL) (2016) *Recommendations on Good Practice in Applied Linguistics*. 3rd edn. British Association for Applied Linguistics. <https://baalweb.files.wordpress.com/2016/10/goodpractice_full_2016.pdf> (last accessed 14 September 2018).

Brown, P. and Levinson, S. C. (1987) *Politeness: Some Universals in Language Usage*. Cambridge: Cambridge University Press.

Brownlees, N. (ed.) (2006a) *News Discourse in Early Modern Britain: Selected Papers of CHINED 2004*. Bern: Peter Lang.

Brownlees, N. (2006b) 'Polemic and propaganda in Civil War news discourse', in Brownlees, N. (ed.) *News Discourse in Early Modern Britain: Selected Papers of CHINED 2004*, pp. 17–40. Bern: Peter Lang.

Brownlees, N. (2014) *The Language of Periodical News in Seventeenth-Century England*. Newcastle upon Tyne: Cambridge Scholars Publishing.

Brownlees, N. (2015) 'The beginnings of periodical news (1620–1665)', in Facchinetti, R., Brownlees, N., Bös, B. and Fries, U. *News as Changing Texts: Corpora, Methodologies and Analysis*. 2nd edn, pp. 5–47. Newcastle upon Tyne: Cambridge Scholars Publishing.

Bruti, S. and Zanotti, S. (forthcoming) 'Representations of stuttering in subtitling: a view from a corpus of English language films', in Ranzato, I. and Zanotti, S. (eds) *Linguistic and Cultural Representation in Audiovisual Translation*. New York and London: Routledge.

Burchfield, R. [1985] (2006) *The English Language*. London: The Folio Society.

Burke, M. (2010) 'Why care about pedagogical stylistics?', *Language and Literature* 19(1): 7–11

Burnard, L. (2004) 'Metadata for corpus work', in Wynne, M. (ed.) *Developing Linguistic Corpora: A Guide to Good Practice*, pp. 30–46. Oxford: Oxbow.

Burnard, L. (2014) *What is the Text Encoding Initiative?* Marseille: Open Edition Press.

Burrows, J. (1987) *Computation into Criticism: A Study of Jane Austen's Novels and an Experiment in Method*. Oxford: Clarendon Press.

Buse, J. E. (1974) 'R. A. Wisbey (ed.): *The Computer in Literary and Linguistic Research: Papers from a Cambridge Symposium*. (Publications of the Literary and Linguistic Computing Centre, University of Cambridge, Vol. 1.) XV, 309 pp. Cambridge: University Press, 1971', *Bulletin of the School of Oriental and African Studies* 37(1): 273–4.

Busse, B. (2010) *Speech, Writing and Thought Presentation in a Corpus of Nineteenth-Century English Narrative Fiction*. Bern: University of Bern.

Busse, B. (2015) '(New) historical stylistics', in Burke, M. (ed.) *The Routledge Handbook of Stylistics*, pp. 101–17. London: Routledge.

Busse, B. and McIntyre, D. (2010) 'Language, literature and stylistics', in McIntyre, D. and Busse, B. (eds) *Language and Style*, pp. 3–14. Basingstoke: Palgrave.

Butler, C. (1985) *Statistics in Linguistics*. Oxford: Blackwell.

Bywood, L., Volk, M., Fishel, M. and Panayota, G. (2013) 'Parallel subtitle corpora and their applications in machine translation and translatology', *Perspectives: Studies in Translation Theory and Practice* 21(4): 595–610.

Cain, W. (2014) 'Sentencing: Hemingway's aesthetic', *Culture and Society* 52: 80–5.

Calzada Pérez, M. (2018) 'What is kept and what is lost without translation? A corpus-assisted discourse study of the European Parliament's original and translated English', *Perspectives: Studies in Translation Theory and Practice* 26(2): 277–91.

I've borrowed this from the library

Carter, R. (1982) *Language and Literature: An Introductory Reader in Stylistics*. London: George Allen & Unwin.

Carter, R. (2010) 'Methodologies for stylistic analysis: practices and pedagogies', in McIntyre, D. and Busse, B. (eds) *Language and Style: In Honour of Mick Short*, pp. 55–68. Basingstoke: Palgrave.

Carter, R. and McCarthy, M. (1995) 'Grammar and the spoken language', *Applied Linguistics* 16(2): 141–58.

Carter, R. and Nash, W. (1990) *Seeing Through Language: A Guide to Styles of English Writing*. Oxford: Wiley Blackwell.

Chapman, S. (2008) *Language and Empiricism: After the Vienna Circle*. Basingstoke: Palgrave.

Charles, M. (2017) 'Do-it-yourself corpora in the EAP classroom: views of students and teachers', in Wong, L. L. C. and Hyland, K. (eds) *Faces of English Education: Students, Teachers, and Pedagogy*. Oxford: Taylor & Francis.

Cheng, W., Warren, M. and Xun-feng, X. (2003) 'The language learner as language researcher: putting corpus linguistics on the timetable', *System* 31(2): 173–86.

Chomsky, N. (1957) *Syntactic Structures*. The Hague: Mouton.

Church, K., Gale, W., Hanks, P. and Hindle, D. (1991) 'Using statistics in lexical analysis', in Zernik, U. (ed.) *Lexical Acquisition: Exploiting On-line Resources to Build a Lexicon*, pp. 115–64. Hillsdale, NJ: Lawrence Erlbaum.

Clark, U. and Zyngier, S. (2003) 'Towards a pedagogical stylistics', *Language and Literature* 12(4): 339–51.

Clarke, B. (2004) *From Grub Street to Fleet Street*. London: Ashgate.

Clear, J. (1993) 'From Firth principles: computational tools for the study of collocation', in Baker, M., Francis, G. and Tognini-Bonelli, E. (eds) *Text and Technology: In Honour of John Sinclair*, pp. 271–92. Amsterdam: John Benjamins.

Cohen, J. (1994) 'The Earth is round (p < .05)', *American Psychologist* 49(12): 997–1003.

Conrad, J. (1910) 'The secret sharer', *Harper's Magazine*. New York: Harper's Magazine Foundation.

Conrad, S. and Biber, D. (eds) (2001) *Variation in English: Multi-Dimensional Studies*. London: Longman.

Coupland, N. (2007) *Style: Language Variation and Identity*. Cambridge: Cambridge University Press.

Craig, H. (1999) 'Contrast and change in the idiolects of Ben Jonson characters', *Computers and the Humanities* 33(3): 221–40.

Crisp, P. (2006) 'E-learning and *Language and Style* in Hong Kong', *Language and Literature* 15(3): 277–90.

Croft, W. A. (2001) *Radical Construction Grammar: Syntactic Theory in Typological Perspective*. Oxford: Oxford University Press.

Crystal, D. and Davy, D. (1969) *Investigating English Style*. London: Longman, Green.

Culpeper, J. (2001) *Language and Characterisation: People in Plays and Other Texts*. London: Longman.

Culpeper, J. (2002) 'Computers, language and characterisation: an analysis of six characters in *Romeo and Juliet*', in Melander-Marttala, U., Ostman, C. and Kytö, M. (eds) *Conversation in Life and in Literature: Papers from the ASLA Symposium*, Association Suédoise de Linguistique Appliquée (ASLA) 15, pp. 11–30. Universitetstryckeriet: Uppsala.

Culpeper, J. (2009) 'Keyness: words, parts-of-speech and semantic categories in the character-talk of Shakespeare's *Romeo and Juliet*', *International Journal of Corpus Linguistics* 14(1): 29–59.

Culpeper, J. and Kytö, M. (2010) *Early Modern English Dialogues: Spoken Interaction as Writing*. Cambridge: Cambridge University Press.

Culpeper, J. and McIntyre, D. (2010) 'Activity types and characterisation in dramatic discourse', in Eder, J., Jannidis, F. and Schneider, R. (eds) *Characters in Fictional Worlds: Understanding Imaginary Beings in Literature, Film and Other Media*, pp. 176–207. Berlin: De Gruyter.

Davies, M. (2004–) *BYU-BNC*. (Based on the British National Corpus from Oxford University Press). <https://corpus.byu.edu/bnc/> (last accessed 1 July 2018).

Davies, M. (2012) *Oppositions and Ideology in News Discourse*. London: Bloomsbury.

de Linde, Z. (1995) 'Read my lips: subtitling principles, practices and problems', *Perspectives: Studies in Translatology* 3: 9–20.

de Linde, Z. and Kay, N. (1999) *The Semiotics of Subtitling*. Manchester: St Jerome.

Demjén, Z. (2015) *Sylvia Plath and the Language of Mental States*. London: Bloomsbury.

Demmen, J., Semino, E., Demjén, Z. Koller, V., Hardie, A., Rayson, P. and Payne, S. (2015) 'A computer-assisted study of the use of violence metaphors for cancer and end of life by patients, family carers and health professionals', *International Journal of Corpus Linguistics* 20(2): 205–31.

Denby, D. (2012) 'We are all Smiley's people', *The New Yorker*, 28 February. <https://www.newyorker.com/culture/culture-desk/we-are-all-smileys-people> (last accessed 9 April 2018).

Depraetere, I. and Reed, S. (2006) 'Mood and modality in English', in Aarts, B. and McMahon, A. (eds), *The Handbook of English Linguistics*, pp. 269–90. Malden, MA: Blackwell.

Díaz-Cintas, J. and Remael, A. (2007) *Audiovisual Translation: Subtitling*. Abingdon: Routledge.

Dunning, T. (1993) 'Accurate methods for the statistics of surprise and coincidence', *Computational Linguistics* 19(1): 61–74.

Economic and Social Research Council (ESRC) (2015) *ESRC Framework for Research Ethics (Updated January 2015)*. ESRC. <https://esrc.ukri.org/files/funding/guidance-for-applicants/esrc-framework-for-research-ethics-2015/> (last accessed 14 September 2018).

Edmondson, W. (1997) 'The role of literature in foreign language learning and teaching: some valid assumptions and invalid arguments', *AILA Review* 12: 42–55.

Eisner, W. (1996) *Graphic Storytelling & Visual Narrative*. Tamarac, FL: Poorhouse Press.

Enkvist, N. E. (1964) 'On defining style', in Enkvist, N. E., Spencer, J. and Gregory, M. (eds) *Linguistics and Style*, pp. 1–56. Oxford: Oxford University Press.

Enkvist, N. E. (1973) *Linguistic Stylistics*. The Hague: Mouton.

Erman, B. (1987) *Pragmatic Expressions in English: A Study of 'you know', 'you see' and 'I mean' in Face-to-Face Conversation*. Stockholm: Almqvist & Wiksell.

Evans, M. (2013) *The Language of Queen Elizabeth I: A Sociolinguistic Perspective on Royal Style and Identity*. Chichester: Wiley Blackwell.

Evans, M. (2018) 'Style and chronology: a stylometric investigation of Aphra Behn's dramatic style and the dating of *The Young King*', *Language and Literature* 27(2): 103–32.

Evert, S. (2005) *The Statistics of Word Cooccurrences: Word Pairs and Collocations*. Dr. Phil. dissertation. Institut für maschinelle Sprachverarbeitung, University of Stuttgart.

Eysenck, M. W. and Keane, M. T. (2010) *Cognitive Psychology: A Student's Handbook*. 6th edn. Hillsdale, NJ: Lawrence Erlbaum.

Fens-De Zeeuw, L. and Straaijer, R. (2012) 'Long-s in Late Modern English manuscripts', *English Language and Linguistics* 16(2): 319–38.

Field, A. (2000) *Discovering Statistics: Using SPSS for Windows*. London: SAGE.

Fillmore, C., Kay, P. and O'Connor, C. (1988) 'Regularity and idiomaticity in grammatical constructions: the case of *let alone*', *Language* 64: 501–38.

Firth, J. R. (1955) 'Structural linguistics', in Palmer, F. R. (ed.) (1966) *Selected Papers of J. R. Firth 1952–1959*, pp. 32–52. London: Longman.

Firth, J. R. (1957) *Papers in Linguistics 1934–1951*. Oxford: Oxford University Press.

Fischer-Starcke, B. (2010) *Corpus Linguistics in Literary Analysis: Jane Austen and Her Contemporaries*. London: Continuum.

Fish, S. (1980) *Is There a Text in This Class?* Cambridge, MA: Harvard University Press.

Fisher, R. A. (1924) 'On a distribution yielding the error functions of several well known statistics', *Proceedings of the International Congress of Mathematics, Toronto* 2: 805–13.

Flowerdew, L. (2009) 'Applying corpus linguistics to pedagogy: a critical evaluation', *International Journal of Corpus Linguistics* 14(3): 393–417.

Fogal, G. G. (2015) 'Pedagogical stylistics in multiple foreign language and second language contexts: a synthesis of empirical research', *Language and Literature* 24(1): 54–72.

Fowler, R. (ed.) (1966) *Essays on Style and Language*. London: Routledge and Kegan Paul.

Fowler, R. (1977) *Linguistics and the Novel*. London: Methuen.

Fox Tree, J. E. and Schrock, J. C. (1999) 'Discourse markers in spontaneous speech: oh what a difference an *oh* makes', *Journal of Memory and Language* 40: 280–95.

Francis, G. (1993) 'A corpus-driven approach to grammar: principles, methods and examples', in Baker, M., Francis, G. and Tognini-Bonelli, E. (eds) *Text and Technology: In Honour of John Sinclair*, pp. 137–57. Amsterdam: John Benjamins.

Francis, W. N. and Kučera, H. [1964] (1979) *Manual of Information to Accompany a Standard Corpus of Present-Day Edited American English, for Use with Digital Computers*. Department of Linguistics, Brown University.

Frankenberg-Garcia, A. (2010) 'Raising teachers' awareness of corpora', *Language Teaching* 45(4): 273–96.

Frankenberg-Garcia, A. (2012) 'Learners' use of corpus examples', *International Journal of Lexicography* 25(3): 273–96.

Fraser, B. (1999) 'What are discourse markers?', *Journal of Pragmatics* 31: 931–52.

Freddi, M. (2013) 'Constructing a corpus of translated films: a corpus view of dubbing', *Perspectives: Studies in Translation Theory and Practice* 21(4): 491–503.

Freeman, D. C. (1970) 'Linguistic approaches to literature', in Freeman,

D. C. (ed.) *Linguistics and Literary Style*, pp. 3–17. New York: Holt, Reinhart and Winston.

Friedl, J. (2006) *Mastering Regular Expressions*. Newton, MA: O'Reilly Media.

Fries, U. and Lehmann, H. M. (2006) 'The style of 18th century English newspapers: lexical diversity', in Brownlees, N. (ed.) *News Discourse in Early Modern Britain*, pp. 91–104. Bern: Peter Lang.

Fries, U., Lehmann, H. M., Ruef, B., Schnieder, P., Studer, P., auf dem Keller, C., Nietlispach, B., Engler, S., Hensel, S. and Zeller, F. (2004) *Zen: Zurich English Newspaper Corpus, Version 1.0*. Zurich: University of Zurich. <http://www.es.uzh.ch/en/Subsites/Projects/zencorpus.html> (last accessed 20 August 2018).

Fujimura, I. and Aoki, S. (2015) 'A new score to characterise collocations: log-r in comparison to Mutual Information', in *Proceedings of Europhras2015 – Computerised and Corpus-Based Approaches to Phraseology: Monolingual and Multilingual Perspectives*, pp. 271–82. <https://www.researchgate.net/publication/315653005_A_New_Score_to_Characterise_Collocations_Log-r_in_Comparison_to_Mutual_Information> (last accessed 16 August 2018).

Gabrielatos, C. (2005) 'Corpora and language teaching: just a fling or wedding bells?', *TESL-EJ* 8(4). <https://files.eric.ed.gov/fulltext/EJ1068106.pdf> (last accessed 16 August 2018).

Gabrielatos, C. and Marchi, A. (2012) 'Keyness: appropriate metrics and practical issues', CADS (Corpus-Assisted Discourse Studies) International Conference. 13–14 September. University of Bologna, Italy.

Garside, R. (1987) 'The CLAWS word-tagging system', in Garside, R., Leech, G. and Sampson, G. (eds) *The Computational Analysis of English: A Corpus-Based Approach*, pp. 30–41. London: Longman.

Garside, R. (1996) 'The robust tagging of unrestricted text: the BNC experience', in Thomas, J. and Short, M. (eds) *Using Corpora for Language Research: Studies in Honour of Geoffrey Leech*, pp. 167–80. London: Longman.

Garside, R. and Smith, N. (1997) 'A hybrid grammatical tagger: CLAWS4', in Garside, R., Leech, G. and McEnery, A. (eds) *Corpus Annotation: Linguistic Information from Computer Text Corpora*, pp. 102–21. London: Longman.

Gavins, J. and Steen, G. (eds) (2003) *Cognitive Poetics in Practice*. London: Routledge.

Gavioli, L. (2005) *Exploring Corpora for ESP Learning*. Amsterdam: John Benjamins.

Gilmore, A. (2008) 'Using online corpora to develop students' writing skills', *ELT Journal* 63(4): 363–72.

Gilquin, G. and Granger, S. (2010) 'How can DDL be used in language teaching?', in Biber, D. and Reppen, R. (eds) *The Cambridge Handbook of English Corpus Linguistics*, pp. 418–36. Cambridge: Cambridge University Press.

Goff, M. (2007) 'Early history of the English newspaper', *17th–18th Century Burney Collection Newspapers*. Detroit: Gale. <http://find.galegroup.com/bncn/topicguide/bbcn_03.htm> (last accessed 21 March 2018).

Gold, E., Earnshaw, K. and Ross, S. (2017) 'An introduction to the WYRED database', *Transactions of the Yorkshire Dialect Society*.

Goldberg, A. (1995) *Constructions: A Construction Grammar Approach to Argument Structure*. Chicago: University of Chicago Press.

Goldberg, A. (2006) *Constructions at Work: The Nature of Generalization in Language*. Oxford: Oxford University Press.

Gottlieb, H. (1992) 'Subtitling: a new university discipline', in Dollerup, C. and Lindegaard, A. (eds) *Teaching Translating and Interpreting 2: Insights, Aims, Visions: Papers from the Second Language International Conference. Elsinore, Denmark 4–6 June 1993*, pp. 161–70. Amsterdam: John Benjamins.

Gotz, S. (2012) 'Testing task types in data-driven learning: benefits and limitations', in Biebighäuser, K., Zibelius, M. and Schmidt, T. (eds) *Aufgaben 2.0 – Konzepte, Materialien und Methoden für das Fremdsprachenlehren und lernen mit digitatlen Medien*, pp. 249–76. Tübingen: Narr.

Green, C. (2017) 'Introducing the *Corpus of the Canon of Western Literature*: a corpus for culturomics and stylistics', *Language and Literature* 26(4): 282–99.

Gregory, I., Cooper, D., Hardie, A. and Rayson, P. (2015) 'Spatializing and analysing digital texts: corpora, GIS and places', in Bodenhamer, D., Corrigan, J. and Harris, T. (eds) *Deep Maps and Spatial Narratives*. Bloomington, IN: Indiana University Press.

Grice, H. P. (1975) 'Logic and conversation', in Cole, P. and Morgan, J. (eds) *Syntax and Semantics, Volume III: Speech Acts*, pp. 41–58. New York: Academic Press.

Gries, S. Th. (2005) 'Null hypothesis significance testing of word frequencies: a follow-up on Kilgarriff', *Corpus Linguistics and Linguistic Theory* 1: 277–94.

Gries, S. Th. (2010) 'Corpus linguistics and theoretical linguistics: a love–hate relationship? Not necessarily ...', *International Journal of Corpus Linguistics* 15(3): 327–43.

Guthrie, G. (2010) *Basic Research Methods: An Entry to Social Science Research*. London: SAGE.

Hall, G. (2005) *Literature in Language Education*. London: Palgrave.

Hall, G. (2007) 'Stylistics in second language contexts: a critical perspective', in Watson, G. and Zyngier, S. (eds) *Literature and Stylistics for Language Learners*, pp. 3–14. Basingstoke: Palgrave Macmillan.

Halliday, M. A. K. (1966) 'Lexis as a linguistic level', in Bazell, C. E., Catford, J. C., Halliday, M. A. K. and Robins, R. H. (eds) *In Memory of J. R. Firth*, pp. 148–62. London: Longman.

Halliday, M. A. K. and Matthiessen, C. M. I. M. (2004) *An Introduction to Functional Grammar*. London: Arnold.

Hanauer, D. I. (2001) 'The task of poetry reading and second language learning', *Applied Linguistics* 22(3): 295–323.

Hanks, P. (2008) 'The lexicographical legacy of John Sinclair', *International Journal of Lexicography* 21(3): 219–29.

Hardie, A. (2014) 'Log ratio: an informal introduction', Blog post. ESRC Centre for Corpus Approaches to Social Science (CASS). <http://cass.lancs.ac.uk/?p=1133> (last accessed 23 March 2018).

Hardie, A. and McEnery, T. (2010) 'On two traditions in corpus linguistics, and what they have in common', *International Journal of Corpus Linguistics* 15(3): 384–94.

Harmer, J. (2001) *The Practice of English Language Teaching*. London: Longman.

Hennemann, A. (2015) 'Construction Grammar and Corpus Linguistics: the example of Spanish *con respecto a/de* "with respect to"', *Procedia: Social and Behavioral Sciences* 198: 183–93.

Henri, A. (1967) 'Tonight at noon', in Henri, A., McGough, R. and Patten, B. *The Mersey Sound*. London: Penguin.

Henri, A., McGough, R. and Patten, B. (1967) *The Mersey Sound*. London: Penguin.

Herce, B. (2017) 'The diachrony of Spanish haber/hacer + time: a quantitative corpus-based approach to grammaticalization', *Journal of Historical Linguistics* 7(3): 276–321.

Heritage, J. (1984) 'A change-of-state token and aspects of its sequential placement', in Atkinson, J. M. and Heritage, J. (eds) *Structures of Social Action: Studies in Conversation Analysis*, pp. 299–345. Cambridge: Cambridge University Press.

Hilpert, M. (2014) *Construction Grammar and Its Application to English*. Edinburgh: Edinburgh University Press.

Ho, Y. (2011) *Corpus Stylistics in Principles and Practice: A Stylistic Exploration of John Fowles'* The Magus. London: Continuum.

Ho, Y., McIntyre, D., Xu, Z., Lugea, J. and Wang, J. (forthcoming) 'Text-world annotation and visualization for crime narrative reconstruction', *DSH: Digital Scholarship in the Humanities*.

Hoey, M. (2004) *Lexical Priming: A New Theory of Words and Language*. London: Routledge.

Hoey, M. (2007) 'Lexical priming and literary creativity', in Hoey, M., Mahlberg, M., Stubbs, M. and Teubert, W. (2007) *Text, Discourse and Corpora*, pp. 7–30. London: Continuum.

Holmes, J. (2013) *An Introduction to Sociolinguistics*. 4th edn. London: Routledge.

Honga, H., Kimb, S. and Chunga, M. (2014) 'A corpus-based analysis of English segments produced by Korean learners', *Journal of Phonetics* 46: 52–67.

Hoover, D. (2017) 'The microanalysis of style variation', *Digital Scholarship in the Humanities* 32 (Issue Supplement 2): ii17–ii30.

Hoover, D., Culpeper, J. and O'Halloran, K. (2014) *Digital Literary Studies: Corpus Approaches to Poetry, Prose and Drama*. Abingdon: Routledge.

Hopcraft, A. (1979) *Tinker Tailor Soldier Spy*. Unpublished BBC scripts. AHP/1/18, Arthur Hopcraft Papers, University of Salford Archives and Special Collections.

Huddleston, R. (1976) 'Some theoretical issues in the description of the English verb', *Lingua* 40: 331–83.

Hughes, J. A. and Sharrock, W. W. (1997) *The Philosophy of Social Research*. 3rd edn. London: Longman.

Hunston, S. (2002) *Corpora in Applied Linguistics*. Cambridge: Cambridge University Press.

Hunston, S. (2007) 'Semantic prosody revisited', *International Journal of Corpus Linguistics* 12(2): 249–68.

Hunston, S. (2015) 'Lexical grammar', in Biber, D. and Reppen, R. (eds) *The Cambridge Handbook of Corpus Linguistics*, pp. 201–15. Cambridge: Cambridge University Press.

Hunston, S. and Francis, G. (1999) *Pattern Grammar: A Corpus-Driven Approach to the Lexical Grammar of English*. Amsterdam: John Benjamins.

Hunston, S. and Su, H. (2017) 'Patterns, constructions, and local grammar: a case study of "evaluation"', *Applied Linguistics* 1–28.

Jakobson, R. (1960) 'Closing statement: linguistics and poetics', in Sebeok, T. A. (ed.) *Style in Language*, pp. 350–77. Cambridge, MA: MIT Press.

Jeffries, L. (2001) 'Schema affirmation and White Asparagus: cultural multilingualism among readers of texts', *Language and Literature* 10(4): 325–43.

Jeffries, L. (2007) *Textual Construction of the Female Body*. Basingstoke: Palgrave.

Jeffries, L. (2010a) *Critical Stylistics*. Basingstoke: Palgrave.

Jeffries, L. (2010b) *Opposition in Discourse: The Construction of Oppositional Meaning*. London: Continuum.

Jeffries, L. and McIntyre, D. (2010) *Stylistics*. Cambridge: Cambridge University Press.

Jeffries, L., O'Driscoll, J. and Evans, M. (2018) 'Language in conflict: linguistics in mediation', in McIntyre, D. and Price, H. (eds) *Applying Linguistics: Language and the Impact Agenda*, pp. 124–36. London: Routledge.

Jeffries, L. and Walker, B. (2018) *Keywords in the Press: The New Labour Years*. London: Bloomsbury.

Jenset, G. B. and McGillivray, B. (2017) *Quantitative Historical Linguistics: A Corpus Framework*. Oxford: Oxford University Press.

Johansson, S., Leech, G. N. and Goodluck, H. (1978) *Manual of Information to Accompany the Lancaster-Oslo/Bergen Corpus of British English, for Use with Digital Computers*. Department of English, University of Oslo.

Johns, T. (1991) 'Should you be persuaded: two examples of data driven learning', in Johns, T. and King, P. (eds) *Classroom Concordancing*. *ELR Journal* 4: 1–16.

Johns, T. (1994) 'From printout to handout: grammar and vocabulary teaching in the context of data-driven learning', in Odlin, T. (ed.) *Perspectives on Pedagogical Grammar*, pp. 293–312. Cambridge: Cambridge University Press.

Johnson, K. (2008) *An Introduction to Foreign Language Learning and Teaching*. Abingdon: Routledge.

Johnson, K. (2016) *The History of Early English*. London: Routledge.

Johnston, J. E., Berry, K. J. and Mielke, P. W. (2006) 'Measures of effect size for chi-squared and likelihood-ratio goodness-of-fit tests', *Perceptual and Motor Skills* 103(2): 412–14.

Jucker, A. H. (1993) 'The discourse marker "well": a relevance theoretical account', *Journal of Pragmatics* 19: 435–52.

Jucker, A. H. (2006) '"but 'tis believed that …": speech and thought presentation in Early English newspapers', in Brownlees, N. (ed.) *News Discourse in Early Modern Britain: Selected Papers of CHINED 2004*, pp. 105–25. Bern: Peter Lang.

Jucker, A. H. (ed.) (2009) *Early Modern English News Discourse*. Amsterdam and Philadelphia: John Benjamins.

Kaplan, A. (1964) *The Conduct of Inquiry: Methodology for Behavioural Science*. Scranton, PA: Chandler Publishing.

Kehoe, A., Renouf, A. and Banerjee, J. (2006) 'WebCorp: an integrated system for web text search', in Hundt, M., Nesselhauf, N. and Biewer, C. (eds) *Corpus Linguistics and the Web*, pp. 47–67. Amsterdam: Rodopi.

Kilgarriff, A. (1996) 'Comparing word frequencies across corpora: why chi-square doesn't work, and an improved LOB-Brown comparison', in *Proceedings of the ALLC-ACH Conference*, pp. 169–72. Bergen, Norway.

Kilgarriff, A. (2005) 'Language is never, ever, ever random', *Corpus Linguistics and Linguistic Theory* 1: 263–75.

Kilgarriff, A. and Tugwell, D. (2001) 'WASP-Bench: an MT lexicographers' workstation supporting state-of-the-art lexical disambiguation', in *Proceedings of the MT Summit VIII*, pp. 187–90. September. Santiago de Compostela, Spain.

King, B. (2009) 'Building and analysing corpora of computer-mediated communication', in Baker, P. (ed.) *Contemporary Corpus Linguistics*, pp. 301–20. London: Continuum

Kitchin, R. (2014) *The Data Revolution: Big Data, Open Data, Data Infrastructures and Their Consequences*. London: SAGE.

Knight, D. (2011) *Multimodality and Active Listenership: A Corpus Approach*. London: Bloomsbury.

Knight, D., Adolphs, S., Tennent, P. and Carter, R. (2008) 'The Nottingham Multi-Modal Corpus: a demonstration', in *Proceedings of the 6th Language Resources and Evaluation Conference*. 28–30 May. Palais des Congrès Mansour Eddahbi, Marrakech, Morocco.

Knight, D., Evans, D., Carter, R. and Adolphs, S. (2009) 'HeadTalk, HandTalk and the corpus: towards a framework for multi-modal, multi-media corpus development', *Corpora* 4(1): 1–32.

Kučera, H. and Francis, W. N. (1967) *Computational Analysis of Present-Day American English*. Providence, RI: Brown University Press.

Lakoff, G. and Johnson, M. (1980) *Metaphors We Live By*. Chicago: University of Chicago Press.

Lang, A. (2009) 'Reading race in *Small Island*: discourse deviation, schemata and the textual encounter', *Language and Literature* 18(3): 316–30.

Lavrakas P. J. (ed.) (2008) *Encyclopedia of Survey Research Methods*. London: SAGE.

Le Carré, J. (1963) *The Spy Who Came in from the Cold*. London: Victor Gollancz.

Le Carré, J. (1974) *Tinker Tailor Soldier Spy*. London: Hodder and Stoughton.

Le Carré, J. (2017) *A Legacy of Spies*. London: Penguin.

Leech, G. (1993) 'Corpus annotation schemes', *Literary & Linguistic Computing* 8(4): 275–81.

Leech, G. (1997) 'Teaching and language corpora: a convergence', in Wichmann, A., Fligelstone, S., McEnery, T. and Knowles, G. (eds) *Teaching and Language Corpora*, pp. 1–23. London: Longman.

Leech, G. (2003) 'Modality on the move: the English modal auxiliaries 1961–1992', in Facchinetti, R., Krug, M. and Palmer, F. R. (eds) *Modality in Contemporary English*, pp. 223–40. Berlin: Mouton de Gruyter.

Leech, G. (2004) 'Recent grammatical change in English: data, description, theory', in Aijmer, K. and Altenberg, B. (eds) *Advances in Corpus Linguistics: Papers from the 23rd International Conference on English Language Research on Computerized Corpora (ICAME 23)*, pp. 61–81. Amsterdam: Rodopi.

Leech, G. (2008) *Language and Literature: Style and Foregrounding*. London: Longman.

Leech, G., Garside, R. and Bryant, M. (1994) 'CLAWS4: the tagging of the British National Corpus', *Proceedings of the 15th International Conference on Computational Linguistics (COLING 94)*, pp. 622–8. Kyoto, Japan.

Leech, G. and Short, M. (1981) *Style in Fiction: A Linguistic Introduction to English Fictional Prose*. London: Longman.

Leech, G. and Short, M. (2007) *Style in Fiction: A Linguistic Introduction to English Fictional Prose*. 2nd edn. London: Pearson.

Lehmann, H. M., auf dem Keller, C. and Ruef, B. (2006) 'Zen Corpus 1.0', in Facchinetti, R. and Rissanen, M. (eds) *Corpus-Based Studies of Diachronic English*, pp. 135–55. Bern: Peter Lang.

Leighton, J. (1971) 'Sonnets and computers: an experiment in stylistic analysis using an Elliott 503 computer', in Wisbey, R. A. (ed.) *The Computer in Literary and Linguistic Research*, pp. 149–58. Cambridge: Cambridge University Press.

Lemon, L. T. and Reiss, M. J. (eds) [1917] (1965) *Russian Formalist Criticism: Four Essays*. Lincoln, NE: University of Nebraska Press.

Lin, Y.-L. (2017) 'Co-occurrence of speech and gestures: a multimodal corpus linguistic approach to intercultural interaction', *Journal of Pragmatics* 117: 155–67.

Locke, R. (1974) 'The spy who spied on spies', *The New York Times*, 30 June. <https://archive.nytimes.com/www.nytimes.com/books/99/03/21/specials/lecarre-tinker.html> (last accessed 9 April 2018).

Lodge, D. (1984) *Small World*. London: Secker & Warburg.

Louw, B. (1989) 'Sub-routines in the integration of language and literature', in Carter, R., Walker, R. and Brumfit, C. (eds) *Literature and the Learner: Methodological Approaches*. British Council ELT Documents 130, pp. 47–54. London: MEP.

Louw, B. (1993) 'Irony in the text or insincerity in the writer? The diagnostic potential of semantic prosodies', in Baker, M., Francis, G. and Tognini-Bonelli, E. (eds) *Text and Technology: In Honour of John Sinclair*, pp. 157–76. Amsterdam: John Benjamins.

Louw, B. (2000) 'Contextual Prosodic Theory: bringing semantic prosodies to life', in Heffer, C. and Sauntson, H. (eds) *Words in Context: A Tribute to John Sinclair on His Retirement*, pp. 48–94. Birmingham: University of Birmingham.

Louw, B. (2008) 'Consolidating empirical method in data-assisted stylistics: towards a corpus-attested glossary of literary terms', in Zyngier, S., Bortlussi, M., Chesnokova, A. and Auracher, J. (eds) *Directions in Empirical Literary Studies*, pp. 243–64. Amsterdam: John Benjamins.

Louw, B. (2011) 'Philosophical and literary concerns in corpus linguistics', in Viana, V., Zyngier, S. and Barnbrook, G. (eds) *Perspectives on Corpus Linguistics*, pp. 171–96. Amsterdam: John Benjamins.

Love, R., Dembry, C., Hardie, A., Brezina, V. and McEnery, T. (2017) 'The Spoken BNC2014: designing and building a spoken corpus of everyday conversations', *International Journal of Corpus Linguistics* 22(3): 319–44.

Luyken, G.-M. (1991) *Overcoming Language Barriers in Television: Dubbing and Subtitling for the European Audience*. Manchester: The European Institute for the Media.

Lyons, J. (1978) *Semantics. Vols. I and II*. Cambridge: Cambridge University Press.

McArthur, T. (1981) *Longman Lexicon of Contemporary English*. London: Longman.

McClarty, R. (2014) 'In support of creative subtitling: contemporary context and theoretical framework', *Perspectives: Studies in Translation Theory and Practice* 22(4): 592–606.

McCloud, S. (1994) *Understanding Comics: The Invisible Art*. New York: HarperCollins.

McEnery, T. (2009) 'Keywords and moral panics: Mary Whitehouse and media censorship', in Archer, D. (ed.) *What's in a Word List? Investigating Word Frequency and Keyword Extraction*, pp. 93–124. Farnham: Ashgate.

McEnery, T. and Hardie, A. (2012) *Corpus Linguistics: Theory, Method, Practice*. Cambridge: Cambridge University Press.

McEnery, T. and Wilson, A. (2001) *Corpus Linguistics*. 2nd edn. Edinburgh: Edinburgh University Press.

McEnery, T., Xiao, R. and Tono, Y. (2006) *Corpus-Based Language Studies: An Advanced Resource Book*. Abingdon: Routledge.

McIntyre, D. (2003) 'Using foregrounding theory as a teaching methodology in a stylistics course', *Style* 37(1): 1–13.

McIntyre, D. (2006) *Point of View in Plays: A Cognitive Stylistic Approach to Viewpoint in Drama and Other Text-Types*. Amsterdam: John Benjamins.

McIntyre, D. (2009) *History of English*. Abingdon: Routledge.

McIntyre, D. (2010) 'Dialogue and characterisation in Quentin Tarantino's *Reservoir Dogs*: a corpus stylistic analysis', in McIntyre, D. and Busse, B. (eds) *Language and Style*, pp. 162–82. Basingstoke: Palgrave.

McIntyre, D. (2011) 'The place of stylistics in the English curriculum', in Jeffries, L. and McIntyre, D. (eds) *Teaching Stylistics*, pp. 9–29. Basingstoke: Palgrave.

McIntyre, D. (2012) 'Corpus stylistics in the classroom', in Burke, M., Csábi, S., Zerkowitz, J. and Week, L. (eds) *Pedagogical Stylistics: Current Trends in Language, Literature and ELT*. London: Continuum.

McIntyre, D. (2013a) 'Corpora and literature', in Chapelle, C. A. (ed.) *Wiley Blackwell Encyclopedia of Applied Linguistics*. Oxford: Wiley Blackwell.

McIntyre, D. (2013b) 'Language and style in David Peace's *1974*: a corpus-informed analysis', *Etudes de Stylistique Anglaise* 4: 133–45.

McIntyre, D. (2014) 'Characterisation', in Stockwell, P. and Whiteley, S. (eds) *The Cambridge Handbook of Stylistics*, pp. 149–64. Cambridge: Cambridge University Press.

McIntyre, D., Bellard-Thomson, C., Heywood, J., McEnery, A., Semino, E. and Short, M. (2004) 'Investigating the presentation of speech, writing and thought in spoken British English: a corpus-based approach', *ICAME Journal* 28: 49–76.

McIntyre, D. and Culpeper, J. (2010) 'Activity types, incongruity and humour in dramatic discourse', in McIntyre, D. and Busse, B. (eds) *Language and Style*, pp. 204–22. Basingstoke: Palgrave.

McIntyre, D. and Lugea, J. (2015) 'The effects of deaf and hard-of-hearing subtitles on the characterisation process: a cognitive stylistic study of *The Wire*', *Perspectives: Studies in Translatology* 23(1): 62–88.

McIntyre, D. and Price, H. (2018a) 'Stylistics: studying literary and everyday style in English', in Hewing, A., Seargeant, P. and Pihlaja,

S. (eds) *The Routledge Handbook of English Language Studies*, pp. 327–44. Abingdon: Routledge.

McIntyre, D. and Price, H. (2018b) 'Linguistics, language and the impact agenda', in McIntyre, D. and Price, H. (eds) *Applying Linguistics: Language and the Impact Agenda*, pp. 3–14. Abingdon: Routledge.

McIntyre, D. and Walker, B. (2011) 'Discourse presentation in Early Modern English writing: a preliminary corpus-based investigation', *International Journal of Corpus Linguistics* 16(1): 101–30.

Mackay, R. (1996) 'Mything the point: a critique of objective stylistics', *Language and Communication* 16(1): 81–93.

Mackay, R. (1999) 'There goes the other foot: a reply to Short et al.', *Language and Literature* 8(1): 59–66.

McKenna, W. and Antonia, A. (1996) '"A few simple words" of interior monologue in Ulysses: reconfiguring the evidence', *Literary and Linguistic Computing* 11(2): 55–66.

Mahlberg, M. (2007a) 'Corpus stylistics: bridging the gap between linguistic and literary studies', in Hoey, M., Mahlberg, M., Stubbs, M. and Teubert, W. *Text, Discourse and Corpora*, pp. 219–46. London: Continuum.

Mahlberg, M. (2007b) 'Lexical items in discourse: identifying local textual functions of *sustainable development*', in Hoey, M., Mahlberg, M., Stubbs, M. and Teubert, W. *Text, Discourse and Corpora*, pp. 191–218. London: Continuum.

Mahlberg, M. (2013a) 'Corpus analysis of literary texts', in Chapelle, C. A. (ed.) *Wiley Blackwell Encyclopedia of Applied Linguistics*. Oxford: Wiley Blackwell.

Mahlberg, M. (2013b) *Corpus Stylistics and Dickens's Fiction*. Abingdon: Routledge.

Mahlberg, M. and McIntyre, D. (2011) 'A case for corpus stylistics: Ian Fleming's *Casino Royale*', *English Text Construction* 4(2): 204–27.

Mahlberg, M., Stockwell, P., de Joode, J., Smith, C. and O'Donnell, M. B. (2016) 'CLiC Dickens: novel uses of concordances for the integration of corpus stylistics and cognitive poetics', *Corpora* 11(3): 433–63.

Mahlberg, M., Stockwell, P. and Sikevland, R. (2014) 'CLiC Dickens: towards a cognitive corpus stylistics of characterisation'. Paper presented at ICAME 35. 30 April. University of Nottingham, UK.

Manning, C. D. and Schütze, H. (1999) *Foundations of Statistical Natural Language Processing*. Cambridge, MA: MIT Press.

Mason, O. (1999) 'Parameters of collocation: the word in the centre of gravity', in Kirk, J. M. (ed.) *Corpora Galore: Analyses and Techniques in Describing English*, pp. 267–80. Amsterdam: Rodopi.

Melia, D. F. (1974) 'Review of *Essays on Style and Language* edited by Roger Fowler', *Foundations of Language* 11: 591–4.

Meurman-Solin, A. (1999) 'Point of view in Scottish and English Genre Styles', in McMillan, N. and Stirling, K. (eds) *Odd Alliances: Scottish Studies in European Contexts*, pp. 25–51. Glasgow: Cruithne Press.

Meyers, J. (1985) *Hemingway: A Biography*. New York: Harper & Row.

Mikhailov, M. and Cooper, R. (2016) *Corpus Linguistics for Translation and Contrastive Studies*. Abingdon: Routledge.

Millar, N. (2009) 'Modal verbs in *TIME*: frequency changes 1923–2006', *International Journal of Corpus Linguistics* 14(2): 191–220.

Miller, D. L. and Brewer, J. D. (2003) *The A–Z of Social Research: A Dictionary of Key Social Science Research Concepts*. London: SAGE.

Minsky, M. (1975) 'A framework for representing knowledge', in Winston, P. H. (ed.) *The Psychology of Computer Vision*, pp. 211–77. New York: McGraw Hill.

Moore, C. (2002) 'Reporting direct speech in Early Modern slander depositions', in Minkova, D. and Stockwell, R. (eds) *Studies in the History of the English Language: A Millennial Perspective*, pp. 399–416. Berlin: Mouton de Gruyter.

Morley, J. and Partington, A. (2007) 'A few *frequently asked questions* about semantic – or *evaluative* – prosody', *International Journal of Corpus Linguistics* 14(2): 139–58.

Mukařovský, J. [1932] (1964) 'Standard language and poetic language', in Garvin, P. L. (ed.) *A Prague School Reader on Esthetics, Literary Structure, and Style*, pp. 17–30. Washington, DC: Georgetown University Press.

Murphy, S. (2015) '"I will proclaim myself what I am": corpus stylistics and the language of Shakespeare's soliloquies', *Language and Literature* 24(4): 338–54.

Nevalainen, T. (2012) 'Gender differences in the evolution of Standard English: evidence from the Corpus of Early English Correspondence', in Biber, D. and Reppen, R. (eds) *Corpus Linguistics, Vol 1: Lexical Studies*, pp. 219–38. London: SAGE.

Nevalainen, T., Vartiainen, T., Säily, T., Kesäniemi, J., Dominowska, A. and Öhman, E. (2016) 'Language Change Database: a new online resource', *ICAME Journal* 40(1): 77–94.

Neves, J. (2005) 'Audiovisual Translation: Subtitling for the Deaf and Hard-of-Hearing'. Unpublished PhD thesis. University of Roehampton.

Ninan, D. (2005) 'Two puzzles about deontic modality', in Gajewski, J., Hacquard, B. and Yalcin, S. (eds) *New Work on Modality*. MIT Working Papers in Linguistics, 51, pp. 149–78. Cambridge, MA: Deptartment of Linguistics, MIT.

Nobel Foundation (2018) 'The Nobel Prize in Literature 1954', Nobelprize.org. <http://www.nobelprize.org/nobel_prizes/literature/laureates/1954/index.html> (last accessed 20 February 2018).

Nowottny, W. (1962) *The Language Poets Use*. London: Athlone Press.

Oakes, M. (1998) *Statistics for Corpus Linguistics*. Edinburgh: Edinburgh University Press.

Ofcom (2015) *Ofcom's Code on Television Access Services*. <https://www.ofcom.org.uk/__data/assets/pdf_file/0016/40273/tv-access-services-2015.pdf> (last accessed 28 April 2018).

O'Halloran, K. A. (2007) 'Corpus-assisted literary evaluation', *Corpora* 2(1): 33–63.

Ohmann, R. (1966) 'Literature as sentences', *College English* 27: 261–7; reprinted in in Love, G. A. and Payne, M. (eds) (1969) *Contemporary Essays on Style*, pp. 149–57. Glenview, IL: Scott Foresman.

Paesani, K. (2006) '"Exercices de style": developing multiple competencies through a writing portfolio', *Foreign Language Annals* 39(4): 618–39.

Palmer, F. R. (2001) *Mood and Modality*. Cambridge: Cambridge University Press.

Paquot, M. and Bestgen, Y. (2009) 'Distinctive words in academic writing: a comparison of three statistical tests for keyword extraction', in Jucker, A., Schreier, D. and Hundt, M. (eds) *Corpora: Pragmatics and Discourse*, pp. 247–69. Amsterdam: Rodopi.

Paran, A. (2008) 'The role of literature in instructed foreign language learning and teaching: an evidence-based survey', *Language Teaching* 41(4): 465–96.

Partington, A. (2004) 'Utterly content in each other's company: semantic prosody and semantic preference', *International Journal of Corpus Linguistics* 9(1): 131–56.

Peace, D. (1999) *1974*. London: Serpent's Tail.

Phillips, M. (1989) *Lexical Structure of Text*. Discourse Analysis Monograph 12. Birmingham: English Language Research.

Piao, S., Archer, D., Mudraya, O., Rayson, P., Garside, R., McEnery, T. and Wilson, A. (2005) 'A large semantic lexicon for corpus annotation', in *Proceedings of the Corpus Linguistics Conference*

Series 1(1). 14–17 July. Birmingham, UK. <https://bit.ly/2I1MDde> (last accessed 23 March 2018).

Piao, S., Wilson, A. and McEnery, T. (2002) 'A Multilingual Corpus Toolkit'. Paper presented at 4th American Association of Applied Corpus Linguistics (AAACL) Conference, Indianapolis, Indiana, USA.

Plummer, P. and Busse, B. (2006) 'E-learning and *Language and Style* in Mainz', *Language and Literature* 15(3): 257–76.

Polchinski, J. (1998) *String Theory*. Cambridge: Cambridge University Press.

Poole, J. (2006) 'E-learning and learning styles: students' reactions to web-based *Language and Style* at Blackpool and The Fylde College', *Language and Literature* 15(3): 307–20.

Popper, K. [1959] (2002) *The Logic of Scientific Discovery*. London: Routledge.

Porter, M. F. (1971) 'Designing a programming language for use in literary studies', in Wisbey, R. A. (ed.) *The Computer in Literary and Linguistic Research*, pp. 259–69. Cambridge: Cambridge University Press.

Price, H. (2018) 'Navigating the peripheries of impact: public engagement and the problem of kneejerk linguistics', in McIntyre, D. and Price, H. (eds) *Applying Linguistics: Language and the Impact Agenda*, pp. 41–52. Abingdon: Routledge.

Quirk, R., Greenbaum, S., Leech, G. and Svartvik, J. (1985) *A Comprehensive Grammar of the English Language*. London: Longman.

Ramsay, S. (2013) 'Who's in and who's out?', in Terras, M., Nyhan, J. and Vanhoutte, E. (eds) *Defining Digital Humanities: A Reader*, pp. 239–42. London: Ashgate.

Raymond, J. (1996) *Invention of the Newspaper: English Newsbooks 1641–49*. Oxford: Clarendon Press.

Raymond, J. (ed.) (1999) *News, Newspapers and Society in Early Modern Britain*. London: Frank Cass.

Rayson, P. (2003) 'Matrix: A Statistical Method and Software Tool for Linguistic Analysis Through Corpus Comparison'. Unpublished PhD thesis. Lancaster University.

Rayson, P. (2008) 'From key words to key semantic domains', *International Journal of Corpus Linguistics* 13(4): 519–49.

Rayson, P. (2009) *Wmatrix: A Web-Based Corpus Processing Environment*. School of Computing and Communications, Lancaster University. <http://ucrel.lancs.ac.uk/wmatrix/> (last accessed 1 July 2018).

Rayson, P., Berridge, D. and Francis, B. (2004) 'Extending the Cochran Rule for the comparison of word frequencies between corpora', in Purnelle, G., Fairon, C. and Dister, A. (eds) *Le poids des mots: Proceedings of the 7th International Conference on Statistical Analysis of Textual Data* (JADT 2004), pp. 926–36. 10–12 March. Louvain-la-Neuve, Belgium.

Rayson, P. and Garside, R. (2000) 'Comparing corpora using frequency profiling', in *Proceedings of the Workshop on Comparing Corpora*, pp. 1–6. 38th Annual Meeting of the Association for Computational Linguistics. 1–8 October. Hong Kong.

Renouf, A., Kehoe, A. and Mezquiriz, D. (2004) 'The accidental corpus: some issues in extracting linguistic information from the web', *Language and Computers* 49(1): 403–19.

Rissanen, M. (2000) 'The world of English historical corpora: from Cædmon to the computer age', *Journal of English Linguistics*, 28(1): 7–20.

Rissanen, M., Kytö, M. and Heikkonen, K. (eds) (1997) *English in Transition: Corpus-Based Studies in Linguistic Variation and Genre Styles*. Berlin: Mouton.

Romer, U. (2006) 'Pedagogical applications of corpora: some reflections on the current scope and a wish list for future developments', *ZAA (Zeitschrift fur Anglistik und Amerikanistik)* 54(2): 121–34.

Ross, L. (1977) 'The intuitive psychologist and his shortcomings: distortions in the attribution process', in Berkowitz, L. (ed.) *Advances in Experimental Social Psychology, Vol. 10*, pp. 173–220. New York: Academic Press.

Rumelhart, D. E. (1984) 'Schemata and the cognitive system', in Wyer, R. S. and Srull, T. K. (eds) *Handbook of Social Cognition, Vol. 1*, pp. 161–88. Hillsdale, NJ: Lawrence Erlbaum.

Rumelhart, D. E. and Norman, D. A. (1976) *Accretion, Tuning and Restructuring: Three Modes of Learning*. San Diego, CA: Centre for Human Information Processing, University of California.

Rutherford, W. and Sharwood Smith, M. (1985) 'Consciousness raising and universal grammar', *Applied Linguistics* 6: 274–82.

Ryan, D. (1995) 'Dating Hemingway's early style/parsing Gertrude Stein's modernism', *Journal of American Studies* 29: 229–40.

Sabin, R. (1996) *Comics, Comix & Graphic Novels: A History of Comic Art*. London: Phaidon Press.

Sadoski, M., Paivio, A. and Goetz, E. T. (1991) 'A critique of schema theory in reading and a dual coding alternative', *Reading Research Quarterly* 26(4): 463–84.

Sandford, A. and Emmott, C. (2012) *Mind, Brain and Narrative*. Cambridge: Cambridge University Press.

Saraceni, M. (2003) *The Language of Comics*. London: Routledge

Saugera, V. (2011) 'Scriptwriting as a tool for learning stylistic variation', *Foreign Language Annals* 44(1): 137–52.

Schank, R. C. and Abelson, R. P. (1977) *Scripts, Plans, Goals and Understanding: An Inquiry into Human Knowledge Structures*. Hillsdale, NJ: Lawrence Erlbaum.

Schiffrin, D. (1987) *Discourse Markers*. Cambridge: Cambridge University Press.

Schneider, R. (2001) 'Toward a cognitive theory of literary character: the dynamics of mental-model construction', *Style* 35(4): 607–39.

Scott, M. (2000) 'Focussing on the text and its key words', in Burnard, L. and McEnery, T. (eds) *Rethinking Language Pedagogy from a Corpus Perspective*, vol. 2, pp. 103–22. Frankfurt: Peter Lang.

Scott, M. (2010) 'Problems in investigating keyness, or clearing the undergrowth and marking out trails …', in Bondi, M. and Scott, M. (eds) *Keyness in Texts*, pp. 43–57. Amsterdam: John Benjamins.

Scott, M. (2016) *WordSmith Tools, Version 7*. Stroud: Lexical Analysis Software.

Scott, M. and Tribble, C. (2006) *Textual Patterns: Key Words and Corpus Analysis in Language Education*. Amsterdam: John Benjamins.

Seale, C., Charteris-Black, J., MacFarlane, A. and McPherson, A. (2010) 'Interviews and internet forums: a comparison of two sources of qualitative data', *Qualitative Health Research* 20(5): 595–606.

Semino, E. (2001) 'On readings, literariness and schema theory: a reply to Jeffries', *Language and Literature* 10(4): 345–55.

Semino, E. and Short, M. (2004) *Corpus Stylistics: Speech, Writing and Thought Presentation in a Corpus of English Writing*. London: Routledge.

Shaw, K. (2010) *David Peace: Texts and Contexts*. Brighton: Sussex Academic Press.

Shaw, K. (ed.) (2011) *Analysing David Peace*. Newcastle upon Tyne: Cambridge Scholars Publishing.

Shen, D. (2012) 'Stylistics in China in the new century', *Language and Literature* 21(1): 93–105.

Shklovsky, V. [1917] (1965) 'Art as technique', in Lemon, L. T. and Reiss, M. J. (eds) *Russian Formalist Criticism: Four Essays*, pp. 3–24. Lincoln, NE: University of Nebraska Press.

Short, M. (1996a) *Exploring the Language of Poems, Plays and Prose*. London: Longman.

Short, M. (1996b) 'Stylistics upside down: using stylistics in the teaching of language and literature', in Carter, R. and McRae, J. (eds) *Language, Literature and the Learner: Creative Classroom Practice*, pp. 41–64. London: Longman.

Short, M. (2006) 'E-learning and *Language and Style* in Lancaster', *Language and Literature* 15(3): 234–56.

Short, M. (2007) 'Thought presentation 25 years on', *Style* 41(2): 225–41.

Short, M. (2012) 'Discourse presentation of speech (and writing but not thought) summary', *Language and Literature* 21(1): 18–32.

Short, M. and Archer, D. (2003) 'Designing a world-wide web-based stylistics course and investigating its effectiveness', *Style* 37(1): 27–46.

Short, M. and Breen, M. P. (1988) 'Innovations in the teaching of literature: putting stylistics in its place', *Critical Quarterly* 30(2): 1–8.

Short, M., McIntyre, D., Jeffries, L. and Bousfield, D. (2011) 'Processes of interpretation: using meta-analysis to inform pedagogic practice', in Jeffries, L. and McIntyre, D. (eds) *Teaching Stylistics*, pp. 69–94. Basingstoke: Palgrave.

Short, M. and van Peer, W. (1999) 'A reply to Mackay', *Language and Literature* 8(3): 270–5.

Simpson, P. (2011) '"That's not ironic, that's just stupid!" Towards an eclectic account of the discourse of irony', in Dynel, M. (ed.) *The Pragmatics of Humour Across Discourse Domains*, pp. 33–50. Amsterdam: John Benjamins.

Simpson, P. (2014) *Stylistics: A Resource Book for Students*. Abingdon: Routledge.

Sinclair, J. (1966) 'Taking a poem to pieces', in Fowler, R. (ed.) *Essays on Style and Language*, pp. 68–81. London: Routledge.

Sinclair, J. (1991) *Corpus, Concordance, Collocation*. Oxford: Oxford University Press.

Sinclair, J. (1998) 'The lexical item', in Weigand, E. (ed.) *Contrastive Lexical Semantics*, pp. 1–24. Amsterdam: John Benjamins.

Sinclair, J. (2004) *Trust the Text: Language, Corpus and Discourse*. London: Routledge.

Sinclair, J. (2005) 'Corpus and text – basic principles', in Wynne, M. (ed.) *Developing Linguistic Corpora: A Guide to Good Practice*, pp. 1–16. Oxford: Oxbow.

Sinclair, J., Daley, R. and Jones, S. (2004) *English Collocational Studies: The OSTI Report*. Ed. R. Krishnamurthy. London: Continuum.

Southall, H., Von Luenen, A. and Aucott, P. (2009) 'On the organisation of geographical knowledge: data models for gazetteers and historical GIS', in *Proceedings of the 2009 5th IEEE International Conference on e-Science Workshops*, pp. 162–6. Oxford: Institute of Electrical and Electronics Engineers (IEEE).

Sperberg-McQueen, C. M., Huitfeldt, C. and Renear, A. (2000) 'Meaning, interpretation and markup', *Markup Languages: Theory and Practice* 2(3): 215–34.

Spitzer, L. (1948) *Linguistics and Literary History*. Princeton, NJ: Princeton University Press.

Stockwell, P. (2002) *Cognitive Poetics: An Introduction*. London: Routledge.

Stockwell, P. (2010) 'The eleventh checksheet of the apocalypse', in McIntyre, D. and Busse, B. (eds) *Language and Style: In Honour of Mick Short*, pp. 419–32. Basingstoke: Palgrave.

Stockwell, P. and Mahlberg, M. (2015) 'Mind-modelling with corpus stylistics in *David Copperfield*', *Language and Literature* 24(2): 129–47.

Stuart, K. (2017) 'Methods, methodology and madness: digital records management in the Australian government', *Records Management Journal* 27(2): 223–32.

Stubbs, M. (2005) 'Conrad in the computer: examples of quantitative stylistic methods', *Language and Literature* 14(1): 5–24.

Stubbs, M. (2007) 'Quantitative data on multi-word sequences in English: the case of the word *world*', in Hoey, M., Mahlberg, M., Stubbs, M. and Teubert, W. (eds) *Text, Discourse and Corpora: Theory and Analysis*, pp. 163–89. London: Continuum.

Student (1908) 'The probable error of a mean', *Biometrika* 6: 1–25.

Studer, P. (2008) *Historical Corpus Stylistics*. London: Continuum.

Taavitsainen, I. (1994) 'Subjectivity as a text-type marker in historical stylistics', *Language and Literature* 3(3): 197–212.

Taavitsainen, I. (1999) 'Personality and style of affect in *The Canterbury Tales*', in Lester, G. (ed.) *Chaucer in Perspective: Middle English Essays in Honour of Norman Blake*, pp. 218–34. Sheffield: Sheffield Academic Press.

Teranishi, M., Saito, A., Sakamoto, K. and Nasu, M. (2012) 'The role of stylistics in Japan: a pedagogical perspective', *Language and Literature* 21(2): 226–44

Thomas, J. (1995) *Meaning in Interaction*. London: Longman.

Thompson, G. (1996) 'Voices in the text: discourse perspectives on language reports', *Applied Linguistics* 17(4): 501–30.

Tieken-Boon van Ostade, I. (2009) *An Introduction to Late Modern English*. Edinburgh: Edinburgh University Press.

Tilney, M. (2018) 'Cohesive harmony and theme in Peter Carey's "The last days of a famous mime"', *Language and Literature* 27(1): 3–20.

Timmis, I. (2015) *Corpus Linguistics for ELT: Research and Practice*. Abingdon: Routledge.

Timucin, M. (2001) 'Gaining insights into alternative teaching approaches employed in an EFL literature class', *CAUCE, Revista de Filología y su Didáctica* 24: 269–93.

Tinker Tailor Soldier Spy, DVD. London: BBC Worldwide, 2003.

Tognini-Bonelli, E. (2001) *Corpus Linguistics at Work*. Amsterdam: John Benjamins.

Tomlinson, B. (2001) 'Materials development', in Carter, R. and Nunan, D. (eds) *The Cambridge Guide to Teaching English to Speakers of Other Languages*, pp. 66–72. Cambridge: Cambridge University Press.

Toolan, M. (2009) *Narrative Prospection in the Short Story: A Corpus Stylistic Approach*. Amsterdam: John Benjamins.

Toolan, M. (2011) 'Teaching the stylistics of prose fiction', in Jeffries, L. and McIntyre, D. (eds) *Teaching Stylistics*, pp. 178–99. Basingstoke: Palgrave.

Trodd, Z. (2007) 'Hemingway's camera eye: the problem of language and an interwar politics of form', *The Hemingway Review* 26(2): 7–21.

Unser-Schutz, G. (2011) 'Developing a text-based corpus of the language of Japanese comics (*manga*)', in Newman, J., Baayen, H. and Rice, S. (eds) *Corpus-Based Studies in Language Use, Language Learning, and Language Documentation*. pp. 213–38. Amsterdam: Rodopi.

van Gelderen, E. (2014) *A History of the English Language*. Amsterdam: John Benjamins.

van Peer, W. (1986) *Stylistics and Psychology*. London: Croom Helm.

van Peer, W., Hakemulder, F. and Zyngier, S. (2012) *Scientific Methods for the Humanities*. Amsterdam: John Benjamins.

Vendler, H. (1966) 'Review of *Essays on Style and Language* edited by Roger Fowler', *Essays in Criticism* 16(4): 457–63.

Viana, V. and Zyngier, S. (2017) 'Exploring new territories in pedagogical stylistics: an investigation of high-school EFL students' assessments', *Language and Literature* 26(4): 300–22.

Viola, R. (2017) 'A corpus-based investigation of language change in Italian: the case of grazie/ringraziare di and grazie/ringraziare per', *Journal of Historical Linguistics* 7(3): 372–88.

Wales, K. (2011) *A Dictionary of Stylistics*. 3rd edn. Harlow: Pearson.

Walker, B. (2011) 'Character and Characterisation in Julian Barnes's *Talking It Over*: A Corpus Stylistic Analysis'. Unpublished PhD thesis. Lancaster University.

Walker, B. and McIntyre, D. (2015) 'Thinking about the news: thought presentation in early modern English news writing', in Baker, P. and McEnery, T. (eds) *Corpora and Discourse Studies*, pp. 175–91. Basingstoke: Palgrave.

Wallot, S., O'Brien, B. A., Haussmann, A., Kloos, H. and Lyby, M. S. (2014) 'The role of reading time complexity and reading speed in text comprehension', *Journal of Experimental Psychology: Learning, Memory and Cognition* 40(6): 1745–65.

Walsh, J. A. (2012) 'Comic book mark-up language: an introduction and rationale', *Digital Humanities Quarterly* 6(1). <http://www.digitalhumanities.org/dhq/vol/6/1/000117/000117.html> (last accessed 1 July 2018).

Wang, J., Xu, Z., McIntyre, D., Lugea, J. and Ho, Y. (2016) *Worldbuilder 1.0*. Department of Informatics, University of Huddersfield. <http://viv-research.info/TWT/system/index.html> (last accessed 1 July 2018).

Warner, C. (2012) 'Literary pragmatics in the advanced foreign language literature classroom: the case of Young Werther', in Burke, M., Csábi, S., Zerkowitz, J. and Week, L. (eds) *Pedagogical Stylistics: Current Trends in Language, Literature and ELT*, pp. 142–57. London: Continuum.

Warren, M. (2016) 'Data-driven learning', in Farr, F. and Murray, L. (eds) *Routledge Handbook of Language Learning and Technology*, pp. 337–47. London: Routledge.

Watts, R. and Trudgill, P. (eds) (2001) *Alternative Histories of English*. London: Routledge.

Welch, B. L. (1947) 'The generalization of "Student's" problem when several different population variances are involved', *Biometrika* 34(1–2): 28–35.

Werth, P. (1999) *Text Worlds: Representing Conceptual Space in Discourse*. London: Longman.

West, D. (2010) *I. A. Richards and the Rise of Cognitive Stylistics*. London: Continuum.

Widdowson, H. G. (1984) 'The incentive value of theory in teacher education', *English Language Teaching Journal* 38(2): 86–90.

Widdowson H. G. (1990) *Aspects of Language Teaching*. Oxford: Oxford University Press.

Williams, C. (2007) *Tradition and Change in Legal English: Verbal Constructions in Prescriptive Texts*. Berlin: Peter Lang.

Willis, J. (1996) *A Framework for Task-Based Learning*. Oxford: Longman.

Wilson, A. and Thomas, J. (1997) 'Semantic annotation', in Garside, R., Leech, G. and McEnery, T. (eds) *Corpus Annotation*, pp. 53–65. London: Longman.

Wisbey, R. A. (ed.) (1971) *The Computer in Literary and Linguistic Research*. Cambridge: Cambridge University Press.

Włodarcyzk, M. (2007) *Pragmatic Aspects of Reported Speech: The Case of Early Modern English Courtroom Discourse*. Frankfurt: Peter Lang.

Wright, D. (2003) 'Stylistic variation within genre conventions in the Enron email corpus: developing a text-sensitive methodology for authorship research', *International Journal of Speech, Language and the Law* 20(1): 45–75.

Yañez Prieto, M. C. (2010) 'Authentic instruction in literary worlds: learning the stylistics of concept-based grammar', *Language and Literature* 19(1): 59–75.

Zerkowitz, J. (2012) 'Stylistics for language teachers', in Burke, M., Csábi, S., Zerkowitz, J. and Week, L. (eds) *Pedagogical Stylistics Current Trends in Language, Literature and ELT*, pp. 193–209. London: Bloomsbury.

Zipf, G. (1935) *The Psychobiology of Language*. Boston: Houghton-Mifflin.

Index